Property and Trust Law in Japan

Property and Trust Law in Japan

Hiroshi Matsuo

This book was originally published as a monograph in the International Encyclopaedia of Laws/Property and Trust Law.

Founding Editor: Roger Blanpain
General Editor: Frank Hendrickx
Volume Editors: Alain Verbeke, Vincent Sagaert

Wolters Kluwer

Published by:
Kluwer Law International B.V.
PO Box 316
2400 AH Alphen aan den Rijn
The Netherlands
E-mail: international-sales@wolterskluwer.com
Website: lrus.wolterskluwer.com

Sold and distributed by:
Wolters Kluwer Legal & Regulatory U.S.
7201 McKinney Circle
Frederick, MD 21704
United States of America
E-mail: customer.service@wolterskluwer.com

ISBN 978-94-035-3475-6

e-Book: ISBN 978-94-035-3480-0
web-PDF: ISBN 978-94-035-3481-7

This title is available on www.kluwerlawonline.com

The Author

Hiroshi Matsuo was born on November 19, 1962, in Nagano Prefecture, Japan. He graduated from Keio University in 1985 and completed the master program at Keio University in 1987 and doctor program at Hitotsubashi University in 1990. He was employed by Yokohama City University as Lecturer in 1990 and by Yokohama National University as Associate Professor in 1994. He moved to Keio University as Professor of Law in 2003. Since 2017 he is the Director of Keio Institute for Global Law and Development (KEIGLAD). He lectures separate courses on civil law, and law and development. In addition, since 2002, he has been participating in Legal Cooperation Programs arranged by Japan International Cooperation Agency (JICA) in Asian countries, including Vietnam, Laos, Cambodia, Nepal, and Myanmar. He has lectured Japanese Legal System at the University of Sydney and the University of Jena as Visiting Professor from 1997 to 2005. His publications (only books by single author) include: *Yoi Touchi To Ho No Shihai* [*Good Governance and the Rule of Law*] (Nihonhyoronsha, 2009); *Minpo No Taikei* [*A System of the Civil Law*], 6th edn (Keio University Press, 2016); *Zaisanken No Hosho To Sonshitsu Hosho No Hori* [*Guarantee of Property Rights and Compensation for Takings*] (Taiseishuppansha, 2011); *Minpo Kaisei Wo Yomu* [*Reading the Civil Law Reform*] (Keio University Press, 2012); *Kaihatsu Hogaku No Kiso Riron* [*A Basic Theory of Law and Development*] (Keisoshobo, 2012); *Hatten Suru Ajia No Seiji Keizai Ho* [*Politics, Economics, and Law in Developing Asia*] (Nihonhyoronsha, 2016); *Saiken Ho Kaisei Wo Yomu* [*Reading the Obligation Law Reform*] (Keio University Press, 2017); *Kazoku Ho Kaisei Wo Yomu* [*Reading the Family and Succession Law Reform*] (Keio University Press, 2019).

The Author

Table of Contents

List of Abbreviations

§1. Laws and Regulations

CC	Civil Code of Japan
CE	Constitution of the Empire of Japan
CJ	Constitution of Japan
FCC	Civil Code of France
GCC	Civil Code of Germany
LCSPPR	Law on the Contract of Security Preserved by Provisional Registration
LDUOB	Law on the Divided Unit Ownership of Building
LLLB	Law on the Lease of Land and Building
LRIP	Law on the Registration of Immovable Property
SMLDU	Special Measures Law for the Public Use of Deep Underground

The number of Article of Constitution is abbreviated as follows:

Article 29 (3) CJ means Article 29, section 3 of Constitution of Japan.

The number of Section, Subsection, Item, etc. of laws and regulations is abbreviated as follows:

Section 330 (1) [3] CC means section 330, Subsection 1, Item 3 of the Civil Code of Japan.

§2. Judgments of the Court

DCJ	Judgment of the District Court
HCD	Decree of the High Court
HCJ	Judgment of the High Court
SCD	Decree of the Supreme Court

List of Abbreviations

SCJ	Judgment of the Supreme Court
SCJ (FB)	Judgment of the Supreme Court, Full Bench
STD	Decree of the Supreme Tribunal (1875–1947)
STJ	Judgment of the Supreme Tribunal (1875–1947)
STJ (FB)	Judgment of the Supreme Tribunal, Full Bench (1875–1947)

Judgment and decree of the court are cited by the date and the source of publication. For example:

> SCJ (FB) Jul. 13, 1977 Minshu 31-4-533 means Judgment of the Supreme Court, Full Bench, on July 13, 1977 Minshu [Report on Civil Cases of the Supreme Court], Vol. 31, No. 4, p. 533.

§3. Law Reports

Dai-min	Daishin-in-saibanrei, Minpo [Collection of Decisions by Supreme Tribunal on Civil Law]
Gyosai	Gyosei-jiken-saibanrei-shu [Report on Administrative Cases]
Hanji	Hanrei-jiho [Cases-News Report]
Hanketsuzenshu	Daishin-in Hanketsu Zenshu [Comprehensive Collection of the Supreme Tribunal Decisions]
Hanta	Hanrei-taimuzu [Cases-Reports]
Kagetsu	Kateisaibansho-geppo [Monthly Report of Family Court]
Keiroku	Daishin-in-keiji-hannketu-roku [Record of Criminal Cases of the Supreme Tribunal]
Keishu	Saiko-saibansho-keiji-saibanrei-shu [Report on Criminal Cases of the Supreme Court]
Kinpo	Kin-yu-homu-jijyo [Financial Law News]
Kinsho	Kin-yu-shoji-hanrei [Financial and Commercial Cases]
Minroku	Daishin-in-minji-hannketu-roku [Record of Civil Cases of the Supreme Tribunal]
Minshu	Saiko-saibansho-minji-saiban-reishu [Report on Civil Cases of the Supreme Court]
Saimin	Saibanshu-minji [Collection of Decisions in Civil Matters]
Shogetsu	Shomu-geppo [Monthly Report on Litigation]
Shinbun	Horitsu-shinbun [Law News]

Law Reports are cited by the number and pages. For example:

> DCJ (Sapporo) Mar. 27, 1997 Hanji 1598-33 means Judgment of the District Court of Sapporo on March 27, 1997 Hanji [Cases-News Report], No. 1598, p. 33.

§4. Books

Books are cited by the family name of the author(s) and the publication year from the list of Selected Bibliography.

If there are two or more publications by the same author in the same year, they will be identified by adding "a," "b" to the year.

For example:

Ishida 2008: p. 324 means Ishida, Minori, *Minpo Taikei II: Bukken Ho [System of Civil Law II: Law of Real Rights]* (Shinzansha, 2008), page 324.

Dogauchi 2017b: pp. 77–78 means Dogauchi, Hiroto, *Tanpo Bukken Ho* [The Law of Real Rights for Security] (Yuhikaku, 2017b), pp. 77–78.

List of Abbreviations

General Introduction

§1. General Background of the Country

I. Geography and Climate

1. Japan is an island country which consists of 6,852 islands including Hokkaido, Honshu, Shikoku and Kyushu as the four largest islands. It is surrounded by the North Pacific Ocean, the Sea of Japan, the East China Sea and the Philippine Sea. It locates at between 20 and 45 degrees north latitude and between 123 and 154 degrees east longitude extending approximately 3,000 kilometers from northeast to southwest. The easternmost tip is *Minami-tori-shima*, the westernmost tip is *Yonaguni-jima*, the northernmost tip is *Etorohu-to*, and the southernmost tip is *Okino-tori-shima*. The total land area, if it includes the Northern Territories, is 377,974 square kilometers.[1]

According to the statistics from 2010 to 2017, the land use was categorized as cultivated land (11.8%), forest (66.3%), grassland (0.9%), water area, rivers and channels (3.5%), roads (3.7%), residential land (3.2%), industrial land (0.4%), other lands for building (1.6%) and others (8.7%).[2]

2. Northern areas of Japan lie in the subarctic zone, middle areas in the temperate zone and southern areas in the subtropical zone. There are relatively large differences in climate within the country. The average monthly mean temperature from 1981 to 2010 in Tokyo, for example, was 27.4 degrees in August and 6.1 degrees in January. It was 27.1 degrees in August and 5.2 degrees in January since 1961–1990. It shows the tendency of gradual warming. Except for the northern part of the country, there is a rainy season lasting for about a month and a half from the middle of June to the end of July.[3]

1. As of Oct. 1, 2018. Statistics Bureau 2020: 1.1, available at http://www.stat.go.jp/english/data/nenkan/ (accessed Nov. 1, 2020); Geospatial Information Authority of Japan, Ministry of Land, Infrastructure, Transport and Tourism, Maps & Geospatial Information, available at http://www.gsi.go.jp/ENGLISH/page_e30031.html (accessed Nov. 1, 2020).
2. Statistics Bureau 2020: 1.6.
3. Statistics Bureau 2020: 1-9.

II. Cultural Situation

3. According to the twentieth National Census conducted in 2015, the population of Japan as of October 1, 2015, was 127.09 million (61.84 million for male and 65.25 million for female).[4] It showed a decline of 0.96 million (0.8%) from the previous census conducted in 2010. The latest population is estimated to be 126.15 million (61.39 million for male and 64.75 million for female).[5]

The number of foreign residents usually living in Japan was 1.75 million in 2015. By nationality, Chinese was the largest (0.51 million, 29.2% of the foreign residents), followed by Korean (0.38 million, 21.5%), the Philippines (0.17 million, 9.8%), and Brazilian (0.13 million, 7.2%). It increased 0.1 million from that in 2010 showing around 1.24% increase on an annual basis.[6] The number of foreign workers is rapidly increasing. It was estimated to be 1.46 million in October 2018 showing an increase of 0.18 million (14.2%) from the number in October 2017.[7] It is closely related to the decreasing population in Japan as confirmed above.

4. The population composition of Japan has been changing. The birth rate (rate per thousand persons) has been declining from 34.9 in 1925, through 18.8 in 1970, to 8.0 in 2015. The total special birth rate (the average number of children one woman gives birth to in her life) was 5.10 in 1925, 2.13 in 1970, 1.26 in 2005 (the lowest record) and 1.45 in 2015.[8]

But the life expectancy has been increasing from 46.92 for male and 49.63 for female in 1935, through 71.73 for male and 76.89 for female in 1975, to 80.75 for male and 86.99 for female in 2015.[9] As a result, the aging index (the ratio of the population aged 65 or older to that aged 0–14) has been considerably increased from 14.4% in 1920, through 29.4% in 1970, 66.2% in 1990, and 91.2% in 1995, to 210.6% in 2015.[10] Thus the aging of society is progressing in Japan.

5. The number of marriages was about 521 thousand in 1925 and increased to about 1,100 thousand in 1972. However, since the middle of the 1970s it has been decreasing to about 789 thousand in 1979 and it was about 635 thousand in 2015.[11] The average age of the first marriage has also been changing from 27.1 for male and 23.1 for female in 1925, through 26.9 for male and 24.2 in 1970, to 33.3 for

4. The Population Census has been taken every five years since 1920 regularly with one exception of the sixth census scheduled for 1945. It was suspended due to the Pacific War and was replaced by the Extraordinary Population Census in 1947. The censuses up to the fifth census (1940) were based on the Law on the Population Census, and those after the sixth census were conducted by following the provisions of the Statistics Law (Law No. 18, 1947).
5. Statistics Bureau 2020: 2-1, B.
6. Statistics Bureau, 2015 Population Census, Summary of the results and statistical tables, https://www.stat.go.jp/english/data/kokusei/2015/final_en/pdf/s01.pdf (accessed Nov. 1, 2020).
7. Ministry of Health, Labor and Welfare, Report on the Employment of Foreign Workers, 2018, available at https://www.mhlw.go.jp/content/11655000/000472891.pdf (accessed Nov. 1, 2020).
8. Statistics Bureau 2020: 2-19.
9. Statistics Bureau 2020: 2-21.
10. Statistics Bureau 2020: 2-6.
11. Statistics Bureau 2020: 2-16.

male and 31.1 for female in 2015.[12] The tendency of decreasing marriage and late marriage together with the negative attitude of the couples toward having children due to the lasting economic recession, the increasing costs for education, unfavorable working conditions for parents, etc. are thought to have contributed to the decreasing birth rate.[13]

6. Japan is not an ethnically homogeneous nation. As migrants from Ryukyu Islands (Okinawa prefecture since 1879) and Korean Peninsula increased after the 1910s, unequal treatments by the employers and community members caused serious discrimination issues.[14] As for the Korean residents, the government has simplified the procedures to grant permanent residence and limited the causes of deportation by enacting the Special Law on the Immigration Control for Persons Who Resigned from Japanese Nationality Based on the Peace Treaty with Japan in 1991 (Law No. 71, 1991). The Alien Registration Law was partially amended in 1993 and the fingerprinting requirement was abolished.

7. As for the Ainu people who are the ancestors of aboriginal inhabitants in the northern reaches of Honshu and the northern island of Hokkaido, the Law for the Promotion of Ainu Culture and the Dissemination and the Enlightenment of Knowledge of Ainu Traditions and Others was enacted in 1997 (Law No. 52, 1997). As the main purpose of this law is limited to the protection and teaching of Ainu culture, it does not recognize any indigenous rights, nor cultural rights, which had been recognized by the lower court decision.[15] The Law acknowledges the legal status of Ainu people under the unified sovereignty of the Japanese government. Consequently, the land of Ainu people is also to be subject to the state power of eminent domain (compulsory purchase power) prescribed by Article 29 (3) CJ. In 2019, the Law on the Promotion of Measures to Realize a Society That Respects for the Pride of Ainu People (Law No. 16, 2019) articulated for the first time in legislation that the Ainu people are "indigenous people" in Japan (section 1). However, it did not stipulate the widespread principle of "Free, Prior and Informed Consent" (FPIC) to

---

12. Ministry of Health, Labor and Welfare, Survey Report on Marriage, 2016, available at https://www.mhlw.go.jp/toukei/saikin/hw/jinkou/tokusyu/konin16/index.html (accessed Nov. 1, 2020).
13. Cabinet Office, White Paper on Declining Birthrate, 2004, Ch. 2, Paragraph 1. White Paper on Declining Birthrate (in Japanese) is issued every year after 2004 on the basis of s. 9, Basic Law on Policies for Declining Birthrate (Law No. 133, 2003), available at https://www8.cao.go.jp/shoushi/shoushika/whitepaper/index.html (accessed Nov. 1, 2020)
14. Gordon 2014: pp. 153–154. Okinawans were said to be less assertive than the Koreans in claiming a separate ethnic identity (ibid, p. 154).
15. DCJ (Sapporo) Mar. 27, 1997 Hanji 1598-33. The court declared that the expropriation decided by the Hokkaido Land Expropriation Commission was illegal. The court applied s. 27 of the International Covenant on Civil and Political Rights and held that "the Ainu people had inhabited mainly Hokkaido and maintained their distinct culture and identity before Japan extended its rule over them, and they still form a social group with a distinct culture and identity even after suffering social and economic damage caused by policies carried out by the majority Japanese who incorporated the Ainu into Japan." However, it dismissed the plaintiff's claim to rescind the decision of the expropriation by applying s. 31 of the Administrative Litigation Law to the case.

be obtained before adopting and implementing legislative or administrative measures that may affect the indigenous people.[16]

8. The major religions in Japan are Shintoism and Buddhism. The number of followers of each religion as of December 31, 2018 was: 87,219,808 for Shintoism, 84,336,539 for Buddhism, 1,921,484 for Christianity, and 7,851,545 for others.[17] The total number of followers was 181,329,376, and it exceeds the population, mainly because one person can be both Shintoist and Buddhist. The reason would be that, on the one hand, Shintoism originated in the natural and indigenous belief from the ancient times and it has been polytheistic. Shinto Gods are usually worshipped at "jinja" [Shinto shrines], but the natural objects such as trees, rocks, and land and the natural phenomena such as rain, wind, and thunder have also been considered as having "kami-gami" [Gods], which are numerous and uncountable as they are called "Yaoyorozu-no-kamigami" [Eight Millions of Gods]. In addition, there have been no specific leaders nor any books of fixed scripture in Shintoism.

On the other hand, Buddhism was introduced into Japan around the sixth century by way of Korea. It was supported by the state and developed throughout the country so that many temples were constructed. There is no specific God in Buddhism, but there are some scriptures written by the Japanese Buddhist priests such as Kukai, Saicho, Honen, Shinran, and Nichiren.

As a result, Shintoism and Buddhism have been syncretized and worshipped at the same place as it was called "shin-butsu-shugo" [syncretism of Shintoism and Buddhism].[18]

However, they were separated by the Decree on the Separation of Shintoism and Buddhism issued on March 28, 1868, by the Meiji government. It aimed to establish Shintoism as the national religion of Japan by deifying the Emperor, which led to the anti-Buddhism movement.

But, after the Pacific War (1941–1945), the practice of religion was separated from the function of state, and Article 20 CJ guarantees religious freedom and it prohibits the state from any religious activities. As a result, there is no state religion, and religious instruction is forbidden at public schools. However, the Supreme Court held that the disbursement from a local government's treasury for a Shinto-style "ji-chin-sai" [groundbreaking ceremony] for constructing a public school was constitutional since the ceremony was a "traditional custom," not a "religious ceremony."[19]

---

16. United Nations Declaration on the Rights of Indigenous People, Sep. 13, 2007 (A/RES/295), Art. 19.
17. Agency for Cultural Affairs, *Shukyo Nenkan* [*Religious Yearbook*] *2019*, p. 49.
18. Shinto practice extends to the worship of ancestors as well. The Buddhists also pray their ancestors by putting their ancestral tablets in the Buddhist alter at an individual's house.
19. SCJ (FB) Jul. 13, 1977 Minshu 31-4-533. The Japanese consciousness that spirits dwell in the land is quite old. However, five judges, including the Chief Judge, out of fifteen judges at full bench of the Supreme Court presented the dissenting opinions by the strict interpretation of the principle of church-state separation stipulated by Art. 20 CJ.

9. Confucianism was also introduced into Japan since the fourth or fifth century from Korea and China. As a result, the Japanese are said to be tolerant toward religions. According to the Survey on the Religious Consciousness of the Japanese,[20] about 65% of the respondents confessed that they had no religion to believe. However, those who worshiped Shinto alters or Buddhist alters were more than 50%, and those who visited regularly Shinto shrines or Buddhist temples were more than 80%. This implies that the Japanese are not indifferent to religion even though they answered in the Survey that they were not believers of a certain religion, and it is due to the behavioral features of the Japanese Shintoism and Buddhism which are diffused into various activities of their daily life.[21] People go to shrines occasionally, for instance, when a child is born, and marriage ceremonies are often conducted according to Shinto rites. A small Shinto altar has traditionally been placed in an individual's house, and families go to famous shrines on New Year's Day. Many families go to temples on New Year's Day and have also a Buddhist altar in their homes where they place offerings, burn incense and pray for the repose of their ancestors and for the health, safety and peace of their family. When people die, they are usually buried according to Buddhist rites and are given posthumous Buddhist name.

III. Political System

A. *The Constitutional Monarchy as a Basic Structure*

10. The basic structure of government is a constitutional monarchy, which was established by the promulgation of the Constitution of the Empire of Japan (CE) on February 11, 1889. Japan was the first Asian country that adopted a written constitution and created a constitutional monarchy with an elected parliament (the Imperial Diet) and an independent judiciary, which enabled Japan to be benefitted from the Industrial Revolution in Asia.[22] The CE was totally amended in 1946 by the Constitution of Japan (CJ) that introduced popular sovereignty. Article 15 (3) CJ guarantees the universal adult suffrage with regard to the election of public officials, which is given to the people aged 18 years or over. The state power is divided into legislative, executive and judicial power, and they are given to the Diet, the Cabinet and the Courts, respectively (Article 41, 65 and 76 (1) CJ). The "Tenno" [the Emperor] shall perform "kokuji-kooi" [acts in matters of state], but the Emperor "shall not have powers related to government" (Article 4 (1) and 7 CJ). The acts of the Emperor shall include appointment of the Prime Minister as designated by the Diet and appointment of the Chief Judge of the Supreme Court as designated by the Cabinet (Article 6 CJ), and other acts to be performed with the advice

20. NHK Hoso-Bunka-Kenkyusho Yoron-Chosa-Bu [Public Opinion Research Department, Broadcasting Culture Research Institute, Japan Broadcasting Corporation], *Nihonjin-no-Shukyo-Ishiki* [Religious Consciousness of the Japanese], 1984.
21. Masaaki Ikeda, "Bukkyo-ga-sabakareru" ["Buddhism is Judged by the Court"], Juristo, No. 829, 1985, pp. 66–67.
22. Daron Acemoglu & James A. Robinson, *Why Nations Fail* 297 (Profile Books 2012).

and approval of the Cabinet such as promulgation of amendments of the Constitution, laws, cabinet orders and treaties, convocation of the Diet, dissolution of the House of Representatives, proclamation of general election of members of the Diet, attestation of the appointment and dismissal of Ministers of State and other officials as provided for by law, and of full powers and credentials of ambassadors and Ministers, attestation of general and special amnesty, commutation of punishment, reprieve, and restoration of rights, awarding of honors, attestation of instruments of ratification and other diplomatic documents as provided for by law, receiving foreign ambassadors and Ministers, and performance of ceremonial functions (Article 7 CJ). Thus under the current constitutional system of Japan, the Emperor shall play a nominal, symbolic, ritual and ceremonial role and have no substantial power in political decision-makings.

B. The Diet

11. Article 41 CJ provides that "Kokkai" [the Diet] is "the highest organ of the state power" as well as "the sole law-making organ of the state." It qualifies the Diet to be the "highest" and "sole" organ which decides the general will of the people as the state will by representing the nation. The Diet shall designate the Prime Minister among the members of the Diet (Articles 6 and 67 (1) CJ). The Diet can establish the impeachment court to decide the dismissal of the judges (Article 64 CJ). However, it does not mean the predominance of the Diet over the Cabinet and the Courts. For instance, if a fight or scuffle occurred in the Diet, the power of indictment exercised by prosecutor can reach into the Diet.[23] The Cabinet can dissolve the House of Representatives of the Diet (Articles 7 [3] and 69 CJ). The legislation adopted by the Diet is subject to the constitutional review by the courts (Articles 81 and 98 (1) CJ).

12. The Diet is bicameral and it consists of two Houses: "Shugiin" [the House of Representatives] and "Sangiin" [the House of Councilors] (Article 42 CJ). The House of Representatives has 465 seats, 289 of which are directly elected in single-seat constituencies by simple majority vote, and 176 of which are elected in multi-seat constituencies by proportional representation vote. The term of its members is four years. The House of Councilors has 248 seats, 148 of which are directly elected in multi-seat constituencies by majority vote, and 100 of which are elected according to the order of the candidate list decided by each political party within the number of seats which shall be allocated by proportional representation vote. The term of its members is six years, and a half of them renewed every three years (Articles 42–47 CJ; section 4 (1) and (2) Election Law). The House of Representatives has the greater power than the House of Councilors on such matters as: (a) passing a bill (Article 59 (2) and (4) CJ), (b) determination of the budget (Article 60 CJ), (c) conclusion of treaties (Article 61 CJ), and (d) designation of the Prime Minister (Article 67 (2) CJ). For instance, when a bill had been passed by the House of Representatives, but the House of Councilors made a different decision from it, the bill

---

23. DCJ (Tokyo) Jan. 22, 1962 Hanji 297-7.

may become a law when it is passed again by the House of Representatives by a majority of two-thirds or more of the members present (Article 59 (2) CJ). Thus the relation between the two Houses is called "the lame bicameralism."

13. In addition to the Diet, local public entities such as prefectures, cities, towns, and villages have the right to enact "joorei" [bylaws enacted by the local public entity as its own regulations] within the scope provided by law (Article 94 CJ). Article 93 CJ recognizes that the local public entities shall establish assemblies as their deliberative organs, in accordance with law. The members of their assemblies are to be elected by direct popular vote within their communities. According to the Local Autonomy Law, the local public entities of general nature include "Tokyo-to" [Tokyo Metropolitan Government], "Hokkai-doo" [Hokkaidoo Government], "Kyoto-fu" and "Osaka-fu" [the Kyoto and Osaka Government] and the other forty-three "ken" [Prefectures]. Within each prefecture there are "shi" [cities], "choo" [towns] and "son" [villages]. Local public entities of special nature include "tokubetsu-ku" [special wards] within Tokyo-to, Yokohama-shi, Osaka-shi, etc. (sections 1, 2 (3) and 281 Local Autonomy Law). All of them are local public entities which are empowered to enact bylaws.

C. The Cabinet

14. According to Article 65 CJ, the executive power is vested in the Cabinet. The concrete content of the Cabinet's power is enumerated in Article 73 CJ. The Cabinet consists of "Naikau-sori-daijin" [the Prime Minister] as its head, and the other "kokumu-daijin" [Ministers of the State]. They must be civilians, i.e., non-military personnel (Article 66 CJ). Ministers are usually the head of departments or other administrative organizations.[24]

However, there are some organizations which are independent of the Cabinet, though they may exercise a part of the executive power, such as "Jinji-in" [the National Personnel Authority],[25] "Kaikei-kennsa-in" [the Board of Audit], "Kosei-torihiki-iinkai" [the Fair Trade Commission], and the local public entities.[26]

15. Article 66 (3) CJ provides that the Cabinet has to be collectively responsible to the Diet for the exercise of executive power. This means that the Cabinet is based on the confidence of the Diet. This is called "giin-naikaku-sei" [the parliamentary system of the government]. It reflects on the failure of "chozen-shugi" [the indifference of the government to the Diet] under the CE, which accentuated the independence of the government from the Diet. The parliamentary system, which

24. But there can be Ministers who have no such post. They are called "Muninsho-daijin" ["Ministers Without Portfolio"].
25. DCJ (Fukui) Sep. 6, 1952, Gyosai 3-1823.
26. Local public entities are vested with the right to manage their property, affairs and administration (Art. 94 CJ).

followed the English type of parliamentary regime, tried to make much of the influence of political parties to function through the decision-making in the Diet.[27]

D. The Judiciary

16. Article 76 CJ provides that the whole judicial power is vested in the Supreme Court and the lower courts which are established by law (Article 76 CJ). It means that the present Constitution introduced a unitary court system which consists of a single hierarchy of courts, at the top of which the Supreme Court is located. There was the Administrative Court specifically established by the law in accordance with Article 61 CE. However, there are no extraordinary courts or tribunals independent of the control of the Supreme Court. There is no constitutional court in Japan. The only exception is the impeachment court provided by Article 64 CJ.[28]

17. The court system in Japan consists of: (i) "Saiko-saibansho" [the Supreme Court], (ii) "Koto-saibansho" [the High Courts], (iii) "Chiho-saibansho" [the District Courts], (iv) "Katei-saibansho" [the Family Courts] and (v) "Kan-i-saibansho" [the Summary Courts]. In general, the Japanese court system adopts a three-tier court system. In the ordinary case, the District Court has jurisdiction at first instance in both civil and criminal cases. However, there are several exceptions.[29]

18. There is only one Supreme Court located in Tokyo. It has its jurisdiction in matters of: (i) the further appeal from the judgments, in principle, of the High Courts; and (ii) the other appeals provided by the procedural laws (section 7 Court Law). The Supreme Court is vested with the power of judicial review as the last resort to maintain the constitutionality of any laws, orders, regulations, and other government actions (Articles 81 and 98 (1) CJ). It unifies the interpretation of laws and regulations carefully and thus contributes to the implementation of the rule of law.

19. There are eight High Courts located in major cities. They are, from north to south, Sapporo, Sendai, Tokyo, Nagoya, Osaka, Hiroshima, Takamatsu and Fukuoka. They have their own territorial jurisdiction over one of the eight parts of Japan. In addition, there are six branches and one Intellectual Property High Court, which was established in 2005 as a special branch of the Tokyo High Court, that treats cases only concerned with intellectual property. In the case of offenses against state security (sections 77–79 Penal Code), the High Court has the jurisdiction at first instance. However, in the main, the High Court is an appellate court from judgments given by the District Courts at first instance.[30]

---

27. Noda 1976, pp. 98–99.
28. *See* para. 11 *supra*.
29. *See* paras. 19, 20 and 21 *infra*.
30. But decisions given by the Summary Court at first instance are heard on appeal in the District Court, and further (and final) appeals are brought to the High Court.

20. There are fifty District Courts which have their own territorial jurisdiction over their respective areas. They are identical to those of forty-seven prefectures except for Hokkaido which is divided into four areas. In addition, there are 203 branches. The District Court is generally the court of first instance, except for matters specifically coming under the exclusive original jurisdiction of other types of court. It also has appellate jurisdiction over appeals in civil cases lodged against judgments of the Summary Courts and appeals lodged against orders and directions made at the Summary Courts. In District Courts, cases are handled by a single judge in principle.[31]

21. The Family Courts are specialized in dealing comprehensively with family cases and juvenile cases for the purpose of maintaining the welfare of family members concerning family matters and seeking for the sound upbringing of juveniles. They have jurisdiction over cases which involve domestic relations and juvenile delinquency, and over litigations which involve personal status, such as the relationship between husband and wife and parents and children. It conducts the conciliation procedure and the adjudication procedure according to the Family Cases Procedure Law (Law No. 52, 2011) and the Personal Status Litigation Law (Law No. 109, 2003). The Family Courts and their branches are located at the same places of the District Courts and their branches as mentioned above.[32] In addition, they have their local offices at the sites of seventy-seven Summary Courts.

22. The Summary Courts have jurisdiction over the civil cases which involve claims for an amount not exceeding JPY 1,400,000[33] and over the minor criminal cases such as offenses punishable by fines or lighter punishment and other offenses such as theft and embezzlement (section 33 Court Law). It does not have jurisdiction over administrative cases. As a rule, it cannot impose sanctions such as imprisonment without work or severer punishment. Exceptionally, it may impose imprisonment with work not exceeding three years concerned with cases of offenses specifically provided by the provisions of law. When the Summary Court deems it appropriate to impose punishment exceeding those limits, it must transfer the case to the District Court. In Summary Courts all cases are handled by a single judge. There are 438 Summary Courts in Japan, so that they are the most accessible courts for the people.

23. The power of judicial review over the constitutionality of legislation vested with the court by Articles 81 and 98 (1) CJ may be controversial when it is considered how the judicial review can be balanced with the supremacy of the Diet as the "highest" state organ as provided by Article 41 CJ.[34] The question is whether laws enacted by the Diet which directly represents the people should be subjected

---

31. Exceptionally, however, a three-judge panel is required in particular cases as provided by law such as appeals against judgments in civil cases rendered by Summary Courts and appeals against orders and directions made at Summary Courts in civil cases.
32. There are 253 District Court offices (50 District Courts and 203 branches) in total. *See* para. 20 *supra*.
33. It amounts to about USD 13,333 if it is calculated as USD 1 equivalent to JPY 105.
34. *See* para. 11 *supra*.

to the control of the court that is composed of a small number of persons who are not directly responsible to the nation, and whether it might contradict with the principle of popular sovereignty and democracy.

But, the principle of judicial supremacy is thought to be not in contradiction with democracy and popular sovereignty, first because the control of the constitutionality of laws by the court through its principled deliberation has actually been playing a role to protect the people from the abuse or deviation of power by the Diet under the influences of political fever.

Second, the appointment of the judges of the Supreme Court is reviewed by the people at the first general election of members of the House of Representatives following the judges' appointment. It shall be reviewed again at the first general election of the members of the House of Representatives to be held ten years after the first review, and reviewed in the same manner thereafter. When the majority of the voters favors the dismissal of a judge, he/she is dismissed (Article 79 (2), (3) and (4) CJ).[35]

Third, even if the Supreme Court exercised the power of judicial review and held a legislation or a part of it unconstitutional, the law would not be nullified. That is, the court cannot annul a law which it thinks unconstitutional, but it can only refuse applying the law to the particular case before them. The court has no power to give an abstract judgment or a judgment for future case on the constitutionality.[36] The law continues to be valid even after the decision that held it to be unconstitutional unless it is amended or abrogated by the Diet. Consequently, the principle of judicial supremacy to be applied through the careful judicial review is thought to be compatible with the constitutional status of the Diet as the "highest" state organ and harmonized with the democratic principle in the Constitution.

24. Besides, the court's consideration of the constitutionality of a particular clause of a particular law or a government action will not appear in the judgment section of the decision but in the reasoning. Thus the Supreme Court is not a constitutional court but an ordinary court which treats the concrete case even if it considers the constitutionality of the legal provision to be applied to the case. In addition, the Supreme Court has been careful to exercise its power of judicial review, especially when it treats highly political issues. The self-restriction by the court on the power of judicial review is due to the intention to maintain its tense relationship with the Diet and the Cabinet, which would lead to judicial autonomy in Japan. However, the judicial independence ultimately rests on the public trust in the court.[37]

35. The detailed procedure is provided by Law on the Popular Review of the Supreme Court Judge (Law No. 136, 1947).
36. SCJ (FB) Oct. 8, 1952 Minshu 6-9-783.
37. Haley 1995a: pp. 1–15; Haley 1995b: pp. 98–115.

IV. Economy

25. After the rapid economic growth through the 1960s and 1970s, the growth speed of the Japanese economy has gradually declined since the end of the 1970s. As a result of the collapse of asset price bubble since the beginning of the 1990s due to the excessive investments to the immovable property beyond their substantive value through the 1980s, the economic growth slowed down markedly in the 1990s. The Japanese economy was also affected by the Asian financial crisis in 1997, by the Lehman Brothers bankruptcy in 2008 and by the Tohoku massive earthquake in 2011. The growth rate of Gross Domestic Product (GDP), which was 12.5% in 1969, has been declined to 5.5% in 1979, 4.9% in 1989, –0.25% in 1999, –5.4% in 2009, and 1.9% in 2019.[38] In 2019 the GDP was USD 5.415 trillion and GDP per capita was USD 42,798.[39] Japan has been struggling for economic reform under the adverse conditions of population decline and aging society.

26. The GDP by sector composed of (a) agriculture, forestry and fishing (1.2%); (b-1) manufacturing (20.8%); (b-2) construction (5.8%); (b-3) electricity, gas and water supply and waste management service (2.6%); (b-4) mining (0.06%); (c-1) wholesale and retail trade (14.0%); (c-2) real estate (11.4%); (c-3) professional, scientific and technical activities (7.5%); (c-4) human health and social work activities (7.0%); (c-5) transport and postal services (5.1%); (c-6) public administration (5.0%); (c-7) information and communications (4.9%); (c-8) finance and insurance (4.2%); (c-9) education (3.6%); (c-10) accommodation and food service activities (2.5%); and (c-11) other services (4.3%) in 2017.[40] Thus currently (b-1) manufacturing, (c-1) wholesale and retail trade, and (c-2) real estate are the top three industries in Japan.

27. The labor force population was 65.90 million in 2010 and 68.30 million in 2018. Among them, the ratio of the workers who aged 65 or over has increased from 8.9% in 2010 to 12.8% in 2018, whereas the ratio of workers under the age of 34 has decreased from 28.2% in 2010 to 25.5% in 2018.[41] The unemployment rate had decreased from 5.1% in 2010 to 2.4% in 2018.[42]

---

38. GDP Growth (annual %), the World Bank, World Development Indicators, Japan, at http://data.worldbank.org/country/japan (accessed Nov. 1, 2020).
39. GDP and GDP per capita, Purchasing Power Parity (current international USD), the World Bank, *supra* (footnote 38).
40. Statistics Bureau 2020: 3-4 (accessed Nov. 1, 2020).
41. Statistics Bureau 2020: 19-2 (accessed Nov. 1, 2020).
42. Statistics Bureau 2020: 19-2 (accessed Nov. 1, 2020).

§2. Legal Background of the Country

I. Legal Family or Tradition

A. Overview

28. The Japanese legal system has developed through several steps:[43]

(i) Before the sixth century when there were local powers competing with each other for political hegemony, indigenous rules had evolved in local regions, but unified legal rules that bridge them had not been developed.
(ii) Since the end of the sixth century the integration of political powers has been promoted under the Yamato Dynasty which was originated in the western part of Japan. In the seventh century, the government introduced the Chinese legal concepts and legal rules such as "ritsu" [penal rules] and "ryo" [administrative regulations] from China directly and indirectly by way of Korea so as to strengthen the foundation of the emerging state of Japan.
(iii) After the reception and assimilation of the ritsu-ryo legal system, as the wealthy nobles, shrines and temples began to privatized manors, the ritsu-ryo legal system has been declined at the beginning of the tenth century, the armed tribes in the regions called "bushi" or the warrior class called "samurai" have gained strength. They developed their own legal concepts and rules based on the customary laws in each region. At the end of the twelfth century, the Shogun was appointed by the Emperor as the head of samurai families, and the feudal legal system has been established at the beginning of the seventeenth century after the long civil wars.
(iv) In the middle of the nineteenth century, the Shogun's government was replaced by the more centralized imperial government as a result of the restoration. Since then the Western legal concepts and legal rules were comprehensively introduced from the U.K., France, Germany, etc. to facilitate the modernization of the state and legal system, including the promulgation of Constitution.
(v) The imperial government embarked on foreign expansion by colonizing Asian countries since 1894, but it was defeated by the Allied Forces in August 1945. In 1946 the Constitution was amended and the democratic constitutional system was strengthened by the legal reform under the supervision of the U.S. occupying force even though the constitutional monarchy was kept.

43. As for the history of Japan, *see* Gordon 2014; Henshall 2012; Huffman 2010; Mason and Caiger 1997; Totman 2005.
As for the Japanese legal history in general, *see* Dean 2002: pp. 55–127; Jones and Ravitch 2018: pp. 13–38; Noda 1976; Oda 2011: pp. 13–25; Röhl (ed.) 2005; Carl Steenstrup, "New Knowledge Concerning Japan's Legal System before 1868, Acquired from Japanese Sources by Western Writers since 1963," in: Foote (ed.) 2007: pp. 7–33.

(vi) Since the 1990s, the impact of globalization has been increasing on legal reform such as the protection of environment, the strengthening of rights of children, women and minorities, and the judicial reform to promote the rule of law.

29. The unique structure of the Japanese legal system is a combination of indigenous elements which had traditionally evolved and foreign elements which have been received from China, Korea, the U.K., France, Germany, other European countries, the U.S. etc. Foreign legal rules which were sometimes combined with themselves have been assimilated with existing rules so that they could be applied to the practices. As a result, the Japanese legal system became a hybrid of various legal rules of different origins, including traditional rules and received rules. It has created a unique legal culture characterized as a "gray" legal culture.[44]

B. Unification of Political Powers by the Imperial Government Through the Introduction of the Ritsu-Ryo Legal System

30. Since the seventh century, the emerging unified government of Japan introduced the ritsu-ryo legal codes which had originally developed in China. It was available by the introduction of a writing system using "Kanji" [the Chinese characters] by way of the Korean Peninsula. Japan also received Buddhism and the political philosophy based on Confucianism and the Absolute Legalist thought. Confucianism taught that rulers should instruct the ignorant people with virtue and courtesy, whereas Absolute Legalism stressed that political leaders should rule by a system of reward and punishment based on the law.[45] On the basis of the ritsu-ryo legal system and the political thought based on Buddhism, Confucianism and Absolute Legalism, the Emperor and his/her officials established the nationwide-uniform system of rule at the beginning of the eighth century. The original concept of law ("ho" in Japanese) represented nothing but a political instrument for the ruling class to justify orders and sanctions to be given to the ruled, and the legal codes included a catalogue of obligations on the part of subjects so as to establish the society to be governed by the rulers. This original conception of law has lasted long and influenced deeply the people's consciousness of law which seems to remain still now. Under the ritsu-ryo system, all the land and people shall belong to the Emperor, which was called "ko-chi ko-min."[46]

31. Even before Buddhism, Confucianism, Absolute Legalism and the ritsu-ryo legal code were introduced from Korea and China, indigenous norms had developed in Japan. The respect for conformity was developed influenced by the collective labor structure for rice production and the development and management of irrigation system. Shintoism has been the indigenous religion developed gradually

44. Katsuta 1996: p. 249.
45. Katsuta 1996: p. 250.
46. It meant that any privatization of the land and people shall be prohibited as was stipulated in s. 2 of the Imperial Edict in 646.

in Japan from the time unknown in detail. It originated from a kind of animism in which trees, rocks, mountains and other natural objects are worshipped as Gods resided within them. It has no fixed scriptures or metaphysical doctrines. Shintoism was used to strengthen the Emperor's authority by explaining that the Emperor came from heaven down to the earth as a God. This became the very basis of the political structure of Japan as a kind of kingdom, the ultimate authority of which shall be drawn from the Emperor.[47] It coexisted with Buddhism and was embedded in the ritsu-ryo legal system.[48]

C. Development of the Feudal Legal System under the Bakufu Government

32. Since the tenth century, the ritsu-ryo system was shaken by the development of private manors collected by the wealthy nobles and clergy of shrines and temples and the rise of "bushi" [the armed tribes in the regions] or "samurai" [the warrior class] who gained the political powers in their regions through the delegated administration of public land and private manors.[49] It led to political struggles between the imperial government and the competing nobles, and it brought about fights between bushi families who supported different sides of the imperial struggles. In 1180, Taira clan, the most powerful bushi family at that time based on the western part of Japan, was defeated by Minamoto clan which was another powerful bushi family based in the eastern part. Yoritomo Minamoto, the head of Minamoto clan, acquired the right to appoint the head of each region from the Emperor in 1185 and established the Shogun's government called "Bakufu" in Kamakura, about 50 km south of Tokyo. He was appointed by the Emperor as the Shogun, the head of bushi families, in 1192. Then the real political power shifted from the imperial government to the Shogun's government.[50]

The "Bakufu" government developed the bushi law, as represented by the Joei Shikimoku [Joei Code] in 1232. It was enacted by the agreement between the Shogun, the lord, and his main vassals who had benefices from the Shogun and the lords in reward for their military service. It was an important and unique law dealing with conflicts among bushi based on the bushi justice, which was the morality called "dori" [the reason] or "giri" [the right reason]. Joei Shikimoku became part of the general legal system and remained one of the major sources of law until the collapse of the feudal regime in 1868.[51]

47. The imperial family legitimized itself through the God of Shinto. *See* Henshall 2012: p. 22.
48. The Department of Worship provided in the Taiho Ritsu-Ryo Code was concerned with Shinto. *See* Mason and Caiger 1997: pp. 39, 44.
49. In order to distinguish the private manors ruled by the nobles, temples, shrines and bushi from the public land held by the imperial government, the registration offices were established by the Imperial government since the eleventh century.
50. Henshall 2012: pp. 29–37.
51. Maison and Caiger 1997: p. 135. Its central norms such as "dori" and "giri" have been generalized in the society and become the basic norms of various kinds of organizations such as family, school, company, and bureaucracy in Japan.

33. The political power of Bakufu government was gradually strengthened, and the areas under its control gradually expanded from the eastern part to the other territories in the country through the thirteenth to seventeenth century. However, this process was not promoted in a straight line. During the period of Kamakura Bakufu (1180–1338), there was the restoration by Emperor Godaigo called "Kenmu-no-chuko" since 1333. Although Takauji Ashikaga took back the political power from Emperor Godaigo in 1336 and established Muromachi Bakufu government in Kyoto, the Bakufu government weakened again around the end of the fifteenth century. Since then, small independent states ruled by the regional bushi families emerged all around the country, and "sengoku jidai" [the Age of Civil Wars] began. The ruler of each state was called "sengoku daimyo" [the lords in Civil War period]. The Age of Civil War lasted until 1603 when Ieyasu Tokugawa established a unitary feudal regime of Tokugawa Bakufu government.[52] It lasted until 1868 when the Restoration by the Imperial government took place again.

34. After the establishment of the Tokugawa Bakufu government, all areas of Japan including Hokkaido and Okinawa were united under the feudal regime. The Bakufu government devised the solid structure of the political regime by keeping the nominal authority of the Emperor as the ultimate source of legitimacy. Fiefs were divided among the "daimyo" [the feudal lords] into "Han" [the territorial state governments] in which daimyo enjoyed their political and legal autonomy. There were the Han laws in each territorial domain to govern the land and people. Therefore each Han was a decentralized local government, although the control by the Shogun as the head of the central government was maintained and the law of Bakufu presided over the laws of Han when there was an inconsistency between them. This system was called "Baku-Han-taisei" [the governance system by the combination of Bakufu and Han], and the centralization of political power was yet to be completed.[53]

35. The Bakufu government established the strict hierarchical order that consisted of the court noble, the clergy, "shi" [bushi], "no" [peasants], "ko" [artisans], "sho" [merchants] and pariahs. The commoners were ranked below "shi" in such an order as "no," "ko" and "sho." Although the peasants ("no") were officially ranked at the highest status among the commoners, they were actually imposed very heavy burdens, obliged to live frugally, neither allowed to change their place of residence nor their occupation. In order to maintain this rigid class distinction, the Bakufu government adopted Confucianism as its official ideology, and issued "hatto" [the basic regulations], "furegaki" [the orders] and "tasshi" [the circulars] on the basis of Confucianism.[54] Among basic regulations, "Kinchu narabini-kuge-sho-hatto" [the General Status Code of the Court Nobles] of 1615, "Buke-sho-hatto" [the General Status Code of Bushi Family] of 1615, and "Kujigata-osadame-gaki" [the Written Rules of Procedure] of 1742 were most famous and important in practice. They

52. Henshall 2012: pp. 41–50.
53. Mason and Caiger 1997: pp. 196–202.
54. In Confucian thought it was emphasized that the people's fate is determined by heaven from their birth.

were not promulgated codes which provided rights of the people but administrative manuals and penalties for the interest of government officials.[55]

D. The Restoration by the Imperial Government and Modernization of Legal System

1. The Shift of Political Power from the Bakufu to the Imperial Government

36. In the middle of the nineteenth century, the Bakufu government confronted with the frequent requests to open the country by the foreign governments and with the internal defiance to overthrow the Bakufu by means of the imperial authority. In 1867, the 15th Shogun Yoshinobu Tokugawa proposed to hand back the "Taisei" [the great political power] including the domain and the people which had been directly governed by the Bakufu to the Emperor and it was accepted by the Emperor.[56] Then the newly built Imperial government under the authority of the Meiji Emperor (Meiji government) promoted a set of policies to centralize the political power into the hands of the Emperor. It confiscated the former Shogun's territories called "Tenryo" in 1868,[57] and demanded the head of other Han, the territorial state governments, to return their land and people to the imperial government in 1871.[58] These measures were the fundamental basis of the centralization policy to be promoted by Meiji government.

37. Some of the territorial states such as Aizu Han, Sendai Han, and Nagaoka Han together with the supporters of the former Bakufu resisted the Meiji government, but they were repressed by June 1869. As a result of the return of land from Han to the imperial government, the former samurai lost their status and financial source. Some dissatisfied samurai rebelled against the government, but they were suppressed by November 1877 when "Seinan" War was suppressed. This marked the restoration process called "Meiji-ishin." However, there are controversies about what the substance of "Meiji-ishin" was. It may be difficult to characterize it as a revolution because it was carried out by the limited groups consisting mostly of the lower class bushi of some great territorial states in the southwest of Japan such as "Satsuma," "Choshu," "Tosa" and "Hizen" so that it was not associated with a popular movement element of a revolution. Rather, it would be appropriate to understand that it was a coup d'etat by the progressive political leaders to strengthen the centralization of state power to cope with the international imperialistic movement of colonization by the Western powers.[59]

38. The Meiji government began a set of campaigns to unite the people under the centralized authority of the Emperor so as to keep independence against foreign

55. Dean 2002: pp. 58–59.
56. It was called "Taisei-Hokan" [the restoration of the great political power].
57. It terminated the Bakufu as an institution of national government. Mason and Caiger 1997: p. 260.
58. It was called "Han-Seki-Hokan" [the restoration of the domination of land and people].
59. Noda 1976: p. 42 and note 2; Mason and Caiger 1997: pp. 258–259.

powers. This can be seen as a process of modernization initiated by the state following the model of modernized countries. A series of comprehensive legal reform modeled on the Western legal system can be realized in this modernization context. The Japanese style of modernization can be characterized by policy slogans such as: (a) "bunmei-kaika" [the enlightenment for civilization], (b) "fukoku-kyohei" [the wealthy state and strong army] and (c) "shokusan-kogyo" [the investment to encourage new industries].

In the field of law, the modernization process can be divided into three stages.[60] They are: (1) the transition period (1868–1871),[61] (2) the liberalization period (1871–1890),[62] and (3) the nationalization period (1890–1898).[63]

39. In the first few years after the restoration, the Meiji government issued basic laws and regulations for rebuilding the nation, while it proclaimed that it should keep "institutions of Tokugawa ancestors, graceful customs and good laws."[64] In April 1868, it issued fundamental norms of "Gokajo-no-goseimon" [the Imperial Covenant of Five Articles] which provided the policy of decision-making through discussion by holding meetings and "Seitai-sho" [the Code of the Form of Government] which included the rule of separation of powers into the legislative, executive and judiciary,[65] though the Constitution was enacted after twenty years.[66] They were followed by administrative and criminal laws such as Public Officials Order in 1870, Civil Registration Law in 1871, and Penal Code in 1868 (amended in 1871 and 1873).

2. Codification of Civil Code and Other Basic Codes

40. The codification project to introduce civil law was initiated by the government officials since the beginning of the 1870s. However, it was not promoted straightforwardly. In 1870, Rinsho Mitsukuri, a member of the study group of the codification of civil law headed by Shinpei Eto, who became the Minister of Justice in 1872, within the Meiji government, translated the French word "droit civil" as "min-ken." "Min" means citizen and "ken" means right, so that their combination means the citizen's right. It indicated that the citizen can have a right. But the conservative members of the group raised strong objections against such translation, for they could not believe that the ordinary citizen can have a right as the subject of

60. In the Japanese context, however, the modernization of law resulted in a formal discontinuity of the state law between the modernized state law and the former Japanese law developed before the Meiji Restoration. *See* Noda 1976: p. 39.
61. *See* para. 39 *infra*.
62. *See* paras. 40 to 44 *infra*.
63. *See* paras. 45 to 51 *infra*.
64. The Great Command of the Restoration of Imperial Rule issued in January 1868.
65. However, they were not independent organizations but branches of the government. The Diet was introduced in 1890 after the Constitution was promulgated in 1889. Before that the Senate called "Genro-in" and the Supreme Court called "Daishin-in" were established in 1875, and the Cabinet system called "Naikaku" was adopted in 1885. In addition, the Privy Council called "Sumitsu-in" was introduced in 1888.
66. It was promulgated in February 1889. *See* para. 50 *infra*.

right. As the discussion could not reach a conclusion, Mr. Eto winded it up that they should keep Mitsukuri's translation, for it might be utilized in the future.[67]

41. In the early stage of modernization of legal system, the liberal legal thoughts introduced from European countries and U.S. were influential. Some laws were enacted modeled on the British and French laws. Among them, for example, "Soto-bunrei" [the Order Concerning Procedural Documents] in 1873 and "Shusso-kigen-kisoku" [the Regulation on Limitation] in 1873 were influenced by the English law. However, the English common law system was considered to be too complicated to introduce and incorporate into the existing law within a short period of time.[68]

42. In the field of criminal law, the Penal Code of 1880 and the Criminal Procedure Code of 1880 were drafted by Gustave Boissonade, who was Professor at the Faculty of Law, the University of Paris and came over to Japan in 1873 in response to the invitation of the Meiji government. These codes were challenged by conservatives in "Genro-in" [the Senate] and officials who supported the former penal codes based on the ritsu-ryo legal system[69] and the traditional customs. But they won the promulgation and were put into effect in 1882.[70]

43. In 1879 (or 1880), the Minister of Justice Takato Ohki asked French Professor Gustave Boissonade[71] to draft the Civil Code except for the parts of family law and succession law that were reserved in the hands of Japanese drafters. Once this project was interrupted in the middle, the new Minister of Justice Akiyoshi Yamada appointed Boissonade as a drafter of the Civil Code again in 1887. His draft was written in French and translated into Japanese as it was drawn up. The translated drafts were discussed and modified by the Committee for the Investigation of Law, and then by "Genro-in" [the Senate], and finally by "Sumitsu-in" [the Privy Council]. In 1889 parts of the bills drafted by Boissonade (Book on Property; Book on the Methods of Acquiring Property except for Chapters on (1) succession, (2)_ inheritance property and (3) marriage contract; Book on the Securities for Guaranteeing Performance of Obligations; and Book on the Methods of Proof) were adopted and promulgated on April 21, 1890. The other parts drafted by the Japanese drafters (remaining three Chapters in Book on the Method of Acquiring Property (from (1) to (3) above), and Book on the Persons) were also adopted and promulgated on October 7, 1890. These five Books were combined into a single

---

67. Nobushige Hozumi, *Hoso Yawa* [Night Stories on Legal Matters] (Iwanami-bunko, 1980), p. 214.
68. Dean 2002: p. 62.
69. *See* paras. 28 and 31 *supra*.
70. Dean 2002: pp. 62–63.
71. Boissonade came to Japan in November 1873 and gave lectures on natural law and French law at the law school in the Ministry of Justice from April 1874 until August 1879. Yoshihiko Kawaguchi, *Nihon Kindai Ho Shi* [A Modern Japanese Legal History] (Shinseisha, 1998), p. 111.

code as the Civil Code of the Empire of Japan (1890) and to be brought into effect on January 1, 1893. It followed the French style of codification called "Institutiones" system.[72]

44. In addition, other basic codes were also adopted: Commercial Code was drafted by Hermann Roesler following the German style, promulgated on April 27, 1890, and to be brought into effect on January 1, 1893; Court Organization Law was drafted by Otto Rudolf on the model of German Law of 1877, promulgated on February 10, 1890, and took effect on November 1, 1890; Code of Civil Procedure was drafted by Hermann Techow modeled on the German system almost exactly, and came into effect on January 1, 1891.[73]

45. However, the Civil Code of 1890 and the Commercial Code of 1890 did not come into effect as it was scheduled on January 1, 1893, because the newly established Diet[74] adopted a bill on November 22, 1892, to the effect that both Codes needed to be amended so that their enforcement shall be postponed until December 31, 1896, unless amendment bills would be approved by the Diet before that date. Only Chapters on company and partnership, bills of exchange and checks, and bankruptcy in the Commercial Code were amended and put into effect in July 1893. The other parts of Commercial Code and the Civil Code were still under review. This postponement was a result of the hot dispute on the enforcement of the Civil Code which was thought to have a gap with the existing laws and traditional norms, especially in the provisions of family and status relationship.[75] The Commercial Code drafted by the German adviser was also felt to hold a gap with the existing laws and customs so that it was necessary to put into the comprehensive review before enforcement.[76]

46. In order to promote the revision and redrafting of the Civil and Commercial Code, the Council for Codification Studies was set up by the Imperial Ordinance on February 22, 1892, and chaired by Prime Minister Hirobumi Ito. He made the Guideline for the Study of Codification and appointed drafters who were all Japanese. Within the Council, the draft was submitted to the Chief Investigation Committee and then to the Plenary Committee for discussions and revisions in accordance with the Guideline. The Council adopted the Policy for the Study of

72. It consisted of: (i) Book on Persons, (ii) Book on Property, (iii) Book on the Methods of Acquiring Property, (iv) Book on the Securities for Guaranteeing Performance of Obligations, and (v) Book on the Methods of Proof.
73. To note is that the procedural laws were put into effect and applied earlier than the Civil Code and Commercial Code. *See* Noda 1976: p. 55.
74. It was established in November 1890 after the promulgation of the Constitution in February 1889 and the first national election in July 1890.
75. Dean 2002: pp. 65–66.
76. Dean 2002: pp. 66–67.

Codification which included the structural change of the Civil Code from the "Institutiones" system of the former Civil Code of 1890 to the "Pandekten" system based on the German Civil Code.[77]

47. However, the Policy did not change the purpose of the codification, which had been adopted by the Minister of Justice Takato Ohki. In his proposal to the government in September 1876, he articulated that the purpose of compiling "the complete Civil Code" was to facilitate the communications among human beings on the basis of "tennen-no-risei" [natural reason] or natural law. He emphasized the importance to provide rights and duties between the persons in comprehensive legal relations through codification. He also established the Bureau for the Investigation of Local Customary Rules in 1876 and published the Collection of Customary Rules in Civil Matters in 1878, which was revised in 1880. It was often consulted by the drafters of the new Civil Code and reflected in their drafts. The purpose of the Minister of Justice was to increase the integrity of national legal system on the basis of the combination of traditional rules and the newly introduced rules based on the natural law.[78]

48. The Guideline and the Policy for the Study of Codification confirmed that the purpose of the Council was the necessary "modification and revision" of the Civil Code of 1890. As a result, the newly drafted bill of the new Civil Code retained some provisions of the former Civil Code with certain revisions. But it also adopted new provisions with some modification from the first and second draft of the German Civil Code, and referred to the civil code of Austria, the Netherlands, Italy, Spain, Portugal, Switzerland, Belgium, Russia, California, Louisiana, etc., and statutes and case law of U.K., U.S.A., India, etc. The drafters often combined elements from those different sources to arrange new provisions so that the new Civil Code was characterized as "a fruit of comparative jurisprudence."[79]

49. The bill of the new Civil Code for the first three Parts (Part 1: General Provisions, Part 2: Real Rights and Part 3: Claim Rights) was adopted by the Diet and promulgated on April 27, 1896, and that for the last two Parts (Part 4: Family Relations and Part 5: Succession) was adopted and promulgated on June 21, 1898. They came into effect on July 16, 1898. It was almost the same timing as the German Civil Code was promulgated on August 24, 1896, and shall be put into effect on January 1, 1900. After the enforcement of the Japanese Civil Code which followed the German "Pandekten" system, the German legal science became popular, and it strongly influenced the interpretation of the Japanese Civil Code. It was called "gakusetsu-keiju" [reception of legal theory] which led to the predominance of German legal science until the end of World War II.[80]

---

77. As a result, the new Civil Code consisted of Books of: (i) the General Provisions, (ii) Real Rights, (iii) Obligations, (iv) Family Relations and (v) Succession.
78. The natural law called "sei-ho" in Japanese was recognized as a source of law when the judge could not find any provision of law and customary law in civil matters (s. 3, Ordinance No. 103 in 1875).
79. Hozumi 1912: p. 22.
80. Michiatsu Kaino, "Some Introductory Comments on the Historical Background of Japanese Civil Law," *International Journal of Sociology of Law*, Vol. 16, 1988, pp. 385–389.

3. Enactment of Constitution

50. The Germanization of Japanese legal science was also closely related to the enactment of the first Constitution. The drafting of Constitution started in 1886 under the initiative taken by Hirobumi Itoh who became the first Prime Minister in November 1885. Kowashi Inoue was a central figure among the drafters. He consulted with German Jurist Herman Roesler and Albert Mosse who admired the Prussian Constitution of 1850, and completed the draft by 1888. However, it was not discussed in the Senate but only in the Privy Council. On February 11, 1889, the Constitution of the Empire of Japan was promulgated or "granted" by the Emperor as a sovereign to his subjects, and came into effect on November 29, 1890.[81] This Constitution is called the Meiji Constitution.

51. Under the Meiji Constitution, Japan shall be reigned by the Emperor who held "the rights of sovereignty" (Articles 1 and 3 CE) and exercised the legislative power "with the consent of the Imperial Diet" (Article 5 CE). The Imperial Diet was a collaborative organ with the Emperor (Article 37 CE), whereas the Imperial Ordinance was to be applied as law in an emergency and when the Diet was out of session (Articles 8 and 9 CE). The power of the Imperial Diet was considerably weakened by the Cabinet as well.[82] If the Diet would not adopt the bill of the budget submitted by the Cabinet, the budget of the previous year was to be enforced again (Article 71 CE).[83] In addition, the military power was not prescribed and controlled by the Constitution. Because of the immature independence of the Diet and incomplete control over the military force, the constitutionalism of the Meiji Constitution was "only in an appearance."[84]

52. However, judicial independence has gradually grown even under the political pressures of the Cabinet under the Meiji Constitution. In May 11, 1891, when the Russian Prince, the future Czar Nicholas II, visited Japan, a policeman, named Sanzo Tsuda, suspected that the Prince had come to spy, and he attacked and stabbed the Prince in a small-town Otsu (Otsu Incident). This incident bothered the government because it would complicate the relation between Japan and Russia so that Prime Minister Masayoshi Matsukata strongly required the Minister of Justice Akiyoshi Yamada that the death penalty should be given to the offender Tsuda. The Meiji Emperor unconventionally called on the Prince in hospital, and the Minister of Foreign Affairs Shuzo Aoki had given an assurance to the Russian Embassy that Tsuda must be sentenced to die. However, the head of the Supreme Court Iken Kojima

81. Dean 2002: pp. 68–69.
82. The Cabinet system had been established in 1885. Through the enactment of Communes Law of 1888 and Departments Law of 1890, the central and local administration were perfected along the Prussian line.
83. *See also* Art. 54 CE which stipulated that the Ministers of State and the Delegates of the Government may, at any time, take seats and speak in either House of Representatives or House of Lords. It was in contrast with the parliamentary system adopted by the present Constitution under which Prime Minister and a majority number of the Ministers of State must be chosen from among the members of the Diet (Art. 67 (1) and 68 (1) CJ).
84. Noda 1976: p. 57.

refused to yield to such political pressure with the support by the members of the bar and, on May 27, 1891, the court sentenced Tsuda to life imprisonment for the reason that the Criminal Code did not provide the death penalty for attempted murder (sections 112 and 116 the former Criminal Code) and that the high treason (section 2 the former Criminal Code) could not be applied to this case as alleged by the government leaders. This reasoning based on the rule of law could persuade Russia, and it is said that the Kojima installed the "principle of judicial independence" in Japan and he was honored as the "Guardian of Constitution." The political pressures and incentives for agents to follow their principal's wishes seemed to be restrained by the growing rule of law.[85]

E. The Postwar Reforms

1. Series of Reform under the Occupation

53. On August 10, 1945, the government of Japan decided to accept Potsdam Declaration, and it proclaimed the unconditional surrender on August 15, 1945.[86] After that, the government was placed under the control of Allied Forces. However, it was not a direct rule so that the government of Japan was allowed to act under the supervision of "Rengokoku-saiko-shireikan" [the Supreme Commander of the Allied Powers: SCAP]. In order to help SCAP to control the Occupational Forces, the General Head Quarter (GHQ) was set up. Over SCAP there was "Tai-nichi-rijikai" [the Allied Council for Japan: ACJ] to supervise SCAP, and ACJ was under the control of "Kyokuto-rijikai" [the Far Eastern Committee: FEC]. In the first stage of the occupation, from August 1945 to summer 1948, the following reforms were suggested or required by GHQ: (a) demilitarization; (b) fundamental reform of the Constitution; and (c) "Five Major Reforms" concerned with the promotion of liberalization and democratization such as: (1) equalization of the sexes, (2) encouragement of the labor union, (3) liberalization of education, (4) abrogation of institutions related to the police state, and (5) democratization of the economy. These reforms meant a radical change of the political, economic and legal system of the Meiji regime, which were carried out under the supervision of GHQ in which the role of civilian advisors mainly from the U.S.A. was crucial.[87] I will focus on the amendment to the Constitution and Five Major Reforms as follows.[88]

54. The Constitution of the Empire of Japan (Meiji Constitution) was transformed into the Constitution of Japan (present Constitution) through the "amendment" clause of Article 73 CE, which was promulgated on November 3, 1946, and put into effect on May 3, 1947. Although the present Constitution has kept the constitutional monarchy, it changed the fundamental principles of the Meiji Constitution:

85. Ramseyer and Rosenbluth 1997: pp. 142–143.
86. The instrument of surrender was signed on Sep. 2, 1945.
87. Dean 2002: pp. 70–71.
88. As for the demilitarization, *see* Oda 2011: p. 21.

(a) There was a transformation of sovereignty from the Emperor to the people. The will of the people shall be represented by the Diet, the members of which are to be elected by the universal election. The universal election had been for the first time held on April 10, 1946, by the amendment to the Election Law before the promulgation of the present Constitution.[89] But the present Constitution was enacted by way of an "amendment" to the Meiji Constitution in accordance with Article 73 CE. As a result, the validity of the present Constitution was challenged because it would be questioned whether the fundamental principle of the Constitution on the holder of sovereignty could be changed by way of its "amendment." In order to justify the validity of the present Constitution, the "August Revolution" Thesis was presented,[90] which regarded the constitutional change that took place in August 1945 as a revolution.[91] However, it cannot deny the lack of social reality corresponding to the "revolution." Rather, it should be to affirm the continuity of the legal system between the Meiji regime and the present regime by recognizing the confirmation by the people of the constitutional change, including the holder of sovereignty. The Constitution is a part of the working legal system that can change the Constitution, including the holder of sovereignty,[92] and the legal system itself is one of the aspects of social system that includes people's consciousness, religions, customary rules, political system, tribes, etc.[93]

(b) The present Constitution guarantees the fundamental human rights (Articles 11–29, 31–40, and 97 CJ) and safeguards them through the introduction of the judicial review (Articles 81 and 98 CJ). It also needed the revision of the Code of Criminal Procedure, which was enacted in 1948 on the underlying principle of due process of law based on the U.S. adversarial system.[94]

(c) Article 9 CJ provides the renunciation of war, which is also the salient feature of the present Constitution based on pacifism.[95]

---

89. Before the amendment to the Constitution, the right to vote and the right to be elected in the national election were given to women for the first time by the amendment to the Election Law for Members of the House of Representatives promulgated on Dec. 17, 1945.
90. Toshiyoshi Miyazawa, "Hachigatsu-kakumei-to-kokuminshuken-shugi" [August Revolution and the Principle of Popular Sovereignty], *Sekai-bunka* [World Culture], Vol. 1, No. 4, 1946, pp. 64–71.
91. On this dispute, *see* Yasuo Hasebe, *The August Revolution Thesis and the Making of the Constitution of Japan*, in *Rule of Law, Rechtstheorie, Beiheft 17* 335–342 (Werner Krawietz, Enrico Pattaro and Alice Erh-Soon Tay eds, Duncker & Humblot 1997).
92. Such a legal system was called "nomos" by the legal philosopher Tomoo Odaka in his book, *Kokumin-shuken-to-tenno-sei* [*Popular Sovereignty and Emperor System*] 60–61 (Kokuritu-shoin 1947).
93. Joseph Raz, *The Concept of a Legal System: An Introduction to the Theory of a Legal System* 188 (Clarendon Press 2nd ed. 1980).
94. The prewar criminal procedure was based on the German inquisitorial system. *See* Oda 2011: p. 436.
95. The pacifist nature of the present Constitution appears in its Preamble as well. "We, the Japanese people, ... resolved that never again shall we be visited with the horrors of war through the action of government, ... desire peace for all time and are deeply conscious of the high ideals controlling human relationship, and we have determined to preserve our security and existence, trusting in the justice and faith of the peace-loving peoples of the world." *See also* Jones and Ravitch 2018: pp. 188–192.

55. Among the "Five Major Reforms,"[96] the promotion of gender equality and the agricultural land reform as a measure to promote economic democratization should be worth explaining in more detail:

(a) In order to realize the equality between men and women in accordance with the revised Constitution to be enforced on May 3, 1947 (Article 14 (1) CJ on the equality under the law and Article 24 CJ on the essential equality of the sexes in marriage, property rights, inheritance and other matters pertaining to the family), provisions which contradicted with the gender equality were excluded from the Civil Code by the Amendment Law to the Civil Code promulgated on December 22, 1947. For example, sections 14–18 of the former Civil Code which provided the limited capacity of wife (and a necessary consent by her husband) to do a juridical act concerning valuable property such as a transaction of immovable property were abrogated.[97]
(b) The agricultural land reform had been the crucial problem because the disputes between landlord and tenant had been increasing after the recognition of private ownership to land. The legal reform was interrupted by the Pacific War, but revived just after the War. In October 1946, the Special Measures Law for Establishing Independent Farmers was enacted and the absentee landlords and the resident landlords who owned exceeding 1 hectare of tenant farmland were forced to sell the land to the state, and tenant farmers were given the opportunity to buy the land from the state at a lower price than the market value. By October 1952, an area of about 1,988,000 hectares of tenant land had been bought by the state, about 2,500,000 landowners sold their tenant land, and about 4,260,000 tenant farmers had purchased the farmland. Farm families without self-owned land decreased from around 26% in 1938 to around 4% in 1952, and farm families which worked as tenant farmers decreased from around 70% to 40% in the same period. The number of owner cultivators increased from 31% (about 1,656,000 farm families) in 1941 to 70% (4,200,000 farm families) in 1955, while tenant farmers, who owned little farmland (farmers who own less than 10% of their cultivating land), decreased from 28% (1,516,000 farm families) to 4% (239,000 farm families) during the same period.[98]

Against the agricultural land reform, the landlords who were forced to sell their land at a lower price than the market value challenged the constitutionality of the land reform legislation in accordance with Article 29 (3) CJ which stipulates "Private property may be taken for public use upon just compensation therefor." The Supreme Court (majority opinion) said that "fair compensation should be based on a price that could be thought of as fair considering the economic conditions of the

---

96. *See* (3) in para. 53 *supra*.
97. The legal reform to implement the gender equality was based on the respect for the dignity of individuals which appears in Art. 13 and Art. 24 CJ, s. 2 JCC, etc. so that the Amendment Law to the Civil Code also totally revised Part IV (Family Relations) and Part V (Succession). It dissolved "ie-seido" [the family system] under the Meiji regime.
98. Toshihiko Kawagoe, "Agricultural Land Reform in Postwar Japan: Experiences and Issues," Policy Research Working Paper 2111, the World Bank, 1999, pp. 33, 54.

time, and be an appropriate amount rationally calculated," and it was "not necessary for it to correspond exactly to any price which might usually apply." It was to promote the cultivation of agricultural land, and to maintain and improve the stability of the cultivator's position, and agricultural output. Looked at from the viewpoint of the "purpose" of the land reform legislation, this pricing was "just."[99]

2. Change of the Original Occupation Policy

56. In the second stage of the occupation since around the summer in 1948 until the conclusion of the Peace Treaty in 1951, the early occupation policy, however, was significantly altered influenced by the increasing tensions between the U.S. and the states of the Eastern Bloc. Due to this policy shift, disarmament, encouragement of the labor union, and dissolution of the business conglomerates were looked over again, and some reactionary revisions were carried out.

For instance, the labor standards of the public officials were considerably diminished by the Order of 1948 (Order No. 201), and the right of officials to participate in the union, which had been guaranteed by Labor Union Law of 1945, was denied by its revision in June 1949.

The Anti-Monopoly Law of 1947 was amended in 1953 in order to adapt it to the situation in Japan, which meant the relaxation of regulation.[100]

The outbreak of the Korean War and the growing worse of the Cold War promoted the shift of disarmament policy to rearmament, which led to the introduction of the Police Auxiliary Force. It grew up into the Self Defense Force. This shift in the reform policies brought about a serious contradiction of the actual existence of the Self Defense Force and the explicit clause of the renunciation of war in section 9 CJ. This political framework has been firmly fixed by the U.S.-Japan Security Treaty concluded on September 8, 1951. The Supreme Court has avoided deciding on the constitutionality of the existence of the Self Defense Force because its decision would affect the highly political decisions of the executive and legislative and it would break the balance of powers. As far as this question is concerned, the Supreme Court has been very cautious.

3. After the Conclusion of Peace Treaty

57. Japan signed the Peace Treaty with the Allied Nations on September 8, 1951, which took effect on April 28, 1952. It marked the end of occupation by the Allied Forces. The government accelerated the implementation of development policies. The government had a policy of supporting industry and pursued productivity which was combined with the expansion of employment (the policy of "growth with

99. SCJ (FB) Dec. 23, 1953 Minshu 7-13-1523. However, four justices had dissenting opinions that anything other than the objective market price was against the Constitution. Majority opinion acted as a precedent and guided later decisions relating to agricultural land reform (SCJ Jan. 22, 1954 Minshu 8-1-225; SCJ Nov. 10, 1954 Minshu 8-11-2034; SCJ Oct. 26, 1955 Minshu 9-11-1690).
100. Oda 2011: p. 34.

equity").[101] It promoted the formation of a virtuous circle of achieving economies of scale through increasing workers' income, and demand and supply. On the one hand, in order to put in place the needed industrial base, the government enacted laws such as Temporary Measures Law for Textile Industry Equipment of 1956, Temporary Measures Law for Machinery Industries Promotion of 1956, Special Measures Law for the Synthetic Rubber Industry of 1957, Temporary Measures Law for the Electronics Industry Promotion of 1957, and Law for the Aircraft Industry Promotion of 1958. On the other hand, the government facilitated the stability of employment and improved the well-being of employees by enacting the Law on the Agency for the Promotion of Employment in 1961 and the Law on the Promotion of the Modernization of Medium- and Small-Sized Firms in 1963. They were strategic laws which gave a legal basis for implementing the policy of "growth with equity" as mentioned above.

Once the policy was written into the laws: (a) they prevented frequent changes, reversals and cancelations of that policy due to the intervention by political parties and pressure groups; (b) they also secured financial resources for the policy implementation; (c) further, they promoted public understanding of that policy and gave the people incentives for cooperation with government and industries. Those industrial and economic laws acted together with the Plan to Double Citizens Income (to be attained within ten years from 1961 to 1970) which was announced in December 1960 and created the institutional circumstance for the rapid economic development.[102]

The Cabinet decision issued in June 1960 stipulated a detailed schedule for liberalization of markets. Private firms understood that they could not avoid the liberalization of trade and investment. They strongly desired free investments, while they cooperated with the government by following the administrative guidance which led to the merger of big companies such as in heavy industries, paper industries, and automobile industries. It had to be adjusted to the competition policy administered by the Fair Trade Commission.[103] There has always been a tense relationship between the government and private sector on the backside of public-private cooperation.

F. Conditions for Economic Development and Legal Reform

1. Initial Conditions

58. Japan embarked on the reforms for modern economic growth in the middle of the 1880s. In 1886, the Gross National Product (GNP) per capita was only USD 136 as converted into USD in 1965. It was still USD 876 in 1965.[104] However, the

101. Ministry of Finance, *Basic Ideas of the Future Economic Policy* (August 1954).
102. Shinji Asanuma and Hirohisa Kohama, *Kindai Keizaiseicho Wo Motomete* [*In Search of Modern Economic Growth*] 324–326 (Keiso-shobo 2007).
103. Asanuma and Kohama, *supra* (note 102), pp. 330-336.
104. Ryoshin Minami, *Nihon no Keizai-hatten* 4 [*Economic Development in Japan*] (Toyokeizai-shinposha 3rd ed. 2002).

economic growth has been accelerated since the 1960s as a result of the government policies to promote economic activities. The government facilitated the private firms to introduce new technologies from developed countries by providing financial support. But those private activities could be promoted on the basis of institutional infrastructures which had developed before and after the modernization. The initial conditions for economic growth included:[105] (i) the fairly high literacy rate which is estimated to have been about 86% in Edo (now Tokyo) and more than 80% in rural areas around the 1880s might have been due to the education system in Buddhist temples; (ii) the irrigation system had been developed by using not only ponds but also rivers together with the establishment of an association to manage the distribution of water; (iii) the transportation system was developed by the "hikyaku" [the express messenger] who delivered documents, money, promissory notes, luggage, silk, flowers, etc. about four days between Edo and Osaka. It had become the basis of postal service system established in 1871, distribution of goods, and financial system; (iv) the shipping system was developed around the coast, mainly between Edo and Osaka; (v) the market system was developed mainly for rice. The rice market opened around 1660 in Dojima, Osaka. It adopted the securitization system and treated the futures transactions, which was authorized in 1730 by the Bakufu government. The price information was delivered by the hikyaku as mentioned above.

2. Government Policies and Laws and Regulations

59. The Meiji government recognized the private landownership for all individuals in exchange of collecting land tax from the landowner which created the market for immovable property transaction and established the financial basis of the government. Then it took the policy of "shokusan-kogyo" [the investment to encourage new industries][106] which needed to introduce new technologies and institutional innovation, including engineering education. It was implemented by a series of education laws promulgated in 1886 which covered primary, secondary and higher education.[107] By the government's initiative, the economic structure has been transformed from indigenous sectors such as agriculture, fishing, forestry, silk industry, textile manufacturing, brewing industry, paper manufacturing, and oil manufacturing into modern sectors such as mining industry, railway business, shipping industry, machine industry, and chemical industry by the cooperation between government and private firms.

60. After World War II, democratization was strongly promoted under the initiative of the Allied Forces. The democratization of political decision-making was implemented by the fundamental revision of the Constitution in November 1946

---

105. Asanuma and Kohama, *supra* (note 102), pp. 15–23.
106. *See* para. 38 *supra*.
107. Before that, the predecessors of private universities had been opened since 1858. The Institute of Technology was established in 1873 and the University was established in 1877. The preceding institutes had already been established within Ministries.

and other related laws. The dissolution of zaibatsu and the agricultural land reform were crucial measures to democratize the economy by reducing asset inequality. The agricultural land reform redistributed private landholding for agriculture by implementing the Special Measures Law for Establishing Independent Farmers enacted in October 1946. On the basis of these democratization policies, the government took the effort to manage the macroeconomy and to keep the stability of society on the one hand, and to integrate the Japanese economy into the international economy on the other. In August 1954, the Ministry of Finance announced the Basic Ideas of the Future Economic Policy and required the private firms both to reduce the costs of production and to increase employment by creating job opportunities. In January 1960, the government concluded the Japan-U.S. Security Treaty to secure the national defense; then in December 1960, the Cabinet headed by Prime Minister Hayato Ikeda adopted the Plan to Double Citizens Income to be attained within ten years from 1961 to 1970. For that purpose, it was necessary to increase the productivity in private sector so that the government implemented the policy of "growth with equity" by enacting a series of industrial and economic laws.[108] The gross GDP doubled in 1966, and the gross GDP per capita doubled in 1967 as that in 1961.

61. In the development process after World War II, the simultaneous advancement of economic growth, socioeconomic equality, and democracy promotion has been sought by the government: (i) the government implemented the socioeconomic policy by increasing the spending in certain fields of agriculture, light industries and then heavy industries; (ii) which led the more socioeconomic development; (iii) that enabled the government to redistribute income from the more privileged to the less privileged groups which resulted in the reduction of income inequality to around one-tenth of that before World War II; (iv) which facilitate the more socioeconomic equality; and (v) the more supportive participation in the government decision-making and the stability of government.[109]

62. However, on the back of the rapid economic growth driven by the manufacturing companies, the environmental pollution had been getting worse quite seriously. The "Big Four" pollution cases were the Itai-itai Disease caused by cadmium occurred around 1910 and lasted until the 1970s in Toyama, the Minamata Disease caused by organic mercury occurred around 1956 in Kumamoto, the Yokkaichi Asthma caused by sulfurous acid gas around 1960 in Aichi, and the Niigata Minamata Disease caused by organic mercury around 1964 in Niigata. Air pollution also seriously affected the residents of the heavily industrialized cities such as Yokohama, Kawasaki, and Amagasaki.[110] The government was slow to prevent these diseases and help victims to be compensated for their damages. It enacted the Basic

108. *See* para. 57 *supra*.
109. Ikuo Kabashima, *Supportive Participation with Economic Growth: The Case of Japan*, 36 *World Politics* 332–338 (1984).
110. Gordon 2014: pp. 282–283.

Law on the Prevention of Environmental Pollution in 1967 and the Law on the Special Measures for the Remedy for Pollution-Related Disease in 1969.[111] However, it was too late to prevent the spread of damages. The government established the fund to provide compensation, but it could not cover all the victims because the requirements to be confirmed as affected by the disease are fairly strict.[112]

G. The Role of Law for Development in Japan

1. The Government's Instrument to Centralize Powers and Promote Development

63. Legal reform has contributed to political, economic and social development step by step: (a) legal reform associated with political reform until the Meiji Restoration has been a long process to centralize the political powers. The Meiji government introduced private landownership together with the land registration system which was combined with the comprehensive reform of tax system.[113] It consolidated the financial basis of the government, on the basis of which the Meiji Constitution confirmed the basic structure of the unitary state.[114] The centralization of political powers was the necessary condition for an effective legal system; (b) the codification of Civil Code and Commercial Code gave the foundations for the private transactions. It extended the market system to cover various properties which fostered private sector;[115] (c) legal reform after World War II has been a further promotion of liberalization and democratization of the legal system on the basis of private property system introduced under the Meiji regime. There is a continuity between the institutions before and after the War, even though fundamental reform of the Constitution and progressive reforms such as Five Major Reforms were taken under the Allied Forces.[116] Enactment of industrial and economic laws was used as a strategic measure to implement development policies. It stabilized the development policies of the government by preventing political interventions. It was characterized as an "anchor" which secured economic policies from the political instability or as a "check valve" which prevented backflow of the policies.[117]

111. It was abrogated by the Law on the Compensation for the Pollution-Related Disease enacted in 1973.
112. Many cases were brought to the court by the victims or their successors to claim for compensation on the basis of the provision of the Law on the Compensation for the Pollution-Related Disease or the general provision of tort liability (s. 709 CC and s. 1 (1) State Compensation Law). Supreme Court recognized the victims' claim for compensation for damages caused by the omission by the State and prefecture to regulate corporate activities and restrict the pollution (SCJ Oct. 15, 2014 Minshu 58-7-1802).
113. *See* para. 70 *infra*.
114. *See* para. 50 *supra*.
115. *See* paras. 40–49 *supra*.
116. *See* paras. 53–54 *supra*.
117. *See* para. 57 *supra*.

2. The People's Measure to Protect Their Rights and Promote the Rule of Law

64. Legal reform also fostered the rights consciousness of the Japanese people and strengthened the protection of their rights. The Civil Code was taken seriously by the people, and they used its provisions in the courts to pursue their own interests. But it was not welcomed by the political leaders, and they tried to restrain the people's rights through the legislation since the 1920s. It was totally revised after the War as explained above. However, when a litigation campaign broke out such as due to environmental disputes caused by the serious pollution, the government restrained the use of litigation by making new laws for prevention and compensation and creating informal justice system to channel disputes from the courts to bureaucratically managed compensation and mediation schemes. As a result of these restrictive measures, the use of litigation, which was common in the 1960s, peaked in 1971 and decreased by two-thirds in a decade. Litigation rates dropped by 75% between 1883 and 1990. It was correlated with the shrinkage of legal sector in the number of judges, prosecutors and lawyers per capita terms and the share of the national budget allocated to the court system, which interestingly occurred at a time of rapid economic growth. It saved the social costs to use formal justice system, which had become "massively expensive" in the U.S.[118]

However, the further promotion of access to justice by improving the protection of people's rights was required to establish the rule of law. This was the reason why the Justice System Reform Council was established in the Cabinet by the Law concerning Establishment of Justice System Reform Council in June 1999. Its agenda included: (i) realization of a more accessible and user-friendly justice system, (ii) public participation in the justice system, and (iii) redefinition of the legal profession and reinforcement of its function. After investigations and deliberations, it submitted the report to the Cabinet in June 2001: *Recommendations of the Justice System Reform Council.*[119] On the basis of the Recommendation, the Japan Legal Support Center was established to improve legal aid in April 2006 (Law on the Comprehensive Legal Aid, June 2, 2004), the law school education was introduced to foster candidates for National Legal Examination in April 2004 (Law on the Relation Between Law School Education and National Legal Examination, December 6, 2002), and the saiban-in (lay judge) system was adopted as a means of popular participation in criminal trials in May 2009 (Law on the Criminal Trials with the Participation of Saiban-In, May 28, 2004).

---

118. Frank Upham, *Mythmaking in the Rule-of-Law Orthodoxy*, in *Promoting the Rule of Law Abroad: In Search of Knowledge* 92–99 (Thomas Carothers ed., Carnegie Endowment for International Peace 2006).

119. The Justice System Reform Council, *Recommendations of the Justice System Reform Council: For a Justice System to Support Japan in the 21st Century*, on Jun. 12, 2001. It is available in English at https://japan.kantei.go.jp/policy/sihou/singikai/990612_e.html (accessed Nov. 1, 2020).

H. *The Concept of Law in Japan*

1. The Relationship Between Law and Right

65. The traditional notion of "ho" [the law in the Japanese consciousness] connoted a penalty to be imposed on the people or an admonitory norm to be given to the subjects by the government associated with the sanction of pain and penalty; the Japanese generally conceive of law as an instrument of constraint that the government uses when it wishes to impose its will on the subjects.[120] It was different from the Western notion of law (droit, Recht, dirrito, derecho, etc.) which is closely related to and undivided from the notion of right (droit, Recht, dirrito, derecho, etc.). At the end of the nineteenth century, the Western terms corresponding to law and right were translated into Japanese as "ho" [law] and "kenri" [right], respectively. Originally the Japanese concept of "kenri" or "ken" implied the power to be held by the government, not by the people in general, as an instrument of governance.[121] However, through the legal reform since the Meiji period, the Western concept of right originated in the individual has gradually taken root in the consciousness of the Japanese, and the concept of law as a measure to protect the people's right has become popular among the citizens. As a result, the understanding of "ho" and "kenri" has been coming closer to that between law and right, though the original concept still remained and mixed with the new one.

2. The Distinction Between Private Law and Public Law and Criminal Law

66. The mixture of the traditional concept of law understood as primarily administrative and criminal law and the new concept of law which included private law defining and protecting private rights influenced the Japanese legal discipline, and it led to the fairly strict distinction between public law and private law and between criminal law and private law. For instance, in the Osaka International Airport Case, inhabitants who lived around the Osaka International Airport (before it moved to Kansai International Airport) entered a lawsuit according to civil procedure against the state who managed the national airport claiming the injunction of takeoff and landing permission at the airport from 9:00 p.m. to 7 a.m. based on their personhood right because they had suffered from physical and mental damages caused by the noise, vibration and exhaust gas from aircraft. The High Court of Osaka affirmed the plaintiffs' claim. However, the Supreme Court, responding to the appeal by the state, reversed the High Court judgment and dismissed the claim without prejudice. The reason was that the plaintiffs could not make a claim against the state concerning the exercise of the administrative power to manage the aviation of national airports through civil procedure because the power to manage the aviation should be

120. Noda 1976: pp. 159–160. *See also* para. 30 *supra.*

121. This was the reason why when Mr. Mitsukuri, a progressive government official, translated "droit civil" as "min-ken" [right of the citizen] and presented it at the study group of the codification of civil law, most of his colleagues felt unpleasant and strongly objected by asking how the people could have a right. *See* para. 40 *supra.*

exercised so as to implement the national policy of aviation, and it could not be subject to the civil procedure.[122] The Supreme Court affirmed the compensation for the actual damages which plaintiffs suffered in the past due to the negligence of the state in exercising the power to manage the facilities of national airport. Thus the Supreme Court separated the state's power to manage the aviation as a matter of public law from that to manage the airport facilities as a matter of private law. However, there were four dissenting opinions which criticized the strict distinction between the power to manage the aviation and airport facilities.

As far as the distinction between private law and criminal law which had been strict so far, criminal procedure law was amended in 2000 so as to enable the criminal victims and their family to use the evidence which had been collected by the police and prosecutor for the criminal procedure also in the civil procedure under certain conditions as provided by law.[123] It relaxed the strict distinction between private law and criminal law for the protection of victim's right.

II. Relation and Hierarchy Between the Sources of Law

A. *Statutory Laws and Regulations*

67. There is a broad spectrum of sources of law in Japan if it includes justiciable and non-justiciable law, written law and custom, because the Japanese legal system is essentially a "hybrid" of the civil law tradition through the codification, and the common law element through the post War reform, and the customary rules by retaining traditional concept of law, which is characterized as a "grey" legal culture.[124] It is an example of legal pluralism.[125]

However, the sources of law reflect on the integrity of law under the constitutional system of a state. In this sense they are the substantial ground of the rule of law in each country.[126] The followings are the major sources of law in Japan:

(i) The primary source of law in Japan is "Kenpo" [the Constitution] (Article 98 (1) CJ) and "horitsu" [statutory law] which is adopted by the Diet in accordance with the provisions of the Constitution (Articles 41, 59 CJ) is the central source of law. This is the reason why Japan is regarded as adopting a civil law tradition.

(ii) "Kisoku" [regulation] can be decided by the Supreme Court, each House of the Diet, the National Personnel Authority and the Board of Audit in accordance with the provisions of Constitution (Articles 58 (2) and 77 CJ).

---

122. SCJ (FB) Dec. 16, 1981 Minshu 35-10-1369.
123. Section 3 of the Law Concerning the Measures Appurtenant to Criminal Procedure for the Protection of Rights and Interests of the Crime Victims, etc. (May 19, 2000).
124. *See* paras. 28–57 (para. 29 in particular) *supra*.
125. Dean 2002: pp. 129–130.
126. As for the sources of law in Japan, *see* Oda 2011: pp. 26–52.

(iii) "Meirei" [decree or ordinance] is the delegated legislation to be made by the Cabinet, Ministries and other administrative organizations and is also recognized as an important source of law.
(iv) "Jorei" [bylaw] enacted by the local public entities in accordance with the Constitution (Article 94 CJ).
(v) "Joyaku" [treaty] concluded by the Cabinet must be ratified by the Diet (Article 61 CJ). Once the treaty is concluded by Japan, it must be faithfully observed together with established laws of nations as provided by the Constitution (Article 98 (2) CJ).

B. Case Law

68. Different from common law countries, "hanrei" [judicial precedents, case law] are not explicitly recognized as a source of law, and the principle of stare decisis is not formally acknowledged. However, judicial precedents, especially those of the Supreme Court, cannot be neglected in the interpretation of laws and regulations and other sources of law which were treated by those judicial precedents. If the Supreme Court needs to change its precedents, it must handle the case by full bench.[127] Substantially the judicial precedents reflect on the public policy of the state through the ontological interpretation of law on the one hand, and on the customary usages created in the society through the recognition as customary laws on the other. Japanese judges are regarded as fairly active in creating "law" in the form of judicial precedent through the "interpretation" of law even though they sometimes deviate from the wording of law instead of adhering to the literal meaning of law when they cannot find any alternative way to achieve an equitable solution. It is characterized as the anti-positivist approach in the application of law which is the uniqueness of Japanese law.[128]

C. Customary Law

69. "Kanshu" [customs] can become the source of law ("kanshu-ho" [customary law]): (i) where it is explicitly recognized in the provisions of laws and regulations[129] or (ii) where customs which are not against public policy and which relate to matters not provided for in laws and regulations. In these cases, customs may have the same effect as laws (section 3 Law on General Rules for Application of Laws). In addition, (iii) in cases there is any custom which is inconsistent with a provision of law or regulation not related to public policy, if it is found that any

127. Section 10 (3) of the Court Law provides that the Supreme Court cannot handle in a petty bench but must handle by full bench the case where an opinion concerning interpretation and application of the Constitution or of any other laws and regulations is contrary to that of a judicial decision previously rendered by the Supreme Court.
128. Oda 2011: p. 7.
129. For instance, custom is directly referred to as a source of law in ss. 217, 219 (3), 228, 236, 268 (1), 269 (2), 263, 294 CC, etc.

party to a juridical act has the intention to abide by such custom, such custom shall prevail over that provision of law or regulation (section 92 CC).[130] Customary laws can be recognized by the court and transformed into judicial precedents (case laws).[131]

§3. Introduction to the Law of Property and Trust

I. Historical Origins and Evolution

70. The institutional basis of the modern property law in Japan was the introduction of private ownership to land and building. In September 1871, the government alleviated the restrictions on the cultivation of land, and in December of that year it began to issue "chiken" [the certificate of landownership] by measuring and evaluating every piece of land starting from Tokyo and Osaka area. By issuing this certificate, the government recognized the landownership for the holder of the land and each owner of the land had to pay "chiso" [land tax] in money. On February 15, 1872, the government removed the ban of the transaction of the land for cultivation which had been prohibited so far under the Bakufu government. Besides, it stipulated that "from now on every person regardless of their classes may own, sell and purchase the land."[132] It contributed to create the land market through which land price has emerged. On February 24, the Ministry of Finance issued the Regulations on the Issue of Certificate of Land Ownership on Occasion of Sale and Donation of the Land which provided the procedure of issuing the land certificate to cover not only the urban area but also rural area.[133] On July 23, 1873, the Decree on Land Tax Reform was issued and it imposed "chiso" [land tax to be paid with money] on the owner of a piece of land at 3% of the land price which was recognized by the government.[134] Since 1877 the tax rate was reduced to 2.5%. As a result of this land tax reform, the financial basis of the government transformed from "nengu" [the annual tax in kind paid with rice by the holder of land for cultivation] to a land tax in money to be paid with money by the owner of the land including that in urban area which had been tax free under the Bakufu government. The revenues from land tax accounted for around 78% of the ordinary revenue of the Meiji government on average between 1868 and 1881 (the highest was around 93%), which has decreased to about 50% in 1890 and about 30% in 1897, because of the introduction of other tax sources such as tobacco tax, liquor tax, and business tax, though land tax was

130. Section 92 CC is interpreted by case law to the effect that if one of the parties to contract proved that there is a particular custom in this type of transaction known to both parties, the custom is binding unless the other party proves that he/she did not agree to abide by that custom. STJ Jun. 2, 1921 Minroku 27-1038.
131. *See* note 136 *infra* and corresponding text.
132. No. 50 of "Daijokan-hukoku" [the Decree of the Grand Council of the State].
133. No. 25 of Ordinance by Ministry of Finance.
134. No. 272 of "Daijokan-hukoku" [the Decree of the Grand Council of the State].

the largest single source of revenue until the turn of the century.[135] The tax reform undertaken by the Meiji government ensured stable tax revenue and improved the fair taxation.

71. Property law in Japan has developed through the codification of Civil Code and the enactment of concerned special laws. The major source of property law is Part 2 "Bukken" [Real Rights] of the Civil Code of 1896 (sections 175-398-22 CC). In addition, special laws have been enacted to meet the needs of the business and society. They include the Law on the Lease of Land and the Law on the Lease of Building of 1921, which are combined and amended by the Law on the Lease of Land and Building of 1992, the Agrarian Land Law of 1952, the Law on the Divided Unit Ownership of Building (Condominium) of 1962, the Law on the Special Provisions, etc. of the Civil Code Concerning the Opposability Requirements for the Conveyance of Movables and Claims of 1998, etc. Certain customary laws are recognized in cases such as those concerning the land use by the neighboring persons.[136] In addition, judicial precedents (case laws) are also very important to understand the meaning and interpretation of those provisions on property rights. For instance, "jyoto-tanpo" [conveyancing mortgage] and "shoyuken-ryuho" [reservation of ownership] are popular types of collateral in secured transaction and regulated by the concerned judicial precedents.[137]

II. The Concept of Ownership

A. Unity and Fragmentation

72. Ownership right is called "Shoyu-ken" in Japanese. "Shoyu" means to own and "Ken" means a right. The term "Shoyu-ken" was created and began to be used in laws and regulations by the Meiji government since the late nineteenth century.[138] Section 206 CC provides "[A]n owner has the rights to freely use, obtain profit from and dispose of the thing owned, subject to the restrictions prescribed by laws and regulations." In this provision "the thing" ("mono" or "butsu" in Japanese) means the corporeal thing because section 85 CC defines that the term "mono" (or "butsu") used in the Civil Code shall mean only "yutai-butsu" [the corporeal thing] such as immovable property and movable property (section 86 CC). Thus the ownership is defined as the right to freely use, make profit of and dispose of a corporeal thing. The present Civil Code adopts the concept of ownership in a narrow

135. Mason and Caiger 1997: pp. 276–277.
136. *See* ss. 217, 219 (3), 228, 236 CC, etc.
137. *See* paras. 79, 493, 524, 526 *infra*. Initially, the conveyance mortgage was invented and used in the business transactions as a kind of customary law. Then it was recognized by the court under certain conditions which was articulated in the judicial precedents (case laws).
138. "Shoyu-ken" corresponds to "propriété" in French and "Eigentum" in Germany. It was used to translate these terms and introduce Western laws and legal thoughts. It was first used in laws and regulations to introduce landownership by the Meiji government such as in the Proclamation of 1874, and s. 4 of the Regulation on Sales and Transfer of Land of 1880. The Meiji Constitution of 1889 provided "Shoyu-ken of every Japanese subject shall remain inviolate" (Art. 27 (1) CE).

sense by following the German Civil Code (sections 90, 903 GCC).[139] An incorporeal thing is not the object of "ownership" provided by the Civil Code. In a case where A bought a photo image of the calligraphy work by the famous calligrapher in Tang Dynasty (AD 8 c.) and published a book by using that photo image without the consent of B who owned that calligraphy. B claimed against A to stop selling the book on the basis of ownership of the calligraphy. However, the court dismissed A' s claim for the reason that the object of ownership is limited to a corporeal thing so that owner of the calligraphy is not entitled to directly take exclusive control of its photo image as an incorporeal thing. The copyrighted work, if any, shall return to public domain after the copyright ceased to exist.[140] The interests to be drawn from the incorporeal thing may be protected as far as the special laws provide remedies for the misuse of it. They include the Copyright Law, the Patent Law, the Utility Model Law, the Design Law, the Trade Mark Law, the Commercial Code,[141] the Unfair Competition Prevention Law,[142] etc.[143]

73. Section 30 of Book on Property in the former Civil Code of 1890 defined ownership by dividing it into two Subsections: "(1) Ownership is a right to freely use, obtain profit from and dispose of the thing. (2) This right may not be limited by way of law, agreement or testamentary will." Subsection (1) was the principle and Subsection (2) was the exception. This definition of ownership was based on the liberal thought influenced by its drafter G. Boissonade and government leaders in the 1870s.[144]

However, section 206 of the present Civil Code of 1896 changed the definition of ownership. "An owner has the rights to freely use, obtain profit from and dispose of the thing owned, subject to the restrictions prescribed by laws and regulations." This is not just the combination of two Subsections in the former Civil Code. The new definition implies that ownership shall be inherently recognized within "laws and regulations." It was influenced by the nationalistic thought which was strengthening among government leaders when they were drafting the Meiji Constitution in the late 1880s under the Germanization movement of Japanese legal science.[145]

But, after World War II, the Meiji Constitution was amended and Article 29 CJ provides the guarantee of private property: "(1) The right to own or to hold property is inviolable. (2) Property rights shall be defined by law, in conformity with the public welfare. (3) Private property may be taken for public use upon just compensation therefor." Sub-article (2) stipulates that property rights shall be defined by "law," in conformity with the public welfare, while section 206 CC which provides that ownership may be recognized within the restrictions by "laws and regulations"

139. The former Civil Code of 1890 similarly defined ownership as the right to freely use, take profit of and dispose of the thing (s. 30 Book on Property). However, it adopted broader definition of the thing which included not only corporeal things but also incorporeal things (s. 6 Book on Property) so that ownership could be extended to the incorporeal object.
140. SCJ Jan. 20, 1984 Minshu 38-1-1. *See also* para. 224 *infra*.
141. Trade name is defined and protected by ss. 11 to 13 of the Commercial Code.
142. Trade secret is protected by the Unfair Competition Prevention Law.
143. As for the intellectual property law in Japan, *see* Oda 2011: pp. 363–380.
144. *See* paras. 43, 47 *supra*.
145. *See* para. 50 *supra*.

was not amended. In order to correct the inconsistency between Article 29 (2) CJ and section 206 CC, the meaning of "laws and regulations" in section 206 CC is interpreted to mean laws and regulations delegated by laws in conformity with section 29 (2) CJ.[146]

The content of ownership is now restricted by many laws from various aspects. They include the Urban Planning Law, Standards of Construction Law, Land Expropriation Law, Mining Law, Agrarian Land Law, Basic Law for Land,[147] Cultural Properties Protection Law, etc.

B. *Immovable and Real Property*

74. Immovable property is called "fu-do-san" in Japanese. "Fu-do" means immovable, and "san" means property. "Fu-do-san" (immovable property) shall consist of land and fixtures to it (section 86 (1) CC).[148] Immovable property shall be generally registered one by one in accordance with LRIP. Some provisions of law shall be applied only to "Fu-do-san."[149] However, it is difficult to define "Fu-do-san" accurately from its connotation so as to identify which property belongs to immovable absolutely. Big stones on the land, a building or facilities under construction, for instance, are sometimes problematic. Most stones can be moved no matter how heavy they are, while even a garden stone can be an immovable property when it turned into a part of the landscape as a fixture to the land (section 86 (1)).[150] A building under construction can be an immovable property as a fixture to the land when it has a roof and walls so that it can withstand wind and rain even before the completion of construction works.[151] From the practical purpose of transactions, "Fu-do-san" is understood as the thing to be used and transacted without presupposing the change of place on the land.

146. Matsuo and Kozumi 2008: pp. 161–162.
147. Basic Law for Land (hereinafter "BLL") was amended in March 2020 (promulgated on Mar. 31, 2020, Law No. 12) and the new s. 6 BLL strengthened the duty and responsibility of landowner to use, manage and transact the land in accordance with the ideals of land (ss. 2 to 6 BLL), take measures to clarify the name and address of the right-holders and the border with the neighboring land, and to cooperate with the state and local public entities for the implementation of their land policies. In the background of this amendment, the land area whose owner and/or its address became unknown is increasing significantly in the movement of declining birth rate and aging population.
148. *See* para. 82 *infra*.
149. For example, in the Civil Code ss 177 (registration necessary for opposability), 265 (superficies), 270 (emphyteusis), 280 (servitude), 369 (hypothec), 239 (2) (ownerless property), 241 (accession), etc. *See* para. 83.
150. A garden stone can be an immovable property as a fixture to the land as provided by s. 86 (1) CC (25 Ju. 1934 STJ Hanketsuzenshu 1-8-6), Mar. 38, 1969 Minshu 23-3-699. *See also* paras. 82 and 94 *infra*.
151. STJ Oct. 1, 1935 Minshu 14-1671. *See also* para. 91 *infra*.

C. Movable and Personal Property

75. Movable property is called "do-san" in Japanese. "Do" means movable, and "san" means property. Section 86 (2) CC defines "do-san" [the movable property] as all sorts of "mono (butsu)" [the thing] other than immovable property. To note is that the term "mono (butsu)" [the thing] used in the Civil Code shall mean "yutai-butsu" [the corporeal thing] (section 85 CC).[152] Thus movable property means corporeal thing other than immovable property.[153] Movable property can be registered only if special laws provide registration for particular movables such as automobiles, cars, ships, boats, and construction machines.[154]

III. Estate and Patrimony

A. Unity and Fragmentation

76. Property rights in Japanese law are classified into "bukken" [real rights] and "saiken" [claim rights]. This distinction was received from that between "Sachenrecht" and "Forderung" in German jurisprudence and took root in Japanese legal discipline and legal practice. In the present Civil Code Book 2 is "bukken" and Book 3 is "saiken." "Bukken" [real rights] are the rights of a person over a thing such as ownership.[155] They allow him/her to take control of and make profits from that specified thing so that they can be asserted against all persons. "Saiken" [claim rights] are the rights of a person to require another person to deliver something or to do something (or not to do something). They arise from contract, quasi-contract, tort, unjust enrichment and other obligational relationship so that they can obligate only the parties involved in that relation. This distinction has practical consequences in cases of infringement. For instance, a holder of real right is entitled to demand the removal of disturbance caused by any person to the thing, while a holder of claim right does not have such power against a third party but only the person in that obligational relationship.[156]

77. No real rights shall be established other than those prescribed by the Civil Code and other laws (section 175 CC). It means that the kinds and content of real rights cannot be created and altered by the agreement between the parties to transaction of the property, but they must be provided by law. It is called "bukken-hotei-shugi" [the principle of numerus clausus of real rights]. It aims to unify the kinds and content of real rights so as to avoid conflicts due to different understanding of the real rights which are to be transacted and to reduce the costs of transaction of

152. *See* para. 72 *supra*. This conception of a thing relates with the concept of ownership which is defined as a right to use, take profits from and dispose of a "thing," i.e., a corporeal thing (s. 206 CC). Thus the right of ownership is recognized only on corporeal things in the Japanese Civil Code, which adopted the concept of ownership in a narrow sense.
153. *See* paras. 215 to 267 *infra*.
154. *See* para. 218 *infra*.
155. *See* para. 78 *infra*.
156. Oda 2011: p. 154.

real rights. In this sense, the predictability of real rights and the stability of transactions are the reasons for the existence of the numerus clausus principle.[157]

78. The Civil Code provides ten sorts of real rights. They are "shoyu-ken" [ownership] (section 206 CC), "chijo-ken" [superficies] (section 265 CC), "eikosaku-ken" [emphyteusis] (section 270 CC), "chieki-ken" [servitude] (section 280 CC), "iriai-ken" [the right of commons] (section 263, 294 CC), "ryuchi-ken" [the right of retention] (section 295 CC), "sakidori-tokken" [right of lien] (section 303 CC), "shichi-ken" [the right of pledge] (section 342 CC), "teito-ken" [the right of hypothec] (section 369 CC), and "sen-yu-ken" [the right of possession] (section 180 CC).

In addition, there are other real rights recognized by special laws. They include "saiseki-ken" [the stone-quarrying right] (section 4 of the Quarrying Law), "kogyo-ken" [the mining right] and "soko-ken" [the mining lease right] (sections 12 and 71 of the Mining Law), "gyogyo-ken" [the fishing right] and "nyugyo-ken" [the piscary] (sections 23 and 43 of the Fishery Law), "damu-shiyo-ken" [the right to use a dam] (section 20 of the Specified Multipurpose Dam Law), "karitoki-tanpo-ken" [the security right by the use of provisional registration] (Law on Contract for Establishment of Security Interests by the Use of Provisional Registration), "kokyo-shisetsuto-un-ei-ken" [the managing right of public facilities] (section 24 of the Law on the Promotion of Public Facilities by the Private Finance Initiative), etc.[158]

79. According to the principle of numerus clausus of real rights (section 175 CC),[159] it is controversial whether real rights may be recognized by customary law. On the one hand, a judicial precedent denied a claim brought into the court by the holder of "uwatsuchi-ken" [the right to use surface of a land for the purpose of holding a building on the basis of customary law] prevailed in Osaka district should be recognized as a special type of real right so that it should not follow a rule of raising a rent for "chijo-ken" [superficies] provided as a real right in the Civil Code.[160] On the other hand, however, other judicial precedents have recognized certain types of rights based on customary law as real rights such as "ryusui-shiyo-ken" [the right to use water flow][161] and "onsen-senyo-ken" [the right to use hot spring].[162] In addition, "jyoto-tanpo" [conveyancing mortgage][163] and "shoyuken-ryuho" [reservation of ownership][164] have been recognized as real rights for the security purpose by a series of judicial precedents.

---

157. Oda 2011: p. 166.
158. Matsuo 2016: pp. 22–23.
159. *See* para. 77 *supra*.
160. STJ Feb. 10, 1917 Minroku 23-138.
161. STJ Feb. 6, 1917 Minroku 23-202. It recognized the claim by the landowner of downstream who held a customary right to use water flow to confirm his right against the landowner of upstream.
162. STJ Sep. 18, 1940 Minshu 19-1611. It held that the right to use hot spring should be recognized a real right based on customary law so that it should follow the similar requirement for the transfer of that right with s. 177 CC which applied to the transfer of real right to immovable property.
163. STJ Nov. 2, 1914 Minroku 20-865. *See* paras. 493 and 524 *infra*.
164. SCJ Jul. 18, 1974 Minshu 28-5-743. *See* para. 526 *infra*.

According to the judicial precedents, real rights based on customary law may be recognized under the following conditions:[165] (i) first, the alleged right has been traditionally maintained, but the Civil Code had failed to include it even though it should have been recognized as a real right when it was enacted, or after the Civil Code came into effect the new type of right has evolved in the practice which should be recognized as a real right even though the legislation has not yet adopted it; (ii) second, the recognition of the alleged right as a real right based on customary law would not affect the reasons for the principle of numerus clausus prescribed by section 175 CC:[166] the recognition of the real right based on customary law would not bring a confusion to transactions like "uwatsuchi-ken" which might be confused with the existing real right such as "chijo-ken" [superficies] (the predictability of real rights), and it would not increase the cost of transaction of that right (the stability of transactions). "Ryusui-shiyo-ken" [the right to use water flow], "onsen-sen-yo-ken" [the right to use hot spring], "jyoto-tanpo" [the conveyancing mortgage] and "shoyuken-ryuho" [the reservation of ownership] seem to have met these conditions.

The recognition of real rights based on customary law by the judicial precedents implies that the principle of numerus clausus (section 175 CC) is not strictly applied by the court. Then the question arises whether this practice is against the rule of law or not. However, as I have confirmed the conditions under which the customary-law-based real rights are recognized by the court, the principle can be compatible with them because of the limits of legislation. According to the prevailing legal doctrine, section 175 CC should be interpreted that it allows the legitimate exception of the numerus clausus principle if the alleged right is not against the reasons for the principle[167] and the customary rule that bases the alleged right is "not against public policy" and it relates to "matters not provided for in laws and regulations" as provided by section 3 of the Law on General Rules for Application of Laws.[168]

B. Trust and Fiduciary Mechanisms

80. The distinction between "bukken" [real rights] and "saiken" [claim rights] was received from German jurisprudence by the Japanese legal discipline as the basic structure of property rights system, adopted by the present Civil Code (Book 2 on "Bukken" and Book 3 on "Saiken"), and took root in the legal practice.[169] It is a popular classification of property law in civil law countries which adopted Pandekten system originated in German legal science in the nineteenth century.

However, trust laws such as Trust Law and Trust Business Law were received from common law countries by referring to Indian Trust Law, related provisions in

165. Matsuo and Kozumi 2008: pp. 25–26.
166. *See* para. 77 *supra*.
167. They are the predictability of real right and the stability of transactions as explained in para. 77 *supra*.
168. *Ibid*. *See also* para. 69 *supra*.
169. *See* para. 76 *supra*.

the Civil Code of California in the U.S. and case laws and legal doctrines developed in England, where the strict distinction between real rights and claim rights is not adopted. The rights and interests of beneficiary would be beyond claim rights and come closer to real rights, although the title of property right is transferred to the trustee from the settlor. But the Japanese legal doctrine assimilated trust relations into the basic framework of property rights system by protecting the interests of beneficiary as a special type of claim right.[170] This arrangement of legal institutions of different origins into the consistent legal system also shows the hybrid nature of Japanese law.[171]

As far as the trust laws are concerned, the Trust Law (Law No. 62) and Trust Business Law (Law No. 65) were enacted in 1921. Interestingly before the enactment of general law of trust, the Secured Bond Trust Law of 1905 (Law No. 52) was adopted in the Diet due to the necessary introduction of foreign capital for restoration after the war between Japan and Russia in 1904. The Loan Trust Law (Law No. 195, 1952) was introduced to regulate the loan trust business. In 2006, the new Trust Law was enacted to modernize the trust relations (Law No. 108). The Trust Business Law was also amended in 2004 (Law No. 154) and in 2006 (Law No. 109).[172]

IV. Possession and Title

81. Japanese law makes a clear distinction between "senyu-ken" [the right of possession] and "hon-ken" [title, the right to possess] (section 202). Possession of a thing is conceived as a kind of real rights in the Japanese Civil Code (Book II Real Rights, Chapter 2 Right of Possession). However, the right of possession (possessory right) is a special type of real right because it is conceived as a "kari-no-kenri" [provisional right] to protect the current state of possession tentatively until the conflict could be solved by deciding to whom the right to possess the thing should belong. The right to justify the possession of a thing is called "hon-ken" [title, the right to possess][173] in Japanese. It includes not only real right such as ownership, the right of superficies, and the right of pledge but also claim right such as the right of lease. It is also called "ken-gen" [justified source of right]. The right of possession (possessory right) is recognized when a person takes hold of a thing with the intention to do so for his/her interest even though he/she does not have any title to possess it (section 180 CC). It is protected by the possessory actions (sections 198–202 CC) against infringement even by the owner of the thing who exercises a self-help. It will contribute to the maintenance of peaceful state of possession to be kept by the possessor's voluntary change of possession or by the force of law, which restricts the self-help by the holder of a title to possess the thing.[174]

170. *See* paras. 377–381 *infra.*
171. *See* para. 29 *supra.*
172. *See* para. 374 *infra.*
173. The term "hon-ken" [title] is used in s. 202 (1) and (2) CC on the relation between the action based on the right of possession and that on the right to justify the use of a thing. *See* paras. 304 and 305 *infra.*
174. *See* paras. 296–305 *infra.*

Part I. Immovable Property

Chapter 1. General Classification

§1. The Concept of Immovable Property

82. Immovable property is called "fu-do-san" in Japanese.[175] Section 86 (1) CC stipulates that "fu-do-san" [the immovable property] shall be land and any fixtures to it.[176] Movable property is defined as all the corporeal things other than immovable property (sections 85 and 86 (2) CC).[177] The definition of immovable and movable property was received from French and German law. But it was more simplified consciously by the drafters of the present Civil Code in order to avoid confusions.[178]

83. In Japanese law, the distinction between immovable and movable property matters in the following provisions: (i) a person under curatorship cannot acquire and dispose of immovable property without the consent of curator, while he/she can do so for movables unless they are valuable (section 13 (1) [3] CC); (ii) acquisition, disposition, and any changes in real rights on immovables cannot become opposable against a third person unless they are registered in accordance with LRIP (section 177 CC), while transfer of real rights on movable property can be opposable against a third person if the property is delivered to the acquirer (section 178 CC); (iii) if a person acquires a possession of a movable property from the other party through a transaction peacefully, openly and in good faith without fault that the property belongs to that party, he/she can acquire a right corresponding to the transaction immediately (the immediate bona fide acquisition for movables: section 192 CC); (iv) not only superficies and emphyteusis but also servitude cannot be established on movables but on land (sections 265, 270, 280 CC); (v) some special types of right of lien are provided for movables (section. 311 CC), while certain types of right of lien are recognized for immovables 325 CC); (vi) acquisition and effects of right of pledge are differently provided for movables (section 352–355 CC) from immovables (sections 356–361 CC); (vii) right of hypothec can be established only on immovables (section 369 CC) unless other laws provide for special types of

175. As for the general introduction to the concept of immovable property, *see* para. 74 *supra*.
176. Section 2 [1] LRIP adopts a narrower definition of immovable property as "land or building" for its own purpose.
177. *See* para. 75 *supra*.
178. Ume 1911 (I): pp. 182–185.

hypothec on movables; (viii) jurisdiction for litigation and execution over immovable property shall depend on the location of the property (section 5 [12] Civil Procedure Law, section 44 Civil Execution Act), etc. Thus the different treatment of immovable and movable property depends not only on the difference of technical handling method due to the nature of property but also on the different interests in property from the viewpoint of legal policies. For instance, certain movables such as cars, ships, aircraft, machines for construction and agriculture can be registered and treated like immovable property.[179]

§2. Land

84. Land is a typical "immovable" property (section 86 (1) CC). However, to be precise, land can move though very slowly because it is the earth's crust so that it is always moving little by little in a strict sense due to the tectonic movements. In the event of some huge earthquakes such as the Hanshin-Awaji Earthquake on January 17, 1995, in the western part of Japan and the East Japan Earthquake on March 11, 2011, many pieces of land around the seismic center moved toward certain directions from several tens of centimeters to a few meters at a time. The movement of the land as a result of the earthquakes raised a question of whether a piece of land may move or the original space before the movement should be recognized as the land. In response to this question, the Ministry of Legal Affairs announced quickly just after the Hanshin-Awaji Earthquake in 1995 that pieces of land with their boundaries "moved" so that ownership and other rights to the land before the earthquake shall follow that land which moved with the tectonic movement by the earthquake.[180] It meant that the owner of the land cannot claim to keep the domination of a space on and beneath the land before it moved even though it had been measured by the global positioning system. But the announcement also confirmed that the tectonic movements must be distinguished from the movements of the soil and sand on the surface of the earth such as a landslide. In this case, the land is never recognized as moved so that the landowner should return to the original position. This authentic confirmation of the legal meaning of "land" by the Ministry of Legal Affairs could avoid serious conflicts among the owners of land over the boundaries of their land.

85. According to LRIP, land shall be divided into each piece which is called "hitsu" in Japanese, the counting unit for land. It is measured by the qualified land surveyor authorized by the state and registered in the land registry at each registration office according to jurisdiction on the site of the land so as to establish and maintain the cadaster which is renewed by the government time and again. The land registration system has been improved step by step on the basis of the cadaster. The land registration consists of two parts. One is the registration of description of the land and the other is that of rights on the land. The registration of land description

---

179. *See* paras. 258 *infra.*

180. The Response by the Director-General of the Civil Affairs Bureau, the Ministry of Legal Affairs, No. 2589, dated on Mar. 29, 1995.

contains basic information of that land, including its location, land number, width, and classification of land usage to be fixed from certain categories so as to identify each piece of land. The registration of rights on the land shall record the establishment, transfer, change, restriction and extinction of ownership, superficies, emphyteusis, servitude, rights of lien, right of pledge, hypothec, right of lease and stone-quarrying right (sections 2 [4], 3 LRIP).[181]

§3. Building and Other Fixtures to Land

I. Building

86. Building is a typical immovable property as a fixture to land (section 86 (1) CC). One of the features of the Japanese property law is that a building is regarded as an independent and separate property from a land on which the building is constructed. This rule reflects on the traditional treatment of the building. The wooden building could be moved from one place to another. The right of hypothec has often been established only on the house when the house owner needed a certain finance as equivalent to the value of the house.

The Civil Code defines immovable property as the land and the fixtures to it (section 86 (1) CC), and a building is regarded as one of the fixtures to the land, so that the building is in no doubt regarded as an immovable property. However, the building is treated not as an integrated immovable property to the land but as an independent and separate immovable property from the land. This means that Japanese law did not adopt the principle of "superficies solo cedit" which was created in Roman law and widespread in European laws. Instead, Japanese law adopted the principle of land and building as separate property. It is evident from the following treatment by laws.

(i) The building shall be registered in the building registry which is independently and separately compiled from the land registry.[182] The building registry also consists of two parts like the land registry as stated above. One is the registration of the description of the building and the other is that of rights on that building. The registration of building description provides basic information of the building, including its location, building number, width, story, structure, and classification of building usage from certain categories so as to identify each building. The registration of rights on the building shall record the establishment, transfer, change, restriction and extinction of ownership, rights of lien, right of pledge, hypothec, right of lease and right of a widowed spouse to residence (sections 2 [4], 3 LRIP).[183]

181. As for registration of transactions of immovable property, *see* para. 242 *infra*.

182. LRIP presupposes that building registry shall be compiled independently from the land registry. *See* ss. 44–58 LRIP.

183. The spouse's right to residence shall be established by the deceased spouse's testamentary will, agreement of the heirs (s. 1028 (1)) or the judgment at the family court (s. 1029).

(ii) The principle of land and building as separate property is also evident from some provisions in the Japanese Civil Code. For instance, if A, the owner of a piece of land, owned a building on that land, A can establish a right of hypothec on both the land and the building at the same time, which is mostly the case in practice, or only on the building or only on the land. If you read section 370 CC you can understand that it presupposes the situation in which the right of hypothec is established only on a piece of land even though there is a building on it:

> Sec. 370 CC A hypothec shall extend to the things that are recognized to constitute an integral part of the object of the hypothec (hereinafter referred to as "hypothecated immovable property") except for the building on the hypothecated land; provided, however, that this shall not apply in cases where the action establishing the hypothec provides otherwise or the creditor can rescind the action of the debtor in accordance with the provisions of Sec. 424 CC.

Sec. 370 CC is analogically interpreted to be applied also to the case in which the right of hypothec was established only on the building. In this case, the right of hypothec cannot extend to the land on which the hypothecated building was constructed.

87. However, when the right of hypothec was established only on the land and not on the building on it, and the hypothec was executed, the buyer of the land at the auction, if any, cannot use the building because the hypothec shall not extend to the building on the land as provided by section 370 CC. Also, the building owner can no longer use the land if he/she can agree with the buyer of the land using it. On the contrary, when the right of hypothec was established only on the building and the hypothec was executed, the buyer of the building at the auction cannot use the land and maintain the building on that land because the hypothec shall extend only to the building and not to the land by the analogical interpretation of section 370 CC. In order to avoid these inconveniences, section 388 CC is added and provides as follows:

> Sec. 388 CC In cases where a land and a building on the land belong to the same owner, if a hypothec is established with respect to that land or building, and the execution of that hypothec results in the creation of different owners, it shall be deemed that a superficies has been established with respect to that building. In such cases, the rent shall be fixed by the court at the request of the parties.

As Sec. 388 CC stipulates, if a hypothec was established only on the land, the buyer of the land at the auction shall bear the statutory superficies for the interest of the building owner, although the rent shall be paid to the land owner as fixed by the court. This solution may be justified, because the person who established the hypothec on the land could have recognized the existence of the building, nevertheless he/she did not establish a hypothec on that building so that the collateral value should not be extended to the building but limited only to the land and the buyer at the auction of the hypothecated land can acquire only that limited collateral value.

88. On the other hand, as is provided in section 388 CC, the owner of the building can keep ownership of the building on that land on the basis of the statutory superficies, though he/she should pay the rent to be fixed by the agreement with the landowner or by the court decision. The same shall apply *mutatis mutandis* in the case where the owner of the land and the building established the hypothec only on the building. In this case, when the hypothec is executed, the buyer of the building shall acquire the statutory superficies on that land by the analogical interpretation of section 388 CC. In this case, the owner of the land who established the hypothec only on the building could foresee this result so that he/she should bear the statutory superficies.

89. However, from the viewpoint of legal policy, there was another choice for the Japanese Civil Code instead of adopting the principle of land and building as separate property. Originally the drafters of the present Civil Code prepared the draft to the effect that fixtures to land including a building shall be a part of land unless otherwise provided. It was based on the principle of "superficies solo cedit" so that a building shall be a part of land on which the building was constructed. This principle had prevailed in the European countries where the Japanese drafters had studied law.[184] However, in the meeting to examine the draft there were strong oppositions that it was against the customary law in Japan according to which the building had been transacted and hypothecated independently from the land. The drafter, Masaaki Tomii, answered that it was not always good to follow the traditional rule, and the other two drafters, Nobushige Hozumi and Kenjiro Ume, supported Tomii to defense the original draft. But, as a result of the vote, the opponents in favor of the customary law narrowly won the supporters of original draft. Just after that, the drafter had to change the original draft and prepared the new draft provisions which resulted in the provisions of sections 370 and 388 CC as introduced above.[185]

90. Another important consequence of adopting the principle of land and building as separate property is that a landowner cannot remove for himself/herself a building on the land once it was constructed or maintained by another person even without any title to possess the land, because the building is a separate property from the land. Of course, the landowner may claim against the building owner without holding title to possess the land for removal of the building and vacation of the land on the basis of ownership of that land (section 206 CC). Also, as the landowner he/she can claim against the building owner for return of fruits or payment

184. The drafter of concerned provisions on the relation between land and building was Masaaki Tomii who studied law in France. The other two drafters Nobushige Hozumi who studied in the U. K. and moved to Germany and Kenjiro Ume who studied France also agreed to Tomii's original draft.

185. As for legislative history, *see* Matsuo 2016: p. 162.

of profits to be drawn from the use of the land until the vacation is completed on the basis of unjust enrichment (sections 189 and 190 CC), and claim for compensation for additional damages if any on the basis of tort liability (sections 191 and 709 CC).[186] However, the landowner has to take a legal action by proving his/her landownership against the building owner instead of removing it directly for himself/herself. For that purpose, he/she has to find the building owner. But it is not always easy and sometimes difficult and costly. In order to lighten the cost for the landowner to find the building owner, a judicial precedent upheld the claim of a landowner against a person who is registered as a building owner in building registry for removal of the building and vacation of the land if the holder of ownership title in building registry had acquired building ownership and made the registration for himself/herself.[187] In this case, he/she cannot make a defense by stating that the building ownership has already been transferred through agreement with a third party though it is not registered in building registry because it should have been easy for him/her to change the title in building registry if he/she had actually transferred the building so that he/she had lost his/her ownership.[188]

91. If the building is an independent and separate immovable property from the land, a clear standard is necessary to judge from when the collection of movables put on the land shall become an immovable property in the process of building construction. Although there is no explicit provision in the Civil Code and other laws, judicial precedents have given certain standards. In response to a claim for confirmation of a building ownership, the court decided that the building under construction might be recognized as an independent immovable property if it was equipped with a roof on and walls around the property so that it could protect its inside from rains and winds and thus it can provide its own function beyond the collection of movables fixed to the land even though the construction work was not completed.[189]

92. However, in the case where the government claimed for payment of fixed assets tax (real estate tax) against an owner of an unfinished building which had not been registered, the court decided that in order to collect fixed assets tax a series of construction work was completed so that the building was able to be registered.[190] But, in this case the issue was the proper timing of taxation on the building so that the meaning of "building" seemed to be interpreted in the light of the purpose of taxation, which could be different from the standard meaning of "building." For the general standard of building to be owned as an independent immovable property, the former judgment explained in the previous paragraph is recognized to maintain the status of judicial precedent. It is also followed by the registration office in its

186. As for remedies against infringement of ownership, *see* paras. 103 to 110 *infra*.
187. SCJ Feb. 8, 1994 Minshu 48-2-373. For more detail, *see* paras. 105 and 106 *infra* concerned with claim for removal of building and vacation of land.
188. Ownership may be transferred only by the declaration of will of the parties (s. 176 CC) unless a third party makes a defense based on the lack of registration. *See* paras. 230, 237 and 238 *infra*.
189. STJ Oct. 1, 1935 Minshu 14-1671.
190. SCJ Dec. 7, 1984 Minshu 38-12-1287.

practical treatment of building registration (section 136 of the Regulation on the Treatment of Immovable Property Registration Procedure).

II. Other Fixtures to Land

93. Fixtures to land as immovables in the sense of section 86 (1) CC are classified into three categories in the practice: (i) the first category of fixture: there are fixtures which are always regarded as an independent immovable property from the land. They include a building as stated in the preceding paragraphs and a cluster of trees which are registered in tree registry as provided by the special law (section 2 (1) Law on Tress, Law No. 22, 1909). If a cluster of trees are registered and recognized as an independent immovable property, the owner of trees may sell, mortgage, or establish a hypothec on only trees or both trees and land on which those trees are planted (section 2 (2) Law on Trees). If the owner sells only trees on land, it is normal for him/her to negotiate with the buyer of trees about establishing the right to use the land such as a superficies or a right of lease for the purpose of owing trees. However, if the owner established a hypothec only on trees and it was executed and a person who bought trees at the auction was different from the landowner, then it shall be regarded that a superficies was established for the purpose of owning those trees (a statutory superficies). In this case, the rent and duration of the statutory superficies shall be fixed by the court at the request of the parties in consideration of the customary law widespread in the region (section 5 (1) Law on Trees).[191]

94. (ii) The second category of fixture: there are other fixtures which are fixed to land. They include trees that are not registered by Law on Trees as stated in the previous paragraph, seeds and plants maintained on land, a machine, a statue, a garden stone, etc. which are firmly fixed to land, railways locked on land, tubes imbedded in land, etc. In principle, these fixtures are regarded as parts of the land. However, they may be exceptionally transacted independently from the land if they have any commercial value and need to be sold or mortgaged by keeping them on the land under the condition that those transactions are publicly noticed in accordance with the customary law (publicity method based on customary law). For instance, trees which are not registered in tree registry may be sold by notification about the sale on a notice board set up around those trees when the transaction was made and kept after that in accordance with the customary law in the region.[192]

95. (iii) The third category of fixture: there are still other fixtures which are always regarded as incorporated parts of land as long as they are fixed to the land.

191. The same rule shall be applied to the case of compulsory execution on the registered trees (s. 5 (2) Law on Trees).
192. SCJ May 4, 1961 Minshu 15-5-1253.

They include stone walls, fences,[193] ditches, pavements, wells, tunnels, etc. They are always treated and transacted as a part of the land unless they are removed from the land because they have little commercial value if they are separated from the land so that it is not advantageous for the landowner to transact them independently from the land.[194]

§4. Collective Assets

I. The Principle of One Real Right in One Thing

96. In principle, a real right in one object is not compatible with another real right which has the same effect as the former one. It is called the principle of "haita-sei" [the exclusivity] of real rights. The priority between the two or more real rights the effect of which is not compatible with each other shall be determined by the provisions of law. For example, if A owned a piece of land and made a sales contract of the land with B and agreed to transfer ownership immediately though the registration was not completed (section 176 CC). Then A made a sales contract of the same land with C and agreed to transfer ownership and registered it. In this case the priority of ownership on the land between B and C shall be determined by the registration (section 177 CC) so that C's ownership shall prevail over B's ownership even though the agreement to transfer ownership between A and B was earlier than that between A and C.[195] Thus priority provisions are necessary for transactions of real rights due to the principle of "haita-sei" [the exclusivity]. However, in the absence of those provisions, the real right established earlier shall prevail over that established later.[196] On the other hand, an object of a real right should be specific, unitary and independent. It is called the principle of "tokutei-sei" [the specificity], "tan-itsu-sei" [the unity] and "dokuritsu-sei" [the independence] of the object of real rights. According to the traditional legal doctrine in Japan, the principle of specificity, unity and independence of the object of real rights is the natural consequence of the principle of exclusivity of real rights because the holder of real rights can exclude others and directly control the profits resulting from the object so that the object of exclusive and direct control should be specified, unitary and independent from other things. In other words, if the object is an unspecified thing, collective things or a part of a thing, it would be difficult for the right-holder to make a direct control of and exclude others from the object because the scope of the object

193. However, a wall and a fence on the border of land can be an independent immovable property which is presumed to be co-owned by the landowners unless they agree otherwise (s. 229 CC). If one of the landowners increased the height of the wall in his/her own expense, the increased part of wall shall belong to him/her (s. 231 CC).

194. The landowner can remove those fixtures from the land, but after that they are no longer immovables but become movables though they still belong to the landowner. If the other person removes them from the land without the consent of landowner, it is the infringement of landownership and the removed property still belongs to the landowner, even though it has become movable property.

195. This rule applies to the transaction of immovable property. For movable property, the priority shall be determined by the delivery of property in principle (s. 178 CC).

196. It is the fundamental principle of "prior tempore, potior iure."

becomes unclear if the object is unspecified and includes lots of things and the direct and exclusive control becomes difficult if the object is limited to a part of a thing. In this sense, the traditional legal doctrine integrated the principle of exclusivity as the fundamental nature of real rights and the principle of specificity, unity and independence of the object of real rights into the principle of "Ichibutu-ikken-shugi" [the principle of one real right in one thing].[197] This simplified and integrated principle became popular as a dogmatic explanation about the basic nature of real rights and their object in legal education.

II. Exceptions to the Principle of One Real Right in One Thing

97. However, several exceptions to the principle of one real right in one thing have been created by special laws and judicial precedents in response to the demand of the business practice. The Law on Hypothec in Factory (Law No. 54, 1905)[198] enabled the owner of land and buildings of a factory to establish a hypothec on the land and buildings comprehensively by which the effect of hypothec shall extend not only to the land and buildings but also to machines, facilities and other tangible things to be used in that factory. If the inventory of those things as the objects of the hypothec is made in accordance with the provisions of law, it shall be regarded as registration by which the creditor shall be able to assert his/her right of hypothec against a third party who acquired any rights to those objects from the owner of the factory after the inventory was arranged (sections 2 and 3 Law on Hypothec in Factory). The creditor may be able to pursue the objects which are removed and carried out of the factory unless they are acquired by a bona fide third party without negligence who is protected by the rule of immediate acquisition as provided in sections 192–194 CC (section 5 Law on Hypothec in Factory).[199] In this case, the principle of one real right in one thing, especially the principle of unity, is relaxed by the provision of special law and judicial precedent.

98. Several statutes enabled the company to establish a hypothec on the company's assets more comprehensively. For instance, the Law on Hypothec in Railway (Law No. 28, 1909) regards all the assets owned by the railway company to be used for the operation of railway including power plants, communication facilities, and other immovable and movable properties as "one thing" so that the company may be able to establish a hypothec on those assets regarded as one thing at a time by submitting the inventory of those assets to the Minister of Transportation and acquiring its permission (sections 2 and 3 Law on Hypothec in Railway). This special law also relaxed the principle of one real right in one thing, especially the principle of specificity and unity for the purpose of promoting the finance of railway companies on the basis of government policy to improve the basic infrastructure like railway.

197. Wagatsuma and Ariizumi 1983: para. 23; Funabashi 1960: p. 11; Matsuo 2016: para. 3.2.
198. In this period, the government needed to promote the finance for factories after the Russo-Japanese War in 1904.
199. SCJ Mar. 12, 1982 Minshu 36-3-349.

99. Further, the Law on Enterprise Collateral (Law No. 106, 1958) enabled a stock company to establish a collateral for the creditor of its corporate bond on "all the assets" of that company which include not only specific immovable and movable properties but also floating commodities. It is established by registration in the registry for stock company at the registration office which has jurisdiction over the main office of that company (sections 1, 2, 3 and 4 Law on Enterprise Collateral). This special law aimed to promote finance for stock companies by using its profitability at the beginning of high economic growth after World War II. It also relaxed the principle of one real right in one thing, especially the principle of specificity and unity for the purpose of promoting the finance of stock companies on the basis of government policy to facilitate the production by stock companies. However, the availability of this special type of collateral was limited to stock companies and for the security of their creditors of corporate bond so that it was not enough for small and medium companies which did not issue corporate bond to access finance more easily. The financial demand of small and medium companies has become evident since the middle of the 1950s, and it led to the recognition of a special type of mortgage in the form of transfer of ownership (conveyancing mortgage) on current assets of a debtor, including floating commodities and claim rights to be generated by the debtor in the future. This extension of collateral measure was not done by legislature but was led by judicial precedent.[200]

---

200. As for the role of judicial precedent in creating "law" in the Japanese legal system, *see* para. 68 *supra*.

Chapter 2. Legal Interests

§1. The Concept of Ownership in Immovable Property

I. Ownership in Immovable Property

100. Ownership, "shoyu-ken" in Japanese, is a typical real right in the sense that an owner has a right to "freely use, obtain profit from and dispose of the thing which he/she owns subject to the restrictions prescribed by laws and regulations" (section 206 CC).[201] It is a right to control its object most exclusively. However, as already confirmed, the "thing" in this provision means "corporeal thing" (section 85 CC) so that ownership cannot be extended to an incorporeal thing, which may be the object of intellectual property rights in accordance with the special laws.[202] For corporeal things, "shoyu-ken" [ownership] shall be equally recognized for both immovable and movable properties (section 86 (1) and (2) CC). The Japanese can say "Watashi-wa-kono-tochi-no-shoyu-ken-wo-motte-imasu" [I have ownership in this piece of land] in the same way as "Watashi-wa-kono-tokei-no-shoyu-ken-wo-motte-imasu" [I have ownership in this watch]. The concept of "Shoyu-ken" [ownership right] for itself abstractly has the same connotation for land and watch though the substance of ownership is totally different between them. But, in practice, ownership of immovable property, especially landownership, has special features. As a general rule of landownership, section 2 of the Basic Law for Land (1989, Law No. 84) explicitly announced "public welfare shall take precedence with regard to land" because land is particularly related to public interest for the following reasons. First, land is a finite resource; second, it is an indispensable basis for citizens' activities; third, the use of a piece of land is closely linked with that of other pieces of land; fourth, the value of land fluctuates depending on the trends of population, industry and land use, development of social infrastructure and other socioeconomic conditions. In order to implement this general rule, special laws provide restrictions on landownership.[203]

101. Ownership of land shall extend to the space both above and beneath the surface of land, subject to the restrictions prescribed by "laws and regulations" (section 207 CC). The meaning of "laws and regulations" in section 207 CC should be strictly interpreted to mean laws and delegated regulations by laws in conformity with section 29 (2) CJ which provides that property rights must be defined by "laws."[204] Although there are no specific limits articulated generally in the Japanese Civil Code on the effect of landownership about the use of space above and beneath the surface of land,[205] legal doctrine interprets section 207 CC that ownership of

201. As for the concept of ownership in general in Japanese law, *see* para. 72 *supra*.
202. *See* para. 72 *supra*.
203. For instance, Mining Law (1950, Law No. 289), Forest Law (1951, Law No. 249), Agricultural Land Law (1952, Law No. 229), Urban Planning Law (1968, Law No. 100), etc.
204. *See* para. 73 *supra*.
205. Section 905 GCC and s. 667 Swiss Civil Code explicitly limit the scope of landownership within which the interests of the owner exist.

land cannot extend beyond the scope in which the interests of the owner exist.[206] Within the scope of landownership, if a person other than the landowner wants to use the space above or beneath the land, he/she has to obtain any titles such as superficies or servitude in accordance with the purpose, scope and form of the use of the land.[207] However, minerals in the ground listed in Mining Law are included in the mining area which is the object of the mining right or the mining lease right; the landownership cannot extend to them.[208]

II. The Deep Underground

102. The Special Measures Law for the Public Use of Deep Underground (hereinafter "SMLDU, Law No. 87, 2000") enabled the service operator who acquired an approval by the Minister of Land, Infrastructure and Transport to use the underground space deeper than the points which are prescribed by this law and the delegated regulation for the purpose of public use without any prior compensation. This special underground space is called "daishindo-chika" [the deep underground].[209]

The Deep Underground is defined as the underground space deeper than 40 meters from the surface of the land and deeper than 10 meters from the underground bed which can sustain the foundation pillar for construction which has the allowable bearing capacity more than 2,500 newtons per square meter (section 2 SMLDU, and sections 1 and 2 Enforcement Regulation for SMLDU). After the public notice of the Minister's approval for the service, the approved service operator may use the Deep Underground to build tunnels, to construct stations and other facilities necessary for the provision of service without any prior compensation. A landowner and holders of other rights in land (such as superficies, emphyteusis, servitude, land lease right, etc.) are restricted to use the land that would affect the approved service. When a landowner suffers any actual loss due to the restriction of his/her use of the land, he/she may claim for compensation against the approved service operator only within one year after the public notice of the Minister's approval (sections 21, 25 and 37 SMLDU).[210]

206. Funabashi 1960: p. 345; Matsuo and Kozumi 2008: p. 166.
207. *See* para. 120 and 151 *infra*.
208. Sections 2, 5 to 8 Mining Law.
209. This law (SMLDU 2000) was enacted as a special law of Land Expropriation Law (Law No. 219, 1951), which provides for the general rules for public takings procedure and the general standard of compensation for compulsory purchase.
210. The SMLDU was applied to big infrastructure projects such as those undertaken by Nippon Express Way Company (NEXCO) East for the construction of deep underground expressway in Tokyo, by Japan Railway Company (JR) Central for the construction of a linear motor train's railway and stations from Tokyo to Osaka, etc.

§2. Remedies Against Infringement on Ownership of Immovable Property

I. General Rules

103. There are no specific provisions in the present Civil Code for remedies against infringement on ownership of immovable property.[211] However, legal doctrine and judicial precedents have recognized a series of remedies available against infringement on ownership modeled on those against infringement on possession for which the Civil Code provides from sections 197–202 CC. They include: (i) a recovery of the original state (section 200 CC), (ii) discontinuance of disturbance and removal of obstacle (section 198 CC), and (iii) prevention of future infringement by providing preventative measure (section 199 CC).[212] These are the typical models of remedies, and drafters seem to have thought flexibly about the availability of appropriate remedies in accordance with the content of substantive rights such as ownership.

104. Remedies for ownership may be available against a person who infringed, are infringing or will infringe on ownership of immovable property even in bona fide and without negligence. It is different from tortious remedies (section 709 CC). For example, A, an owner of a building, once leased it to B and B installed a machine which was borrowed from C in the building. But, B terminated the building lease with A, left the machine in A's house and disappeared. Then A claimed for removal of the machine from A's house against C on the basis of ownership of the building. A alleged that C was the owner of the machine so that C should be regarded as a possessor of the building with C's machine placed in A's building without any title to possess the building. C made a defense that C did not place the machine in A's building and did not know about it at all without fault so that C was not responsible for removal. The court upheld A's claim for removal of the machine based on ownership of A's building even though C did not place the machine and

211. The former Civil Code provided in Book on Property for remedies against infringement of ownership (s. 36), usufruct (s. 67), right of lease (s. 136) and servitude (s. 269). They were not succeeded to the present Civil Code. Three reasons were given by a drafter, Kenjiro Ume, for the exclusion of those remedies from the present Civil Code. First, it should go without saying that appropriate remedies must be given when a right was infringed in accordance with its content. Second, it would be too complicated if remedies were to be provided for all the substantive rights. Third, remedies were to be concerned with right of actions which should not be included in the Civil Code, although the possessory actions were taken in ss. 197 to 202 CC (Record of Discussions of the Council for Codification Studies on Jun. 8, 1894, Oct. 9, 1894 and Jun. 18, 1895).

212. However, these possessory actions are available only within certain period of time (s. 201 CC. For instance, within one year after the removal of possession) and cannot exclude remedies on the basis of ownership and other substantive rights (s. 202 CC).

did not know that B installed the machine in A's building and left it there.[213] Judicial precedent made it clear that the remedy based on ownership must be recognized without consideration of the personal responsibility of an actor who caused the infringement on ownership.[214]

II. Claim for Recovery

105. A landowner may claim for vacation of the land against the possessor without any right to possess it. If there is a building on the land without any title to hold it there, the landowner may claim for removal of the building and vacation of the land against the owner of the building who is regarded as "a possessor of the land" by owning the building.[215] This is a result of the Japanese law which regards a building as an independent immovable property from the land on which the building is constructed.[216] For instance, A owns a piece of land and B owns a building on that land without any valid title to hold it there,[217] and B lent the building to C. In this case, A has to claim for removal of the building and vacation of the land against B and claim for leave from the building against C.

106. However, it is not always easy for the landowner to find the building owner without title in the following case. A owns a piece of land and lent it to B by concluding a contract of lease for the purpose of owning a building. B constructed the building and registered it in the building registry. The contract of lease was terminated by A due to the non-payment of rent. B sold the building to C but the transfer of ownership was not registered. C lent the building to D and D occupied it. In this case, it is difficult and costly for A to find C because A cannot refer to the building registry to confirm C's address before the registration. The Supreme Court held that B cannot make defense against A based on the transfer of ownership of the building to C unless B registered the transfer of ownership (including the address of the new owner) of the building to C in accordance with section 177 CC.[218] This judicial precedent may prevent the owner of a building who possesses the land without any title

213. STJ Oct. 31, 1930 Minshu 9-1009.
214. After C removed the machine form A's building, C may claim for compensation for damages against B on the basis of contractual or tortious remedies (ss. 415, 709 CC). If A refuses C to remove the machine from A's house, then C may claim against A for recovery of C's machine based on ownership of the machine (rei vindicatio).
215. SCJ Jun. 16, 1960 Minshu 14-8-1396; SCJ Dec. 7, 1972 Minshu 26-10-1829.
216. The principle of "*superficies solo cedit*" was not adopted so that the building shall not merge into the land even if it is constructed or maintained without any title to be kept on the land. *See* paras. 86–90 *supra*.
217. This will happen: (i) when B constructed the building without A's approval, or (ii) when B borrowed the land from A by concluding a contract of lease for the purpose of holding a building and constructed the building, but A terminated the contract due to the non-payment of rent, but B did not vacate the land in spite of A's claim for vacation and recovery of the land.
218. SCJ Feb. 8, 1994 Minshu 48-2-373. Normally s. 177 CC is applied for the acquisition of an immovable property right to be opposed against a third party. But in this case it was applied for the loss of an immovable property right (a building ownership) to be opposed to a third party. For the opposability by registration of the change of immovable property rights based on s. 177 CC, *see* paras. 238 and 243 *infra*.

to escape easily his/her duty to remove the building by making excuse that he/she has transferred ownership of the building to another person.

III. Claim for Discontinuance of Disturbance

107. In the case where a landowner suffers any disturbance in the land by someone else who has no right to do so, then the landowner may claim for discontinuance of the disturbance against the person who causes the disturbance. It includes the case where the registered title on the land is not correct for some reasons in such a way that the title was registered due to the forged transaction, the rescinded transaction, etc. Then the landowner may claim against the current holder of the registered title to transfer it to the true landowner.[219]

108. A claim for discontinuance of disturbance may be used as a remedy for illegal nuisance. It sometimes can be used by combining with personal right. For instance, in the case where A owned a piece of land and lived in a house on that land adjacent to another piece of land owned by B which was lent to C. C constructed a Karaoke-shop on this land and kept it open until very late at night with emitting a terrible noise. A claimed for discontinuance of Karaoke-business operation from 1 a.m. to 4 a.m. against C on the basis of C's infringement on A's ownership of his land and house and his personal right to live in tranquility. The court upheld A's claim for the reason that C's business operation infringed on A's ownership of his house which included a function as a rest facility as well as on A's personal right.[220]

IV. Claim for Prevention of Disturbance

109. A remedy for prevention of possible infringement is available when an owner of immovable property is likely to be disturbed by his/her ownership. The remedy may include measures to remove the cause of danger or install the preventive facility. For example, A owned a piece of land and a house on the land, and B, an owner of an adjacent land, dug down about 1 meter near the boundary with A's land. B sold the land to C. Then A claimed against C for reinforcing a wall at the boundary with A's land to prevent a possible danger based on A's ownership of the land and house because A's land was about to collapse toward C's land and A's house about 2 meters from the border was about to decline toward the boundary. C made a defense that B caused the danger, not C. The court upheld A's claim. However, the court reserved an exception when A had agreed to B's action or the danger was caused by force majeure.[221]

219. SCJ Jul. 7, 1955 Minshu 9-9-1002.
220. DCJ (Sapporo) May 10, 1991 Hanji 1403-94.
221. TSJ Nov. 19, 1923 Minshu 16-1881. The similar thinking of cost sharing between the owners of adjacent land is found in ss. 223 to 226 CC.

110. When the danger of likely collapse of land was brought about by force majeure such as a typhoon, an earthquake, or other unexpected natural disasters, then the owner of a land (A) may claim against the owner of adjacent land (B) for putting up with a preventive measure such as reinforcing the wall to be taken by A within A's land near the boundary with B's land. In this case, A may claim for reimbursement of a part (e.g., a half) of costs spent for taking the preventive measure which is recognized to be in the interest of B.[222]

V. Accompanying Rights and Duties with Remedies for Ownership

111. When A, an owner of a piece of land, claims for removal of disturbances against B, a possessor of the land without title, A may also claim against B for recovery of fruits taken from the land or profit taken by B's own use of the land (use profit), which were to be taken by A if B had not infringed on A's land (sections 189 and 190 CC). The recovery of fruits and use profit are regarded as a part of recovery of the land based on ownership.[223]

112. However, if B was a possessor in good faith, i.e., B believed that he/she had a right to use the land, then he/she shall be exempt from the duty to return fruits or use profit[224] derived from the land (section 189 (1) CC). But, if A sued B for the return of the land and B lost the suit even though B believed that he/she had a right to use the land until the final decision, B shall be deemed to be a possessor in bad faith from the time when that action was brought into the court (section 189 (2) CC).

113. If B was a possessor in bad faith, i. e., B was aware that he/she did not have a right to use the land, or who possessed the land through violence, duress or concealment, then A may claim against B to return fruits, to pay the price of fruits that he/she has already consumed, damaged due to negligence or failed to collect (section 190 CC), or to pay the price equivalent to use profit.[225]

114. When a property such as land and building owned by A but possessed by B without any title was lost or damaged due to reasons attributable to B, if B was the possessor in bad faith, then A may claim B for compensation to recover the entire loss, and if B was a possessor in good faith, then A may claim B for compensation to recover the loss to the extent that B is actually enriched as a result of the loss or damage of the thing possessed by B (section 191 Main Text CC).[226] However, if B was a possessor who did not have an intention of holding the property as an owner

222. HCJ (Tokyo) Mar. 17, 1983 Hanta 497-117.
223. Matsuo and Kozumi 2008: p. 46; Matsuoka 2017: pp. 39–40. There is another view that the attribution of fruits and use profit is not the effect of ownership but the effect of possession of a thing by which a possessor in good faith can acquire fruits and use profit and a possessor in bad faith is required by law to return them to the owner of the thing. Hirano 2016: pp. 243–247.
224. STJ Jan. 20, 1925 Minshu 4-1.
225. Matsuo and Kozumi 2008: p. 47; STJ Jan. 20, 1925 Minshu 4-1.
226. Section 191 Main Text CC is a special rule of the tortious liability (s. 709 CC) by reducing the duty of compensation for the possessor in good faith. Hirano 2016: p. 247.

must compensate the entire loss, even if B was in good faith (section 191 Proviso CC). The reason for this exception by section 191 Proviso CC would be that the possessor without the intention as the owner such as a tenant has a duty to possess the property with due care of a prudent manager until he/she returns the property to A.[227]

115. When a possessor of a property owned by another person without any title had spent "necessary expenses" including costs to preserve the property, he/she may claim for reimbursement of the expenses when he/she returns the property to the owner. Until the owner of the property reimburses the expenses, the possessor may retain the property in his possession (section 295 CC). However, if the possessor has acquired fruits or use profit during the possession of that property, he/she has to bear ordinary necessary expenses (section 196 (1) CC). This is regarded as a special rule of unjust enrichment (sections 703, 704 CC).[228]

116. When the possessor of another person's property without any title spent "beneficial expenses" such as those to improve the property during his/her possession and there remains an increase in value at the time of recovery by the owner of the property, the possessor may claim for reimbursement of the amount actually paid by him/her or the amount of increased value of the property depending on the choice by the owner of that property (section 196 (2) CC).[229] The possessor may retain and refuse to return the property until the owner reimburses the expenses (section 295 CC). However, if the property was lost before the recovery by the owner, the possessor cannot have the beneficial expenses reimbursed even though the possessor had already claimed for reimbursement.[230] The reason is that there is no unjust enrichment on the part of the owner.

117. However, if the possessor was in bad faith about the absence of his/her right to possess the property, the court may grant a reasonable time to reimburse the beneficial expenses at the request of the owner. In this case, the mala fide possessor cannot retain the thing until the owner reimburses the expenses but must return it immediately after the owner's claim (section 196 (2) Proviso CC).[231]

---

227. This is regarded as an application of the general rule for the responsibility of a possessor of another person's property. According to s. 400 CC, a possessor who has a duty to deliver the property must keep the property with due care of a prudent manager until the completion of such delivery.
228. To note is that not only the possessor in good faith but also the possessor in bad faith can claim for reimbursement of necessary expenses. The reason is that this claim is based on the unjust enrichment on the part of the owner who recovered the property.
229. This claim is also available either by the possessor in good faith or by the possessor in bad faith, because it is also based on the unjust enrichment on the part of the owner.
230. SCJ Jul. 17, 1973 Minshu 27-7-798.
231. In this case, the possessor cannot refuse to return the property based on the right of retention (s. 295 CC) even before the owner reimburses the expenses. This exceptional rule may be justified as a sanction to the bad faith possessor.

Chapter 3. Equitable Interests

118. Japanese law did not receive the common law distinction between legal interests and equitable interests. In the Japanese legal system, influenced by the legal system of civil law countries, justiciable interests are simply unified simply and prescribed in the Civil Code and other special laws in a fairly systemic way. They are judged and protected by the unitary court system. However, certain interests which are not stipulated by law may be still recognized by customary law and protected by judicial precedents such as "ryusui-shiyo-ken" [the right to use water flow] and "onsen-senyo-ken" [the right to use hot spring], "jyoto-tanpo" [the conveyancing mortgage] and "shoyuken-ryuho" [the reservation of ownership].[232] An interest of a purchaser or other transferee of an immovable property which was not registered as provided by section 177 CC may be protected against a third party who acquired the same property and registered his/her title in a manner contrary to the principle of good faith and fair dealing.[233] An interest of a seller or other transferor of an immovable property who rescinded the contract with a buyer or other transferee for the reason of mistake, fraud or duress may be protected by legal doctrine and judicial precedent against a third party who has not registered his/her title acquired from the buyer or other transferee even if the third party had acquired the property in good faith and for value without notice.[234]

232. *See* paras. 68, 69, 79 *supra.*
233. *See* paras. 232, 243 *infra.*
234. *See* paras. 253, 254 *infra.*

Chapter 4. Limited Interests

§1. Usufruct

119. The former Civil Code of 1890 provided the right of usufruct, the right of usage and habitation, the right of lease, the right of emphyteusis, the right of superficies, and the right of easement as the rights corresponding to limited interests. But the present Civil Code of 1896 succeeded only the right of superficies, emphyteusis, and the right of easement (servitude) from the former Civil Code of 1890 for the practical necessity. However, the present Civil Code newly recognized the right to commons based on customary law as a type of limited interest.[235] Restrictive covenants and licenses are foreign to the Japanese law.

§2. Building and Planting Rights (Superficies)

I. The Concept of Superficies

120. Superficies is a real right of a person (superficiary) to use another person's land for the purpose of owning "structures" such as a building, or "trees or bamboo" on that land (section 265 CC). As explained above, Japanese law did not adopt the principle of "superficies solo cedit"[236] so that a building is regarded as an independent immovable property from the land on which the building exists. Still, it is necessary for the owner of a building on another person's land to hold an appropriate right to use the land for the purpose of owning the building, trees and other facilities without being claimed for recovery and vacation of that land. As a result, the concept of superficies in Japanese law is focused on a real right to use another person's land (a land use real right) rather than ownership of the building and other facilities on the land.[237]

II. Acquisition of Superficies

121. Normally a real right of superficies is established by an agreement between the parties.[238] It can be established by a testamentary will (section 960 CC). It may

235. There are two types of right to commons. One is the right to commons as a collective ownership of community (s. 263 CC) and another is that as a limited interest to be recognized on the other person's property (s. 294 CC). *See* paras. 171–182 *infra.*
236. *See* para. 86 *supra.*
237. Funabashi 1960: pp. 396–397.
238. If there is no explicit agreement on the nature and content of a land use right between the parties, the interpretation of the agreement will be necessary (SCJ Jan. 20, 1966 Minshu 20-1-22). *See* para. 122 *infra.*

be also acquired through an acquisitive prescription (section 163 CC). Finally, a statutory superficies is established by the effect of provisions of law (section 388 CC and section 5 Law on Trees).[239]

122. A contract of establishing superficies may be made explicitly or implicitly. In the case where A, a person who succeeded a land and a building on that land from the deceased person P, donated the building to B who was a common law wife of P but there was no explicit agreement about the right to use the land. After that A sold the land to C and B sold the building to D. Then C claimed against D for removal of the building and vacation of the land alleging that the right of B to use the land was the loan for use (section 593 CC) and the landowner may claim for return of the land because B had completed to use the land in accordance with the purpose of the loan for use as provided by section 597 (2) CC. However, D refused to return the land alleging that the land use right of B was a superficies or land lease right which could not cease to exist even when B ended to use it and sold the land use right with the building. The court held that the right of B was neither the superficies nor the land lease right but the loan for use which ended when the landowner claimed for returning it after the use of B had completed in accordance with its purpose.[240]

123. Once a superficies is established, it should be registered in the land registry. If the registration for the superficies is not completed, a third party such as a person who bought ownership of the land from the landowner may deny the acquisition of the superficies (section 177 CC, sections 3 [2], 78 LRIP).[241] The application for registration of a right of superficies must be made jointly by the landowner and the superficiary (section 60 LRIP). However, if the landowner refused to cooperate for the application, the superficiary may claim for registration, bring the case to the court and make application for himself/herself alone with judgment in his/her favor (section 63 (1) LRIP).[242]

124. Alternatively, if the purpose of superficies is to own a building and the superficiary constructed the building and registered it as its owner in building registry, then his/her right of superficies shall become opposable against a third person (section 10 (1) LLLB). This building registration has an equal effect as the registration of superficies in the land registry (section 177 CC and sections 3 [2] and 78 LRIP). The advantage of the latter is that the building registration can be applied only by the building owner without the landowner's cooperation.[243]

---

239. As for the statutory superficies due to the adoption of the principle of land and building as separate property, *see* paras. 87, 88 *supra* and 482 *infra*.
240. SCJ Jan. 20, 1966 Minshu 20-1-22.
241. As for the inopposability of unregistered transaction of real rights, *see* para. 238 *infra*.
242. For a superficies, the purpose, duration, rent and its payment time, etc. (s. 78 [1] to [3] LRIP). *See* para. 125 *infra*.
243. This special procedure was introduced to strengthen the interest of a building owner by the provision of law since 1909.

125. When the superficies is registered in the land registry, the purpose of the superficies (such as to own a building and to own a certain kind of trees), a term of duration, an amount and payment mode of rent, special agreements such as a land lease right with a fixed term (section 22 LLLB), a land lease right for a business purpose (section 23 (3) LLLB), etc. shall also be registered.[244]

126. Normally in the contract to establish a superficies, parties agree about the purpose of superficies, amount and payment method of a rent, a term of duration, etc. However, different from a right of emphyteusis as will be stated below, an agreement of the rent is not necessary element of a right of superficies.[245] But, once it is agreed among the parties, it can be registered in the land registry (sections 59 and 78 LRIP), and it becomes a part of the superficies and will be effective against a third party. For instance, in the case where a landowner established a superficies for B and registered the right of superficies, the rent was not registered though agreed between A and B. Afterward, A sold the land to C. C claimed against B to raise the amount of the rent in accordance with the price increase alleging that C should not be bound by the rent amount which had been agreed between A and B unless it had been registered in the land registry. However, the court denied C's claim for the reason that once the rent is agreed between A and B, it had become the content of the superficies so that rights and duties concerned with the rent should be assumed by both a person who acquired ownership of the land from the landowner and a person who acquired the superficies from the former superficiary.[246]

127. In the case where A, the landowner, established a superficies for B and B agreed with A about payment of a certain amount of rent, the rent was not registered. Then B sold the superficies to C. A claimed C for payment of the rent as it had been agreed with B, but C refused to pay alleging that the rent is not registered in the land registry even though A could register it. There was a judgment of appellate court which denied the A's claim, because A failed to register the rent.[247] But if B's superficies was not registered but B's building ownership was registered, in that case the rent cannot be registered in building registry so that A's claim can be affirmed.[248] Or there is another view that if C was aware of the rent agreement between A and B, A's claim may be recognized against C.[249] However, recent legal doctrines affirm generally A's claim, because, as indicated by the judicial precedent in the previous paragraph, once the rent is agreed between A and B, it had become the content of the superficies so that rights and duties concerned with the rent should

244. Details of the registration items are provided by s. 78 LRIP. Matsuo and Kozumi 2008: p. 214.
245. Section 265 CC on the right of superficies does not refer to the rent, while s. 270 CC on the right of emphyteusis refers to it as an essential content of emphyteusis. Thus the rent is a necessary element of emphyteusis, while it is optional for superficies. *See also* para. 120 *supra* and para. 145 *infra*.
246. STJ Jul. 5, 1906 Minroku 12-1074; STJ Jun. 12, 1916 Minroku 22-1189. Matsuo and Kozumi 2008: pp. 211–212.
247. Judgment of Appellate Court of Osaka Dec. 4, 1906 Shinbun 403-10.
248. Wagatsuma and Ariizumi 1983: p. 375.
249. Ishida 2008: p. 442.

be assumed not only by a person who acquired ownership of the land from the landowner but also by a person who acquired the superficies from the former superficiary.[250]

128. As for the term of duration of a superficies, there is no restriction in law. The judicial precedents recognized that there might be superficies the duration term of which was agreed as "indefinite" or "forever."[251] However, there is a room to interpret the meaning of "indefinite" or "forever" in accordance with the concrete circumstances in each case. It may be interpreted to mean that the superficies shall continue until the business as the purpose of superficies is terminated.[252] Or it may just mean that the duration term is "not fixed."[253] In this case, the superficiary may renounce his/her right of superficies at any time unless a different custom prevails. However, if a rent must be paid, the superficiary must give notice one year or more in advance or pay the rent for one year that has not yet become due (section 268 (1) CC). If the superficiary does not renounce his/her right of superficies, the court may, by the request of either party, fix a duration between twenty and fifty years by taking into consideration the kind and the status of the structures of a building, trees or other facilities and circumstances at the time of establishment of the superficies (section 268 (2) CC). The term of duration is interpreted to be fixed by the court from the time of establishment of the superficies, not from the adjudication.[254]

III. Effects of Superficies

129. A superficiary may use, take profits from or dispose of the land within the purpose of the superficies to own structures or trees (section 265 CC). For example, if the purpose of superficies is to own a house for thirty years, then the superficiary may use the land for himself/herself during the term. The provisions concerning neighborhood relations (sections 209–238 CC) shall apply *mutatis mutandis* between a superficiary and a landowner of adjacent land or between superficiaries of adjacent pieces of land (section 267 CC).[255]

Within the scope of that purpose of the superficies, the superficiary may also transfer the right of superficies together with ownership of the house to a third party, establish a hypothec on the right of superficies (section 369 (2) CC) or lend the land with the house to a third party without the permission of the landowner.[256] The landowner may agree with the superficiary to restrict the transfer, the establishment of

250. Matsuo and Kozumi 2008: p. 211; Kawakami 2012: p. 349.
251. STJ Nov. 16, 1903 Minroku 9-1244; STJ Apr. 14, 1925 Shinbun 2413-17.
252. STJ Aug. 14, 1941 Minshu 20-1074.
253. STJ Jun. 26, 1940 Minshu 19-1033.
254. Funabashi 1960: p. 401.
255. *See* Ch. 7, paras. 194–208 *infra*.
256. It is different from the right of lease, for which the lessee is required to have permission from the landowner in order to transfer the right of lease or to sublease the land to a third party (s. 612 CC).

hypothec or mortgage or the sublease of the superficies. But, the restriction cannot be registered in the land registry so that it will not bind the third party.[257]

130. If a superficiary suffers any infringement by anybody on the enjoyment of the land within the purpose of the superficies, then the superficiary may claim against the person who infringes on the right of superficies directly for any necessary remedies in accordance with the form of infringement. This claim for remedies is based on the right of superficies as a real right similar to that for ownership.[258] The superficiary may also claim for compensation for damages on the basis of tort liability.[259]

IV. Extinction of Superficies

131. A superficies shall end when the term of duration has passed. A renewal of the term depends on the negotiation between the landowner and the superficiary. However, if the superficies is established for the purpose of owning a building on the land, it is regarded as a type of "Shakuchi-ken" [the land lease right to own a building] and the term of duration may be renewed in accordance with the special rules provided by the LLLB.[260]

132. If the term of duration was not fixed by the contract or testamentary will that established the superficies, and there is no custom on the duration term, the superficiary may waive his/her right at any time. However, when a rent must be paid, the superficiary must give notice one year or more in advance or pay the rent for one year in advance (section 268 (1) CC). But, if the superficiary must pay a rent periodically to the landowner, but he/she has gained no profit for more than three years consecutively or has gained profit less than the rent for more than five years consecutively due to force majeure, he/she may waive his/her right of superficies without any payment (sections 266 (1) and 275 CC). In any case, however, if the superficiary had established a hypothec on his/her right of superficies, he/she cannot assert that he/she waived the right of superficies against the creditor who had acquired the right of hypothec on the superficies (section 398 CC). In this case, if the hypothec is executed, a person who bought the right of superficies at auction will become a new superficiary in place of the former one.

133. If the superficies was established by the contract, the right of superficies may be terminated for the reason of breach of the contract (sections 541 and 542 CC), unless the termination is restricted by law for the interest of the superficiary. For instance, when a superficiary fails to pay the rent for more than two years consecutively, the landowner may claim for extinction of the superficies (sections 266

257. It is different from the right of emphyteusis, for which the restriction on the transfer of the right of emphyteusis or the sublease of the land may be registered in the land registry and thus opposable against a third party (s. 272 Proviso CC; s. 79 [3] LRIP).
258. As for the remedies based on ownership, *see* para. 103 *supra*.
259. This claim for compensation for damages is based on s. 709 CC.
260. *See* paras. 137 and 139 *infra*.

(1) and 276 CC). This provision is interpreted to mean that the special agreement between the parties which is less favorable than this provision to the superficiary (e.g., that the landowner may terminate the superficies when a superficiary fails to pay the rent for six months) should be void.[261]

134. When the right of superficiary is extinguished, the superficiary has a right to remove structures, facilities or trees on the land (section 269 (1) Main Text CC). However, if the landowner gives notice that he/she will purchase those fixtures by offering to pay an amount equivalent to the market price, the superficiary may not refuse the landowner's offer without justifiable grounds (section 269 (1) Proviso CC). But, if there are any other customs, they shall prevail (section 269 (2) CC).

According to the legal doctrine, it is also a duty of the superficiary to restore the land to its original condition by removing those structures when the right of superficiary is extinguished. However, from the viewpoint of keeping the social values of those fixtures, the superficiary do not have a duty to remove the structures which increase the value of the land.[262] But, there is a different opinion that the superficiary cannot be exempted from the duty to remove them even though they increase the value of the land unless the landowner gives notice to buy them at a market price.[263]

V. Superficies for Specified Space Above Ground or Underground

135. When a landowner and a superficiary agree to establish a superficies to own structures such as overpass for roads, monorail tracks, and tunnels for roads and railways in a specified space above ground or underground of a piece of land by identifying limits in the vertical dimension, "kubun-chiijo-ken" [the superficies in a separated space in the land] may be established (section 269-2 (1) First Sentence CC).[264] In the agreement between the landowner and the superficiary, any necessary restrictions on the use of land may be stipulated by the landowner for the interest of superficiary (section 269-2 (1) Second Sentence CC). It will enable to maximize the potential use value of land particularly in urban areas. Those restrictions may be registered in the land registry at the same as the registration of establishment of the superficies (section 78 [5] LRIP).

136. However, if there are interested persons who have already had a right to use or take profits from the land, the superficies can be established by the approval of all persons who hold those rights and who hold a right on those rights. For instance, A, the landowner, had established a superficies for B for the purpose of owning a

261. Wagatsuma and Ariizumi 1983: p. 383; Funabashi 1960: p. 408.
262. Still, the superficiary keeps the right to remove it. Wagatsuma and Ariizumi 1983: p. 370.
263. Ishida 2008: p. 440.
264. Superficies for specified space may also be established by the force of law (s. 388 CC). For instance, if a person A established a right of hypothec for his/her creditor B on a particular basement room owned by A, and the right of hypothec was executed, the superficies for a specified underground shall be established for the interest of the buyer C and the amount of rent shall be fixed by the court (s. 388 CC). Wagatsuma and Ariizumi 1983: p. 388; Ishida 2008: p. 450.

house. B built a house on the basis of the superficies and established a hypothec on that superficies for creditor C and lent the house to D. E, the subway company, asked A to use the land between 20 meters and 35 meters under the ground. In this case, in order to establish a superficies for E in the specified space as described above, it is necessary for E to have approval not only of A but also of B and C.[265] If one of them did not agree to establish the superficies for E, E cannot use the underground of A's land even though it would not affect the use or taking the profit of the land.[266] Once they approved to establish the superficies for E, they cannot disturb the exercise of the superficies of E (section 269-2 (2) Second Sentence CC).

§3. Land Lease Right

137. "Shakuchi-ken" [the land lease right to own a building] is a claim right to use another person's land for the purpose of owing a building through the contract of lease by section 2 [1] of the Law on the Lease of Land and Building (LLLB). The LLLB strengthened the right to use another person's land for owning a building even though it is a claim right. The LLLB created the concept of land lease right to protect the interests of a holder of the land lease right who own a building either for residence or for business and the value of the building from the viewpoint of social economy.[267] In addition, if the purpose of a superficies is to own "tatemono" [the building] on that land, such superficies is included in the category of a "shakuchi-ken" [the land lease right] as defined (section 2 [1] LLLB).

138. In the case of a land lease right, that is, the superficies or the land lease for the purpose to own a building (section 2 [1] LLLB),[268] the minimum term of duration is thirty years (section 3 LLLB). The parties can agree to a longer term of duration such as forty or fifty years. Before the enactment of LLLB in 1991, the Law on the Lease of Land of 1921 provided that the land lease right shall be extinguished when the building decays even before the expiration of the duration term (section 2 (1) Proviso and section 5 (1) Second Sentence Law on the Lease of Land). However, the LLLB deleted those provisions so that the land lease right shall not cease to exist even though the building decays before the expiration of the term. It strengthened the effect of agreement between the parties. This special rule aims to protect the interest of holder of the land lease right.[269]

139. The term of duration of the land lease right may be extended through a renewal of the contract or due to a reconstruction of the building. If the parties to a land lease contract renew the contract, the minimum period for the renewal shall

265. E does not need to have an approval of D, because D has neither a right to use the land or to take any profits from the land nor a right on these rights. *See* s. 269-2 (2) First Sentence CC.
266. There is a view that E can claim for the establishment of the superficies for the specified space if it should not affect any right of A, B and C. Ishida 2008: p. 452.
267. Yamanome 2012: p. 185.
268. As for the land lease right, *see* para. 137 *supra*.
269. Matsuo 2016: pp. 417–418.

be ten years from the date of renewal.[270] In the case where the parties could not reach an agreement for the renewal, but the holder of land lease right requests the renewal of the contract and there is a building on the land, the contract is deemed to have been renewed with the same conditions as those of the previous contract unless the lessor (landowner) makes an objection without delay (section 5 (1) LLLB). To note is that, however, the objection of the landowner cannot be recognized unless there are "seito-jiyu" [the justifiable grounds] for it upon consideration of: (i) the necessity of using the land on the part of the lessor (landowner) and the holder of land lease right (including the holder of a land sublease right), (ii) the history of the leased land, (iii) the circumstances of the land use, and (iv) the payment of property benefits which the lessor (landowner) has offered to the holder of land lease right as a condition for vacation of the land (section 6 LLLB). The last factor of payment for vacation (Item (iv) above) is interpreted as only a complementary reason to strengthen the necessity for the landowner to use the land for him/herself (Item (i) above). If the landowner rejected the lessee's request to renew the contract only by offering the payment for vacation without any reasonable reason for the use of land, "seito-jiyu" [the justifiable ground] cannot be met.[271]

140. In the case where the building is lost before the duration term of the land lease right expires, including the demolition by the holder of land lease right or the holder of land sublease right,[272] and the holder of land lease right reconstructs a building which will survive more than the remaining period, if the lessor (landowner) gives a consent to the reconstruction, then the land lease right shall continue to exist for twenty years from the date of the consent or the date when the building is reconstructed, whichever is the earliest unless the remaining period is longer than that or the parties have agreed a longer period (section 7 (1) LLLB).

141. There are three types of special land lease right provided by the LLLB. First, when parties to a land lease contract agree that: (i) the duration term of the land lease right is fifty years or the term is longer than that, (ii) there will be no renewal of the contract and no extension of the duration term due to the reconstruction of building,[273] and (iii) no request is to be made to the landowner to purchase

270. However, it is twenty years in the first renewal after the establishment of the land lease right (s. 4 LLLB).
271. SCJ Nov. 25, 1971 Minshu 25-8-1343.
272. The land lease right shall end even when the building is lost before the term of duration expires. *See* para. 138 *supra*.
273. *See* para. 140 *supra*.

the building at the expiration of the term;[274] the agreement shall be valid in accordance with these conditions. In this case, a special contract stating those three conditions must be concluded in writing such as, for instance, by means of a notarial deed (section 22 (1) LLLB).[275] This is called "teiki-shakuchi-ken" [the fixed term land lease right].[276]

142. Second, if parties to the contract of land lease right agree by a notarial deed that: (i) the purpose of the land lease contract is to own a building solely for the business purpose and (ii) the duration term of the land lease right is certain years between ten years (minimum) and thirty years (maximum), then the land lease right shall not be renewed or extended by any reasons and the lessee may not request the lessor (landowner) to buy the building when the term of duration expires (section 23 (2) LLLB). This type of land lease right was aimed to be used for certain businesses such as a restaurant in the suburbs, convenience store, and shopping center which can recover invested capital in a relatively short period of time.

However, there was a need to establish a longer land lease right for the business purpose because for some companies it was difficult to recover investment within such a shorter period.[277] As a result of the amendment to the LLBL in 2007, a new provision was added to create another type of land lease right for the business purpose. If parties to the contract of land lease right agree by a notarial deed that: (i) the purpose of the land lease contract is to own a building solely for the business purpose and (ii) the duration term of the land lease right is certain years between thirty years (minimum) and fifty years (maximum), then they can also specifically agree in that notarial deed that (iii) there shall be no renewal of contract and no extension of the duration term due to the reconstruction of building and (iv) no request to be made to the landowner to purchase the building at the expiration of the term (section 23 (1) LLLB). It is called "jigyoyo-teiki-shakuchi-ken" [the fixed term land lease right for the business purpose].

143. Third, the parties to the land lease contract may agree that the building on the land will be transferred to the lessor (landowner) for a reasonable price and the land lease right will be extinguished on the date which is more than thirty years after the land lease right is established (section 24 (1) LLLB). For instance, when A, a landowner, concluded a land lease contract with B to the effect that ownership of the building shall be transferred from B to A on the fixed date which is thirty-five years after the conclusion of the contract, and on that date B's land lease right will be extinguished. Or A and B may stipulate that the ownership of the building will be transferred from B to A and the land lease right will be extinguished when A asks B to transfer ownership of the building after thirty years since the conclusion of the

274. In the normal type of land lease right, when the duration term expires and the term is not renewed, then the holder of the land lease right may request the landowner to buy the building and other fixtures to the land at the current price (s. 13 LLLB).

275. Different from the second type of special land lease right (*see* next para.), the notarial document is one of the examples of document required for contracting the first type.

276. It is expected to give an incentive for the landowner to lend his/her land for building construction without worrying about the return of the land.

277. Tayama et al. (eds.) 2019: p. 143.

contract. Or A and B may agree that the building on the land will be transferred from B to A on the later date either after thirty-five years since the conclusion of the contract or B or B's spouse dies.[278]

144. When the term of duration of the land lease right expires and the land lease contract is not renewed, then the holder of land lease right may request the lessor (landowner) to purchase the building which he/she constructed at the current market price (section 13 LLLB). This special rule will enable the holder of land lease right to collect the value of his/her investment in the land by his/her own initiative.[279]

§4. Emphyteusis

I. Concept of Emphyteusis

145. Emphyteusis is a right of a person (an emphyteuta) to use another person's land for the purpose of engaging in cultivation or livestock farming by paying a rent (section 270 CC). Different from superficies, payment of a rent is a necessary element of emphyteusis and to be registered in the land registry (section 270 CC; section 79 [1] LRIP). It is a real right for a person who carries out agriculture. However, the landowners have preferred to establish a land lease right for the purpose of agriculture by way of contract of lease because the land lease right is a claim right so that it is less restrictive on the rights of landowners than the emphyteusis as a real right.[280] Emphyteusis has been established, for instance, by the landowner for his/her relatives or among coheirs as a means of partition of inheritance[281] though the number of the establishment of emphyteusis has been decreasing.[282]

II. Acquisition of Emphyteusis

146. Emphyteusis may be established through contract and testament to that effect. Different from superficies, the term of duration of emphyteusis is limited by the provision of law and it shall be determined between twenty years and fifty years. If the term of duration is stipulated in an act of establishing emphyteusis for a period longer than fifty years, it shall be regarded as fifty years (section 278 (1) CC).

278. As a result of the transfer of the building ownership, the land lease right shall cease to exist (s. 24 (1) LLLB). *See also* Tayama et al. (eds.) 2019: p. 149.
279. As explained in the previous para., s. 269 (1) Proviso CC provides the landowner's right to purchase the fixtures from the superficiary, while s. 13 LLLB gives the superficiary a right to sell the fixtures to the landowner at the market price. It will facilitate the recovery of invested capital.
280. As for the land lease for agriculture, *see* Ch. 8.
281. Inamoto 1983: p. 362.
282. According to the Statistics of Registration taken by Ministry of Justice, the number of registration of emphyteusis was 17 in 2013, but it has been 0 from 2014 to 2018. The number of superficies has been 8,415 in 2013; 16,746 in 2014; 20,716 in 2015; 24,261 in 2016; 29,737 in 2017; and 23,379 in 2018 [https://www.e-stat.go.jp/dbview?sid=0003268726] (accessed on Nov. 1, 2020).

Emphyteusis may be renewed, but the duration may not exceed fifty years from the time of the renewal. The reason for restricting the duration was that the emphyteusis longer than fifty years was thought to affect the transaction and maintenance of the land.[283]

If the term of duration is not stipulated in an act of establishing emphyteusis, then the duration shall be thirty years unless there is a customary law to the contrary (section 278 (2) and (3) CC).[284]

147. A right of emphyteusis shall become effective when it is established by an agreement between the contracting parties (section 176 CC) or when a testamentary will take effect by the death of a testator (sections 176 and 985 (1) CC). However, it is not opposable against a third party unless it is registered in the land registry (section 177 CC, and section 3 [3] and 79 LRIP). The amount of rent and a term of duration are also registered and becomes opposable against a third party (section 177 CC and section 79 [1] and [2] LRIP).[285]

In addition, the special agreement between a landowner and an emphyteuta that the emphyteuta cannot transfer the right of emphyteusis to a third person or lend the land to a third person is also valid and registrable (section 272 CC and section 79 [3]). Once it is registered, the landowner can deny the transfer of the emphyteusis or the sublease of the land (section 177 CC). This is a restriction on the free transaction of emphyteusis for the interest of agricultural landowners.[286] However, if there are any different customs, they shall prevail (section 277 CC).

III. Effects of Emphyteusis

148. An emphyteuta may use and take profits from the land in accordance with the act of establishing emphyteusis. However, an emphyteuta is not a landowner so that he/she may not make any alteration to the land which will result in irreparable damage (sections 270 and 271 CC). In principle, the emphyteuta, as a holder of a real right, may transfer the emphyteusis to another person and lend the land to another person within the duration of his/her right to cultivate or farm livestock without any permission of the landowner. However, the right to transfer the emphyteusis or lend the land may be prohibited by the act of establishing the emphyteusis (a special agreement between the contracting parties or a special provision in the testamentary will), which is to be registered (section 272 CC and section 79 [3]). This is the restriction on the privilege of emphyteusis, though the different customary law prevails if any (section 277 CC).[287]

---

283. Tomii 1923: pp. 226–227.
284. The term of thirty years is a provision for convenience between twenty and fifty years by referring to the prevailing customs. If there is a different custom of duration in a particular region, it shall prevail over this provision even though it is less than twenty years or more than fifty years. Tomii 1923: p. 280.
285. As for the validity of an unregistered agreement on the rent, the interpretation of s. 177 CC for superficies may be applied to emphyteusis. *See* para. 127 *supra*.
286. There is no corresponding provision for superficies.
287. *See* para. 147 *supra*.

An emphyteuta may not claim for exemption from the rent or reduction of the rent even though a loss of profits has been suffered due to force majeure unless the different customary law exists (section 274 and 277 CC). This is a strict rule for the emphyteuta to protect the interest of the landowner. It was understood as the possible risk to be taken by the holder of a real right.[288]

In order to keep the balance of interest between the tenant farmer, including the emphyteuta and the landowner, the Agrarian Land Law provides that when the amount of rent including that of emphyteusis becomes unreasonable as a result of the increase or decrease in the price of agricultural production or in the production costs or the other change of economic circumstances, or in comparison to the amount of rent, etc. for the similar agrarian land in the vicinity, the parties may, notwithstanding the contract conditions, request future increases or decrease in the amount of rent (section 20 Agrarian Land Law).[289]

IV. Extinction of Emphyteusis

149. The right of emphyteusis shall end when the term of duration expires. A renewal within the duration of fifty years (section 278 (2) CC) may be made depending on the negotiations between the emphyteuta and the landowner.

Besides, if an emphyteuta has gained no profit for more than three years consecutively or has gained profits less than the rent for more than five years consecutively due to force majeure, he/she may waive his/her rights of emphyteusis (section 275 CC).[290] However, if the emphyteuta had established a hypothec on his/her right of emphyteusis, he/she cannot assert against the creditor who had acquired the right of hypothec on the emphyteusis that he/she had waived the right of emphyteusis (section 398 CC). In this case, if the hypothec is executed, a person who buys the right of emphyteusis will become a new emphyteuta in place of the former one.

When an emphyteuta fails to pay the rent for "more than two years consecutively," the landowner may claim for extinction of the emphyteusis (section 276 CC). This provision aims to protect the emphyteuta because the landowner cannot terminate the emphyteusis without collecting the rent for such a long time as two years consecutively. However, the drafter thought that section 276 CC shall not be a compulsory provision so that the landowner and emphyteuta may agree differently through their negotiation.[291] But the majority of legal doctrines interpret that it is a compulsory provision to protect the interest of emphyteuta.[292] In any case, if different customs exist, they shall prevail over the provisions of law (section 277 CC).

---

288. Record of Discussions of the Council for Codification Studies on Oct. 2, 1894 [a remark by Rinsho Mitsukuri].
289. This provision applies to a right of emphyteusis as not only a real right but also an agricultural land lease which is a claim right based on the contract of lease concluded by a landowner and a tenant farmer (s. 20 (1) Agrarian Land Law).
290. Even in that case, the reduction of rent may not be recognized (s. 274 CC). *See* para. 148 *supra*.
291. Ume 1911 (II): p. 251. STJ Jan. 29, 1902 Minroku 8-1-90; STJ Mar. 11, 1904 Minroku 10-264.
292. Wagatsuma and Ariizumi 1983: p. 405; Suekawa 1956: 347-348; Funabashi 1960: 423.

The landowner may terminate the contract of establishing emphyteusis for the reason that the emphyteuta has altered the land which will result in irreparable damage (sections 271, 541 and 543 CC). When the landowner exercised the right to terminate the contract of emphyteusis, the emphyteuta is obliged to restitute the land into its original condition.[293]

When the right of emphyteusis is extinguished, the emphyteuta has a right and a duty to remove any things on the land and restitute the land into its original condition.[294] However, if the landowner gives notice that he/she will purchase those things offering to pay an amount equivalent to the market price, the emphyteuta may not refuse the offer without justifiable grounds. But, if there are any other customary laws, they shall prevail (sections 279 and 269 CC).

§5. Habitation

150. The Law on the Lease of Land and Building (LLLB) strengthens a right of a tenant of building to protect the interests of the tenant. When a lessor of building and a tenant concludes a contract of lease for the period of more than a year, the building lease shall end only if the lessor proposes to refuse a renewal in six to twelve months before the duration period is over and the lessor must have "seito-jiyu" [the justifiable grounds] to refuse the renewal. It can be recognized upon consideration of: (i) the necessity of using the building on the part of the lessor and the tenant, (ii) the history of the building lease, (iii) the circumstances of the building use, and (iv) the payment of property benefits which the lessor has offered to the tenant as a condition for vacation of the building (sections 26 (1) and 28 LLLB). When the duration period is less than a year, the building lease shall end only if the lessor proposes to cease the lease after six months from the proposal and the lessor must have "seito-jiyu" [the justifiable grounds] to cease the lease (section 27 (1) and 28 LLLB).

However, before a lessor and a tenant conclude a building lease for a fixed period, the lessor has explained to the tenant with document to the effect that the lease shall end at the expiration of the fixed period and not be renewed, and then they concluded the lease contract. In this case, the building lease shall end at the expiration of the fixed period (section 38 LLLB).

Article 31 (1) LLLB provides to the effect that if the building was delivered to the tenant on the basis of the building lease, it can be opposable against a third party who has acquired ownership or other real rights on that building after the building lease, even if the building lease is not registered. It protects the interest of a tenant who possesses the building but cannot acquire the necessary approval of the landlord to register the building lease.

293. However, if a customary rule exists which is different from s. 271, it shall be applied (s. 277 CC).
294. On the relation between a right and a duty to restore the land, *see* para. 134 *supra*.

§6. Easements (Servitude)

I. Concept of Servitude

151. Servitude is a real right by which a person, an owner of the land (dominant land),[295] may use another person's land (servient land) for the benefit of the dominant land in accordance with the purpose prescribed in the act of establishing the servitude (section 280 CC). Thus, servitude in the Japanese Civil Code is defined as a right to use the servient land so as to increase the value of dominant land for itself, not just to increase the personal interest of the dominant landowner.[296] Servitude for the personal interest (servitus personarum) was not adopted in the Japanese Civil Code.

The former Civil Code of 1890 provided servitude by the provisions of law and by the act of persons (section 214 (2) Law on the Property). But the present Civil Code did not adopt the servitude by the provisions of law, because similar provisions such as the right to use adjacent land and the right of passage were included in the subchapter on the coordination of exercise of ownership right between the owners of adjacent land (sections 209–238 CC).[297]

152. Servitude is not an independent right but always appurtenant to and indivisible from the dominant land because it is the right to increase the use value of the dominant land. On the one hand, servitude may not be transferred to another person apart from the dominant land, and it cannot become the object of other rights apart from the dominant land. For instance, servitude cannot be sold, donated or made the object of the right of pledge separated from the dominant land (section 281 (2) CC). This feature is called "fuju-sei" [the obedient nature] of servitude.[298]

On the other hand, if the dominant land is transferred to another person, then the servitude accompanies with (ownership of) the dominant land, and if the dominant land becomes the object of other rights such as a right of pledge or hypothec, then the servitude shall also be the object of those rights unless the act of establishing the servitude provides otherwise (section 281 (1) CC). These features are characterized as "zuihan-sei" [the appurtenant nature] of servitude.[299]

153. If the dominant land is co-owned by several persons, any co-owners of the dominant land cannot extinguish a servitude even with respect to his/her own share

295. The dominant land is the land of a person who is entitled to a servitude and enjoys benefits from another person's land, which is called the servient land.
296. The number of newly established servitude has been around 20,000 every year: 20,649 in 2014; 23,227 in 2015; 23,186 in 2016; 22,189 in 2017; and 23,127 in 2018 (Statistics of Registration by Ministry of Justice [https://www.e-stat.go.jp/dbview?sid=0003268726] (accessed Nov. 1, 2020)).
297. *See* paras. 194 to 208 *infra*.
298. Matsuo and Zozumi 2008: p. 221.
299. Matsuo and Kozumi 2008: p. 222.

(section 282 (1) CC) because the servitude shall exist for the dominant land comprehensively to increase the use value of the dominant land so that it cannot be divided into each share of co-owners of dominant land.[300]

On the other hand, if a servient land is co-owned by several persons, any co-owners of the servient land may not extinguish a servitude even with respect to his/her share (section 282 (1) CC), because the servitude shall exist on the servient land for the benefit of a dominant land so that it should not be limited in relation to particular co-owners of the servient land.[301]

These rules are characterized as the indivisible nature of servitude.[302]

154. If a dominant land is partitioned into several parts or a portion of the dominant land is transferred to another person, a servitude shall exist for every portion of the dominant land (section 282 (2) Main Text CC).[303] However, if the servitude has existed only for a particular portion of the dominant land by its nature, the servitude shall exist only for that portion (section 282 (2) Proviso CC).

On the other hand, if a servient land is partitioned into several parts or a portion of the servient land is transferred to another person, a servitude shall continue to exist in relation to every portion of the servient land (section 282 (2) Main Text).[304] However, if the servitude relates only to a particular portion of the servient land by its nature, the servitude shall exist only on that portion (section 282 (2) Proviso CC).[305]

155. Servitude may be acquired by the acquisitive prescription (section 283 CC).[306] If one of the co-owners of a land acquires a servitude by acquisitive prescription, then the other co-owners of the land (dominant land) shall also acquire the servitude (section 284 (1) CC).[307] In order to prevent the acquisitive prescription of a servitude by a renewal of the passed prescription period, the owner of a servient land has to interrupt the use of the servient land against every co-owner

---

300. Any co-owners of the dominant land cannot extinguish the servitude as a whole, because it corresponds to the alteration of the co-owned object that can be allowed only by the unanimous agreement of all the co-owners (s. 251 CC).
301. The owner of the dominant land cannot identify the limited use of the servient land in relation to a particular co-owner of the servient land. The right of servitude aims to use a servient land physically so that it cannot exist on a share of the ownership of the servient land. This rule applies not only to the servitude but also to the superficies and emphyteusis. Wagatsuma and Ariizumi 1983: p. 415.
302. Similar rules are also provided by s. 282 (2), 284 and 292 CC. *See* paras. 154, 155 and 156 *infra*.
303. In this case, the right of servitude shall jointly belong to all the owners of divided portions.
304. This is a common principle to real rights established on another person's property. This rule applies not only to the servitude but also to the superficies and emphyteusis. Wagatsuma and Ariizumi 1983: p. 415.
305. This exception is characteristic to the servitude. Wagatsuma and Ariizumi 1983: p. 416.
306. As for the acquisitive prescription of a servitude, *see* para. 161 *infra*.
307. This is an extension of the protection for the benefit of the other co-owners of the dominant land. Ume 1911 (II): pp. 279–280.

who exercises the servitude (section 284 (2) CC).[308] If a provisional interruption of the acquisitive prescription is recognized for one of the co-owners of the possible dominant land who uses the possible servient land by exercising the servitude, it does not prevent the acquisitive prescription by other co-owners of the possible dominant land (section 284 (3) CC).[309]

156. Servitude may be extinguished by the extinctive prescription (limitation period) (sections 166 (2), 289, 290, 291 CC).[310] If the dominant land is co-owned by two or more persons, an interruption of extinctive prescription by a renewal of the passed prescription period or by a provisional interruption in favor of one of the co-owners of the dominant land shall also be effective for the benefit of other co-owners (section 292 CC). The reason is that the right of servitude cannot exist only on a share of a co-owner of the dominant land.[311]

If a person who holds a right of servitude has exercised his/her right only on a part of the servient land and the other part has not been used for over the period of extinctive prescription, then the servitude shall be extinguished by extinctive prescription only for the part of the servient land which has not been used (section 293 CC).[312]

II. Acquisition

A. Acquisition by the Act of Establishing Servitude

157. A servitude may be acquired by the act of establishing servitude such as a contract between the owner of dominant land and that of servient land.[313] They may agree about the fee and the term of duration. However, neither the fee nor the term of duration can be registered because both the fee and the term of duration are not necessary elements of a servitude. Land registry does not prepare for the record of the fee and the term of duration.[314]

158. Once a servitude is established, it is to be registered in the land registry. Otherwise, it will not be opposable against a third party such as a purchaser of the servient land (section 177 CC). First, the servitude shall be registered in the land registry of a servient land with the description of: (1) a cause of its acquisition, (2) purpose, (3) scope and (4) location of a dominant land. Then, the servitude shall be

308. In order to prevent the prescriptive acquisition by renewal of the prescription period, the owner of the possible servient land may acquire a final judgment to exclude the use of the his/her land by the owner of a possible dominant land (s. 147 (2) CC) or claim for a recognition by the owner of possible the possible dominant land (s. 152 CC).
309. A provisional interruption of the prescriptive acquisition may be recognized, for instance, by filing a case to the court claiming the exclusion of the use of the servient land (s. 147 (1) CC), etc.
310. The period of the extinctive prescription for the servitude is twenty years (s. 166 (2) CC).
311. *See* para. 153 *supra.*
312. It does not affect the indivisible nature of the servitude as recognized above (*see* para. 153 *supra*).
313. It may be established by a testamentary will by the owner of a servient land for the owner of a dominant land. Wagatsuma and Ariizumi 1983: p. 418.
314. As for the registrable items of a servitude in the land registry, *see* s. 80 LRIP.

registered ex officio in the land registry of a dominant land with the description of: (1) a location of servient land, (2) purpose, (3) scope, etc. (sections 3 [4], 80 (1), (2), (3) and (4) LRIP).[315]

159. An unregistered servitude, however, is held to be opposable against a third party under certain conditions. According to a judicial precedent, in the case A, the owner of pieces of land, developed them as building lots and sold a lot, land α, to B. A agreed with B to establish a servitude on land β (a servient land) owned by A to improve the access for land α (a dominant land) to a public road through land β. But the servitude was not registered. There was a pathway on land β, which was constructed and paved by A when A developed the area as a housing site. A sold land β to C and C did not know about the agreement of establishing the servitude on land β between A and B, though C might have been aware that B was using the pathway on land β as the access to the public road. However, C prevented B to use the pathway on land β by putting obstacles on it based on the ownership of land β. B claimed against C for confirmation of the servitude on land β which had been established by the agreement between A and B before C bought land β from A. But C denied the servitude for the reason that it was not registered so that it could not be opposable against a third party like C (section 177 CC).[316] In response to this defense, B made a counterclaim that C was aware of B's right of servitude (in bad faith) in a matter which was against the general principle of good faith and fair dealing required to exercise the rights, including ownership (section 1 (2) CC).[317]

The High Court affirmed B's counterclaim by applying the established judicial precedents that restricted the application of section 177 CC to a bad faith third party who acted in breach of good faith principle (section 1 (2) CC).[318]

In response to the appeal made by C, the Supreme Court rejected C's appeal and affirmed the result for B, but amended the reason because it was difficult to decide whether C was aware of the agreement on servitude between A and B when C bought land β from A. Instead, the Supreme Court established a new formula that when a third party acquired a servient land, if it was objectively evident from the location, form, structure and other physical conditions of the pathway that the servient land had been used continuously by the owner of dominant land as a passage and the third party knew or could have known about it, then he/she did not deserve to be a third party as provided by section 177 CC who could assert that B had failed to register his/her title.[319] The scope of this judicial precedent should be carefully

315. In both land registry of the dominant land and servient land, neither the name nor the address of the holder of a right of servitude shall be registered because a servitude is for increasing the benefit of the dominant land. *See* s. 80 LRIP.
316. Section 177 CC provides to the effect that the establishment and transfer of real rights cannot be opposable against a third party unless they are registered in accordance with the Law on the Registration of Immovable Property (LRIP). As for the application and interpretation of s. 177 CC *see* paras. 238–241 *infra.*
317. As for the restrictive application of s. 177 CC to a bad faith third party who acted in breach of the general principle of good faith and fair dealing provided by s. 1 (2) CC, *see* para. 254 *infra.*
318. HCJ (Fukuoka, Naha Branch) Jan. 30, 1997 Minshu 52-1-99.
319. SCJ Feb. 13, 1998 Minshu 52-1-65. After that B may claim against C for registration of the servitude (SCJ Dec. 18, 1998 Minshu 52-9-1975). As for the case where C, a third party, had acquired a right of hypothec on the servient land and it was executed and D purchased the servient land, B,

limited to the case where the existence of a servitude for the purpose of passage is objectively evident from the physical conditions when a third party transacted with the former owner of the servient land. As a result, this judicial precedent will apply only to the case where the de facto publicity of the servitude can be recognized even though it is yet to be registered.[320]

160. Not only the owner of a dominant land but also the superficiary and the emphyteuta of that land may exercise the servitude which has already been established by that owner.

Besides, if the servitude has not established when the superficies or the emphyteusis is established on a dominant land and the superficiary or the emphyteuta needs the servitude on a servient land owned by a third person for the purpose of the superficies or the emphyteusis, they may acquire the servitude by concluding a contract with the owner of the servient land or by acquisitive prescription of the servient land for their own interest as the holder of a real right.[321]

However, the lessee of a dominant land who does not have a real right such as a superficies or an emphyteusis but has only a claim right to the owner of the dominant land cannot acquire servitude for himself/herself.[322] The lessee may exercise the servitude which has already been acquired by the owner of dominant land. If it has not yet been acquired by the owner of the dominant land, the lessee may negotiate with the owner of the dominant land for the acquisition of a servitude in accordance with the purpose of the lease contract. Further, the legal doctrine proposes that the lessee should be able to acquire a servitude if the right of lease has already been registered in the land registry.[323]

B. Acquisition by Prescription

161. Servitude can be acquired by acquisitive prescription. Generally, a person who exercises any property right other than ownership peacefully and openly with an intention to do so on his/her own behalf shall acquire that right after twenty years, or ten years when he/she began to exercise that right in good faith (bona fide) without negligence believing that he/she had that right (section 163 CC). In addition, a servitude can be acquired by acquisitive prescription so long as it is "continuously exercised" and "externally recognized" (section 283 CC).

---

the holder of unregistered servitude, had to assert that C, not D, knew or could have known about B's servitude which was objectively evident from the physical conditions when C acquired the hypothec (SCJ Feb. 26, 2013 Minshu 67-2-297).

320. Matsuo 2016: p. 387.

321. Wagatsuma and Ariizumi 1983: p. 413; Funabashi 1960: p. 427. In this case, in order to register the servitude, the superficies or the emphyteusis must be registered in the land registry before the registration of servitude. In the registration of this servitude in the land registry of the servient and dominant land, the registration should include the purpose of servitude which provides information that it was established by the superficiary or the emphyteuta.

322. STJ Apr 22, 1927 Minshu 6-198 (concerning the acquisition of servitude by way of acquisitive prescription).

323. Wagatsuma and Ariizumi 1983: pp. 412–413; Suekawa 1956: p. 354; Funabashi 1960: p. 427.

The requirement of "continuously exercised" can be met by the objective style of exercising the right of servitude to be acquired by prescription. For instance, in order to acquire the servitude for passage by acquisitive prescription, judicial precedents require that a passage must have been established by the owner of dominant land for him/herself who claims for the acquisition of the servitude.[324] However, the Supplementary Opinion to the judicial precedent and majority of legal doctrine are critical to this strict interpretation of section 283, and they recognize that the owner of dominant land who has continued to maintain the passage with his/her expenses or efforts which had been established by anybody else may also acquire the servitude of passage by acquisitive prescription.[325] It seems appropriate from the purpose of section 283 which aims to distinguish the use of another person's land by his/her goodwill or favorable acquiescence and by his/her indifference.

Another requirement of "externally recognized" is judged by the form of servitude, so that the servitude for passage can meet this requirement because the passage can be "externally recognized." On the contrary, the servitude for landscape view, for example, which can require the owner of servient land not to prevent the view by any means such as by constructing a building that will block the view cannot be "externally recognized" because the exercise of this servitude may not be objectively recognized from outside so that the owner of (possible) servient land would not have a chance to interrupt the acquisitive prescription.[326]

162. If one of the co-owners of (possible) dominant land acquires a servitude by prescription, then the other co-owners shall also acquire that servitude (section 284 (1) CC). In favor of the co-owners of the (possible) dominant land, the interruption of prescription shall not have effect against those co-owners unless it is addressed to every co-owner who exercises the servitude (section 284 (2) CC). Further, even though there is a cause to provisionally interrupt the acquisitive prescription with respect to one of the co-owners of the (possible) dominant land who exercise a servitude, the prescription shall run in favor of other co-owners (section 284 (3) CC).[327]

324. SCJ Dec. 26, 1955 Minshu 9-14-2097; SCJ Feb. 14, 1958 Minshu 12-2-268.
325. The Supplementary Opinion to SCJ Feb. 14, 1958 Minshu 12-2-268; Wagatsuma and Ariizumi 1983: p. 421; Suekawa 1956: pp. 356–357; Funabashi 1960: p. 432.
326. The same applies to the servitude for underground sewage which also cannot be objectively recognized from outside. Suekawa 1956: p. 355.
327. These rules are a part of indivisible nature of servitude. *See* para. 155 *supra*.

III. Effects

A. General Effects

163. The owner of dominant land may use servient land in accordance with the purpose of the servitude which was agreed between the parties to contract of establishing servitude or which is presumed to have been implicitly recognized in the servitude acquired by prescription. The superficiary, emphyteuta and lessee of dominant land may also exercise the servitude once it is established.[328]

164. If the exercise of servitude was disturbed by somebody, the holder of servitude may claim against that person for removal of obstacle or suspension (injunction) of disturbance in accordance with the purpose of that servitude and compensation for damages. However, the remedies for a servitude are different from those for ownership, superficies and emphyteusis, all of which have an effect of excluding any disturbances by way of a claim for recovery (rei vindication), because they include the right to possess the object comprehensively, while the servitude does not include the right to possess the servient land comprehensively but to use it as long as it is necessary in accordance with the purpose of that servitude.[329] As a result, the remedies for servitude shall be claim for removal of obstacle and suspension (injunction) of disturbance and claim for taking measure to prevent possible risk of disturbance as long as they are necessary to achieve the purpose of that servitude and claim for compensation for damages.

For instance, A, the owner of dominant land, acquired a servitude of passage on servient land owned by B to the effect that A could pass on that land with a car which was less than 2.8 meters in width and 2.5 tons in weight. A's servitude was registered. B transferred ownership of the servient land to C, the resident association of the area. D owned a house and a piece of land adjacent to the servient land and parked a car on the servient land constantly, which disturbed A's servitude because when A drove a car on the servient land, A had to slow down the speed and take special care to pass by D's car. Both A and D were the members of C. A brought a lawsuit against D claiming for prohibition of parking a car on the servient land. The High Court rejected C's claim for the reason that there remained a minimum space on the servient land to pass a car even if D parked there. In response to A's appeal, the Supreme Court upheld A's claim partly stating that D must refrain from parking a car constantly on the servient land in a manner that it would disturb the passage of a car which was less than 2.8 meters in width and 2.5 tons in weight.[330] It reflects on the characteristics of a servitude which does not include the right to possess the servient land comprehensively, the remedy for which may be available as long as it is actually disturbed in accordance with its purpose.

---

328. *See* para. 160 *supra*.
329. Wagatsuma and Ariizumi 1983: pp. 424–425.
330. SCJ Mar. 29, 2005 Hanji 1895-56.

B. Special Effects of Water Servitude

165. Special provisions are prepared for the water servitude to coordinate the interests of owners of dominant land and servient land. If a water supply which flows on servient land and subject to a servitude of dominant land is insufficient for the demand of dominant land and servient land, the water shall be used first for household purposes in proportion to the demand of dominant and servient land, then the remaining water if any shall be used for other purposes unless the act of establishing the servitude provides otherwise (section 285 (1) CC).[331]

If two or more water servitudes are established on the same servient land, the servitudes which have been previously established may not be disturbed by those established later (section 285 (2) CC). It is a result of the nature of servitude as a real right which includes the principle that the real right established earlier shall prevail over that established later (*prior tempore, potior iure*).[332]

C. Special Effects Concerning Structures Constructed on Servient Land

166. There are also special provisions concerning some structures which are constructed on a servient land for the purpose of exercising a servitude. If the owner of servient land has assumed obligations to install or repair structures for the exercise of a servitude at his/her own expenses by the act of establishing the servitude or by the contract concluded after establishment of the servitude, the transferee of ownership of the servient land shall also assume those obligations (section 286 CC). The owner of a servient land may use those structures installed on the servient land to the extent that would not disturb the servitude. In this case, however, the owner of the servient land must bear the expenses for the installation and preservation of the structures in proportion to the benefit he/she receives (section 288 CC). The owner of the servient land may be exempted from those obligations to install or repair structures as stated above at any time by abandoning the ownership of a necessary part of the servient land for the servitude to the owner of dominant land (section 287 CC). This transfer of ownership of a part of servient land shall take place by the unilateral expression of a will by the owner of servient land.[333]

IV. Extinction

167. The common causes of extinction of real rights as stated before also apply to the servitude.[334]

---

331. Special provisions stipulated in the act of establishing the servitude may be registered in the land registry (s. 113 LRIP). In that case it is opposable against a third party. Wagatsuma and Ariizumi 1983: p. 423.
332. Wagatsuma and Ariizumi 1983: p. 423. *See also* para. 96 *supra*.
333. The servitude existed on the transferred part of former servient land shall cease to exist by the confusion of real rights (s. 179 (1) CC). Suekawa 1956: p. 360.
334. *See* paras. 131 and 149 *supra*.

168. Different from the emphyteusis, the servitude may be eternal depending on the act of establishing servitude or the nature of servitude which has been acquired by acquisitive prescription. However, if the term of duration was stipulated in the act of establishing servitude, then the servitude shall end when the term has expired.[335]

169. The right of servitude may also be extinguished by extinctive prescription in accordance with section 166 (2) which provides that any property right other than claim right and ownership shall be extinguished if it has not been exercised for twenty years. As for the commencement of that period, if the servitude is not to be exercised continuously by its nature, this period shall commence upon the final exercise of it, and if the servitude is to be exercised constantly and continuously, it shall commence upon the occurrence of the fact that prevents the exercise of that servitude (section 291 CC).

Besides, in the case where a dominant land is co-owned by two or more persons, if there is an interruption to renew the already passed period or provisional interruption of extinctive prescription in favor of one co-owner of dominant land, that interruption or provisional interruption shall also be effective for the benefit of other co-owners of dominant land (section 292 CC).[336]

If a person entitled to a servitude has not used a part of servient land, then only that part shall be extinguished by extinctive prescription (section 293 CC).[337]

170. If a possessor of a servient land has continued to possess the land and the requirements for acquisitive prescription (section 163 CC) have been met, the servitude shall be extinguished in favor of the possessor of the servient land (section 289 CC). It is called "an extinctive prescription" of the servitude as well (section 290 CC).[338] This "extinctive" prescription shall be interrupted by the exercise of servitude by the person who holds a right of servitude (section 290 CC). However, even in this case, the possessor of a servient land can acquire the ownership of the servient land if he/she has continued to possess the servient land for twenty years, even though the ownership shall be restricted by the servitude.[339]

---

335. Wagatsuma and Ariizumi 1983: p. 425.
336. Wagatsuma and Ariizumi 1983: p. 426. This rule is advantageous for co-owners of dominant land. It is characterized as a result of indivisibility of servitude (*see* para. 153 *supra*). It can be interpreted to apply to the case of acquisitive prescription of the co-owned dominant land: If there is an interruption to renew the period or provisional interruption of acquisitive prescription in favor of one co-owner of dominant land, that interruption or provisional interruption shall also be effective for the benefit of other co-owners of dominant land.
337. The period of extinctive prescription is twenty years (s. 166 (2) CC) as explained above.
338. The expression of "extinctive prescription" is not correct according to Wagatsuma and Ariizumi 1983: p. 425.
339. Wagatsuma and Ariizumi 1983: p. 425.

§7. RIGHT TO COMMONS

I. Concept of Right to Commons (Iriai-Ken)

171. The right to commons called "iriai-ken" in Japanese is a right of each member[340] of a local community called "iriai-dantai"[341] to use and manage certain fields, plains, forests, hills, mountainside, a land for a community hall, and other lands called "iriai-chi" which all the members of that community collectively own or hold. It has spontaneously evolved and maintained in the long history of each local community together with the development of customary rules concerned with the use and management of the community land. Those rules are often articulated in written form, kept and amended by each community.

The Civil Code contains only two sections which provide for the right to commons. According to section 263 CC, the right to commons which has the nature of co-ownership by the community members shall be governed by local customs and provisions on joint ownership in the Civil Code (sections 249–262 CC) to be applied *mutatis mutandis*. On the other hand, section 294 CC provides that the right to commons which does not have the nature of co-ownership but co-holding of the right to use the land owned by the state, local government or a private person shall be governed by local customs and provisions on servitude in the Civil Code (sections 280–293 CC) to be applied *mutatis mutandis.*[342] Most rules virtually applied to the right to commons are not provisions of the Civil Code but local and customary rules. In addition, some basic rules concerned with rights and duties of the members of community to commons have been confirmed and articulated by the court. As a result, the judicial precedents are now very important sources of law for the right to commons in Japan.

172. For the right to commons which has the nature of co-ownership of the community members, the community land called "iriai-chi" is recognized to belong to all the members of the community as collective property. This type of collective ownership is called "so-yu" in Japanese.[343] The very basic feature of "so-yu" [the

340. A member in this context normally means a representative of each family in the same household within the local community. Hoshino 1981: p. 183.
341. To note is that a local community called "iriai-dantai" is not a branch of local government, but a private body which has spontaneously evolved in each local region. It does not have a legal personality like a legal person but a kind of association without legal personality. There have traditionally been cooperative relations among its members, the standard number of which has been around from hundred to two hundred families (independent households) depending on the regions.
342. One of the reasons why the right to commons without the nature of co-ownership appeared was that in the first stage of Meiji Restoration since 1868 the government divided whole land areas into the government land and the private land. In that process, certain land areas which had been the commons of a particular community was classified into the government land. For the protection of the community members in those cases, the court recognized the persistence of the right to commons even though the land was held to be owned by the central or local government. Wagatsuma and Ariizumi 1983: pp. 435–436.
343. SCJ Nov. 25, 1966 Minshu 20-9-1921.

collective joint ownership] is that each member of the "iriai-dantai" [the local community] shall not have any share in the community land.[344] For instance, if a part of community land which belongs collectively to the "iriai" community is sold to another person by the decision of the "iriai" community, the purchase money also collectively belongs to that community and individual member of the community cannot claim for the partition, even though the purchase money may be divisible.[345] The reason is that each member of the community shall have no share in community property.

173. The basic structure of the right to commons can be captured as a combination of the right belonging to the community collectively and that belonging to each community members.[346] On the one hand, the right to manage and dispose of the commons belongs to the local community as a whole, the decision of which must be unanimous in principle unless the assembly of the local community or the customary law recognizes otherwise. On the other hand, the right to use and take profits from the community land in accordance with the customary law of the community belongs to each member of the community.[347]

174. The right to commons had been regarded as an old and premodern type of landholding, which had been thought to disappear with the modernization of law and society. In the 1960s the government launched a policy to "modernize" the right to commons by dividing the community land into pieces which the community members could privately own or by establishing a legal person who became the owner of the former community land.[348]

However, since the 1980s the importance of maintaining the right to commons have been reconsidered from the viewpoint of its possible contribution to the conservation of a village-vicinity mountain called "satoyama" which had been maintained as a community land, and to the protection of environment to be coordinated with the sustainable development.[349] The area of community land was around two million hectares in 1960 when the modernization policy has been launched. As a result of its implementation, around 850,000 hectares were dissolved into private properties of individuals or legal entities. But there still remain more than one million hectares of land as commons.[350] It implies that the social significance of the right to commons cannot be underestimated. This is the reason why it has been protected by a series of judicial precedents as will be explained below.

---

344. The same principle of "so-yu" applies to the right to commons that does not have the nature of co-ownership but have the nature of co-holding of the right to use community land. In this case, the members of the community do not have any share in that use right.
345. SCJ Apr. 11, 2003 Hanji 1823-55.
346. Wagatsuma and Ariizumi 1983: p. 438.
347. SCJ Jul. 1, 1982 Minshu 36-6-891.
348. In 1966, the Law for Promoting Modernization of the Rights to Commons Land, Forests, etc. (Law No. 126, 1966) was enacted to modernize the right to commons.
349. Kazuhiko Takeuchi et al. (eds.), *Satoyama: The Traditional Rural Landscape of Japan* (Springer 2003).
350. Mitsuru Kikuma et al., *An Empirical Study of Forest Commons*, 15(3) Bulletin of Yamagata University, Agricultural Science 165–166 (2008).

II. Acquisition of Right to Commons

175. Acquisition of right to commons by the "iriai-dantai" [the local community] is distinguished from acquisition by each member of the local community. On the one hand, it is difficult to identify when and how the local community acquired the original "iriai-chi" [the community land] because the formation of the local community should have associated with the possession of the commons as a whole to use it collectively, without which the local community could not survive. The holding of commons by the local community should have evolved in the long history of its formation on the basis of customary law before seventeenth century when the feudal landholding system has been established, in which the local communities had played a crucial role to take joint responsibility to collect tax in kind (by rice crop). The local community can also acquire the land through the acquisitive prescription (section 162 CC) and transactions such as a contract of sale (section 555 CC).[351]

On the other hand, the right to commons as using and taking profits from the community land can be acquired by the representative of each household in the local community. However, it cannot be succeeded or transacted, but mostly it associates with the qualification as the member of that community. Additional requirements may be put on the new comers to the local community such as certain duration of residence, payment of admission fee, and contributions by money and/or work in accordance with customary law, articulated provisions in the articles of association or the decision of the general meeting of the community.[352]

176. Although the right to commons is classified as a type of real rights (sections 263 and 294 CC), it cannot be registered as "the right to commons" in the land registry because LRIP does not have any provision on the registration of right to commons. In the practice, the commons (community land) is registered in the land registry by the nave of representative(s) of the local community for the convenience of its management. But, it is registered as if the private property of the representative(s), so that it happened that the creditor of that representative(s) attached the community land in case of default of the representative(s) and it can be sold to a third party at compulsory auction, or that the representative(s) sold it to a third party just like his/her own property. However, even in those cases, the local community can assert the right to commons in priority against the third party even though that third party registered the transaction of that land because the representative(s) had no private property to commons so that the third party could not acquire any right to commons.[353]

351. Wagatsuma and Ariizumi 1983: pp. 446–448; Funabashi 1960: pp. 455–456.
352. Wagatsuma and Ariizumi 1983: p. 448; Funabashi 1960: pp. 458–459.
353. STJ Nov. 28, 1921 Minroku 27-2045.

III. Effects of Right to Commons

177. The right to manage and dispose of the commons belongs to the local community as a whole. The community may sell (a part of) the commons through the valid decision of its general meeting or by the other procedure in accordance with the customary rules of that community.[354] Also, the community, if necessary, may bring a lawsuit to the court in the name of that community.[355]

178. The right to use and take profits from the commons (community land) may be exercised by each member of the "iriai-dantai" [the local community] in accordance with the concerned rules of that community.[356] The member of the community as a holder of the right to commons may sue individually the other person who disturb the use or taking profits from the commons without any title.[357]

For instance, in the case where a member of the local community claimed deletion of the registration against a person who was registered in the land registry as an owner of the land which was a part of the commons without any valid title, the court held that in principle the individual member of the local community could bring the case to the court when the exercise of his/her right to commons is actually disturbed by someone else. However, in the case before the court it recognized that the incorrect registration for itself would not disturb the use or taking profits from the commons and rejected the claim by the member of the local community.[358] In that case, the local community as a whole needs to take an action for deletion of the false registration.[359]

IV. Extinction of Right to Commons

179. Extinction of the right to commons held by the "iriai-dantai" [the local community] as a whole needs to be examined from two aspects. One is the dissolution of the local community and the other is the division of commons into private property of its members. The right to commons may cease to exist through the dissolution of the "iriai-dantai" [the local community]. The dissolution of the local community will not take place at a time (like the dissolution of the company or other legal persons) but may take place gradually associated with the depopulation of the local community, which has been very seldom so far.[360] However, when it happened, ownership of the commons which had the nature of co-ownership of the

354. SCJ May 31, 1994 Minshu 48-4-1065.
355. Section 29 of the Civil Procedure Code provides that an association or foundation without legal personality like a juridical person may sue or be sued in the name of that association or foundation if its representative or administrator is designated. The "iriai-dantai" [the local community] is regarded as an association without legal personality.
356. SCJ Jul. 1, 1982 Minshu 36-6-891.
357. STJ Mar 9, 1918 Minroku 24-434.
358. SCJ Jul. 1, 1982 Minshu 36-6-891.
359. *See* para. 177 *supra*.
360. But in the tendency of progressing low birth rate and aging society, the dissolution of a local community as a result of the gradual depopulation would be the case. For instance, the case of SCJ Jul. 17, 2008 Minshu 62-7-1994.

community members (section 263 CC) but could not be distributed to them shall belong to the state,[361] while the right to commons which did not have the nature of co-ownership (section 294 CC) shall disappear and the owner of the land (such as the state, prefecture, city, town, village, or a private person) shall recover the right to use the land.[362]

180. The right to commons of the "iriai-dantai" [the local community] will be extinguished where the commons land is divided among the community members into their private ownership by the unanimous decision of that community or by the valid decision in accordance with the customary rules of that community.[363] In this case, the right to commons may disappear, although the community remains to exist.

However, it should be noted that the court is very careful about this type of extinction of the right to commons by recognizing that there can be the case where the community members still keep the right to commons although the ownership of the commons land has been divided into private ownership of those members.[364]

181. The right to commons which does not have the nature of co-ownership may be held extinguished by extinctive prescription when it has not been exercised for twenty years since the occurrence of a fact that prevents the exercise of that right (sections 166 (2), 294 and 291).[365] However, in accordance with the change of the use of commons, the non-exercise of the former style of use does not always mean the non-exercise of the right to commons because the new styles of use such as the preservation of ecological environment may be available or might have already commenced.[366]

182. The right to commons of individual members of "iriai-dantai" [the local community] may be extinguished when he/she loses the membership of that local community by transferring his/her properties in that community to others and

361. Section 239 (2) CC provides that ownership of immovable property without an owner shall vest in the National Treasury.
362. The same result shall take place when the right to commons which did not have the nature of co-ownership ceased to exist by the extinctive prescription due to non-exercise for more than twenty years (s. 166 (2) CC) from the time of occurrence of a fact that had prevented the exercise of that right (ss. 294 and 291 CC). *See* HCJ (Hiroshima) Oct. 20, 2005 Minshu 62-5-984 cited in para. 181 *infra*.
363. SCJ Sep. 13, 1957 Minshu 11-9-1518.
364. SCJ May 20, 1965 Minshu 19-4-822. In this case, the right to commons still remains to exist, but it has been transformed from the right to commons with the nature of co-ownership to that without the nature of co-ownership.
365. HCJ (Hiroshima) Oct. 20, 2005 Hanji Minshu 62-5-984.
366. SCJ Mar. 17, 2006 Hanji 1931-29.

moving to another community.[367] In this case, the member who lost the right to commons cannot claim for partition of the commons land or compensation for it because there is no share of the commons for each member of the community.[368]

367. The member of the "iriai-dantai" [local community] may lose his/her right to commons, when he/she failed to perform the duty to share the costs of the community. However, even if the member of the local community lives in another community, but keeps the property such as agricultural land and cultivate it in the former community, he/she may not lose the right to commons under certain conditions in accordance with the customary rules in the community. *See* Funabashi 1960: p. 458.
368. This is the difference between the right to commons and the right of co-owners and the right of partnership members.

Chapter 5. Security Interests

183. Security interests in immovable property are recognized and protected in the form of right of retention, right of lien, right of pledge, right of hypothec, right of security interests preserved by provisional registration, right of mortgage, right of reservation of ownership. They will be discussed in Part V, Chapter 1 below.

Chapter 6. Joint Ownership

§1. Joint Ownership of Immovable Property

I. In General

A. *Major Types of Joint Ownership*

184. In the Japanese legal doctrines and judicial precedents, three major types of joint ownership of immovable property are recognized. They are: (i) "so-yu" [the collective joint ownership], (ii) "go-yu" [the indivisible joint ownership] and (iii) "kyo-yu" [the divisible joint ownership].[369] However, they are so-called ideal types so that there are atypical types of joint ownership.[370]

"So-yu" [the collective joint ownership] presupposes that co-owners do not have any specific share to the property. As a result, they can neither dispose of share nor claim other co-owners for partition of the co-owned property. This type of joint ownership is typically found in the right to commons where commons land is owned by the "iriai-dantai" [the local community] which has evolved spontaneously in local areas as an association without legal personality, and the members of the local community do not have any specific share but have the right to use and take profits from the land in accordance with the rules of that community.[371]

185. In contrast, co-owners of "go-yu" [the indivisible joint ownership] and "kyo-yu" [the divisible joint ownership] have particular shares to the property. However, co-owners of "go-yu" [the indivisible joint ownership] shall be subjected to certain restrictions on the disposition of share and the partition of co-owned property so as to accomplish the purpose of such indivisible joint ownership, though they have their own shares to the property. One of the typical examples of "go-yu" [the indivisible joint ownership] is the right of partners to partnership property (section 668 CC). A partnership is established by a partnership contract with which parties (partners) promise to engage in joint business by making their contributions (section 667 CC).[372] The partnership property including contributions and other properties acquired by the partners for the purpose of partnership business shall be jointly owned by all partners (section 668 CC). However, if a partner disposes of his/her share of the partnership property, the disposal may not be asserted against

369. Funabashi 1960: pp. 372–374.
370. For instance, inheritance succeeded by coheirs (s. 899 CC), boundary marker, fence, wall, channel and moat installed on boundary lines (s. 229 CC), common areas such as corridors, stairs, and elevators in the condominium (s. 4 Law Condominium), etc. are special types of joint ownership, which are hard to classify into a particular type of joint ownership. Wagatsuma and Ariizumi 1983: pp. 314–319.
371. *See* Ch. 4, §7, Right to Commons.
372. However, judicial precedents have been strict to recognize a contract concluded by the parties to make contributions to buy a land for sharing the use as a partnership contract (SCJ Apr. 19, 1951 Minshu 5-5-256) and for establishing the foundation (STJ Apr. 18, 1917 Minroku 23-799).

any partners and a third party who had transacted with partners for partnership business (section 676 (1) CC). In addition, any partner may not claim for partition of the partnership property before the partnership is dissolved and liquidated (section 676 (3) CC).

186. Co-owners of "kyo-yu" [the divisible joint ownership] can dispose of his/her share and claim for partition of the co-owned property without any restrictions unless any special agreements that stipulate otherwise (sections 206 and 256 (1) Main Text CC).[373] The Civil Code provides for this type of joint ownership in more detail than the other types in Part II, Chapter 3, section 3 (from sections 249 to 264 CC), as will be explained in the following paragraphs.

B. Right to Use

187. Each co-owner of "kyo-yu" [the divisible joint ownership] may "use the entire property in proportion to his/her share" (section 249 CC). The proportion of a share of each co-owner and the way of "shiyo" [the use] of the property jointly owned are usually determined by the agreement among the co-owners. If any specific agreement neither explicitly nor implicitly can be found, the share of each co-owner shall be presumed to be equal (section 250 CC). If one of the co-owners uses alone the property jointly owned, the other co-owners must prove any other agreement to claim for recovery so as to change the way of usage for their benefit, because a possessor shall be presumed to exercise his/her right lawfully with respect to the thing in his/her possession (section 188 CC). Otherwise, the other co-owners may claim neither for recovery[374] nor for any payment based on unjust enrichment and tort.[375] If they cannot prove any reason for the recovery and payment, the last resort is the claim for partition of the property jointly owned.[376]

However, if the possession of the currently possessing co-owner has been acquired after the establishment of joint ownership without any agreement among the co-owners, the other co-owners may claim for payment of any fruits or use benefits in proportion to their share after the claim for recovery and until the recovery will be performed.[377]

373. Co-owners may agree that the co-owned property shall not be divided for a period within five years (s. 256 (1) Proviso CC). The period may be renewed, but it cannot exceed for five years from the time of the renewal (s. 256 CC (2) CC). This agreement can be asserted against a third party who acquired a share of the co-owned property from the former co-owner (*see* s. 254 CC). However, in the case of the immovable property, the agreement cannot be asserted against the third party unless that agreement has not been registered in accordance with s. 177 CC and s. 59 [6] LRIP. Wagatsuma and Ariizumi 1983: p. 331.

374. SCJ May 19, 1966 Minshu 20-5-947.

375. SCJ Feb. 26, 1998 Minshu 52-1-25.

376. Section 256 (1) CC provides that any co-owners may claim for partition of property jointly owned at any time unless they concluded a contract to the effect that a partition will not occur for a certain period within five years.

377. In this case, if the co-owners who have majority shares in total decide to use the property in another way, they can require the possessing co-owner to return the property as well. Matsuo and Kozumi 2008: pp. 197–198.

C. Right to Manage

188. "Kanri" [the management] of a co-owned property shall be determined in principle by a majority value of co-owners' shares (section 252 Main Text CC). For instance, conclusion of a lease contract within the limits of duration provided by section 602[378] and termination of the lease contract, contract for use and other types of contract to use or manage the co-owned property may be determined by the majority value of co-owners' shares.[379]

For instance, A, B and C co-owned a piece of land having an equal share (one-third for each of them), and A and B agreed to rent the land to D for two years for the purpose of using it as a parking lot, but C did not agree to it. However, C shall be bound by the decision made by the majority value of co-owners' shares (section 252 Main Text CC), and the effect of contract of lease shall extend not only to A and B but also to C.[380]

However, there is an exception. Each co-owner of divisible joint ownership may carry out the management without consent of other co-owners when it should be necessary for "hozon" [the preservation] of the property (section 252 Proviso CC). The reason is that it should contribute to the common interest of all co-owners.[381] For example, each co-owner may repair or conclude a contract to fix the property without consent of the other co-owners. He/she may claim for deletion of an incorrect registration of the co-owned immovable property as the preservation of that property as well.[382]

On the contrary, each co-owner cannot carry out any "henko" [the alteration] of the co-owned property unless he/she acquires consent of all the other co-owners (section 251 CC). For instance, the change of use of the property such as the change of land use for cultivation to that for residence cannot be made without unanimous agreement of all the co-owners. The felling trees on the co-owned forest land were recognized as "alteration."[383]

The contract of sale, donation or other transactions which dispose of the property as a hole may not be valid unless all the co-owners approve of it. As for the lease contract, if the term of duration is beyond the limits provided by section 602, all the co-owners have to agree to conclude that contract.[384]

---

378. According to s. 602 CC, a person who has a right to manage the property but does not have a right to dispose of it may make a lease contract that does not exceed the term of ten years for a lease of land for the purpose of planting or felling trees, five years for other lease of land, three years for lease of a building, and six months for the lease of movable property.
379. SCJ Mar. 12, 1954 Minshu 8-3-696 (termination of the contract of loan for use).
380. C cannot deny the claim by D based on the contract of lease even though C did not agree to and participated in the contract concluded between A, B, and D by the force of law (s. 252 Main Text).
381. Therefore the co-owner who spent expenses for preservation can claim the other co-owners for reimbursement in accordance with the share of each co-owner (s. 253 (1) CC).
382. SCJ May 10, 1956 Minshu 10-5-487. This is a different effect from the right to commons of each member of a local community by which the claim for deletion of an incorrect registration can be recognized only if it should disturb the use of commons by the member of the community (SCJ Jul. 1, 1982 Minshu 36-6-891). *See* para. 178 *supra*.
383. STJ Jun. 6, 1927 Shinbun 2719-10.
384. *See* para. 188 *supra*.

D. Right to Claim for Partition

189. Each co-owner of the divisible joint ownership can claim for partition of the co-owned property at any time unless the co-owners have concluded a contract to the effect that a partition will not take place for a period as agreed within five years (section 257 (1) CC).[385] The partition can be made only for the co-owner who claims for partition by dividing a part of the property and the remaining part can be kept as the co-owned property.[386]

The way of partition primarily depends on the agreement among the co-owners. However, if they cannot reach an agreement with respect to the partition, any co-owner may bring the case to the court to claim for partition (section 258 (1) CC). In this case, the court may order: (a) a partition in kind, (b) a partition in money by selling the property to a third person when it cannot be partitioned in kind or its value would be significantly reduced by the partition in kind (section 258 (2) CC), or (c) a partition by assigning the property to one of the co-owners who wants to own it only by him/herself and having him/her to compensate the other co-owners for the amount of each share (the partition with compensation).[387] The court may select one of these measures of partition or combine some of them in accordance with the characteristic circumstances of each case.[388]

E. Duties of Co-owners

190. Each co-owner of the divisible joint ownership must pay the expenses of management and bear any burdens regarding the property in proportion to his/her share. If there is a co-owner who does not perform those obligations within a year, other co-owners may acquire the share of that non-performing co-owner by paying reasonable compensation for his/her share (section 253 CC).

Or when the partition is requested by any co-owners, the co-owner who has paid the expenses which must be paid by another co-owner may claim for appropriation of the partitioned portion of another co-owner who has refused to reimburse the payment of such expenses (section 259 CC).

385. The contract may be renewed within five years from the time of the renewal, as provided in s. 257 (2) CC.
386. SCJ (FB) Apr. 22, 1987 Minshu 41-3-408.
387. The partition with compensation can be recognized where there is a specific reason to do so by taking into consideration of the fact that it should be appropriate to assign the property to the particular co-owner in accordance with the nature, form and cause of the co-owned property, the number and share of the co-owners, the current use of the property, etc., that the value of the share to be compensated is adequately calculated, that the co-owner who will be exclusively assigned the property is afford to pay the amount of compensation, and that the partition with compensation would not affect the fairness among the co-owners. SCJ Oct. 31, 1996 Minshu 50-9-2563.
388. Matsuo and Kozumi 2008: p. 201.

A claim that one of the co-owners holds against other co-owners with respect to the co-owned property may be exercised against a third party who has acquired the share of the property (section 254 CC).[389]

II. Co-ownership Applied to Apartment Buildings

191. The Law on the Divided Unit Ownership of the Building (Law No. 69, 1962: LDUOB) stipulates special provisions on the co-ownership of the building. When a building is structurally divided into multiple units which can be used independently from each other as residences, stores, offices, warehouses, or any other spaces, each unit can be owned under certain restrictions provided by the law (section 1 LDUOB). The divided unit ownership consists of ownership of a unit which the owner can use exclusively, the common areas such as corridors, stairs, and elevators, which the owners of each unit co-own, and the right to use the ground which the owners of each unit jointly hold (section 2 LDUOB). Unit owners have a duty to refrain from any harmful conduct to the preservation of the building or any other conduct which is contrary to the common benefit of other unit owners (section 6 (1) LDUOB).

All of the unit owners may organize an association to manage the building (section 3 LDUOB). The resolution of the association may bind the unit owners. For instance, the resolution at a meeting of the association by at least a three-fourths majority of the unit owners and a three-fourths majority of the votes[390] shall enable the association to alter the common area (section 17 (1) LDUOB). This is a special provision of section 251 CC, which requires unanimous agreements of co-owners to alter the co-owned property. Unit owners can decide "matters among unit owners concerning the management or use of the building, its grounds or ancillary facilities" through the resolution by the association (section 30 (1) LDUOB). However, the meaning of "matters among unit owners" can be interpreted in individual cases. The resolution by the association on the collective contract on the provision of electricity was not recognized as "matters among unit owners" and not binding unit owners who wished to keep the individual contract on the electricity provision.[391]

§2. Joint Ownership of Movable Property

192. Provisions of law on the joint ownership of immovable property[392] can be applied to the joint ownership of movable property unless the law provides otherwise. For instance, the right to commons as a joint ownership of land by the local

389. This claim to be asserted against a third party must be concerned with the co-owned property such as the expenses for management of that property. Wagatsuma and Ariizumi 1983: p. 324.

390. The right to vote can be exercised in accordance with the proportion to the floor space of the divided unit held by each co-owner unless the associations agreement provides otherwise (ss. 14 (1) and 38 LDUOB).

391. SCJ Mar. 5, 2019 Hanji 2424-69.

392. For instance, ss. 249 to 262 CC, and ss. 668, 676, and 677 CC can be applied to the co-owned movable property. *See* paras. 184 to 190 *supra*.

community as an association without legal personality (section 263 CC) is concerned with immovable property. However, any fruits generated from the commons land (sections 88 and 89 CC) and purchase money for the sale of the commons land shall be co-owned by all the members of the association.

§3. Quasi-Co-ownership

193. The provisions on the co-ownership, i.e., from sections 249 to 263 CC, shall apply *mutatis mutandis* to the cases where two or more persons share property rights other than the ownership unless laws and regulations provide otherwise (section 264 CC).

Quasi-co-ownership may be recognized not only for real rights and intellectual property rights but also for claim rights such as the right to rent a forest land[393] and the right to complete the sales contract[394].

393. STJ Feb. 20, 1922 Minshu 1-56.
394. STJ Jul. 27, 1923 Minshu 2-572.

Chapter 7. Neighborhood and Urban Problems

§1. Regulations on Land Use in Neighborhood Relations and Urban Problems

194. The Civil Code stipulates the basic rules on the land use among the owners in "sorin-kankei" [the neighborhood relations] (sections 209–238 CC). They aim to coordinate the land use by extending and restricting the exercise of landownership between the owners of adjacent land, as will be explained below.[395] They seem to be similar to the provisions of servitude. But the coordination of land use in neighborhood relations is understood to be the extension and restriction of the exercise of landownership by the provisions of law, while the servitude shall be established through actions by the parties, mainly by contract.[396] The provisions on the land use coordination in neighborhood relations shall be applied *mutatis mutandis* not only to the right of superficies (section 267 CC) but also to the right of emphyteusis and land lease right because they aim to coordinate the actual use by the holder of land use right.[397]

In order to cope with the increasing demand to coordinate land use, especially in urban areas, legal regulations on the land use have been created since the end of the 1910s. The City Planning Law (Law No. 36, 1919) and the Law on Building in Urban Areas (Law No. 37, 1919) were enacted to restrict land use. The Law on Building in Urban Areas succeeded by the Building Standard Law (Law No. 201, 1950)[398] was enacted to establish the minimum standards of construction in terms of the width of a plot in proportion to the size of the building, facilities and structures of the building on it in accordance with the use of that plot, etc. It aims to maintain the conditions and circumstances for the safe and sound life of the people. For the promotion of the sound development and orderly improvement of cities, the City Planning Law (Law No. 100, 1968)[399] stipulates the details of "toshi-keikaku" [the city planning] and its decision procedures, city planning restrictions, city planning projects and any other matters concerned with city planning. The city planning, according to this law, shall be arranged on the basic principle that the healthy and cultural urban lifestyles and functional urban activities should be secured and balanced with the agriculture, forestry and fishery industries so that the reasonable land use under due regulation should be promoted. It designates "the city planning areas" and provides the requirements for "city planning projects." The restrictions on land use by the Building Standard Law and City Planning Law are public law regulations. However, the provisions may replace the provisions of Civil Code.[400]

395. *See* paras. 195 to 208 *infra*.
396. Wagatsuma and Ariizumi 1983: p. 283; Suekawa 1956: p. 288. The present Civil Code did not adopt servitudes légales.
397. Wagatsuma and Ariizumi 1983: pp. 283–284; Suekawa 1956: p. 288; Funabashi 1960: p. 347. It is recognized by the judicial precedent (STJ Mar. 24, 1961 Minshu 15-3-542, which applied s. 213 CC to the land lease right for the purpose of agriculture).
398. It succeeded to the Law on Building in Urban Areas of 1919.
399. It succeeded to the former City Planning Law of 1919.
400. For instance, *see* para. 207 *infra* relating to the application of s. 234 CC.

§2. Rights to Use the Adjacent Land

I. Right to Use the Adjacent Land

195. The owner of a piece of land may claim for the use of the neighboring land to the extent that it is necessary for constructing or repairing buildings or walls on or in the vicinity of the boundary (section 209 (1) Main Text CC). However, the owner of that land may not enter the dwelling house of the neighbor without his/her approval (section 209 (1) Proviso CC). If the neighbor suffers any damages, he/she may claim for compensation against the owner who used the neighboring land (section 209 (2) CC). For instance, when A needed to use B's land adjacent to A's land for the purpose of repairing A's house on that land and asked B to use a part of B's land, if B refused to accept A's request, A has to bring the case to the court to acquire the judgment on behalf of B's consent (section 414 (1) CC, section 174 Civil Execution Law).[401] But, A cannot claim to enter into B's house if B refuses it, and the court cannot accept A's claim (section 209 (1) Proviso CC).

II. Right of Passage

196. In the case where the owner of land which is surrounded by other persons' land and has no access to public roads or the owner of that land cannot access the public roads without passing through pond, lake, river, waterway, sea, or cliff, then he/she (the owner of the surrounded land) may pass through the surrounding land to reach the public roads (section 210 CC). This is the right of passage by the provision of law.[402] Even though there is a foot path from the land to the public road, the right of passage may be recognized in consideration of the current use and standard usage of the land. If the foot path is not enough to transport necessary materials for the agricultural land or to carry out lumbers from the forestry land, the right of passage other than the foot path can be recognized.[403] The person who holds the right of passage may construct a road if necessary (section 211 (2) CC). However, the location and method of passage must be determined to meet the needs of the person who is entitled to the right of passage and to cause the least damages to the other persons' land (section 211 (1) CC). In addition, the holder of the right of passage must pay compensation for damages caused to the other person's land which he/she passes through (section 212 Main Text CC). However, he/she may pay it on an annual basis except for damages arising from the construction of a road (section 212 Proviso CC).

197. If a partition of land or a transfer of a part of land creates a piece of land which has no access to public roads, the owner of such a piece of land may pass to

401. This is the interpretation by the legal doctrine. Wagatsuma and Ariizumi 1983: p. 286; Suekawa 1956: p. 289; Funabashi 1960: p. 349.
402. In addition, the owner of the surrounded land may negotiate with the owner of surrounding land to establish a servitude for the purpose of passage (s. 280 CC).
403. STJ Aug. 10, 1914 Shinbun 967-31; STJ Jun. 7, 1938 Minshu 17-1331.

the public roads only through the land owned by others who participated in the partition or who transferred a part of his/her land (section 213 (1) First Sentence, section 213 (2) CC). In this case, it is not necessary to pay compensation (section 213 CC (1) Second Sentence, section 213 (2) CC). The reason is that the owner(s) of surrounding land who participated in the partition or who transferred a part of his/her land could foresee the creation of the piece of land which would have no access to public roads so that he/she could have agreed with the new owner of the piece of land to be surrounded by his/her land about the right of passage.

Section 213 CC shall be applied, for example, if the landowner A divided the land into three pieces and sold all of them at a time to B, C and D, respectively, and B's land lost access to the public roads as a result of this division, then B can have the right of passage only on the pieces of land owned by C and D but without any payment.[404] Even if D transferred his/her land to E, B can still assert the right of passage against E because the right of passage shall be recognized by the provision of law in consideration of the physical relation between the adjacent pieces of land.[405]

§3. Treatment of Water

198. In the Japanese Civil Code, there are provisions which deal with the treatment or usage of water among the owners of adjacent land (sections 214–222 CC) because they have been important for the traditional Japanese society. The owner of a land may not interfere with a natural water stream flowing from the neighboring land (section 214 CC). It is a duty of the landowner not to prevent the natural water stream. If the owner of a land prevents the natural water flow, for instance, by putting obstacles on the land, and it changes the water flow which affects the adjacent land, the owner of the adjacent land can claim for removal of those obstacles for the reason that it breaches the duty to pass the natural water stream provided by section 214 CC.[406]

If the stream of natural water is blocked at lower land due to a natural disaster or other unavoidable incidents, an owner of higher ground may carry out necessary work to remove any obstacles to the stream at his/her own expenses (section 215 CC).[407] In this case an approval of the lower landowner is not necessary because the obstacles to the natural water stream at the lower land will infringe on the ownership of higher land, and it is a right of the higher landowner to remove those obstacles. Even if it is not stipulated by the provision of law, the right should be recognized on the basis of ownership of the higher land.[408]

199. If the owner of land suffers or is likely to suffer damages due to destruction or trouble of a facility to store, discharge or draw water installed on the other person's land, the owner of the land affected or to be affected may claim the landowner

404. SCJ Oct. 30, 1962 Minshu 16-10-2182.
405. SCJ Oct. 30, 1962 Minshu 16-10-2182; SCJ Nov. 20, 1990 Minshu 44-8-1037.
406. STJ Jan. 24, 1921 Minroku 27-221.
407. As for the burden of expenses, if there are any other customs, those customs shall prevail (s. 217 CC).
408. Wagatsuma and Ariizumi 1983: pp. 288–289.

on which the facility exists for fixing the facility or removing the obstacles and, if necessary, for prevention of possible damages (section 216 CC).[409] As for the burden of expenses for that work, the customary law shall prevail if any (section 217 CC).

200. The owner of land may not construct any buildings or facilities which will have a roof that discharges rainwater directly onto neighboring land (section 218 CC). This provision shall apply even if the roof does not cross over the boundary with the neighboring land.[410]

201. The owner of the land which faces a stream including a canal, moat or ditch may not change the course or width of the stream if the land on the other side is owned by the other person (section 219 (1) CC).

On the contrary, if the lands on both sides of the stream are owned by the same owner, he/she may change the course or width of the stream. However, he/she cannot change the way out so as to keep the natural course of the stream at the point where the stream meets with neighboring land (section 219 (2) CC).

These are the rules on the right to change the water flow, which had been recognized before the implementation of the Civil Code.[411] However, if any other customary laws exist, they shall prevail over the provisions of law as stated above (section 219 (3) CC).

202. The owner of a higher land may run water through lower lands in order to dry out his/her flooded land, to discharge surplus water for household or agricultural use or industrial use until the water meets a public stream or sewage system. In those cases, the location and method of running the water must be determined so as to cause the least damages to the lower lands (section 220 CC). This is the exceptional rule by the provision of law to recognize the right to drain water artificially affecting another land, which is not allowed in principle, different from the treatment of natural water stream (section 214 CC).[412]

The owner of a land may use a facility constructed by the owner of a higher or lower land to run the water (section 221 (1) CC). In this case, the person who uses the facility constructed by another person must bear the expenses for the construction and maintenance of the facility in proportion to the benefit he/she enjoys (section 221 (2) CC).

203. If the owner of land containing a stream needs to construct a dam, he/she may construct that dam by fixing it to the other side even if the land on the other side is owned by another person (section 222 (1) Main Text CC). However, he/she must pay compensation for damages caused by that construction (section 222 (1) Proviso CC). The owner of the land on the other side may use the dam if he/she

409. The owner of the lower land which is affected or to be affected does not need to endure the water flow, because it is not a natural water stream as provided by s. 214 CC.
410. Wagatsuma and Ariizumi 1983: p. 289; Funabashi 1960: p. 351.
411. STJ Apr. 4, 1906 Minroku 12-507.
412. Wagatsuma and Ariizum 1983: pp. 289–290; Suekawa 1956: p. 291; Funabashi 1960: p. 351.

owns a part of the land under the stream (section 222 (2) CC).[413] In this case, the owner of land on the other side who uses the other person's dam must bear the expenses of the construction and maintenance of that dam in proportion to the benefit he/she enjoys (section 222 (3) CC).

§4. Coordination of Interests of Landowners Around the Boundary

204. A landowner may install the boundary marker by sharing its expenses with the owner of the neighboring land (section 223 CC). The expenses of installation and maintenance of the boundary marker shall be borne equally by the owners of adjacent land (section 224 Main Text CC), while the expenses for measuring the land shall be borne by them in proportion to the sizes of the relevant pieces of land (section 224 Proviso CC). This is the right of a landowner to install the boundary marker.

However, the exercise of the right to install the boundary marker presupposes that "hikkai" [the boundary] has already been fixed. If there is a conflict among the neighbors on the location of their boundary, it must be fixed by the final judgment on the confirmation of the boundary. "Hikkai" [the boundary] is a boundary between pieces of land which are registered in the land registry so that it cannot be changed by the agreement between the parties. It is different from "shoyukenkai" [the border of ownership] which can be fixed by the agreement between the owners or by the acquisitive prescription.[414] As it sometimes takes time to fix "hikkai" [the boundary], there is a special procedure to identify "hikkai" through the investigation by the researcher of "hikkai" on the application of the landowner (sections 123–150 LRIP). Even after the identification of "hikkai" [the boundary], the landowner may bring the lawsuit to confirm the boundary, and the final decision can change the identification of "hikkai" (section 148 LRIP).

If "hikkai" [the boundary] is fixed, and A asked B, the owner adjacent land, to install a boundary marker, but B did not agree to it, then A can sue against B to claim for the cooperation to install the boundary marker by identifying the boundary and material of the marker.[415] It is a different decision from that to decide the boundary as mentioned above.

205. Where two buildings are owned by different owners and there is an open lot between them, each owner may construct a fence on the boundary (section 225 (1) CC). If no agreement can be reached between the parties, the fence to be constructed must be wooden fencing, bamboo fencing or fencing made of similar material and must be two meters high (section 225 (2) CC). The expenses of construction

413. However, even if the owner of the other side of the dam does not own a part of the land under the stream s. 222 (2) CC should be interpreted that he/she can use the dam as long as it is necessary for him/her to use the water flow, which is usually recognized by customary law. Wagatsuma and Ariizum 1983: p. 292; Funabashi 1960: pp. 20, 352.

414. SCJ Feb. 22, 1968 Hanji 514-47. The agreement between the landowners on the boundary can only became one of the materials to confirm "hikkai" by the court decision (SCJ Dec. 26, 1967 Minshu 21-10-2627).

415. Matsuo and Kozumi 2008: p. 173.

and maintenance of the fences shall be borne equally by the neighbors (section 226 CC). But, one of the neighboring owners may construct a fence by using materials better than those provided by section 225 (2) CC above or may increase the height over two meters by bearing the increased expenses (section 227 CC). However, if there are customary laws which are different from the provisions (sections 225, 226 and 227 CC) above, those customary laws shall prevail (section 228 CC).[416]

206. Branches and roots of a tree which grow over the boundary is treated differently. On the one hand, if a branch of a tree or bamboo crosses a boundary line from the neighboring land, the affected landowner may claim the owner of that tree or bamboo for cutting that branch (section 233 (1) CC).[417]

On the other hand, if a root of a tree or bamboo crosses a boundary line from the neighboring land, the affected landowner may cut that root for himself/herself (section 233 (2) CC). The reason is that the root which crosses the boundary is regarded as becoming a part of the neighboring land and thus it is owned by the owner of the affected land.[418]

207. A building to be constructed must be distanced 50 centimeters or more away from the boundary line (section 234 (1) CC). If a person attempts to construct a building in breach of this restriction, the owner of the neighboring land may have construction suspended or changed (section 234 (2) Main Text CC). However, when one year has lapsed from the time when such construction started or when the construction of building has been completed, the owner may only claim compensation for damages (section 234 (2) Proviso CC).[419] If the building was constructed over the boundary, section 234 CC is interpreted to be analogically applied and the owner of the affected land cannot claim for removal of the construction but claim only for compensation.[420]

To note is that there is a special rule to section 234 CC in the Building Standard Law. It provides that in fireproof areas or semi-fireproof areas, buildings with the fireproof outer wall can be constructed in contact with the borderline of adjacent land (section 65 Building Standard Law). This special provision intended to give an incentive to facilitate the construction of fireproof buildings. Supreme Court held that if section 65 of the Building Standard Law applies to a particular case, section 234 CC should not be applied so that it is not necessary to keep a distance of 50 centimeters or more from the boundary for the construction of a building.[421]

---

416. In any case, it should be noted that these provisions are relating to the rules to be applied to the owners of buildings, who are not always the landowners.
417. If the owner of the tree or bamboo refuses to cut the branch, the affected landowner should bring the lawsuit and execute the final judgment by asking a third party to cut off the branch at the expense of the owner of the tree or bamboo (s. 414 (2) CC, s. 171 Civil Execution Law).
418. The root which was cut off is interpreted to belong to the affected landowner. Wagatsuma and Ariizumi 1983: p. 295.
419. If there are any other customary rules, they shall prevail over s. 234 CC (s. 236 CC).
420. Wagatsuma and Ariizum 1983: p. 297; Suekawa 1956: p. 296; Funabashi 1960: p. 356.
421. SCJ Sep. 19, 1989 Minshu 43-8-955. However, it should be noted that the public law purpose of s. 65 of the Building Standard Law to facilitate fireproof building is not identical with the private law purpose of s. 234 CC which aims to secure the interests of living environment such as sunlight, ventilation, and sanitation.

When a person constructs a building and installs a window, porch or veranda which is at a distance of less than one meter (to be measured by the length of a straight line from the point on window, porch or veranda closest to the neighboring land to the boundary line at a right angle) and allows a person to see the residential land of others, then a privacy screen has to be installed (section 235 CC).[422]

208. A well, service water pit, sewage pit or compost pit to be dug must be distanced two or more meters from the boundary line (section 237 (1) CC). A pond, cellar or urine pit to be dug must be distanced one or more meters from the boundary line (section 237 (1) CC). A channel or water pipes to be buried must be distanced at least half the depth of them or one meter from the boundary line (section 237 (2) CC).[423] Any necessary care must be taken to ensure the prevention of earth collapses or leakages of water or contaminated liquids when facilities as stated above are constructed near a boundary line (section 238 CC).

---

422. However, if there are any other customary rules, they shall prevail over s. 235 CC (s. 236 CC).
423. If the construction work violates this regulation, the owner of the adjacent land may claim to stop the work and remove the construction. Suekawa 1956: p. 297.

Chapter 8. Agrarian Problems

§1. Laws on Agrarian Problems

209. The Civil Code provides for rights and duties between a landlord and a tenant farmer in Part II, Chapter 2 on emphyteusis.[424] However, landlords did not prefer to use emphyteusis, and they also used land lease in order to lend the land for the purpose of agriculture. As a result, the landlord and tenant relations are also regulated by the provisions on contract of lease in Part III, Chapter 2, section 7. There have been conflicts between farmers and landlords concerning the increase or decrease of a rent, the transfer of tenant right or sublease of the land, the protection of tenant against a new landlord who has acquired the land from the former landlord and claimed the tenant for vacation of the land, the renewal of the term of duration, etc. According to the Civil Code, the protection of tenant farmer is fairly limited. For instance, the landlord may prohibit the transfer of emphyteusis and the sublease by the act of establishing the emphyteusis (section 272 Proviso CC). An emphyteuta may not claim for exemption from or reduction of a rent even if he/she has been suffered a loss of profits even due to force majeure such as natural disasters (section 274 CC). For the case of the decrease of profits to be collected from the land, section 275 CC provides that when an emphyteuta has gained no profit for more than three years consecutively or has gained profits less than the rent for more than five years consecutively due to force majeure, then he/she may waive his/her rights of emphyteusis. If the farmer is not an emphyteuta but a lessee of the land, the right of tenant cannot be opposable against a third party such as a new landlord unless the right of tenant is registered in the land registry with the approval of the landlord (section 605 CC).[425]

210. The Agricultural Land Law was enacted in 1952 and it regulates not only the transfer of ownership of farming land and grazing land (hereinafter "agricultural land") but also the establishment of superficies, emphyteusis, right of pledge, lease, loan for use, and other forms of use of and taking profits from agricultural land by requiring the parties of those transactions to have a permission of the Agricultural Affairs Committee of each region (section 3 Agricultural Land Law). Through this administrative procedure, the Agricultural Affairs Committee can check the appropriateness of the conditions of contract from the viewpoint of maintaining the efficient use of the agricultural land as an object of the transaction.[426] This law aims to maintain the agricultural production, reduce the conflicts between landlord and tenant farmers, and protect the rights of tenant farmers.[427]

---

424. *See* para. 145 *supra*.
425. *See* para. 147 *supra* and para. 480 *infra*.
426. If the parties to those transactions aim to change the use of agricultural land to that other than agricultural land, they need to have a permission of the head of prefecture (s. 5 Agricultural Land Law).
427. In concluding a lease contract for agricultural land, parties must clearly stipulate in document the duration, amount of a rent, terms of payment and other details concerning the contract (s. 20 Agricultural Land Law). This will contribute to the reduction of conflicts between landlords and tenant farmers. For further details and the protection of farmers, *see* paras. 211 to 213 *infra*.

§2. Protection of the Rights of Farmers and Reduction of Conflicts with Landlords

211. According to the Agricultural Land Law, once a tenant acquires the possession of agricultural land, he/she can assert his/her right of agricultural land lease against a third party such as a new landlord or a person who acquired a hypothec or any other real rights on that land even though the right of agricultural land lease has not been registered in the land registry (section 16 Agricultural Land Law).[428]

212. As for a rent, the Agricultural Land Law provides the claim for increasing or reducing the amount of a rent in accordance with the change of circumstances. When the amount of a rent becomes unreasonable, as a result of the increase or decrease in the price of agricultural production or the cost of production and the other changes in economic circumstances, or in comparison to the amount of a rent for similar agricultural land in the vicinity, the parties may, notwithstanding the contract conditions, claim for the future increase or decrease in the amount of the rent unless special provisions exist to the effect that the amount of the rent will not be increased for a fixed period (section 20 (1) Agricultural Land Law). If no agreement may be reached between the parties regarding the increase in the amount of the rent, it is sufficient for the party who has received the increase request to pay the rent in an amount which is deemed to be reasonable for him/her until the judicial decision on establishing the increased amount as valid becomes final and binding. When the judicial decision becomes final and binding, if the amount that has already been paid is insufficient, the amount of the shortfall shall be paid with the additional interest on delayed payments at the rate of 10% per year (section 20 (2) Agricultural Land Law).

213. If no agreement could be reached between the parties regarding the reduction of the amount of a rent, the landlord may claim for payment in an amount that is deemed to be reasonable until the judicial decision on establishing the reduced amount as valid becomes final and binding. However, when the judicial decision becomes final and binding, if the amount of the rent that has already been paid exceeds the amount which is found to be valid, the amount of the excess is returned to the tenant with the additional interest at the rate of 10% per year from the time the landlord received the payment (section 20 (3) Agricultural Land Law).

428. This is an exceptional rule against s. 605 CC which require the registration in the land registry for a right of lease in immovable property to be asserted against a third party.

Part II. Movable Property

Chapter 1. General Classification

§1. Tangible Movable Property

214. Movable property is defined as all sorts of corporeal things except for immovable property (sections 85 and 86 (2) CC).[429] This narrow conception of movable property relates to the narrow concept of ownership, which can be recognized only for corporeal things (sections 206 and 85 CC).[430] Intangible property cannot be the object of ownership. Therefore, there is no "intangible movable property" in Japanese law because movable property must be the object of ownership (sections 206 and 85 CC). However, intangible property can be the object of rights recognized by special laws, customary laws, and case laws, as will be explained later.[431] Capital fund and investment fund can be treated as collective assets.[432] The concept of chattels personal and chattels real is foreign to Japanese law.

There are movable properties, for which special rules exist to treat them adequately in accordance with their nature. They include money, parts of human body, property for family rituals, etc. Some movable properties are registrable on the basis of law. Certain movables can be collectively the object of a right.

215. Monies such as paper bills and coins are movable property. However, when they are used as currency, which is usually the case, they are instruments to stand for a certain amount of value and to be exchanged with anything that has an equivalent value. In this case, the function of circulation is a crucial feature of monies. In order to maintain and facilitate the circulation function of monies, the court recognized a special rule on monies that "the possession is worthy of ownership."[433] In the case where a certain amount of A's money was stolen and embezzled by B and B paid it to C (B's creditor) to perform B's obligation, A could not claim for returning the money (rei vindication) against C even if A has found that B delivered the money which B had stolen and embezzled from A to C. The reason was that as a result of the change of possession of the money from A through B to C, ownership of the money has already moved from A through B to C. However, the court also

429. *See* para. 75 *supra*.
430. *See* para. 72 *supra*.
431. *See* §2 *infra*.
432. *See* para. 219 *infra*.
433. SCJ Dec. 14, 1964 Hanji 365-26.

recognized that if C was aware (mala fide) that the money he/she received from B had been stolen and embezzled from A or was unaware (bona fide) of it with gross negligence (in the sense of considerable lack of care), then A could claim against C for returning the equivalent value of that money on the basis of unjust enrichment.[434]

216. Parts of a human body such as organs, blood, sperm, and ovum once separated from a person are also movable property. However, there are restrictions on transaction of them on the basis of the principle of public order and good morals (section 90 CC).

Besides, the Law on Organ Transplant (Law No. 104, 1997; amended by Law No. 83, 2009) regulates the treatment of certain organs such as the heart, lung, liver, kidney, eye and other internal organs as specified by the regulation of Ministry of Health, Labor and Welfare. It provides that: (a) where a person either recognizes by document that he/she will provide on his/her death his/her own internal organs which the law and regulation stipulates as mentioned above can be used for organ transplant and his/her bereaved family do not refuse the transplant or there is no bereaved family or (b) in any other cases the bereaved family agrees by document to the transplant; those internal organs may be extracted from "a body of the deceased person including a body of a person who was recognized as brain death" (section 6 (1) Law on Organ Transplant). This law does not recognize the brain death as a general definition of a death of a person, but only permits to extract certain organs from "a body of the deceased person" which shall include "a person recognized as brain death." Thus the brain death is currently recognized in a limited context.

217. Property used for family rituals such as genealogy, equipment to be used in rituals, and grave shall not be subjected to the general rules on succession of property rights, but they are succeeded by the person who shall be the host of rituals for ancestors in accordance with customary laws unless the deceased person had designated a person who shall be the host of those rituals (section 897 (1) CC). In the case where the custom is not evident, the family court shall determine who shall succeed those properties (section 897 CC (2)). Although there are no articulated laws, the same rule will analogically apply to the body of deceased person and the person's ashes through the interpretation.[435]

218. Certain movable properties such as a ship, boat, construction machine, automobile, aircraft, helicopter, and farming machine may be registered for certain transactions in accordance with the provisions of special laws. They include: (i) the Commercial Code (for the transfer of ownership and establishment of hypothec on a ship), (ii) the Law on Registration of Small Boats (for the acquisition and loss of ownership of a small-sized boat), (iii) the Law for Hypothec on Construction Machines (for the acquisition and loss of ownership and hypothec on a construction machine), (iv) the Law for Road Transportation Vehicles (for the acquisition and

434. SCJ Sep. 26, 1974 Minshu 28-6-1243.
435. SCJ Jul. 18, 1989 Kagetsu 41-10-128, Matsuo 2016: 3.23.

loss of ownership on an automobile), (v) the Law for Hypothec on Automobile (for the acquisition, loss and change of hypothec on an automobile), (vi) the Law on Aviation (for the acquisition, loss and change of ownership on an aircraft and helicopter), (vii) the Law for Hypothec on Aircraft (for the acquisition, loss and change of hypothec on an aircraft and helicopter), (viii) the Law on Financing for Farming Machinery (for the acquisition, loss and change of hypothec on a farming machine).

In addition, (ix) the Law on Special Provisions of the Civil Code Concerning Opposability Requirements for the Transfer of Movables and Claim Rights provides the registration for the transfer of ownership on movables and claim rights which a legal person owns (excluding movables for which a warehouse receipt, a bill of lading or a multimodal bill of lading is issued). For example, if a legal person transfers movables or claim rights to another person such as a bank or a creditor, then the acquisition of those movables or claim rights can be made opposable when it is registered in accordance with the provisions of special law (section 3 (1) Law on Special Provisions of the Civil Code Concerning Opposability Requirements for the Transfer of Movables and Claim Rights). It is used only by a legal person who needs to transfer lots of movables or small amount of claim rights comprehensively at a time for the purpose of sales or establishing mortgages. For instance, a company A may be able to borrow certain amounts of money from a bank B by providing movables kept in a warehouse, the content of which is changing comprehensively for collateral (mortgage) by registration in accordance with that special law. A does not need to establish mortgage for each movable one by one but comprehensively through one registration by identifying the particular kind, amount and location of the movables even though the content of which may be always changing by selling some of them and supplementing them in accordance with the economic activity of A. A can save costs for making transaction of each movable.

Movable properties which are registered as explained above shall have special treatment in the application of section 178 CC (on the opposability requirement for movable property) and section 192 CC (on the immediate acquisition of movable property).[436]

219. Collective goods such as certain commodities in a certain warehouse may be the object of a right such as ownership. Since the middle of the 1950s, courts have gradually recognized the validity of "jyoto-tanpo" [the conveyancing mortgage] established on collective assets as a whole such as floating commodities kept at a particular warehouse by the agreement between the mortgager and the creditor.[437] It has been frequently used by the small- and medium-sized enterprises to have finance for their activities.

A special law recognized the transfer of ownership of collective movables owned by a corporation for the reduction of transaction costs and the convenience of the transferor and transferee by introducing the registration system for those collective movables as an object of a certain transaction. It is the Law on Special Provisions

436. *See* paras. 258 and 262 *infra*.

437. DCJ (Osaka) Dec. 6, 1955 Ka-minshu 6-2559; SCJ Feb. 15, 1979 Minshu 33-1-51; SCJ Nov. 10, 1987 Minshu 41-8-1559.

for the Civil Code Concerning the Opposable Requirements for the Transfer of Movables and Assignment of Claims (Law No. 148, 2012). For instance, if company A owns thousand laptop computers of a certain type and kept them at a particular warehouse. A borrowed certain amount of money from B and established the "jyoto-tanpo" [the conveyancing mortgage] and registered it in the registry of movable transfer by identifying the kind, quantity and location of the object. As an effect of this registration, B shall have the same opposable requirement as the delivery of movable property provided by section 178 CC without acquiring the possession of thousand laptop computers which have been kept in a particular warehouse (section 3 (1) Law on Special Provisions for the Civil Code Concerning the Opposable Requirements for the Transfer of Movables and Assignment of Claims).[438] This is a special treatment of collective goods as an object of ownership transfer to be recognized by the provision of law.

§2. Intangible Property

220. As mentioned above, the concept of movable property shall not include intangible property in Japanese law.[439] However, immaterial goods such as intellectual property and certain rights which have financial value such as certain claims to be generated from certain transactions, etc. may be the object of right. Intellectual property such as literary, scientific, artistic or musical works, invention, idea, design, trademark, trade name, service mark, trade secret, etc. may be the object of right if they are recognized as the object of intellectual property rights in accordance with the provisions of law.[440]

221. The right of publicity has been recognized by the court. The Supreme Court defined that the right of publicity is a right to use the customer attracting power of the name, figure, image and portrait of a person who will be able to promote the sale of goods to which his/her name, figure, etc. are attached. The right of publicity is based on the commercial value of the name, figure, etc. of the person, but it is closely related to and generated from the personality right. If the other person uses the customer attracting power of the name, figure, etc. without permission of the right holder would infringe on the right of publicity.[441]

As the right of publicity recognized by the judicial precedents is understood to be generated from the personality right, "the right of publicity of a thing" was denied by the Supreme Court. In this case A, a developer of games software, produced a

438. To note is that the application of this provision is limited only to movables which a corporation owns excluding movables for which a warehouse receipt, a bill of lading or a multimodal bill of lading is issued.
439. *See* paras. 75 and 214 *supra*.
440. Those special laws include the Copyright Law (for literary, scientific, artistic or musical works), Patent Law (for invention), Utility Model Law (for idea), Design Law (for design), Trade Mark Law (for trademark and service mark), Commercial Code (for trade name), and Law on Prevention of Unlawful Competition (for trade secret).
441. SCJ Feb. 2, 2012 Minshu 66-2-89.

software of the horse race game by using the names of existing racehorses including famous ones without consent of B, the owners of those horses. The Supreme Court rejected the claim by B for injunction to sell the software and for compensation for the economic loss. The reason was that ownership of the horse can only cover the corporeal aspect of the horse so that it cannot be extended to the name of the horse.[442]

222. Claim rights which have been generated and will be generated from certain legal relations such as between the landlord and the tenant, the medical doctor and the Medical Fee Payment Fund can be transferred to another person or used for the object of "shugo-ryudo-saiken-jyoto-tanpo" [the conveyancing mortgage on collective, floating and future claims] if they are clearly specified by the cause, amount, term, etc. unless there is a special circumstance to be regarded as against public order and good morals.[443]

If claims for money (monetary claims) belong to a corporation, it can transfer those claims to another person and register the transfer of those claims in the registry of claim rights transfer (assignment) by identifying the debtor, cause and amount of those claims. As an effect of this registration, the acquirer of those claims shall have the same effect of having an opposable requirement against a third party as provided by section 467 (2) CC (section 4 (1) Law on Special Provisions for the Civil Code Concerning the Opposable Requirements for the Transfer of Movables and Assignment of Claims).[444] This is a special provision to treat monetary claim rights held by a corporation as an object of claim rights transfer which will make it opposable against a third party in the easier way than the provision of Civil Code (section 467 (2) CC).

For example, if a company A has hundred monetary claims to be paid by A's debtors B1 to B100, A can transfer these claim rights to C on the basis of sales contract or "shugo-saiken-jyoto-tanpo" [the conveyancing mortgage on collective claims] and have opposable requirement against a third party by registering it in the registry of claim rights transfer at a time. This registration of transfer of claim rights in the registry of claim rights transfer will enable the parties to reduce the transaction cost greatly by the provision of a special law, because according to the Civil Code, the transferor of a claim right has to give notice to a debtor about the transfer of the claim right by way of sending a document on which an official certified date must be put to make it opposable against a third party (section 467 (2) CC). However, it will be costly to give notice by way of sending a document with an official certified date one by one to hundred debtors. The registration of the transfer of hundred claim rights to be made at a time shall replace the notice to a debtor one by one as provided by section 467 (2) CC (section 4 (1) Law on Special Provisions for the Civil Code Concerning the Opposable Requirements for the Transfer of Movables and Assignment of Claims).

442. SCJ Feb. 13, 2004 Minshu 58-2-311.
443. SCJ Jan. 29, 1999 Minshu 53-1-151.
444. To note is that this provision limits its application to claims only for payment of money.

223. As for a claim which is combined with a paper that does not specify any name of the creditor such as a train ticket, admission ticket, and gift certificate has been deemed to be movable property (Old section 86 (3) CC), because the claim combined with the paper must always be exercised by holding and showing that paper so that the claim could not be separated from the paper. However, as a result of the amendment to the Civil Code in 2017,[445] former section 86 (3) was abrogated and the claim combined with the paper that does not specify any name of the creditor has come to be treated as a kind of marketable securities, the holder of which through transactions is to be strongly protected than a movable property (section 520-20 CC).[446]

445. It was brought into effect on Apr. 1, 2020.

446. For instance, the holder of an admission ticket who bought it from the seller who had not been an owner of the ticket does not need to return it to the owner unless the owner succeeded in proving that that the holder of the ticket was aware that it was not owned by the seller or was not aware of it due to the gross negligence (ss. 520-20 and 520-15 CC).

Chapter 2. Legal Interests

§1. Ownership of Movable Property

224. In the Civil Code of Japan, "do-san" [the movable property] is defined as a corporeal thing other than "fu-do-san" [immovable property] (sections 85 and 86 (2) CC), and it is the major object of ownership, an owner of which has the rights, subject to the restrictions prescribed by laws and regulations, freely to use, obtain profits from and dispose of the corporeal thing (section 206 CC).[447]

However, it is controversial whether the right of ownership can be extended to a photo image of the movable property. In the case where A, the owner of a piece of calligraphy which was written by the famous Chinese calligrapher Yang Zhenqing (709–785 AD), claimed against the publishing company B for injunction to stop printing and sale of the photo collection book which contained the photo image of Zhenqing's calligrapher owned by A and compensation for the profit which A might have made. The Supreme Court denied both claims for the reason that the right of ownership can only cover the corporeal aspect of the thing and may not extend to manage the incorporeal aspect of the thing. Otherwise, it would affect the use of intellectual property regulated by special laws such as Copyright Law in the present case, which aim to balance the protection of interest of the creator of intellectual property by fixing the terms of protection and that of the general users. After the protection of the intellectual property law was over, the intellectual property shall belong to the public domain.[448] This problem of the coverage of ownership right is closely related to that of the recognition of the right of publicity of a thing. In the judicial precedents, the right of publicity of a thing such as the right of use of a name of a famous racehorse is not recognized.[449] The name of a thing is independent of and not a part of the thing as an object of ownership. However, the photo image of a thing is more closely related to the thing so that the scope of ownership right to control the use of photo image of a thing is still controversial.[450]

§2. Remedies for Owner of Movable Property

225. Remedies for an owner of a movable property against a person who infringes on it are the same as those for immovable property in principle.[451] They are claim for recovery of dispossessed property (rei vindicatio), claim for removal and injunction of disturbance, and claim for prevention of provable infringement.[452]

The claim for recovery and that for removal and injunction of disturbance against a possessor of the movable property may be accompanied with the additional claim

447. *See* para. 82 *supra*.
448. SCJ Jan. 20, 1984 Minshu 38-1-1.
449. SCJ Feb. 31, 2004 Minshu 58-2-311. *See* para. 222 *supra*.
450. Matsuo and Kozumi 2008: pp. 164–165.
451. *See* para. 103 *supra*.
452. These forms of remedies are modeled on the three types of possessory actions as provided in ss. 198, 199 and 200 CC.

for return of fruits or use profits to be generated from the movable property, and claim for compensation for damages caused by the possessor (sections 189, 190, 191 CC).[453]

The possessor of the movable property may claim for reimbursement of expenses which was spent to maintain or increase the value of the property in accordance with the provisions of law (section 196 CC).[454]

226. A remedy for an owner of movable property needs to be coordinated with that for an owner of immovable property in a particular case. For instance, a landlord A lent his house to B for the purpose of producing goods by using a machine which B had borrowed from C, the owner of that machine. But B became in default and could not pay the house rent so that A terminated the lease contract with B and B left the house without removing the machine and did not return it to C. A claimed against C for removing C's machine on the basis of ownership of the house, the use of which was disturbed by C's machine. C refused to remove it and claimed A for returning the machine with A's expense for the reason that C's machine was dispossessed by A. The court recognized A's claim against C for removing the machine and paying the use profit of the house until the machine will be removed from A's house for the reason that A's house should be regarded as disturbed by C's machine because the machine was not dispossessed by A from C but lent by C to B and placed by B in the house.[455] However, if A refuses C's removal of the machine from A's house without any legitimate reason, then the situation is converted and A is recognized to dispossess C's machine. Accordingly, in this case, C may claim against A for returning the machine with A's expense.[456]

§3. Property Rights Other Than Ownership in Movable Property

227. Real rights other than ownership to be established on movable property are limited compared with those on immovable property. Real rights such as superficies, emphyteusis, servitude, the right to commons are concerned with immovable property. Other than the right of ownership, a movable property may be the object of real rights such as the right of retention, the right of lien, the right of pledge, the right of hypothec recognized by special laws,[457] the mortgage in the form of transfer of ownership, the reservation of ownership, etc. In addition, the right of hypothec established on a forest land is interpreted to reach the trees which are cut off and left on the land, although the trees are movable property.[458] If the right of hypothec on the forest land is executed, the trees cut off from the land and left on the land can be sold at auction with the forest land.[459] If those trees are brought out of the land, they are treated as movables and rules on the movable property shall be

453. *See* paras. 111–114 *supra.*
454. *See* paras. 115–117 *supra.*
455. STJ Oct. 31, 1930 Minshu 9-1009.
456. Matsuo and Kozumi 2008: pp. 43–44.
457. *See* para. 218 *supra.*
458. STJ Apr. 20, 1932 Shinbun 3407-15.
459. Matsuo and Kozumi 2008: pp. 317–318.

applied to them such as section 178 CC (e.g., if they are sold to different purchasers by the owner) and section 192 CC (e.g., if they are sold by a person who does not have ownership and without the approval of the owner).[460]

460. Matsuo and Kozumi 2008: pp. 318–319.

Chapter 3. Equitable Interests

228. The distinction between legal interests and equitable interests is not adopted in Japanese law.

Chapter 4. Security Interests

229. Security interests concerning movable property will be treated in Part V, Chapter 2 below.

Part III. Acquisition of Property Rights

Chapter 1. Transfer of Property Rights *Inter Vivos*

§1. Principles on the Transfer of Property Rights by Contract

230. As the fundamental principle on what legal action causes the transfer of property rights *inter vivos*, the Civil Code of Japan adopted "ishi-shugi" [the principle of agreement] which requires only the agreement between the transferor and transferee to transfer property rights. It was influenced by the French Civil Code.[461] Section 176 CC provides that "the creation and transfer of real rights shall take effect solely by the manifestations of intention of the relevant parties." For instance, if A, the owner of a property, whether immovable or movable, manifests his/her intention to transfer the ownership of the property to B, and B manifests his/her intention to receive it from A, then B becomes the owner of the property only by this agreement. It is not necessary to make the agreement by document such as a notarized deed. Different from the German Civil Code, neither the delivery of the movable property nor the registration for the immovable property is required for the transfer of property rights.[462]

This principle of agreement was introduced into Japan by the drafter of the present Civil Code consciously for both practical and theoretical reasons.[463] From the practical point of view, the drafter thought that the principle of agreement should reduce the transaction costs for both parties. From the theoretical viewpoint, the right of ownership, which is to be distinct from its object, may be able to transfer from the transferor to transferee only by the agreement between them, even though the property is yet to be delivered. It was thought that as the theoretical consequence the concept of ownership right should include the right to transfer of ownership in accordance with the intention of the owner. The principle of agreement, which was based on the voluntarism developed by the natural law theory, has been received into Japan under the influence of a natural law theory on the government officials in the Ministry of Justice, drafters, teachers and students.

461. *See* ss. 711, 1138, 1583 and 1599 FCC.
462. In order to transfer the property rights, the registration for immovable property and the delivery for movable property are required by the Civil Code of Germany (ss. 873, 925 and 929 GCC).
463. Record of Discussions of the Council for Codification Studies on May 22, 1894 [a remark by Nobushige Hozumi].

231. The "intention" to transfer of real rights provided by section 176 CC in Book II on Real Rights is conceptually distinct and separated from the "promise" to sell, donate or exchange of property rights as provided by sections 555, 549 and 586 CC in Book III on Claim Rights. For instance, according to section 555 CC, a contract of sale shall become effective when a seller "promises to transfer a certain property right" and a buyer "promises to pay the purchase money" for it. It means that contract of sale is the agreement to create the seller's obligation and the buyer's claim right to transfer ownership (section 555 CC). It is distinct from the agreement of the transferor's intention solely to transfer ownership and the transferee's intention to receive ownership (section 176 CC).

This distinction is called the principle of separation. The original model of the principle of separation is found in the German Civil Code, where the legal actions to transfer of ownership such as the registration for immovable property and delivery for movable property (sections 873, 925, 929 GCC) are separated from the contract of sale, donation or exchange (sections 433, 480, 516 GCC). It is different from the French Civil Code (sections 711, 1138, 1583, 1599 FCC), where the ownership shall be transferred just as the effect of contract of sale, exchange or donation, which are not separated from the agreement to transfer ownership for itself. It is called the principle of unity.

However, the principle of separation is not strictly maintained in the Japanese Civil Code because it does not require any specific formalities (such as a notarized deed, registration, and delivery) for the agreement to transfer and receive ownership but just requires "the manifestation of intention" (section 176 CC), which is only conceptually distinguished from the contract of sale, exchange or donation (sections 555, 586, 549 CC). Thus the basic principles for the transfer of property rights in the Japanese Civil Code are the combination of the principle of agreement and the principle of (conceptual) separation, which may be characterized as a Franco-German hybrid.[464]

232. According to the principle of (strict) separation, the transfer of ownership remains to be valid even though the contract of sale, exchange or donation becomes invalid as a result of, for instance, avoidance for the reason of mistake, fraud, and duress. The ownership is to be returned to the transferor by the transferee because of the unjust enrichment. It is called the principle of abstraction, which is adopted by the German Civil Code.

On the contrary, according to the principle of unity, the transfer of ownership becomes invalid when the contract of sale, for example, is avoided for the reason of a fraud by the purchaser, and the ownership shall return to the seller at the same time as the avoidance of the sales contract. It is called the principle of causality, which is adopted by the French Civil Code.

---

464. Hiroshi Matsuo "Reception of law and civil law tradition," in: *Law, Legal Culture and Politics in the Twenty First Century* 79–88 (Guenther Doeker-Mach and Klaus A. Ziegert eds., Franz Steiner Verlag 2004).

It is not clear whether the Japanese Civil Code adopts the principle of abstraction or the principle of causality. The judicial precedents and majority of legal doctrines seem to recognize the principle of causality.[465]

233. The timing when ownership transfers from a transferor to a transferee is to be decided by the agreement of the parties. This is a result of the principle of agreement (section 176 CC). Depending on the agreement of intentions between the parties (in the sense of section 176 CC), it may be transferred at the same time as the conclusion of sales contract or it may be deferred until the purchase money is paid in full or in part, or until the delivery or registration is completed. If no specific agreement on the timing of the transfer of ownership can be found in the "manifestation of the intention of the parties," the ownership of a specified property may be interpreted to be transferred at the conclusion of the contract of sale, donation or exchange. The Supreme Court Decision states that in the contract of sale of a specific thing owned by the seller, the transfer of ownership takes place immediately unless the parties stipulate that the ownership will transfer to the purchaser in the future.[466]

234. In the contract of sale of unspecified thing such as goods to be mass-produced, the ownership shall be transferred when the object of that contract is specified by the parties after the conclusion of the sales contract unless they agreed otherwise.[467]

235. In the contract of sale of a thing which is owned not by a seller but by a third party, the ownership of the thing may be transferred when the seller acquires the ownership without making any additional agreement to transfer it to the purchaser unless the seller and the purchaser agreed otherwise.[468]

It should be noted that the contract of sale of a thing which the seller does not own is effective so that the seller owes the purchaser an obligation to acquire the ownership of the thing from the owner and transfer it to the purchaser (section 561 CC). This is a consequence of the principle of (conceptual) separation between the agreement just to transfer the ownership and the contract to promise the transfer of the ownership such as sale, exchange or donation.[469]

236. The intention to transfer ownership of a property may be conditional or unconditional. A transferor and a transferee may be able to agree to the transfer of

465. STJ Dec. 27, 1917 Minroku 23-22366; STJ May 13, 1919 Minroku 25- 770; Wagatsuma and Ariizumi 1983: pp. 68–70; Funabashi 1960: pp. 92–93. The principle of abstraction is supported by Suekawa 1956 pp. 75–81 as the interpretation of s. 176 CC.
466. SCJ Jun. 20, 1958 Minshu 12-10-1585.
467. SCJ Jun. 24, 1970 Minshu 14-8-1528.
468. SCJ Nov. 19, 1965 Minshu 19-8-2003.
469. *See* para. 213 *supra.*

ownership under the condition precedent (section 127 (1) CC)[470] or under the condition subsequent (section 127 (2) CC).[471] For example, if a seller of a thing had agreed with a purchaser to transfer ownership of the thing immediately under the condition subsequent to the effect that the purchaser shall lose the ownership when he/she would not complete a full payment of the purchase money by 4 p.m. on the third day after the conclusion of the contract, and the purchaser did not complete the payment, then the transfer of ownership from the seller to the purchaser shall not be recognized.[472] This is a result of "ishi-shugi" [the principle of agreement] that the parties can agree freely on the transfer of ownership of a thing as long as the agreement should not violate the laws and regulations.

In the Japanese Civil Code, there is no restriction on the transfer of ownership made under the condition like the German Civil Code that the agreement between the transferor and the transferee necessary for the transfer of ownership of a piece of land (Auflassung) which is made subject to a condition or a stipulation as to time is invalid (section 925 (2) GCC). It means that the principle of agreement is strongly implemented in the Japanese law.

§2. Opposability Requirement for the Acquisition of Immovable Property Rights

I. Registration as a Requirement for Opposability

237. The principle of agreement has the advantage of reducing transaction costs for the transfer of property. However, this advantage accompanies a crucial disadvantage of determining the priority when contradictory transactions are taken by the parties, both of which are both sides of the same coin.[473] Under the principle of agreement, for instance, A, the owner of an immovable property, who manifested an intention to transfer the property to B, may manifest an intention to transfer the same property to C because section 176 CC requires neither delivery nor registration but just "manifestation of an intention" to transfer real rights. As a matter of fact, A can agree with C to transfer the property after the same transaction with B. As section 176 CC does not require any notarized document to manifest the intention, it may not be always easy to prove that the acquisition by B was earlier than that by C.

238. Theoretically, according to the principle of agreement, B should prevail over C because when A manifested his/her intention to transfer the property to B, B has become the owner of it and A should have lost ownership of that property. However, practically, it would be hard to identify which manifestation of intention to

470. Section 127 (1) CC provides that a juridical act which is subject to a condition precedent shall become valid upon fulfillment of the condition.
471. Section 127 (2) CC provides that a juridical act which is subject to a condition subsequent shall become invalid upon fulfillment of the condition.
472. SC Mar. 22, 1960 Minshu 14-4-501.
473. The drafter noticed of this problem when he drafted s. 176 CC. Record of Discussions of the Council for Codification Studies on May 22, 1894 [a remark by Nobushige Hozumi].

transfer ownership was earlier than the other, for the manifestation of intention is not combined with any particular forms which are easy to prove. In order to avoid this inconvenience, section 177 CC requires the registration for the acquisition of immovable property and section 178 CC requires the delivery for the acquisition of movable property as a requirement without which the transferee B shall not be able to assert a priority of his/her acquisition against a third party C. That is, according to sections 177 and 178 CC, the manifestation of an intention to transfer ownership "may not be opposable against a third party" unless the manifestation is accompanied by the registration for the immovable property and the delivery for the movable property. The registration for immovable property transaction and the delivery for movable property transaction are called "taiko-yoken" [opposability requirement]. Section 177 CC provides as follows:[474]

> Sec. 177 CC (Opposability Requirement for the Change of Real Rights in Immovable Property)
>
> Acquisitions of, losses of and changes in real rights concerning immovable property may not be opposable against a third party, unless they are registered pursuant to the provisions of the Law of Registration of Immovable Property (Law No. 123, 2004) and other laws regarding registration.
>
> However, there is a room for interpretation concerning the meaning of "may not be opposable" and "a third party". As a result, judicial precedents have been accumulated so as to clarify the meaning of this provision.[475]

239. The phrase "may not be opposable" has special meanings. First, for example, if A, the owner of a piece of land, manifested his/her intention to transfer ownership of that property to B on the basis of a sales contract, and B began to use the land by acquiring the possession from A but did not register the acquisition, and A sold that property to C and manifested his/her intention to transfer that property to C and C registered the acquisition, then C may claim B for vacation of the land alleging that C acquired the property from A. B may make a defense that he/she has already acquired that property before the transaction between A and C. However, C may be able to submit a counterplea that B has lost his/her ownership when C registered his/her acquisition, which is interpreted to be provided by section 177 CC in the sentence that B "may not be opposable against a third party" C.[476]

240. However, under the principle of agreement, the registration is not a necessary requirement for the transfer of ownership but "taiko-yoken" [the opposability requirement]. It means that in the case in paragraph 239 *supra*, if B claims that he/she should be confirmed as the owner of the land against C and C does not make

474. As for s. 178 CC concerning movable property, *see* §3 *infra*.
475. As for the major precedents, *see* III and IV *infra*.
476. Wagatsuma and Ariizumi 1983: pp. 148-151; Funabashi 1960: p. 143.

a defense that he/she would not affirm the acquisition of B for the reason of the lack of registration, then the court cannot deny B's claim even though it is evident that B's acquisition is not registered.[477]

241. In the case in paragraph 239 *supra*, if both B and C have yet to register the acquisition of the immovable property, then neither B nor C can assert the priority of the acquisition of the property right against each other.[478] If B claims against C to confirm B's ownership of the land, then C can make a defense that he/she would not affirm the acquisition of B for the reason of the lack of registration. If C claims against B to vacate the land, then B can make a defense that he/she would not affirm the acquisition of C for the reason of the lack of registration.

II. Registration of Immovable Property

242. While the registration of a description of an immovable property (a piece of land and a building) shall be made by a registrar ex officio (section 28 LRIP), the registration of a right shall be made by the parties' application in principle.[479] The application for a registration of a right must be filed jointly by a person entitled to register (such as a purchaser) and a person obliged to register (such as a seller) unless provided otherwise in laws and regulations (section 60 LRIP). It is called "kyodoshinsei-shugi" [the principle of joint application]. The application needs to be accompanied by: (i) the information necessary for identifying the immovable property to be transacted, the name of the applicants, and the purpose of registration (the application information); (ii) the information of registration identification which is held by the person obliged to register; and (iii) the information certifying the cause of registration (such as the contract of sale) (sections 18, 22, 61 LRIP).[480]

In addition, a provisional registration may be available so as to secure the priority of acquisition of a right in immovable property (sections 105–110 LRIP). It is used in the following two cases. One is when the information necessary to be provided to the registration office for the application of registration is yet to be prepared (section 105 [1] LRIP). Another is when a claim to transfer the right to be

477. Funabashi 1960: p. 148. However, there is a legal doctrine which asserts that once C registered the acquisition of ownership before B registers it, C cannot recognize that B is the owner of the property with keeping C's registration. Wagatsuma and Ariizumi 1983: p. 153.

478. STJ Jan. 24, 1910 Minroku 16-1; STJ Jul. 8, 1921 Minroku 27-1359; Wagatsuma and Ariizumi 1983: p. 151; Suekawa 1956: pp. 99–100; Funabashi 1960: p. 148. The former judicial precedent and a minority legal doctrine recognized that if neither B nor C registered the acquisition, B who had acquired earlier should have a priority. STJ Apr. 12, 1899 Minroku 4-4-22; Tamakich Nakajima, *Minpo Shakugi [Explanation of Civil Law]*, Vol. 2 (1) (Kinshihoryudo, 1927), p. 68.

479. The registration of a right shall include the preservation, establishment, transfer, change, restriction on disposition, or extinction of the following rights in immovable property: a right of: (i) ownership, (ii) superficies, (iii) emphyteusis, (iv) servitude, (v) statutory lien, (vi) pledge, (vii) hypothec, (viii) lease of a land and a building, (ix) residence for a spouse, and (x) quarrying (s. 3 LRIP).

480. However, there exist following exceptions to the principle of joint application. They are the registration of a right based on a final and binding judgment (s. 63 (1) LRIP), by succession of a natural person and merger of a legal person (s. 63 (2) LRIP), and on a compulsory purchase (s. 118 LRIP).

registered is under a certain condition or is yet to be fixed by a person who reserves the right to fix it (section 105 [2] LRIP). If the information is prepared, or the condition is fulfilled or the claim is fixed, the definitive registration shall be made based on the provisional registration, and the priority order of the definitive registration shall follow the same rank in the priority order of the provisional registration (section 106 LRIP). For example, if A, the owner of a piece of land, concluded a pre-contract with B to sell the land by giving the reservation right to B to the effect that B can fix the contract within three months by paying the full amount of purchase money, and a provisional registration was made for B. After that A's creditor C attached the land to execute C's claim right and registered it to prepare for the compulsory auction (section 414 (1) CC, sections 45 and 48 Civil Execution Law). B fixed the contract of sale with A and paid the full amount of purchase money before the due date. Then B, having acquired ownership of the land, can apply for the definitive registration of ownership acquired from A (section 106 LRIP). If A refuses to apply jointly for the registration (section 60 LRIP), B can sue A and register B's ownership based on the judgment (section 63 (1) LRIP). However, B needs to have an approval of C to delete C's registration of attachment (section 109 (1) LRIP). If C refuses it, B can sue C and will have a judgment on behalf of C's approval (section 414 CC, section 174 Civil Execution Law) because the priority between B's ownership and C's attachment shall be fixed in the order of B's provisional registration and C's registration (section 106 LRIP).[481] On the basis of this judgment, B can apply for the definitive registration of ownership (section 63 (1) LRIP) and C's registration of attachment shall be deleted ex officio (section 109 (2) LRIP).

III. Acquisitions of Immovable Property Not Opposable Without Registration

243. Although an acquisition of immovable property right by way of contract such as sale, exchange and donation shall take place when the transferor and transferee agree to it (section 176 CC), it must be registered so as to be opposable against a third party, who challenges the priority concerned with the acquisition of that property (section 177 CC). However, the scope of application of section 177 CC is not limited to the transfer of immovable property right by way of a manifestation of intention such as a contract of sale, donation and exchange and a testamentary will, but also the transfer of immovable property right caused by the acquisitive prescription and succession, and the restoration because of the invalidity, avoidance and termination of those contract such as the sale, donation and exchange. This broad scope of application of Sec 177 CC was a product of the interpretation by legal doctrines and judicial precedents.[482]

481. However, B shall be recognized as the owner of the land not from the time of provisional registration but from the time of fixing the sales contract and full payment of the money as A and B agreed on the transfer of ownership (s. 176 CC). SCJ Jun. 29, 1961 Minshu 15-6-1764.

482. Wagatsuma and Ariizumi 1983: pp. 92–122; Suekawa 1956: pp. 118–131; Funabashi 1960: pp. 158–176; Matsuo and Kozumi 2008: pp. 83–102; STJ (FB) Dec. 15, 1908 Minroku 14-1301.

244. Acquisition of immovable property by way of the acquisitive prescription is not opposable without registration.[483] For example, A was the owner of a piece of land, but the land has been possessed by B peacefully and openly with the intention to own it for more than twenty years (section 162 (1) CC) or for more than ten years if B was in good faith by believing that the land belonged to B without fault when B began to possess it (section 162 (2) CC). However, if A sold the land to C and registered the transfer of ownership from A to C after the acquisitive prescription period had passed for B, and C claimed B to vacate the land, B cannot refuse C's claim. B seems to be able to present a defense that the land had already been acquired by B through the acquisitive prescription. But C can make a counterplea that he/she would not recognize the acquisition of B by way of prescription because of the lack of registration, or that B had lost the ownership of the land acquired through the acquisitive prescription when C has registered his/her acquisition of that land (section 177 CC).

245. However, if C acquired the land from A before the prescription period has passed, B can present a defense that he/she acquired the land by way of acquisitive prescription after A transferred the land to C. In this case, C cannot make a counterplea for the reason of the lack of registration of B because B could not register his/her acquisition by way of prescription until the prescription period should have passed.[484]

246. Besides, the acquisition of immovable property by way of testamentary gift[485] and that by way of partition of inheritance[486] are not be opposable without registration as long as it is beyond the statutory portion of inheritance for coheirs as provided by sections 900 and 901 CC (section 899-2 CC).[487]

IV. Third Parties Against Whom Acquisition May Not Be Opposable

247. Acquisition of immovable property by an acquirer through contract, testamentary will, partition of inheritance, prescription, etc., as stated above, is not be opposable without registration against "a third party" (section 177 CC). There is no restriction on "a third party" in this provision. Just after the enactment of the Civil Code, legal doctrines and judicial precedents interpreted that "a third party" should include all persons except for the parties and their successors so that it included a wrongdoer who infringed on the immovable property and was claimed for restoration and compensation, a person who was registered in the land registry as on owner

483. SCJ Aug. 28, 1968 Minshu 12-12-1963.
484. SCJ Nov. 22, 1966 Minshu 20-9-1901; SCJ Nov. 5, 1971 Minshu 25-8-1087.
485. SCJ Mar. 6, 1964 Minshu 18-3-437. *See* para. 270 *infra*.
486. SCJ Jan. 26, 1971 Minshu 25-1-90. *See* para. 282 *infra*.
487. It was the result of the application of s. 177 CC before the amendment to the Civil Code in 2018 (Law No. 72, 2018). After the amendment, new s. 899-2 CC shall apply to these cases which requires the registration for the acquisition of property rights by way of testamentary will and partition of inheritance as long as it is beyond the statutory portion of inheritance as provided by ss. 900 and 901 CC.

though he did not have ownership and was claimed for deletion of the registration, etc.[488] In the background of this broad interpretation of "a third party," there seems to be the legal policy to give incentive to the acquirer of real rights in immovable property to register the acquisition as fast as possible.[489]

However, the judicial precedent was changed and stipulated that "a third party" in section 177 CC should be interpreted to mean a person who should be recognized to have a "seito-no-rieki" [the legitimate interest] in asserting the lack of registration of acquisition, loss and change of real rights.[490]

248. A typical example of "a third party" is a person who acquired ownership on that property which is not compatible with ownership of the first acquirer who does not register the acquisition of ownership. For instance, if A, the owner of a piece of land, who had sold the land and manifested an intention to transfer ownership in the land to B, did not register the transaction with B, and sold the same property to C and manifested an intention to transfer ownership to C, then C, the second purchaser and transferee are typically "a third party" in section 177 CC.

Likewise, a person who made a contract of establishing real rights other than ownership such as superficies, emphyteusis or servitude and would use the same property as had been acquired by another acquirer without registration is recognized as a third party in section 177 CC.

249. A third party in section 177 CC may be a person not only who has already acquired a real right by the agreement to transfer the right (section 176 CC) but also who has just made a contract of sale (section 555 CC), exchange (section 586 CC) or donation (section 549 CC) and agreed to the future transfer of ownership in the same property as had been acquired by another acquirer.[491]

Besides, a person who made a contract of lease, loan for use or deposit on the property is recognized to be a third party even though they do not acquire real rights on the property which had been acquired by another acquirer without registration, because they have a legal interest to confirm who is regarded as a true acquirer of that property with whom they may need to negotiate on the use of property, the non-performance of obligation, the extension or the renewal of the contract or the return of the property.[492]

250. The problem of whether a third party in section 177 CC should include a person who is a possessor of the property without any title or who is a wrongdoer to that property has been disputed. For instance, A, the owner of a building, sold it to B and manifested an intention to transfer its ownership to B, but they did not register B's acquisition of ownership. However, the building is still occupied by C who

488. Ume 1911 (II): pp. 17–19; Tomii 1923: pp. 60–62; STJ Feb. 27, 1907 Minroku 13-188; STJ Dec. 6, 1907 Minroku 13-1174; STJ Apr. 6, 1908 Minroku 14-395.
489. Matsuo and Kozumi 2008: p. 102.
490. STJ (FB) Dec. 25, 1908 Minroku 14-1276.
491. Wagatsuma and Ariizumi 1983: p. 157; Suekawa 1954: pp. 109–110; Funabashi 1960: p. 190; SCJ Sep. 18, 1953 Minshu 7-955.
492. STJ May 9, 1933 Minshu 12-1123; SCJ Nov. 30, 1950 Minshu 4-11-607; SCJ Mar. 19, 1974 Minshu 28-2-325.

was the former tenant of that building and refused to vacate the building even though the contract of lease had been terminated by A because of the non-performance of rent payment. B claimed against B for the vacation of the building on the basis of ownership which B acquired from A. C made a defense that he would not recognize B's ownership because of the lack of registration in accordance with section 177 CC. The court decided that a person who possesses the property without any title or a wrongdoer is not regarded as a third person in section 177 CC, because they have no "seito-no-rieki" [the legitimate interest] in that property.[493]

251. However, if, in the previous case, A who had transferred ownership of the building to B but had not registered the transfer of ownership to B sold the same building to D and registered the acquisition of ownership by D, and after that B claimed against C for the vacation of that building on the basis of the alleged ownership acquired from A, then C may be able to make a defense that B had lost his/her ownership when D registered his/her acquisition of ownership.[494]

252. It has been controversial whether "a third party" in section 177 CC includes a mala fide (bad faith) third party who knew that the immovable property had already been transferred to another person. section 177 CC provides neither "a bona fide third party" nor "a bona fide third party without fault," but just "a third party." The judicial precedents confirmed that section 177 CC does not require a third party to be bona fide, and a third party who acquired the property and registered the acquisition with the knowledge about the preceding transaction shall not be excluded from "a third party" so that the acquirer by the preceding transaction cannot be opposable against the third party and thus this party may be able to maintain his/her right and is not claimed for any tort liability.[495]

253. There are reasons for those judicial precedents to include a mala fide (bad faith) third party in "a third party" of section 177 CC. First, section 176 CC does not require any particular form to manifest an intention to transfer ownership so that it would be hard to decide what kind of knowledge should be regarded as mala fide which affects the acquisition of property if a mala fide third party shall be excluded from section 177 CC. For instance, A, an owner of a piece of land, had negotiated with B about the sale of that land and agreed to sell the land to B but did not register B's acquisition. After that, A negotiated with C and agreed to transfer ownership of the land to C and registered the acquisition for C. C was aware that A negotiated with B about the transaction of the land. If a mala fide third party is excluded from the third party in section 177 CC, C may be challenged by B as a mala fide and prevented to acquire the property, then the property transaction would be seriously affected.

Second, in order to facilitate the registration of acquisition of immovable property, it would be better not to restrict the meaning of a third party as to be a bona

---

493. STJ (FB) Dec. 15, 1908 Minroku 14-1276; SCJ Dec. 19, 1950 Minshu 4-12-660.
494. Matsuo and Kozumi 2008: p. 106.
495. STJ Dec. 25, 1911 Minroku 17-909; SCJ May 31, 1955 Minshu 9-6-774.

fide third party or a bona fide third party without fault. Third, there is a room to prevent the acquisition by a mala fide third party C, if C knew definitely the preceding acquisition of ownership of the same property by B and registered C's acquisition with the fraudulent intention to prejudice B by applying the general provision of law such as the principle of good faith and fair dealing in the exercise of a right and the performance of a duty (section 1 (2) CC).[496]

254. If a third party who acquired an immovable property and registered the acquisition not only knew the preceding transaction of the same property, but transacted in breach of the general rule which requires a good faith and a fair dealing, then the acquisition of the property by the third party may be denied even though he/she registered the acquisition. For example, A sold and transferred ownership of a piece of land to B and B began to use the land but did not register the acquisition. More than twenty years after the transaction between A and B, C negotiated with the successor of A and bought the land at the price of less than one-twentieth of the market price and registered the acquisition and then asked B to buy the land at the price of more than the market value. The Supreme Court decided that C is not regarded as "a third party" provided in section 177 CC so that B can be opposable against C without the registration and deny the acquisition of the land by C and claim C for deletion of the registration because C should be regarded as acquired the property in breach of the rule on a good faith and a fair dealing when he/she alleged the lack of registration of B's acquisition.[497]

Besides, the Law of Registration of Immovable Property provides that a person who prevented the registration by fraudulent manner or by force, or a person who has an obligation to apply for the registration for another person cannot assert the lack of registration of another person (section 5 (1) and (2) LRIP). These persons shall be excluded from "a third person" in section 177 CC by the special provision of law.

§3. Opposability of Transfer of Movable Property

255. The principle of agreement provided by section 176 CC applies also to the acquisition of movable property. The ownership of a movable property may be transferred from an owner (transferor) to a transferee only by their agreement of manifestations of intention to transfer and accept the property. While the principle of agreement has the advantage of reducing transaction costs for the transfer of property, it accompanies the disadvantage of determining the priority when contradictory transactions are taken by the parties because section 176 CC requires neither notarized document to manifest the intention nor delivery of the property.[498] In order to avoid the inconvenience, section 178 CC provides as follows:

496. *See* the judicial precedents in para. 254 *infra*.
497. SCJ Aug. 2, 1968 Minshu 22-8-1571; SCJ Jan. 16, 1969 Minshu 23-1-18.
498. *See* para. 237 *supra*.

Sec. 178 CC (Opposability Requirement for the Transfer of Real Rights in Movable Property)

The transfer of real rights concerning movables may not be opposable against a third party, unless the movable is delivered.

As for the meaning of "opposable" and "a third party", the preceding paragraphs on the acquisition of immovable property can be applied mutatis mutandis.[499]

256. As for the meaning of "delivered," there are four patterns of delivery,[500] which can make the acquisition of movable property opposable against a third party.

First is "genjitsu-no-hikiwatashi" [an actual delivery] (section 182 (1) CC). It means, for instance, A transfers the actual possession of the property to B and B acquires the actual possession of the property.

Second, if a transferee or his/her agent has already the actual possession of a movable property before the transaction, then the delivery may be effected only by the agreement between a transferor and a transferee. It is called "kan-i-no-hikiwatashi" [the summary delivery] (section 182 (2) CC). If A sold his/her movable to B and transferred ownership which A had already lent to B and B had used it, then the delivery shall be completed only by the agreement between A and B to that effect.

Third, if a transferor manifests an intention that a movable property possessed by him/herself shall be possessed by him/her as an agent on behalf of the transferee as a principal, the principal, that is the transferee, shall acquire a delivery from the transferor just by his/her manifestation of the intention to that effect. It is called "sen-yu-kaitei" [the constructive delivery (transfer of possession)] (section 183 CC).[501]

Fourth, if a movable property is in the possession of an agent C, (1) a transferor A as a principal orders that the agent C should possess the property on behalf of a transferee B as a new principal, and (2) the transferee B agrees to it, then the property shall be delivered to the transferee C. It is called "sashizu-niyoru-sen-yu-iten" [the transfer of possession by way of the order to a possessing third party] (section 184 CC).

In the latter three cases of delivery, the acquisition of property rights in movable property becomes opposable only by the manifestation of intention without changing the place of the movable property.

499. *See* paras. 237 to 241 *supra*.

500. These types of delivery (provided by ss. 182, 183 and 184 CC) can be applied not only to movable property but also to immovable property.

501. For the establishment of "jyoto-tanpo" [the conveyancing mortgage] "sen-yu-kaitei" [the constructive delivery] is usually used. *See* paras. 493 and 524 *infra*.

257. The effect of a delivery is not only making the acquisition of movable property opposable against a third party but also creating a presumption of a title in favor of a transferee who received the delivery and became a possessor.

A possessor is presumed to have a right lawfully that a possessor exercises with respect to a thing in his/her possession (section 188 CC). For example, if A delivered a movable property to B, then B is presumed to have lawfully his/her right (ownership or other rights to possess the thing) which he/she exercises with respect to the movable property (section 188 CC). If C challenges the title (ownership or other rights to possess the property) of B, C bears a burden of proof that B does not have the title.[502]

In addition, a possessor, B in the previous case, is presumed to possess the movable with the intention to own, in good faith, peacefully and in public (section 186 (1) CC). In principle, a possessor is presumed to have ownership unless another presumption is evident. Section 186 CC provides that a possessor is presumed to possess a thing "in good faith" but does not presume it "without fault." However, if B acquired the possession from A by way of delivery, B has a good reason to be presumed to possess the thing not only in good faith but also without fault, because the former possessor A was also presumed to have lawfully his/her right (ownership) and A for himself/herself delivered the thing to B.[503] These presumptions are advantageous for B when he/she needs to prove the acquisition of possession in good faith without fault as the requirement for immediate acquisition (section 192 CC) and acquisitive prescription by the continuous possession of the thing for ten years (section 162 (2) CC).

258. Section 178 CC shall not be applied to certain transactions of movables which are registered in accordance with the special laws.[504] They are: (i) the transfer of ownership and establishment of hypothec on a ship (section 687 and 848 (3) Commercial Code); (ii) the acquisition and loss of ownership of a small-sized boat (section 4 Law on Registration of Small Boats); (iii) the acquisition and loss of ownership and hypothec on a construction machine (section 7 (1) Law for Hypothec on Construction Machines); (iv) the acquisition and loss of ownership and hypothec on an automobile (section 5 (1) Law for Road Transportation Vehicles; section 5 (1) Law for Hypothec on Automobile); (v) the acquisition, loss and change of ownership and hypothec on an aircraft and helicopter (section 3-3 Law on Aviation, section 5 Law for Hypothec on Aircraft); (vi) the acquisition, loss and change of hypothec on a farming machine (section 13 Financing for Farming Machinery Act); (vii) the transfer of ownership on movables which a corporation owns excluding movables for which a warehouse receipt, a bill of lading or a multimodal bill of lading is issued (section 3 (1) the Law on Special Provisions for the Civil Code Concerning the Opposable Requirements for the Transfer of Movables and Assignment of Claims).

---

502. As for immovable property, the presumption of ownership through the registration is interpreted to take precedence over the presumption through the possession. SCJ Jan. 8, 1959 Minshu 13-1-1; Matsuo and Kozumi 2008: p. 74.
503. SCJ Jun. 9, 1966 Minshu 20-5-1011.
504. *See* para. 218 *supra*.

Once they are registered in each registry, thereafter those transactions as specified above shall not be opposable against a third party unless the transaction is registered as provided by the provisions of special laws.[505] For instance, A owned an automobile registered in automobile registry and sold it to B and delivered it, while A borrowed certain amount of money from C and established hypothec on that automobile and registered it in automobile registry. As A could not repay the money to C by the due date, C executed the hypothec and D bought the automobile at the auction and paid the purchase price. In this case, D can claim against B to deliver the car on the basis of ownership of that car. B's defense that B had acquired the ownership of the car (section 176 CC) before A established the hypothec on the car cannot be recognized by the provision of law (section 5 (1) Law for Hypothec on Automobile).

However, if these movables are not registered or once they were registered but the registration was deleted afterward, section 178 shall be applied.

259. Trees separated from the land on which they have been planted and fruits separated from the trees on which they have grown are movables so that section 178 CC shall be applied to them. However, if the owner of trees on the land and fruits on the trees would like to sell them and transfer their ownership by keeping that condition before the separation, it should be hard to deliver them and change the possession of them from the transferor to the transferee. It means that it is difficult to apply sections 177 CC and 178 CC to make those transactions opposable against a third party.[506] For those cases, the judicial precedent recognized that the parties to those transactions would be able to make them opposable by performing "meininhoho" [the publicity method based on customary law] which shall replace the delivery provided by section 178 CC. For example, they can be the signboard built on site which clearly shows the content of the transaction in accordance with the customary law widespread in that region.[507]

505. For instance, ss. 687 and 848 (3) Commercial Code (for the transfer of ownership and establishment of hypothec on a ship); s. 4 Law on Registration of Small Boats (for the acquisition and loss of ownership of a small-sized boat); s. 7 (1) Law for Hypothec on Construction Machines (for the acquisition and loss of ownership and hypothec on a construction machine); s. 5 (1) Law for Road Transportation Vehicles (for the acquisition and loss of ownership on an automobile); s. 5 (1) Law for Hypothec on Automobile (for the acquisition, loss and change of hypothec on an automobile); s. 3-3 Law on Aviation (for the acquisition, loss and change of ownership on an aircraft and helicopter); s. 5 Law for Hypothec on Aircraft (for the acquisition, loss and change of hypothec on an aircraft and helicopter); s. 13 Financing for Farming Machinery Act (for the acquisition, loss and change of hypothec on a farming machine); s. 3 (1) the Law on Special Provisions for the Civil Code Concerning the Opposable Requirements for the Transfer of Movables and Assignment of Claims (for the transfer of ownership on movables which a corporation owns excluding movables for which a warehouse receipt, a bill of lading or a multimodal bill of lading is issued), etc.

506. However, if trees on the land are registered and the transactions such as the transfer of ownership of them and the establishment of hypothec on them are registered in accordance with s. 2 of the Law on Trees, they can be opposable against a third party.

507. STJ Sep. 20, 1916 Minroku 22-1440; STJ May 5, 1920 Minshu 17-1927.

§4. Immediate Acquisition of Movable Property

260. Beyond the presumption and opposability, the effect of delivery of a movable property would include the creation of title in accordance with the legal policy so as to adapt to the economic situation of the country for the purpose of protecting the good faith of a transferee and securing the stability of transaction. According to section 192 CC, a person who begins to possess a movable peacefully and openly by a transaction acquires a right to exercise with respect to the movable immediately if he/she is in good faith without fault. It is called immediate acquisition or bona fide acquisition.

261. A "right to exercise with respect to the movable" can be determined by the legal character of a "transaction." For instance, if the "transaction" is a contract of sale, exchange or donation, then the "right" will be the ownership. If the transaction is a contract of establishing mortgage then the right of mortgage will be acquired. If the transaction is a contract of lease, then the right will be the right of lease.

For example, A sold a movable property, which A had borrowed from X who owns it, and delivered it to B. When X claims B to return the movable on the basis of its ownership, B may make a defense that the movable was acquired by B in accordance with section 192 CC and then X lost its ownership. As stated above, B is presumed to possess the movable peacefully, openly and in good faith without fault.[508] B only has to prove that he/she began to possess the movable and that he/she began the possession by way of transaction. Thus as far as the transaction of movable property is concerned, the transferee is given an advantageous position in principle.

262. Section 192 CC applies to a "movable." However, it is not applicable to registered movables such as a registered ship, small-sized boat, construction machine, automobile, aircraft, helicopter and a farming machine[509] because the transfer of ownership of those registered movables can be provided by the registration and the reliance of an acquirer on the registration should take precedence over that on the possession of them.[510]

The registration of those transactions of those movables is neither given the effect of creating title nor the effect of indefeasibility by the current laws in Japan.[511]

---

508. *See* para. 257 *supra.*
509. SCJ Apr. 24, 1987 Hanji 1243-24.
510. For this reason, s. 192 CC can still be applied to movables which are registered in accordance with s. 3 (1) of the Law on Special Provisions for the Civil Code Concerning the Opposability Requirement for the Transfer of Movables and Claims Rights, because movables to be registered by this law could include collective things which shall be identified by their nature, quantity and location of storage, can be replaced by other movables of the same nature, quantity and location of storage, and which shall be registered without confirming each object.
511. However, there are exceptions. For instance, Law on the Promotion of Countermeasures against Global Warming (1998) regulates the acquisition, holding and transferal of "carbon dioxide equivalent quotas," It provides that the attribution, acquisition and transfer of carbon dioxide equivalent quotas shall be made according to the registration in the quota account inventory (ss. 44, 48 and 50). If the account holder has obtained the registration of an increase in carbon dioxide equivalent quotas in its account inventory due to a transfer pursuant to ss. 48 and 50, then it shall obtain those

263. The protection of acquisition by section 192 CC shall apply to "a person who begins to possess a movable." It is controversial whether the meaning of " … begins to possess" in section 192 CC should include any patterns of the transfer of possession. The judicial precedents exclude the pattern of constructive transfer of possession (section 183 CC) in which the location of property is not changed at all. For instance, A sold a movable property, which A had borrowed from X, the owner of the movable, and delivered it to B by way of the constructive transfer of possession, that is, A manifested an intention that he/she will possess the movable on behalf of B and B agreed to it (section 183 CC). Physically the movable is still located at A's place and kept under the management by A. When X claims A to return the movable on the basis of its ownership, can A and B make a defense that the movable has already acquired by B in accordance with section 192 CC and then X has lost its ownership? The judicial precedents denied the application of section 192 CC to this case and did not recognize the defense based on the bona fide acquisition by B, for the reason that the requirement of " … begins to possess" in section 192 CC should be interpreted to require the acquisition of possession which accompanies "the situational change of the possession that can be confirmed from the outlook" and the constructive transfer of possession without the change of outlook could not be enough to bring about the acquisition of ownership for B in the sacrifice of X.[512]

264. However, there are legal doctrines which recognize the bona fide acquisition by way of constructive transfer of possession under the condition that the transferee acquires actual possession in addition to constructive transfer of possession before the transferor returns the actual possession of the movable to the owner.[513] For instance, A sold a movable property, which A had borrowed from X, the owner of the movable, and delivered it to B by way of the constructive transfer of possession, that is, A manifested an intention that he/she will possess the movable on behalf of B and B agreed to it (section 183 CC). It was known to X and X claimed A to return the movable. But B claimed A to deliver the property though B knew that the movable had been lent by X to A. As A delivered the movable B, X claimed B to return the movable on the basis of his/her ownership. According to the legal doctrines mentioned above B can make defense against X that B had acquired ownership on the basis of section 192 CC when B had concluded the contract with A believing that the movable had belonged to X without negligence even though B knew that the movable had belonged to X when X claimed A to return it to X but A transferred actual possession to B. These legal doctrines are reflecting on the request from the parties of establishing "jyoto-tanpo" [the conveyancing mortgage] where A makes a contract with B to transfer ownership of the movable for the purpose of establishing collateral so that actual possession is held by A and only the constructive transfer of possession is made.

---

carbon dioxide equivalent quotas, provided that this shall not apply in the case of bad faith or gross negligence on the part of the account holder (s. 54). This is a bona fide acquisition of carbon dioxide equivalent quotas.

512. STJ May 5, 1916 Minroku 22-961; SCJ Dec. 27, 1957 Minshu 11-14-2485; SCJ Feb. 11, 1960 Minshu 14-2-168.

513. Wagatsuma and Ariizum 1983: pp. 222–224; Hoshino 1981: pp. 74–75; Hirano 2016: p. 195.

265. There is an exception to the bona fide acquisition provided by section 192 CC. If the movable which was transferred to the bona fide acquirer without negligence was a stolen thing or a lost thing, the victim or the person who had lost the movable can claim against the acquirer for recovery of it within two years from the time of the steal or loss (section 193 CC). The reason for this exception is that the stolen or lost thing was dispossessed from the owner without his/her intention. For the stolen or lost movable, ownership shall be regarded as having been kept by an owner for two years from the time of the steal or loss.[514]

266. There is a further exception to the abovementioned exceptional rule for the stolen or lost movable provided by section 193 CC. If an acquirer of the stolen or lost movable as provided by section 193 CC purchased it in good faith at an auction or in a public market, or from a merchant who sells similar goods, the victim or the person who lost the movable may not recover it unless he/she reimburses the bona fide acquirer without negligence for the price paid by the acquirer (section 194 CC). The purpose of this exception is to protect the interests of the bona fide acquirer who transacted at the market or with the merchant and to secure the reliance on the market or on the transaction with the merchant. This rule shall apply within two years from the time of the steal or loss of the movable because it is an exceptional rule to section 193 CC. After two years have passed, the victim or the person who had lost the movable cannot claim for recovery even though they have an intention to provide reimbursement.[515]

267. One important problem remains concerned with the interpretation of section 194 CC. For example, X owned a used construction machine which was not registered and it was stolen by someone. Two months later, A, a dealer of the construction machines, sold that construction machine to B who was recognized as bona fide without fault. A delivered it to B in exchange of the full payment of the purchase price of JPY 3 million. B has used it for the construction work, when X found it at B's construction site and claimed B for recovery of that machine and bringing the case to the court. It was within two years after the steal. B claimed X to reimburse the purchase money of JPY 3 million which B had paid to A, while X claimed B to return not only the construction machine but also the use value of it for the period from the acquisition of the machine. B returned the machine to X after ten months since X brought the case to the court and claimed X for reimbursement of JPY 3 million. X claimed B to pay the use value of the machine of JPY 4.5 million for ten months (by calculating it as JPY 450,000 per month as equivalent to the average amount of rent for the same property) in accordance with section 189 (2) CC. The District Court held that X should pay JPY 3 million to B and B should pay JPY 3 million to X by estimating the use value of the machine as JPY 300,000 per

514. STJ Jul. 8, 1921 Minroku 27-1373.

515. Still, further exceptional rules exist. If the acquirer (purchaser) was a secondhand dealer or a pawnbroker, the victim or the person who lost the property claim for recovery without any reimbursement within one year from the time of the steal or loss (s. 20 Law on Secondhand Dealer; s. 22 Law on Pawnbroker). After one year, the rule stated in para. 265 *supra* shall apply and they need to reimburse the purchase price, which applies only within two years from the time of the steal or loss.

month. B appealed and the Appellate Court decided that X should pay JPY 3 million, whereas B should pay JPY 2.2 million by estimating its use value of the machine as JPY 220,000 per month. B further appealed.

The Supreme Court reversed the Appellate Court decision in part by confirming B's claim for reimbursement of JPY 3 million while totally denying X's claim for paying the use value stating that B has not been using the machine without title but he has had the right to use the property.[516] The Supreme Court put emphasis of the importance to maintain the stability of acquirer's interests, which will lead to keep the security of market transaction.[517]

516. SCJ Jun. 27, 2000 Minshu 54-5-1737.
517. According to the judicial precedents, during two years after the steal ownership of the machine has been kept by the owner (STJ Jul. 8, 1921 Minroku 27-1373), while the acquirer (B) was held to have had a title to use the machine (SCJ Jun. 27, 2000 Minshu 54-5-1737).

Chapter 2. Transfer of Property by Death

§1. Transfer by Testamentary Will

I. Testamentary Gift

268. Property may be transferred by a testamentary will in certain forms such as a testamentary gift, an appointment of share of successors and an appointment of the way of partition. A natural person can transfer his/her property by testamentary gift to other persons, either natural persons or legal persons, and either successors or any other persons who are not successors. A testator may make a disposition of his/her property, in whole or in part, by way of a comprehensive title or a specific title (section 964 CC).[518]

There was a restriction on the testamentary gift to the effect that the testamentary gift may not violate provisions regarding a legally reserved portion (Old Proviso to section 964 CC). Before the amendment to the Civil Code in 2018, the successor who has a legally reserved portion could claim against the beneficiary for reduction of testamentary gift (Old section 1031 to section 1038 CC). As a result of this claim, the property which was given to the beneficiary by the testamentary will shall become co-owned by the beneficiary and the successor who exercised the right to legally reserved portion. However, this restriction was deleted by the amendment to the Civil Code in 2018 (Law No. 72). There is still the right to a legally reserved portion for certain successors by the provisions of law (sections 1042–1049 CC). But it was transformed from the right to reduce the testamentary gift to the right to claim for paying certain amount of money as equivalent to the legally reserved portion. This amendment aimed to extend the free decision-making by the testator on the disposition of his/her property and strengthen the freedom of testament, which will facilitate the use of testamentary will.[519]

269. There is the legally reserved portion for certain successors provided by law (section 1042–1049 CC). Heirs other than siblings (brothers and sisters) shall be able to receive, as legally reserved portion, an amount equivalent to the ratio prescribed by the provision of law (section 1028 CC).

(i) In the case where only lineal ascendants (such as a father and a mother of the deceased person) are heirs, one-third of the deceased person's property is legally reserved for them in total (section 1028 (1) [1] CC).
(ii) In cases other than the case (i), a half of the deceased person's property is legally reserved for a spouse and children in total (section 1028 (1) [2] CC).

518. The testator may make a testamentary gift in a comprehensive title in such a way as one-third of his/her property shall be given to a certain person, or he/she may make a testamentary gift for a particular property one by one.
519. Matsuo 2019: pp. 42, 58.

Among the spouse and children, the legally reserved portion shall be divided according to the portion of legal inheritance as provided by sections 900 and 901 CC.[520]

270. An acquisition of immovable property rights by way of testamentary gift shall not be opposable against a third party unless it is registered in accordance with the provision of LRIP (section 177 CC).[521] If an acquirer (the beneficiary of the testamentary gift) is one of the heirs, the acquisition more than his/her statutory share shall not be opposable against a third party unless it is registered (section 899-2 (1) CC).[522]

For instance, (1) A, the owner of a piece of land made a testamentary gift to the effect that the land shall belong to B and A died. If C, the only heir of A, sold that land to D and D registered the acquisition before B registers the acquisition of the land based on the testamentary gift, then D prevails over B for the reason of the lack of registration in accordance with section 177 CC. (2) But if B was a wife of A and C was a son of A, then D prevails over B for the acquisition more than B's statutory share (a half of each deceased person's property according to section 900 [1] CC) (section 899-2 (1) CC). It means that the land shall become co-owned by B and D with the share of a half for B and another half for D. B can claim D to correct the registration to that effect.

271. However, in the cases of the preceding paragraph (cases (1) and (2)), if there was an executor of the testamentary will, E, who had been appointed by the testamentary will or by the family court decision before the transaction between C and D, B prevails over D, because an heir, C in this case, may not make a disposition of inherited property or any other actions that interferes with the execution of the testamentary will (section 1013 (1) CC) and the action in violation of section 1013 (1) CC shall be invalid (section 1013 (2) Main Text CC). But if D did not know that the land had been given to B by the testamentary gift and proves that D was in good faith at the transaction with C, then D's acquisition of the land shall be protected (section 1013 (2) Proviso CC).[523]

II. Testamentary Appointment of Share

272. The heirs and their shares in inheritance are provided by the provisions of law. The heirs are blood relatives (sections 887, 889 CC)[524] and a spouse (section

520. If a spouse and two children are heirs, the legally reserved portion shall be divided into a half for the spouse and another half for two children (a quarter for each child) (s. 900 [1] and [4] CC).
521. SCJ Mar. 6, 1964 Minshu 18-3-437.
522. As for the statutory share of the heirs, *see* para. 272 *infra*.
523. However, if B was an heir of A (for example, a wife of A like in the case [2] in para. 270), D can acquire only a half of the share of the land even though D was in good faith, because C had only a half of the share of the land to be transferred to D. SCJ Feb. 22, 1963 Minshu 17-1-235.
524. They shall include an adopted child (s. 809 CC).

890 CC). There is a priority among blood relatives. The first priority is given to children of a deceased person (section 887 (1) CC).[525] A fetus shall be regarded as is born for the purpose of succession unless it is not born alive (section 886 CC). In the lack of the first priority heir, the second priority is given to the direct ancestors such as a father and a mother (section 889 (1) [1] CC).[526] In the lack of the first and second priority heir, the third priority is given to brothers and sisters of the deceased person (section 889 (1) [2] CC).[527]

The shares of the heirs are provided by law. A spouse shall succeed a half of inheritance with the first priority blood relatives (section 900 [1] CC). A spouse shall succeed two-thirds with the second priority blood relatives (section 900 [2] CC). A spouse shall succeed three fourth with the third priority blood relatives (section 900 [3] CC). Among the heirs of the same priority, the inheritance shall be shared equally (section 900 [4] Main Text CC).[528]

A decedent cannot change the heirs and their priorities,[529] but can change and determine the shares in inheritance of joint heirs, or entrust a third party to determine those shares by a testamentary will (section 902 (1) CC). In this case, a beneficiary who acquires more share than that provided by law has to register his/her acquisition so as to be opposable against a third party (section 899-2 CC).

For instance, A, a decent, had two children B and C, and determined their share as two-thirds for B and one-third for C by a testamentary will. A died, and C registered his/her share in a piece of land which belonged to the inheritance of A in accordance with the statutory share according to which the share is equal among children (section 900 [4] CC). Then C sold the share which had been registered as a half in the piece of land to D, and D registered the transfer of the share. After that B claimed against D that the share of the piece of land should be corrected from a half to one-third in accordance with the share determined by a testamentary will of A. D made a counterclaim to the effect that B should have registered his/her share as two-thirds before C registered his/her share as a half and sold it to D, otherwise B's acquisition of two-thirds of the share is not opposable against a third party like D by the effect of section 177 CC.[530] The Supreme Court once decided in favor of B, for the reason that by the effect of A (decedent)'s determination of the share, C had acquired only one-third of the share of the piece of land and had not acquired

525. If a child had died before the decedent but there is his/her child, then this child shall substitute the status of an heir (s. 887 (2), (3) CC).
526. If both parents of the decedent had died but there is ground parent alive, then this person can be the heir (s. 889 (1) [1] Proviso CC).
527. If a brother or a sister had died before the decedent but there is his/her child, then this child shall substitute the status of an heir (ss. 889 (2), 887 (2) CC).
528. However, among the third priority heirs (brothers and sisters), a brother or a sister who has either the same father or mother with the deceased person shall succeed only a half of the share of other brothers and sisters who have the same father and mother with the deceased person (s. 900 [4] Proviso CC).
529. However, if a decedent makes a testamentary gift to the effect that all of his/her inheritance shall be given to a third party who is not an heir by way of a comprehensive title (s. 964 CC), then the beneficiary shall have the same rights and duties with an heir (s. 990 CC).
530. After the amendment to the Civil Code in 2018 (Law No. 72), s. 899-2 CC should be referred to instead of s. 177 CC in this context.

any right more than one-third of the share and the registration must be corrected in accordance with the true share. Section 177 CC was not applied to this case.[531]

However, the interpretation of section 177 CC by this judicial precedent has been changed by the amendment to the Civil Code in 2018 (Law No. 72), which accurately provides that the acquisition of rights through succession more than the statutory share cannot be opposable against a third party unless it is registered (section 899-2 CC).[532]

III. Testamentary Designation of Partition Method

273. A decedent may by a testamentary will designate the way of how to divide the properties included in inheritance or entrust its designation to a third party (section 908 CC). If A, a decedent, had two children B and C and made a will to the effect that a piece of land and a factory on it is "to be succeeded by B," who had worked with A and helped A to manage the factory. A died, and C registered a statutory share of the piece of land and the factory as a half of the share and sold his/her share to D. Then B claimed against D asserting that B had acquired the land and the factory by the testamentary will so that the registration of D's share should be deleted. D made a counterclaim that B should have registered his/her acquisition before D transacted with C and registered his/her acquisition of the share from C; otherwise B's acquisition should not be opposable against a third person like D by the effect of section 177 CC. The Supreme Court decided in favor of B because the land and the factory had been acquired by B and C had no right to the land and the factory when C registered his/her share and sold it to D. Thus section 177 CC was not applied to this case.[533]

However, as already mentioned concerning the case of testamentary appointment of share in the previous paragraph 272, the interpretation of section 177 CC by this judicial precedent has also been changed by the amendment to the Civil Code in 2018 (Law No. 72), which provides that the acquisition of rights through succession more than the statutory share cannot be opposable against a third party unless it is registered (section 899-2 CC).[534] B claimed against D to delete D's registration shall not be recognized because B had not registered the acquisition more than B's statutory share so that B's acquisition should not be opposable against the third party D by the effect of section 899-2 (1) CC.

---

531. SCJ Jul. 19, 1993 Kagetsu 46-5-23.
532. The reason for this amendment can be understood that the beneficiary should have an incentive to register his/her acquisition as fast as possible. It will contribute to the correct publicity of rights through registration and thus consolidate the institutional foundation of the testamentary gift. Matsuo 2019: pp. 85–86.
533. SCJ Jun. 10, 2002 Hanji 1791-59.
534. *See* para. 272 *supra*.

§2. INTESTATE TRANSFER

I. Co-ownership of Inheritance

274. The Japanese law on succession can be characterized by the following principles. First, the intestate succession is supposed to be a general pattern of succession and the succession by a testamentary will is regarded as a special pattern. As a result, heirs cannot be appointed by a testamentary will but provided by law (sections 886, 887, 889, 890 CC) (the principle of intestate succession). Second, the decedent's property shall be succeeded by the heirs upon death of a decedent without any liquidation (the principle of non-liquidation). Third, all the properties included in inheritance shall be succeeded to heirs upon death of the decedent not one by one but comprehensively at a time (the principle of comprehensive succession).

These three principles are implied by section 896 CC. It provides that from the time of commencement of inheritance, that is, upon death of a decedent (section 882 CC), an heir provided by law shall succeed all the rights and duties attached to the property of the decedent (section 896 Main Text CC).

However, exceptionally, rights and duties which are purely personal are not succeeded (section 896 Proviso CC). Also, rights to ownership of a genealogy, equipment to be used in rituals and graves are succeeded by a person who shall preside over rituals for ancestors in accordance with a custom unless the decedent designated a person who shall preside over those rituals (section 897 (1) CC).[535]

275. If there are two or more heirs, the inherited property shall be co-owned by those heirs in accordance with each share in inheritance from the time of death of a decedent (sections 882, 898, 899 CC). Ownership of each immovable and movable property included in inheritance shall be co-owned by heirs. Rights other than ownership such as a right of superficies, intellectual property rights are also co-owned one by one by heirs (quasi co-ownership: section 264 CC).[536] Each heir can dispose of the share of each succeeded property even before the partition of inheritance unless it is prohibited by the testamentary will.[537]

276. It should be noted that according to judicial precedents, a divisible claim right such as a monetary claim shall not be included in inheritance and co-owned by heirs but divided among them upon the death of a decedent in accordance with each share. For example, A, a victim of the accident caused by negligence of B acquired a claim right for compensation for damages of JPY 1,000,000 against B. If A died before the compensation was paid by B. A's successors were only his sons C and D whose share was a half respectively. Then C and D shall acquire the claim

535. If the custom is not evident, the family court shall determine a person who shall succeed the rights of those equipment and graves (s. 897 (2) CC).

536. *See* para. 193 *supra*.

537. If one of the heirs sold his/her share in a particular property in inheritance to a third party, the property shall become co-owned by the remaining heirs and the third party and it is divided in accordance with the partition procedure of co-owned property (s. 258 CC). SCJ Nov. 7, 1975 Minshu 29-10-1525. *See also* para. 191 *supra*.

right for JPY 500,000 against B respectively at the death of A even before the partition of A's inheritance.[538] Also, a right to claim for certain amount of rent to be collected from a tenant of the property of a deceased person is held to be divided among the heirs in accordance with their share even before partition of the property.[539]

277. However, as for the money claim to withdraw a deposited money by a decedent at a bank account, the bank, in practice, would not like to repay the money to each heir who claimed to withdraw the deposited money in accordance with each share unless all other heirs agreed to withdraw the money. The bank wanted to avoid being involved in the conflict among the heirs concerning the partition of inheritance. In response to the request from this business practice, the Supreme Court changed its precedence partly by holding that the claim right to withdraw a deposited money at bank account by a decedent shall be co-owned by heirs as a party of inheritance to be divided by the partition process for two reasons. First, the claim to withdraw money from bank account can be used as an adjustment property in the partition procedure. Second, the amount of the bank account is not fixed but fluctuate even after the death of a decedent due to transfer and withdrawal by debtors and creditors of the decedent.[540]

But, from the viewpoint of each heir, it is not convenient because just after the death of the decedent, certain expenses should be needed such as for holding a funeral and maintaining the life of the bereaved. In order to response to this need for the heirs, the amendment to the Civil Code in 2018 (Law No. 72) provides that each heir shall be able to withdraw the money from bank account of the deceased person up to one-third of his/her share of the total amount of the bank account within the maximum amount to be fixed by the Ordinance of Ministry of Justice for each bank, not for each bank account (section 909-2 First clause CC).[541] Thus the judicial precedents and the legislation have coordinated the practical benefits of banks and heirs.

278. However, money, to be distinguished from the monetary claim, shall not be divided among heirs upon the death of a decedent but co-owned by the heirs in accordance each share. The heirs cannot claim to deliver the amount of money to be divided in accordance with his/her share against the heir who keeps the money upon the death of the decedent because the money must be divided in the partition procedure with other properties in inheritance.[542]

279. Shares of stock company, national bonds, and beneficiary's rights in trust owned by a decedent are also interpreted to be not divided upon the death of the

538. SCJ Apr. 8, 1954 Minshu 8-4-819; SCJ Apr. 20, 2004 Saimin 214-13.
539. SCJ Sep. 8, 2005 Minshu 59-7-1931.
540. SCD (FB) Dec. 19, 2016 Minshu 70-8-2121; SCJ Apr. 6, 2017.
541. The maximum amount for each bank is currently JPY 1,500,000 (Ministry of Justice Ordinance No. 29, 2018). If the heir needs more than that amount before the partition is completed, he/she may be able to apply for the permission of withdrawal of the deposited money from the bank to the family court (s. 200 (3) Law on the Procedure of Family Case).
542. SCJ Apr. 10, 1998 Kagetsu 44-8-16.

decedent among heirs but co-owned by them in accordance with each share until they are divided through the partition process because those rights are indivisible in nature.[543] Until the partition is finalized, the co-owners of the shares of stock company may not exercise their rights in relation to the shares unless they specify one person who exercises the rights and notify the stock company of the name of that person provided that the company would not agree to the exercise of those rights by the co-owners (section 106 Company Law).

II. Partition of Inheritance

280. Heirs who co-own properties in inheritance may at any time divide those properties by agreement unless the partition is prohibited by the decedent's testamentary will for a period not exceeding five years from the time of commencement of inheritance in accordance with section 908 CC (section 907 (1) CC).[544]

If the heirs do not or cannot agree regarding the partition of their co-owned properties in inheritance, each of the heirs may make an application to the family court for a partition of all or a part of the inherited properties (section 907 (2) CC). In the partition of the inherited properties either by agreement among the heirs or by decision of the family court, considerations must be taken to the characteristics and nature of goods or rights belonging to the inheritance, the age, occupation, mental and physical conditions, and financial circumstances of each heir, and all other matters (section 906 CC).

281. Acquisition of a property right by way of the partition of inherited properties more than the statutory share shall not be opposable against a third party unless it has an opposability requirement such as a registration of immovable property and registered movable property, a delivery of unregistered movable property, and a notice to a debtor about the change of a creditor by way of a deed with certified date for a claim right. (section 899-2 (1) CC). For instance, A died and B and C were successors to A who have the same share in inheritance. B and C negotiated about the partition of inheritance and agreed that a particular piece of land included in their inherited properties should belong to B. However, before B registers the acquisition of that land based on the partition in the land registry, C's creditor, D, applied for registration of the succession of that land on behalf of C (section 423 CC) according to the statutory share of B and C and attached C's share and registered the attachment. In this case, if B claims against D for the deletion of registration of attachment alleging that the land had belonged to B as a result of the

543. SCJ Jan. 22, 1970 Minshu 24-1-1; SCJ Feb. 25, 2014 Minshu 68-2-173.

544. Heirs can agree not only to divide all properties in inheritance but also divide only a part of the inheritance. It is articulated in s. 907 (1) CC by the amendment to the Civil Code in 2018 (Law No. 72).

partition of inheritance, then D can make a defense that B has lost C's share which had once acquired through the partition agreement when D registered his/her attachment to that share.[545]

282. How about the case where one of the coheirs sold his/her share of an immovable property included in inheritance to a third party, but before it is registered, the heir agreed with other heirs to the partition to the effect that the immovable property shall belong to another heir, which is in contradiction with his/her previous disposition? section 909 CC provides that "partition of inherited property shall have retroactive effect from the time of the commencement of inheritance, provided that this shall not prejudice the rights of a third party." However, no further requirements are provided for the protection of a third party. For instance, A died and B and C were the heirs who have the equal share. B sold the share of a piece of land included in the inheritance to D, but D did not register the acquisition of the share in that land. After that, B negotiated about the partition of inheritance with C and agreed that the land shall belong to C and C registered the acquisition of that land based on the partition of inheritance. Then D claimed against C that the share, a half of the ownership of that land, had been sold to D so that C should correct the registration. D would make a counterclaim that D has already registered the acquisition of the land based on the partition according to section 899-2 (1) CC so that D's acquisition should be opposable against C. In response to this, D would allege that section 909 CC (see above) stipulates that the retroactive effect of the partition from the time of the commencement of inheritance "shall not prejudice the rights of a third party" (section 909 Proviso CC).

Although there is no judicial precedent on this matter, this problem would occur due to the principle of non-liquidation, under which each heir shall succeed a decedent's property upon death of the decedent in accordance with each share to each property in inheritance without any liquidation so that each heir can dispose of the share to each property even before the partition.[546] This principle is found to be problematic in the case before us. But on the premise of the non-liquidation principle, the share can be transferred even before the partition is made and section 909 Proviso presupposes the possibility of such transaction. However, it does not exclude the further requirement for the protection of the third party such as the registration by section 177 CC and the delivery by section 178 CC. To the previous case, section 899-2 (1) CC should be applied, for C's acquisition was based on the partition.[547] As a result, C can acquire the land including B's share because C has registered the acquisition based on the partition, while D did not register the acquisition of B's share so that D's acquisition is not opposable against C.[548]

545. SCJ Jan. 26, 1971 Minshu 25-1-90. This decision was based on s. 177 CC. However, after the amendment to the Civil Code in 2018 (Law No. 72), s. 899-2 CC shall be applied to this case.
546. *See* para. 274 *supra*.
547. If C's acquisition was the sales contract of B's share, s. 177 CC shall be applied.
548. Matsuo 2016: pp. 730–731.

§3. NON-EXISTENCE OF HEIR

283. If it is not evident whether an heir exists or not, properties of a deceased person shall become a legal person (section 951 CC).[549] In this case: (i) the family court should appoint an administrator of that legal person at the request of an interested party or a public prosecutor (section 952 (1) CC); (ii) the administrator shall make a public notice to confirm whether the heir of the deceased person exists or not (section 952 (2) CC); (iii) if the existence of the heir has not become evident within two months from that public notice, the administrator has to give another public notice to all creditors of the deceased person and beneficiaries of testamentary donation to the effect that a claim for performance should be made within a specified period to be fixed not less than two months (Article 957 (1) CC); (iv) after the expiration of this period, if it is still not evident whether the heir exists or not, the family court has to give a public notice at the request of the administrator or a public prosecutor to the effect that if there is an heir, he/she should assert his/her right within a specified period to be fixes not less than six months (section 958 CC); (v) if there is no person who asserts a right as the heir within this period, neither the heir nor any creditors of the deceased person nor beneficiaries of testamentary donation who are unknown to the administrator shall not be able to exercise his/her right (section 958-2 CC). The administrator should collect debts from the debtors of the deceased person and perform obligations to the creditors and beneficiaries of testamentary donation who have been known to the administrator and thus liquidate the properties of the deceased person; (vi) if the heir has not appeared within the period fixed by the family court as mentioned above, the family court can, if it finds reasonable, at the request of a person who shared a livelihood with the decedent, a person who has contributed to the medical treatment and nursing of the decedent, or any other person who has had a special connection with the decedent,[550] grant such person the remaining amount of the properties after liquidation, in whole or in part (section 958-3 (1) CC); (vii) remaining properties which have not been disposed of in the procedures at (iv) and (v) above shall belong to the state (section 958 CC).

549. But if it becomes evident that there is an heir, the legal person of inherited property (s. 951 CC) shall be regarded not to have been established (s. 955 Main Text CC). However, the effect of actions made by an administrator of inherited property within its authority shall be kept unchanged (s. 955 Proviso CC).

550. This application must be made within three months of the expiration of the period to be fixed by the family court not less than six months in accordance with s. 958 (s. 958-3 (2) CC).

Chapter 3. Possession

§1. The Concept of Possession and the Right of Possession

284. The concept of possession is provided in the Civil Code as "sen-yu" in Japanese. "Sen-yu" [the possession] is defined as "shoji" [holding] of a thing with "jiko-no-tameni-suru-ishi" [the intention to do so for one's own interest] (section 180 CC).

The intention of holding a thing for one's own interest is broadly interpreted to be found in a person who holds a thing not only as an owner but also as a superficiary, tenant, tenant for use, bailee, trustee, etc. For instance, an agent who holds a thing with the intention for the principal's interest shall also have the intention for his/her own interest, and thus these two intentions can be compatible.[551] However, a family member, a servant or a guest of a house who stays there with the owner of the house is not regarded as a possessor but as an assistant possessor because they are not recognized to have the intention of holding the house for their own interest.[552]

The holding of a thing is interpreted as putting a thing under one's actual control. For example, locking the door of a building and keeping the key is regarded as the holding of the building. Placing furniture and household goods in a house can be held as holding the house. Watching a building on a daily basis from the neighboring house is also held to be holding the building.[553]

The right of possession will provide presumption in favor of the possessor, and it will also be the basis of the acquisitive prescription of the "hon-ken" [inherent right] such as ownership, superficies, and right of lease.[554]

§2. Acquisition of the Right of Possession

285. The right of possession is acquired by the actual holding of a thing with the intention to do so for one's own interest (section 180 CC). It is also acquired through the agent who holds a thing with the intention to for the benefit of his/her principal as well as for his/her own interest (section 181 CC).

The possession can be acquired through succession. For instance, A possessed a piece of land and he was claimed by B to return the thing based on B's ownership. A challenged B's ownership and refused to return it. B brought the lawsuit against A, but A died and C and D succeeded A's inheritance. Then B can keep the litigation and claim against C and D to return the thing as successors of the possession of the land even though C and D did not hold the land. In this case C and D were interpreted to possess the thing through the succession of A's properties.[555]

551. SCJ Feb. 19, 1952 Minshu 6-2-95.
552. SCJ Apr. 7, 1960 Minshu 14-5-751.
553. SCJ Feb. 19, 1952 Minshu 6-2-95.
554. *See* paras. 290–295 *infra*.
555. SCJ Oct. 30, 1969 Minshu 23-10-1881.

Another example of the acquisition of possession through succession is that if A had possessed a piece of land peacefully and openly with the intention to own it, though the land was owned by B. Before the period for acquisitive prescription of twenty years (section 162 (1) CC) has passed, B died and C and D succeeded A's inheritance. C and D succeeded the possession of A so that when they have continued the possession for the remaining period of acquisitive prescription, they can acquire ownership of the land, because they can add the period of possession by themselves to that by A (section 187 CC).

A difficult issue is that if in the case mentioned above, if C has held the land because C had lived with A and after A died C has continued to hold the land until the prescription period has passed while D had lived in different place without holding the land since before A died, who acquired the landownership based on the acquisitive prescription? C or C and D? The judicial precedent held that if C believed that only C succeeded the possession and held the land just after the succession and has continued to use and manage the land including paying tax in C's name while D has shown neither interest in that land nor objection to B, C should be regarded as having acquired possession with the intention to own it and acquire ownership on the basis of acquisitive prescription.[556]

286. The right of possession is transferred from the possessor to the other person by "hikiwatashi" [the delivery] of the thing to that person (section 182 (1) CC). However, this style of the transfer of possession will vary depending on the nature of things such as movables, land, building, and trees.[557] It will not always associate with the change of place where the thing has been located. For the land, the transfer of possession shall be made by the change of the use or management. For the building, the delivery of the key to enter into that building may be regarded as the change of the management. As for the transfer of possession of the tees on land, "hikiwatashi" [the delivery] (section 182 (1) CC) can be recognized only by the agreement to change management between the parties without visiting the site.[558] This is called "kan-nen-ka" [the abstraction] of the delivery.[559]

287. If a possessor A (a principal, indirect possessor) possess a thing through another person B (an agent, direct possessor), and A wants to transfer the possession to B who has already acquired the actual holding of the thing, the transfer of the right of possession may be made only by the agreement between the transferor A and the transferee B (section 182 (2) CC). For instance, A is a lessor and B is a lessee of a thing, and then A sold the thing to B, then the delivery, the transfer of

556. SCJ Sep. 8, 1972 Minshu 26-7-1348. In this case, A owned the land and died, and C and D succeeded A's inheritance, but only C has continued to hold the land for more than the period of acquisitive prescription (20 years), while D did not hold the land at all. C claimed against D to register the acquisition of ownership of the land from A to C based on the acquisitive prescription.
557. Wagatsuma and Ariizumi 1983: p. 481; Funabashi 1960: p. 303.
558. STJ Dec. 27, 1920 Minroku 26-2087.
559. Funabashi 1960: pp. 300, 303–304.

possession, can be made only by the agreement between A and B.[560] If the transferee is a tenant who lent it to a subtenant, the transfer of possession may be made by the agreement between the lessor and the tenant (section 182 (2) CC).

288. The transfer of the right of possession can be made even if the transferor of the possession of a thing wants to keep holding the thing only by the agreement between the transferor and transferee to the effect that the transferor will hold the thing on behalf of the transferee (section 183 CC). In this case, the transferor of the possession will become the agent for the interest of the transferee who becomes the principal of the possession, and the transfer of possession shall be completed without any actual delivery of the thing (section 183 CC). This is called "sen-yu-kaitei" [the constructive transfer of possession] and one of the types of abstraction of delivery. This type of delivery is frequently used in practice when A establishes the conveyancing mortgage for B.[561]

289. If a possessor A (a principal, indirect possessor) possess a thing through another person B (an agent, direct possessor), and A wants to transfer the possession to a third party C, the transfer of the right of possession may be made by the order of A to B that B should possess the thing on behalf of C, and the consent of C to accept it (section 184 CC). This is called "sashizu-niyoru-sen-yu-iten" [the transfer of possession by way of the order to a possessing third party] and is also another type of abstraction of delivery. For example, if A concludes a sales contract of 100 bottles of sake (Japanese wine) with C which have been kept in a warehouse managed by B and C wants to keep them in B's warehouse, then the delivery can be completed by the order of A to B to keep them on behalf of C and the consent of C to admit it. B's agreement is not necessary for the transfer of possession. However, in order to continue to keep them in B's warehouse, it is necessary for C to make another contract of bailment, for which B's agreement is indispensable.[562]

§3. Effects of the Right of Possession

I. Presumption of Existence of the Right to Possess

290. The possessor (the holder of possessory right) has some advantages provided by law. The possessor is presumed to have a right to possess the thing lawfully (section 188 CC). For instance, if A possesses a machine and B claims against A that the machine should be returned to B because it is owned by B. In this case, B must prove the ownership of the machine because the machine is possessed by A

560. The transferee of the possession may be not only the agent such as a lessee or a tenant but also the assistant possessor such as a family member or a servant of the possessor. *See* para. 284 *supra*. Funabashi 1960: pp. 300-301.
561. *See* para. 493 *infra*. Funabashi 1960: p. 301.
562. Funabashi 1960: pp. 302–303.

so that A is presumed to be the owner of the machine. This presumption is interpreted to be the presumption of a right based on law (section 188 CC), which cannot be reversed unless the other party (B in the case above) could prove the fact that makes the judge should become confident that the possessor (A in the case above) does not have ownership. However, this presumption cannot be applied between the parties of delivery of a thing, where a transferee who possesses the thing must prove the acquisition of ownership from a transferor.[563]

For immovable property, the presumption of the right to possess based on the registration shall prevail over that based on the possession. This presumption is interpreted to be the presumption of fact which can be reversed if the other party (B in the case above) could prove the fact that makes the judge should become unconfident on the correctness of the registration.[564] Also this presumption cannot be applied between the parties of registration of the immovable property, where a transferee who holds the title in registration must prove the acquisition of ownership from a transferor.[565]

291. The possessor is also presumed to possess a thing with the intention to own it, in good faith, peacefully and openly (section 186 (1) CC). This presumption is advantageous for the possessor who claims the acquisition of ownership of a thing based on the acquisitive prescription (section 162 CC). In order to reverse the presumption that the possessor of a thing has the intention to own it, the other party who would deny the presumption must prove the fact that the possessor did not have the intention to own it from the clear and objective point of view: for instance, the fact that the possessor acquired the possession based on the title by which the possessor should not have the intention to own it by its nature, or the possessor took action which the owner should not usually take or the possessor did not take action which the owner should naturally take during the possession.[566]

The possession by its nature without the intention to own a thing may be transformed to that with the intention to own the thing, when the possessor expresses the intention to own it to the person from whom the possessor acquired the possession, or the possessor initiates the possession by the new "ken-gen" [justified source of the right to possess] such as a sale, gift, and exchange. (section 185 CC).

II. Acquisition of the Right to Possess by Prescription

292. A person who possesses a certain property, either movable or immovable, for twenty years peacefully and openly with an intention to own it shall acquire its ownership (section 162 (1) CC). As explained above, the possessor is presumed to

563. SCJ Mar. 1, 1960 Minshu 14-3-327.
564. SCJ Jun. 29, 1971 Hanji 635-110.
565. SCJ Oct. 15, 1973 Minshu 17-11-1497.
566. SCJ Mar. 24, 1983 Minshu 37-2-131.

possess a thing with the intention to own it, in good faith, peacefully and openly (section 186 (1) CC).[567] The possessor has to prove the continued possession of the property for twenty years.[568]

For instance, if A owned a piece of land and B has possessed a part of that land for twenty-five years. A found B's illegal occupation and claimed against B to return that part of land. B can make a counterclaim that B has acquired that part of land through the acquisitive prescription when twenty have passed since the beginning of the possession.[569]

If the possessor has possessed the property for ten years peacefully and openly with an intention to own it shall acquire its ownership if he/she was not aware that the thing was owned by another person (bona fide) and without negligence when he/she began to possess it (Art 162 (2) CC).

For instance, A sold a piece of land to B and B registered the acquisition and has possessed the land for fifteen years. However, A found that there was a mistake when A concluded the sales contract with B and avoided the contract (section 95 CC). A claimed B to return the land and delete the registration due to avoidance.[570] But B can make a counterclaim that B has acquired ownership of the land when ten years have passed since the beginning of the possession.[571] B's possession is presumed to be with the intention to own it, in good faith (bona fide), peacefully and openly (section 186 (1) CC). In addition, B's possession in good faith began not negligently because the possession of the land was transferred (delivered) from A to B so that B had a good reason to believe the transfer of ownership from A to B by the interpretation of section 188 CC.

293. If there is evidence that a person possessed a thing at two different points in time, it shall be presumed that the possession continued during the interval between those two points (section 186 (2) CC). For example, if B has possessed the land owned by A and prove that B possessed it on July 1, 2000, and on July 1, 2020, then B's possession is presumed to have continued during this period without interruption. In order to prevent the acquisitive prescription A needs to prove that B has lost the possession (section 203, 204 CC) during that time.[572]

This presumption may be available when B initiated the possession of the land on July 1, 2000, but died on July 1, 2010, and the possession was succeeded by C until July 1, 2020. If C proves that B possessed the land on July 1, 2000, and C who

567. *See* para. 291 *supra.*
568. As for the presumption of the continuous possession *see* para. 293 *infra.*
569. However, if B had not registered the acquisition in the land registry after the prescription period has passed and after that A sold the piece of land to C including the part possessed by B and C registered the acquisition, C can claim against B for vacation of that land for the reason of lack of a registration as an opposability requirement (s. 177 CC). *See* para. 244 *supra.*
570. The right to avoid the juridical act may be exercised within 5 years from the time the right-holder may confirm the avoidable action in accordance with s. 124 CC and within 20 years from the time of the action (s. 126 CC).
571. SCJ Jun. 9, 1966 Minshu 20-5-1011. However, if B's possession was initiated not by the delivery from A but B's own action of holding the land, B must prove that he/she began to possess the land without negligence. SCJ Dec. 19, 1968 Saimin 93-707; SCJ Nov. 11, 1971 Hanji 654-52.
572. However, if B recovered the possession by the possessory action for recovery (s. 200), B's possession shall be regarded as not interrupted but continued (s. 203 Proviso CC). *See* para. 297 *infra.*

succeeded B's possession (section 187 CC) possessed the land on July 1, 2020, then the possession is presumed to have continued from July 1, 2000, to July 1, 2020.[573]

294. If a person succeeded the possession of a thing from a predecessor, the successor may assert either his/her own possession only, or in addition to his/her own possession the possession of the predecessor together (section 187 (1) CC). However, if the successor chooses to assert the possession of the predecessor together with his/her own, he/she shall also succeed to defects in the predecessor's possession (section 187 (2) CC). For example, A's land was adjacent to B's land. B possessed a part of A's land by constructing a building which located on B's land and a part of A's land. B knew about it but continued to possess the part of A's land and A claimed nothing about it. After five years have passed since the construction of B's building, B sold the building with the land to C and C continued to possess B's land and the part of A's land on which the building was constructed. C did not know that the building crossed the border with A's land without negligence. After six years have passed since C bought the building and began to possess the land, A sold the land to D and D measured the land and found that C's building crossed the border between C's land and D's land and claimed against C to remove the building. C cannot make a counterclaim that C acquired ownership in the part of D's land by the acquisitive prescription because if C asserts the possession of B for five years in addition to C's possession for six years (eleven years in total) to meet the requirement for ten years possession provided by section 162 (2) CC, C must succeed to a bad faith in B's possession (section 187 (2) CC) so that it is necessary for D to possess fifteen years since D bought the building with the land (section 162 (1) CC).

On the other hand, if B was held to be in good faith without negligence when B began to possess the part of A's land and has possessed for 5 years and C bought the building from B and began to possess the land with the knowledge that the building crossed the border and has continued to possess for 6 years before D who bought the land from A claimed against C to remove the building. C will make a counterclaim that C acquired ownership of the part of D's land by the acquisitive prescription for ten years (section 162 (2) CC), while D will allege that C was in bad faith so that C cannot assert the acquisitive prescription for ten years based on section 162 (2) CC. The judicial precedence recognized C's counterclaim, because if B was in good faith without negligence when B began to possess the part of A's land and became aware that the part of land belonged to A after that, it would not affect B's acquisition of ownership of the part of A's land by the acquisitive prescription for ten years (section 162 (2) CC). The same result should be applied to the case in which the possession which was initiated by B with good faith and without negligence was taken over by C who was in bad faith or with negligence.[574] However, there is a critical opinion in legal doctrines because C was a bad faith or with negligence from the beginning of his/her possession though C took over the possession initiated by B.[575]

---

573. STJ Oct. 14, 1932 Dai-min 6-277.
574. SCJ Mar. 6, 1988 Minshu 32-2-135.
575. Matsuo and Kozumi 2008: p. 142.

295. A person who has continuously exercised property right other than ownership peacefully and openly with an intention to do so for his/her own interest shall acquire such right after twenty years have passed. If he/she was not aware that he/she did not have the right (in good faith) without negligence when he/she began to exercise that property right, he/she shall acquire the right after ten years have passed (section 163 CC). For instance, B lent pieces of land to C for the purpose of the construction of buildings, in which A's land was included and B had no right to lend it to C. C did not know about it and constructed buildings on the land, registered in building registry and has continued to possess the land for ten years with paying a rent to B every month as promised. After that, A claimed against C to vacate A's land by removing the building on that land. C can make a counterclaim that C has acquired a right to lease the land by acquisitive prescription of property right other than ownership as provided by section 163 CC.[576] C's exercise of the right to lease the land is regarded as a type of "jun-sen-yu" [quasi-possession] as provided by section 205 CC.

III. Possessory Actions

A. Action for Recovery of Possession

296. A possessor may bring a possessory action in accordance with the provisions from sections 198 to 201 CC. The agent who takes possession on behalf of his/her principal may also bring the possessory actions (section 197 CC). The possessory actions are different from the actions based on the right to possess a thing such as ownership, superficies, and servitude. because the possessory actions may not need to be based on the right to possess the thing but may be established just proving the fact that his/her possession was infringed or in danger to be infringed. The reasons for the recognition of the possessory actions are: (i) the maintenance of social order, (ii) the prohibition of self-help, (iii) the provision of remedies by simple and quick procedure, and (iv) the protection of claim rights against a third party which cannot be protected by the right to possess a thing to be asserted against a third party such as rei vindicatio.[577]

297. When a possessor A is forcibly dispossessed a thing by another person B, A may claim for the restoration of the thing and compensation for damages against B by bringing an action for recovery (section 200 (1) CC). A does not need to prove his/her ownership but may prove the fact that A was dispossessed the thing by B. If A recovered the possession by the action for recovery, A's possession shall be regarded as not to be interrupted but has continued (section 203 Proviso CC). The dispossession of a thing is interpreted to mean the unintentional removal of the thing from the possessor. If A is delivered a thing to B by the fraud of B, it cannot be held to be "dispossessed," because the delivery was made by the intention of A even though A was forged by B. In this case, A cannot recover the thing from B by the

576. SCJ Oct. 8, 1968 Minshu 22-10-2145.
577. Funabashi 1960: pp. 316–317; Matsuo and Kozumi 2008: p. 145.

possessory action for recovery.[578] On the other hand, if an assistant possessor of a thing did not follow the possessor's will and initiated the possession for his/her own interest, it was held to be regarded as the dispossession of the thing.[579]

298. The action for recovery cannot be filed against a third party in principle. If A was dispossessed a thing by B, and B sold and delivered it to C, A cannot bring the action for recovery against C, because C did not dispossess the thing from A (section 200 (2) Main Text CC).[580] However, if C acquired the thing from B with the knowledge that the thing was dispossessed by B from A, A can bring the action for recovery against C (section 200 (2) Proviso CC) because C was in bad faith and should be equally treated like B who had dispossessed the thing from A. Section 200 CC implies that the possessory action is not based on the right to possess but a sanction against the wrongdoer for his/her bad behavior.[581] As a result, C's bad faith is not enough to be a defendant of the possessory action for recovery if C was aware only of a possibility of the dispossession by B.[582]

299. The action for recovery may be brought only within one year after the thing was dispossessed unlawfully (section 201 (3) CC). After that period, the possessor who had been dispossessed the thing shall lose the possession, and the dispossessor is regarded to acquires the possession instead of A. This restriction on the period of possessory action is also the characteristics different from the action based on the right to possess a thing.[583]

B. Action for Maintenance of Possession

300. When a possessor is not dispossessed but disturbed in his/her possession, he/she may claim for the discontinuation of the disturbance and compensation for damages by bringing an action for maintenance of possession (section 198 CC). The disturbance includes, for instance, construction of building or putting some obstacles on a part of the land without permission of the possessor, disturbance of the possessor's use of a land, etc.[584]

Action for maintenance of possession can be brought during the disturbance is continuing or within one year after the disturbance is extinguished (section 201 (1) Main Text CC).[585] However, if the disturbance is caused by any construction, the action for maintenance of possession may not be brought if one year has passed

578. STJ Nov. 27, 1922 Minshu 1-692.
579. SCJ Mar. 30, 1982 Hanji 1039-61.
580. C is called a "tokutei-shokei-nin" [the specific successor] by s. 200 (2) Main Text CC to be distinguished from a holistic successor such as an heir. It means if C is a successor of B, A can bring the action for delivery against C.
581. Matsuo and Kozumi 2008: pp. 146–147.
582. SCJ Mar. 19, 1981 Minshu 35-2-171.
583. Matsuo and Kozumi 2008: pp. 147–148.
584. Wagatsuma and Ariizumi 1983: p. 506; Funabashi 1960: p. 320; Ishii 2008: p. 558.
585. After the disturbance is extinguished, only compensation can be claimed. Wagatsuma and Ariizumi 1983: p. 507; Funabashi 1960: p. 321; Ishii 2008: p. 560.

from the time when that construction started or if that construction has been completed (section 201 (1) Proviso CC). The purposes of this special rule are to protect the value of the construction and to confirm that the new possession shall be recognized after one year has passed from the construction or the construction has been completed.[586]

C. *Action for Preservation of Possession*

301. When a possessor is neither dispossessed nor disturbed but in danger to be disturbed of his/her possession, he/she may bring an action for preservation of possession and claim either for providing any prevention measure to avoid disturbance or for providing security measure to compensate for possible damages (section 199 CC). For instance, if A piled up stones and sands on the land which caused a possible collapse to the adjacent land possessed by B, B can bring the action for preservation to prevent the collapse against A.

Action for preservation of possession may be brought as long as the danger of disturbance exists (section 201 (2) Main Text CC). However, if the disturbance is likely to be caused by construction activity, action for preservation of possession may not be brought if one year has passed from the time when that construction started or if that construction has been completed (section 201 (2) Proviso CC). The purposes of this special rule are the same as those for action for maintenance of possession.[587]

D. *Relationship Between Possessory Actions and Actions Based on the Right to Possess*

302. Possessory actions shall not prevent actions based on the rights to possess such as an action based on ownership, and actions on the rights to possess shall not prevent possessory actions (section 202 (1) CC). For instance, if the possessor A was dispossessed the thing by the owner B through his/her self-help, A is able to bring the possessory action for recovery, while B can bring the action to claim A to return the thing to B based on his/her ownership. Both actions are compatible.[588]

With respect to possessory actions, a judgment may not be made based on reasons for the right to possess (section 202 (2) CC). For example, if A who had been dispossessed the thing by the owner B through his/her self-help brought the possessory action for recovery against B, the court must not decide the case based on the reason that the thing is owned by B but should decide that the thing is to be returned to A without any other consideration about A's right to possess. Then B needs to bring the action for recovery by proving his/her ownership, against which A can make a defense if he/she has a right to possess B's property such as the right of

586. Wagatsuma and Ariizumi 1983: p. 508; Ishii 2008: p. 560.
587. Wagatsuma and Ariizumfi 1983: p. 508; Ishii 2008: p. 562. *See* para. 300 *supra*.
588. Matsuo and Kozumi 2008: pp. 150–153.

superficies, emphyteusis, and lease. If A does not have any right to possess B's property, the judgment is made in favor of B and A must return the thing to B and the thing is returned to B at last. Thus this rule aims to prevent self-help by the owner.

A difficult question occurred in the mutual dispossessions case. If A in the case above had dispossessed the thing owned and possessed by B before the thing was dispossessed by B from A. A brought the action for recovery (section 200 (1) CC) against B, and B brought the counteraction based on ownership of the thing (section 206 CC). The Supreme Court put emphasis on the prohibition of self-help by B and affirmed the possessory action brought by A.[589] There are legal doctrines which deny A's possessory action if B's self-help was made within one year after the dispossession by A and it should have been difficult for B to find and recover the thing dispossessed by A.[590]

589. STJ May 22, 1924 Minshu 3-224.
590. Matsuo and Kozumi 2008: p. 154.

Chapter 4. Appropriation

§1. Appropriation of Ownerless Things

I. Appropriation of Ownerless Movable Property

303. Japanese law recognizes several patters of initial acquisition of ownership, which means the ownership acquisition of a thing without any burden for another person's interest. They are: (i) appropriation (section 239 CC), (ii) finding of lost property (lost and found: section 240 CC), (iii) discovery of hidden treasure (treasure trove: section 241 CC), (iv) accession (sections 241–245 CC), and (vi) processing (section 246 CC).

Appropriation is the taking possession of a thing by a person with the intention to own it. Appropriation of ownerless movable property by a person can cause the initial acquisition of ownership (section 239 (1) CC).[591] Ownerless movable property is either the movable which has never been owned by anybody (res nullius), or the movable the owner of which had abandoned ownership (res derelicta). The former includes the lawful capture of wild beasts and animals, and lawful collection of wild vegetables. The latter is the appropriation of abandoned items. Lost golf balls left by golfers while driving them into a pond in a golf course were held to have been abandoned by those golfers and possessed by the golf course management company with intention to own them, so that they were no longer ownerless movables.[592]

II. Ownership Acquisition of Ownerless Immovable Property

304. If an immovable property becomes ownerless, it shall belong to the state (section 239 (2) CC). An immovable property shall become ownerless if the owner is recognized to have abandoned his/her ownership of that immovable property. However, abandoning ownership of immovable property such as a piece of land or a building will not always be recognized if it is held to be an action against the principle of public policy and good morals.[593] Judicial precedents generally recognized the possibility to abandon ownership of an immovable property, though they held

---

591. In addition, the establishment of ownership through the acquisitive prescription (s. 162 CC), the immediate acquisition of a movable (s. 192 CC), and the expropriation (public takings) by a public body of private property (Land Expropriation Law) in the sense that the former ownership shall cease to exist upon the establishment of a new ownership. Matsuo and Kozumi 2008: pp. 177–178.
592. SCD Apr. 10, 1987 Keishu 41-3-221.
593. A juridical act with any purpose which is against the principle of public policy and good morals shall be invalid (s. 90 CC).

that it could not be recognized in concrete cases as an abuse of a right of ownership[594] because it might aim to escape responsibility associated with the ownership of the immovable property such as expenses to manage the land administration, and taxes.[595]

§2. Finding of Lost Property (Lost and Found)

305. If the owner of a lost property is not identified within three months after the public notice as provided by the Law on the Lost Property (Law No. 73, 2006), the person who found it shall acquire ownership (section 240 CC). The lost property means a thing whose possession was lost without the intention of a possessor. However, it does not include a stolen thing. But the thing which was mistakenly possessed by someone, the thing which the possessor left, and the livestock which escaped[596] shall be treated like the lost property (section 2 (1), (2) and section 3 Law on the Lost Property).

According to the Law on the Lost Property, the finder of a lost property has to return it to the loser or submit it to the police office "promptly" (section 4 Law on the Lost Property). However, if the lost property was found in a building, car, bus, ship, airplane and other facilities in which an administrator resides, the finder has to submit it to the administrator and the administrator has to return it to the loser or submit it to the police office (sections 4 (2), 14 (1) Law on the Lost Property).[597] If the police office cannot return the lost property to the loser, it shall make a public notice to provide information of lost properties (section 7 Law on the Lost Property). As stated above, if the owner of a lost property cannot be found within three months after the public notice, the finder shall acquire ownership (section 240 CC). However, when the finder would not take the property within two months, he/she shall lose ownership (section 36 Law on the Lost Property), the property shall belong to the prefecture in which the police office is located (section 37 Law on the Lost Property).[598]

If the loser appeared within three months after the public notice, the property shall be returned to him/her. The finder has a right to claim him/her a reward between 5% and 20% of the property value within one month from the return of the property (sections 28 (1) and 29 Law on the Lost Property). The finder at a facility managed by the residing administrator will have a half of the reward and another

594. Section 1 (3) CC provides that no abuse of rights is permitted.

595. HCJ (Tokyo) Apr. 28, 1976 Hanji 820-67; HCJ (Matsue-branch, Hiroshima) Dec. 21, 2016 Shogetsu 64-6-863.

596. As for the wild animal which escaped from the owner, a special provision of s. 195 CC shall be applied. *See* para. 306 *infra*.

597. If the administrator of a facility is recognized by the Cabinet Ordinance to receive a large number of lost properties regularly and to be able to keep them adequately can make a report to the police office within two weeks after the finding instead of submitting them to the police office (ss. 17 to 19 Law on the Lost Property). It is called a special facility administrator.

598. The lost property which has been kept by a special facility administrator as explained in the previous footnote and the finder would not take the property within two months after he/she acquired ownership shall belong to the special facility administrator (s. 37 Law on the Lost Property).

half shall be paid to the facility administrator (section 28 (2) Law on the Lost Property). When the finder and the loser cannot reach the agreement on the amount of the reward, it is determined by the court. For instance, the reward to be paid to the finder of the lost bills and checks should be judged by considering the possible damage due to the good faith acquisition of bills and checks by someone else (sections 16 (2), 77 (1) [1] Law on Bills of Exchange and Promissory Notes; section 21 Law on Checks).[599]

306. A wild animal which was not owned by anyone else can be owned by a possessor who possesses it with the intention to own it (section 239 (1) CC),[600] while a livestock escaped from its owner shall be treated in the same way as the lost property (section 2 (1), (2) and section 3 Law on the Lost Property).[601] Then how to treat "a non-domestic animal," that is, normally a wild animal in each region which, however, is owned by someone else and escaped from its owner? It must be difficult for a possessor of that animal to identify whether it is owned by anyone or not from the outlook. If the possessor does not know that the animal is owned by someone else, he/she cannot be expected to find its owner to return it or to take it to the police office like an escaped livestock. For this reason, a person who began to possess "a non-domestic animal," that is, normally a wild animal in that region which was bred by someone else shall acquire ownership of that animal if he/she did not know that it was bred by someone (in good faith) at the beginning of the possession, and was not claimed for recovery within one month from the time when it left from the owner (section 195 CC). The term "a non-domestic animal" in section 195 CC means an animal which is not usually bred by someone in the region where it was possessed. A Mynah (a kind of bird) was not recognized as "a non-domestic animal" in a region where it was possessed so that section 195 CC could not be applied for the interest of its possessor.[602]

§3. Discovery of Buried Property (Treasure Trove)

307. If "maizo-butsu" [the buried property] is found by a person, but the finder cannot identify whether it is owned by someone or not, it shall be treated in the same way as a lost property (section 1 Law on the Lost Property) so that the finder must submit it to the police office.[603] The police office shall make a public notice (section 7 Law on the Lost Property). If the owner of the property is not identified within six months from the time when the public notice was made, the finder shall acquire ownership of that property (section 241 Main Text CC). However, if the buried property was discovered in a thing such as a land which belonged to another

599. STJ Oct. 26, 1922 Minshu 1-626; STJ Feb. 2, 1928 Minshu 7-33.
600. *See* para. 303 *supra*.
601. *See* para. 305 *supra*.
602. STJ Feb. 16, 1932 Minshu 11-138.
603. *See* para. 305 *supra*.

person, the finder and the owner of that thing shall acquirer ownership of the buried property equally (section 241 Proviso CC).[604]

The term "maizo-butsu" [the buried property] means a property which is buried in another thing so that it cannot be easily found.[605] If an employee of a construction company found a buried property when the employee was engaged in the construction work, the finder of the buried property is interpreted to be the employee, not the construction company.[606] However, if it is considered that the employee found the buried property during the construction work as directed by the construction company, the employee and the construction company (the employer) should be recognized as co-finders.[607]

604. If the owner of the buried property was not found and it was identified as a cultural heritage by an appraisal committee of each prefecture, it shall belong to the prefecture and a reward shall be paid to the finder and the owner of the thing in which it was buried (s. 105 Law on the Protection of Cultural Heritages).
605. SCJ Jun. 1, 1962 Shogetsu 8-6-1005.
606. Wagatsuma and Ariizumi 1983: p. 303; Funabashi 1960: 362.
607. Ishii 2008: p. 342.

Chapter 5. Accession and Processing

§1. Accession

I. Accession of Immovable Property

308. Accession and processing are the causes of the initial acquisition of ownership through the combination of things which had been owned by different owners.

The owner of immovable property shall acquire ownership of a thing that has been attached subordinately, that is, as an accessory, to the immovable property (section 242 Main Text CC). It is called "fugo" [accession]. For instance, when A sowed seeds or planted seedlings on B's land without any agreement with B, and the seeds or seedlings grew so that they cannot be removed without damaging them, then they shall belong to B as a result of accession.[608] Thus B acquires ownership of the accessory, while A loses ownership of it. If A suffers any loss as a result of the accession and B gains any profit caused by the accession, A may claim for compensation in accordance with the provision on the unjust enrichment provided by sections 703 and 704 CC (section 248 CC).

But, if A constructed a building on B's land, A is still recognized as the owner of the building even though it was constructed without any agreement with B, because a land and a building are separate property in Japanese law.[609] Thus the accession cannot take place between the land and the building on it. B has to claim for removal of the building and vacation of the land against A based on ownership of the land.[610]

If two buildings are combined and become one building, the united new building is interpreted to be co-owned by the former owners of old buildings with the shares to be divided in proportion to the value of the old buildings at the time of combination.[611]

309. If an owner of an accessory has a right to reserve ownership of the accessory attached to the immovable property, the accessory shall not be acquired by the owner of the immovable property even though the accessory is subordinately and firmly attached to the immovable property (section 242 Proviso CC). Typical rights to reserve ownership of the accessory are superficies, emphyteusis, land lease right, etc. For instance, when A has a right of lease on a land owned by B to grow a certain plant in accordance with the agreement with B on that land, then the plant remains to be owned by A even though the plant grew, took roots and became attached firmly in that land.

---

608. STJ Jun. 1, 1921 Minroku 27-1032; SCJ Jun. 19, 1956 Minshu 10-6-678; SCJ Nov. 16, 1971 Hanji 654-56.
609. STJ Dec. 26, 1914 Minroku 20-1208; STJ Dec. 9, 1931 Minshu 10-1210. *See* paras. 86–90 *supra*.
610. SCJ Feb. 8, 1994 Minshu 48-2-373. *See* para. 90 *supra*.
611. It is the result of an analogical application of s. 244 CC. SCJ Jan. 25, 1994 Minshu 48-1-18. As for s. 244 CC, *see* para. 311 *infra*.

The right to reserve ownership of an accessory should be made public to secure transactions of the accessory by appropriate measures such as registration or "meinin-hoho" [the publicity method based on customary law].[612] If the right is not made public, the reservation of ownership cannot be opposable against a third party who acquired the accessory from the owner of immovable property by the application of sections 177, 178 and 605 CC.[613] However, it is criticized by another legal doctrine which considers that the holder of the right to reserve ownership of the accessory has not acquired ownership but originally held it so that priority should be given to the holder of the right to reserve it.[614]

310. In the case stated in paragraph 308 *supra*, where A loses the ownership in the accessory and B acquires it as a result of accession (section 242 Main Text CC), even if C who had sold the accessory to A had not received full amount of purchase money from A so that C had held the right of statutory lien in the accessory in accordance with sections 321 and 322 CC, C also shall lose the right of statutory lien in that accessory as a result of accession (section 247 (1) CC). However, C may claim B for compensation money which A may claim B based on section 248 CC[615] as the substitute for the right of statutory lien provided that C attaches the compensation claim of A against B before it is paid or delivered by B to A in accordance with section 304 (1) CC.[616]

However, if two buildings are combined and become one building as a result of accession, a right of hypothec which had been established on the old building shall not be lost but continue to exist on the share of the united new building which is divided in proportion to the value of the buildings at the time of combination.[617]

II. Accession of Movable Property

311. If two or more movables owned by different owners are so firmly combined with each other that they can no longer be separated either without damaging any of them or without spending excessive expenses for separating them, then ownership of the subordinate movable(s) shall vest in the owner of the principal movable (section 243 CC). If wheels and a saddle of a bicycle are attached to another bicycle, they are not recognized to be an accession.[618] If an engine owned by A is installed on a ship owned by B, and there is no specific agreement between A and

612. *See* para. 259 *supra*.
613. Wagatsuma and Ariizumi 1983: pp. 308–309; Funabashi 1960: p. 367; SCJ Mar. 1, 1960 Minshu 14-3-307.
614. Hironaka 1982: pp. 409–410; Matsuo and Kozumi 2008: pp. 185–186. The protection of a third party should be given by the analogical application of s. 94 (2) CC on the good faith acquisition.
615. *See* para. 308 *supra*.
616. Wagatsuma and Ariizumi 1983: p. 306. C may also directly claim B for compensation as unjust enrichment based on s. 248 CC or C may exercise A's claim against B to be acquired on the basis of s. 248 CC by way of the right of a creditor to substitute a debtor (s. 423 CC). However, both these claims must be made before A exercises the claim against B based on s. 248 CC.
617. It is the result of an analogical application of s. 247 (2) CC. SCJ Jan. 25, 1994 Minshu 48-1-18.
618. SCJ Oct. 20, 1949 Keishu 3-10-1660.

B about ownership of the engine and the ship, B as the owner of the principal movable shall acquire ownership of the engine as the subordinate movable.[619] However, in judging which is the principal movable and which is the subordinate movable, not only the size and function of the movables but also the price should be taken into account. For instance, if the price of the engine is considerably higher than that of the ship, the engine may be recognized as the principal thing, while the ship can be regarded as the subordinate movable.[620]

If the distinction of principal movable and subordinate movable(s) cannot be identified, then the owner of each movable(s) shall co-own the combined movable with the shares in proportion to the respective current price at the time of the accession (section 244 CC).[621]

312. The same rule as explained in paragraph 311 *supra* shall be applied to the movables owned by different owners which are not combined but mixed each other so that owners cannot be identified for each of them. For example, a certain amount of rice, wheat, salt, sugar, liquor, etc. owned by different owners are mixed together and can no longer be distinguished to whom they belong (section 245 CC). If the principal movable and the subordinate movable cannot be distinguished, and there is no agreement among the original owners, the mixed things shall be co-owned by them with the shares in proportion to the value of the original movables at the time of mixture.[622] The trashes dumped illegally by A, B and C on the land owned by D were recognized to be co-owned by A, B and C so that they are jointly responsible for the damages suffered by D.[623]

If A was asked by B and C to buy ten pieces of lottery for each of them and A bought thirty pieces of lottery including for himself and kept them collectively without identifying each owner of thirty pieces of lottery so that they were mixed. A found that one of thirty pieces won the lottery and received JPY 12,000,000. If the piece which won the lottery is recognized to be co-owned by A, B and C with the shares in proportion to the expenses at the time of mixture, the benefit shall be divided among them in proportion to each share.[624]

313. As a result of accession, if the owner of the movable suffers any loss, while the owner of the combined movable or mixed movables gains any profit (sections 243 and 245 CC), and there is no specific agreement on the payment for the compensation, the owner who suffers loss may claim for compensation in accordance with the provisions on unjust enrichment (sections 703 and 704 CC) against the owner who gains profit (section 248 CC). For instance, if A, the owner of an engine,

---

619. STJ Jul. 23, 1937 Hanketsuzenshu 4-17-3.
620. STJ May 25, 1942 Minshu 22-411.
621. Section 244 CC is analogically applied to immovables to the effect that if two buildings owned by A and B are combined and become one building and there is no specific agreement between A and B about the ownership of the building, the united new building is interpreted to be co-owned by A and B with the shares in proportion to the value of the old buildings of A and B at the time of combination. SCJ Jan. 25, 1994 Minshu 48-1-18. *See* para. 308 *supra*.
622. HCJ (Tokyo) Feb. 29, 1940 Shinbun 4567-9.
623. DCJ (Tokyo) Jul. 27, 1994 Hanji 1520-107.
624. Matsuo and Kozumi 2008: p. 190.

lost its ownership as a result of its installment on the ship owned by B, and B acquired ownership of the engine (section 243 CC), and there was no agreement between A and B on the compensation, A has a right to claim compensation for loss against B who benefitted by the accession. If B was in good faith about the accession, B is only obliged to return the existing profit at the claim for compensation by A (section 703 CC). If B was in bad faith about the accession, B has to return all the received benefit with interest[625] and to pay compensation for additional damages (section 704 CC).[626]

314. If A loses ownership of the subordinate movable, while B acquired ownership of combined movable or mixed movables as a result of accession, the right established on the subordinate movable owned by A shall be extinguished (section 247 (1) CC). For instance, if C had sold an engine for a ship to A but had not received a part of purchase money from A so that C had kept the right of statutory lien on the engine in accordance with section 321 CC. However, if A lost ownership of the engine as a result of accession, C also lost the right of statutory lien on the engine. In this case, C may claim B for the compensation which A may claim B based on section 248 CC as the substitute for the right of statutory lien by attaching the compensation money before it is paid or delivered from B to A in accordance with section 304 (1) CC.[627]

315. If C had sold a movable to A but had not received a part of purchase money from A so that C had kept the right of statutory lien on the movable owned by A in accordance with section 321 CC. Then that movable owned by A was combined with another movable owned by B and the combined movable was held to be co-owned by A and B with the shares in proportion to the value of each movable at the time of combination (section 244 CC). In this case, C's right of statutory lien shall continue to exist on A's share of the combined movable (section 247 (2) CC).

§2. Processing

316. If a person (processor) attached any work to a movable (material) owned by another person and created a new thing,[628] ownership of the processed thing shall vest in the owner of the materials (section 246 (1) Main Text CC).[629] But there are legal doctrines which do not require the creation of a new thing for the processing but includes the repair of existing material,[630] because the owner of the material

625. It was reduced from 5% to 3% per year (s. 404 (1) CC).
626. Ishii 2008: pp. 359–360.
627. Wagatsuma and Ariizumi 1983: p. 306.
628. STJ Jun. 28, 1917 Keiroku 23-737; STJ Jun. 2, 1915 Keiroku 21-721; STJ Nov. 26, 1919 Minroku 25-2114; STJ Jan. 30, 1924 Keishu 3-38; SCJ Oct. 20, 1949 Keishu 3-10-1660.
629. However, if there was any specific agreement between the processor and the owner of the material on ownership of the processed thing such as an employment contract, it prevails over the provision of s. 246 CC. SCD Apr. 8, 1970 Hanji 590-91.
630. Wagatsuma and Ariizumi 1983: pp. 311–312; Funabashi 1960: p. 371.

shall acquire ownership of the processed thing in principle.[631] This is the general principle on ownership of the processed thing. But there are two special rules which recognize that the processor shall acquire ownership of the processed thing as follow.

317. If the value of the processed thing which is increased by the processing work "significantly" exceeds the value of the material, then the processor shall acquire the ownership of the processed thing (section 246 (1) Proviso CC). However, if the processing requires to create a new thing, the repair of the existing material cannot be recognized as processing even if it increased the value of the material significantly.[632]

318. If the processor supplied a portion of the material(s) to be added to other material(s) owned by another person, the processor shall acquire ownership of the processed thing, if the total value of the material(s) supplied by the processor and the value derived from the processor's work exceeds the value of the material(s) owned by another person (section 246 (2) CC). It will include the case where the processor supplied all the materials.[633]

319. There is a missing rule on the processing in the Japanese Civil Code. Section 246 CC refers only to the processing of "movable" material(s), but does not refer to the processing of an immovable property. But section 246 CC can be analogically applied to the processing of immovable properties. For instance, if A attached any work to the house which was under construction undertaken by B who had contracted with C to build the house on the land owned by C, but B could not complete the construction work because of the bankruptcy of B, so that A completed the work according to the contract with C. In response to the claim by B that the building should belong to B because A added the material (movable) to the building (immovable) under construction by B (section 242 Main Text CC), C claimed that the completed building was owned by A, because the total value of the additional construction work and the additional materials attached by A to the building exceeded the value of the materials provided by B (analogical application of section 246 (2) CC), and then A transferred ownership of the building to C in accordance with the agreement between A and C. The Supreme Court decided in favor of C, however, for the reason that "the house under construction" in this case could not be regarded as the immovable property but movable property, so that section 246 (2) should be applied to the case.[634]

320. However, the problem remains for the case where the house under construction is recognized as an immovable property, which would actually exist,

---

631. The requirement of the creation of a new thing for processing typically corresponds to the specific rule provided by s. 246 (1) Proviso CC which recognizes that the processor shall acquire ownership of the processed thing.
632. Judicial precedents do not recognize the repair as a processing. STJ Nov. 26, 1919 Minroku 25-2114.
633. Wagatsuma and Ariizumi 1983: p. 312.
634. SCJ Jan. 25, 1979 Minshu 33-1-26.

because, according to the case law, the house under construction may be regarded as an immovable property when it has a roof and walls so that it can be protected against the rain and wind even though the construction has not been completed.[635] A new legislation should be expected to cover this case.[636]

321. If A, the processor of a material, did not acquire ownership of the processed thing but B, the owner of the material, B acquired its ownership and thus A suffered the loss and B gained the profit due to the processing, then A may claim B for compensation on the basis of unjust enrichment in accordance with sections 703 and 704 CC (section 248 CC).[637]

322. On the contrary, if A, the processor, acquired ownership of the processed thing and thus gained the profit and B, the owner of the material, suffered the loss, B may claim A for compensation based on the unjust enrichment in accordance with sections 703 and 704 CC (section 248 CC).[638] For instance, if A processed the material with the knowledge that it belonged to B and without any agreement with B, B can claim A for compensation of the value of the material which A received with the payment of interest[639] and compensation for additional damages if any (section 704 CC). There are legal doctrines that if the processor knew that the material belonged to B (in bad faith) the owner of the material can also claim for recovery of the material as an alternative to claim for compensation.[640] However, in response to the claim for recovery of the material, the processor will claim for compensation for the increased value by the processing.

323. If A processed the material owned by B and did not know that it belonged to B without negligence, and acquired ownership of the processed thing, B cannot claim for recovery of the material, but claim only for compensation based on unjust enrichment (section 703 CC), that is, the existing value of the material enjoyed by A at the time when B claims compensation (section 248 CC).[641]

However, if B acquired ownership of the processed thing in the previous case, A may claim for compensation based on unjust enrichment (section 703 CC), that is, the existing value of the processing enjoyed by B at the time when A claims compensation against B (section 248 CC).[642]

324. If A processed the material provided by B which had been the object of the right of C such as the statutory lien for the sale of the material from C to B whose

635. SCJ Oct. 1, 1935 Minshu 14-1671. *See* para. 91 *supra*.
636. Wagatsuma and Ariizumi 1983: pp. 312–313; Funabashi 1960: pp. 370–371; Matsuo and Kozumi 2008: p. 193.
637. However, in many cases there is a specific agreement about the coordination of benefits and expenses between the processor and the owner of the processed thing.
638. If B, the owner of the material, also had provided a processing work on the material, the value of that processing should be taken into account when the loss on the part of B is evaluated.
639. It is 3% per year (s. 404 (1) CC).
640. Hironaka 1982: p. 415; Ishii 2008: p. 365.
641. Ishii 2008: p. 366.
642. Ishii 2008: p. 366.

purchase money had not been paid in full by B, and B acquired ownership of the processed thing in accordance with section 246 (1) Main Text CC or section 246 (2) CC, the right of C shall continue to exist on the processed thing owned by B (section 247 (1) CC).

325. On the contrary, if A processed the material provided by B which had been the object of the right of C such as the statutory lien for the sale of the material from C to B whose purchase money had not been paid in full by B, and B did not acquired ownership of the processed thing in accordance with section 246 (1) Proviso CC or section 246 (2) CC, C's right of statutory lien shall be extinguished (section 247 (1) CC). In this case, C may claim A for the compensation which B may claim A based on section 248 CC as the substitute for the right of statutory lien by attaching the compensation money before it is paid or delivered from A to B in accordance with section 304 (1) CC.[643]

643. Wagatsuma and Ariizumi 1983: p. 306.

Chapter 6. Expropriation

§1. Guarantee of Property Rights

326. The Constitution of the Empire of Japan (the former Constitution, promulgated on February 11, 1889) provided in Article 27 the guarantee of private property within the framework of public interest.[644] Although it did not stipulated the just compensation for the public use of private property, there were government decrees which provided the standards of compensation for public takings since September 1872,[645] just after the private ownership to land was first recognized in Japan.[646] The Constitution of Japan which was totally amended in 1946 guarantees the private property as an essential component of human rights.[647] The present Constitution provides in Article 29 (3) "Private property may be taken for public use upon just compensation therefor."[648] In order to provide the procedure of public takings and the detailed standard of compensation for public takings, Land Expropriation was enacted.[649]

327. Section 3 Land Expropriation Law stipulates the public projects for which land may be acquired or used for the public purpose by compulsory acquisition (public takings). They include projects for constructing facilities such as roads, rivers, bridges, sand control facilities, facilities to prevent disasters, facilities to be used for canals, water-supply and water-drainage machines, railways, tramways, underground, oil pipelines, port facilities, seacoast conservation facilities, electronic communication installations, broadcasting installations, power generation facilities, facilities for fire service, facilities for flood prevention, public halls and museums for the citizens, facilities for furnishing social welfare services, hospitals, sanatoriums, dispensaries, maternity houses, crematories, waste disposal facilities, central and local whole sale markets, parks, green areas, open spaces, playgrounds, cemeteries, conservation projects, and research facilities.[650] These projects have

644. The former Constitution provided in Art. 27 (1) "The right of property of every Japanese subject shall remain inviolable," while in Art. (2) "Measures necessary to be taken for the public benefit shall be provided for by law,"
645. The first two were Decree of Ministry Finance No. 126 (Sep. 4, 1872) and No. 159 (Oct. 31, 1872), which were replaced by Ordinance of Government No. 132 (Jul. 28, 1875). Ozawa 2012 (1): pp. 2–4.
646. As for the introduction of private ownership to land, *see* para. 40 *supra*.
647. As for the amendment to the Constitution, *see* para. 54 *supra*.
648. The present Constitution provides in Art. 29 (1) "The right to own or to hold property is inviolable" and in Art. 29 (2) "Property rights shall be defined by law, in conformity with the public welfare,"
649. Under the former Constitution, the first Land Expropriation Law was enacted in 1889 (Law No. 19, Jul. 30, 1889), which was replaced by Land Expropriation Law in 1900 (Law No. 29, Mar. 7, 1900). Under the present Constitution, Land Expropriation Law was newly enacted in 1951 (Law No. 219, Jun. 9, 1951).
650. Section 3, Item 1 to Item 35 Land Expropriation Law.

been accumulated through amendments to the Land Expropriation Law in accordance with the increase of varieties of facilities which would support the people's lives.[651]

328. Land may be acquired for those public projects as stipulated in section 3 Land Expropriation Law through a voluntary purchase on the basis of agreement between the parties as well. Even in this case, the amount of purchase money should be determined and paid in accordance with the unified rules which is confirmed officially, because it is disbursed from national or local treasury. For that purpose, the Guidelines for Standards of Compensation for Loss Caused by the Acquisition of Land for Public Use was decided by the Cabinet in 1962.[652] In 1967 the Guidelines for Standards of Compensation for Loss Caused to Public Entities by the Public Projects was enacted.[653] As for the compensation standards for a compulsory purchase, the Cabinet Ordinance to Provide Items Delegated by section 88 of the Land Expropriation Law was enacted.[654] On the basis of these guidelines and the ordinance more detailed standards are enacted by the Ministries of Land, Infrastructure, Transport and Tourism, the Central Liaison Council of Taking Measures for Right of Way, the Local Liaison Council of Taking Measures for Right of Way, etc. As a result, quite detailed rules, standards, specifications, unit price lists, and steps to determine the content of just compensation are systemically enacted in the Japanese law for public takings.[655]

§2. Compensation for Expropriation

329. Section 29 (3) CJ provides that "private property may be taken for public use upon just compensation therefor." The necessity and the content of "just compensation" have been much discussed. As for the necessity of compensation, the judicial precedent held that the restriction on the property right to implement the police purpose does not need to be compensated because it is regarded as inherent in the property right, while that to increase the public interest has to be compensated since the increased interest and imposed sacrifice generated by the public project should be fairly shared among the citizens.[656] Taking into account the judicial precedent, the recent legal doctrine stipulates that the just compensation must be paid to a right holder on a land to be taken or used by the project agency for the loss which is recognized to be a special sacrifice in terms of the purpose, the degree and the method of restriction on the property right of that right holder when it is compared with other persons who do not suffer such loss.[657]

651. Ozawa 2012 I: p. 77. While the Land Expropriation Law of 1889 and that of 1900 stipulated the military facilities as the first item in the public projects for which expropriation could be recognized.
652. Cabinet Decision on Jun. 29, 1962, which was amended on Dec. 12, 1967.
653. Cabinet Decision on Feb. 21, 1967.
654. The Cabinet Order No. 248 on Jul. 5, 2002.
655. Matsuo 2011: pp. 27–28.
656. SCJ (FB) Jun. 26, 1963 Keishu 17-5-521.
657. Matsuo 2011: pp. 28–36.

330. As for the content and amount of just compensation, the judicial precedent held that the just compensation should be "the appropriate amount which was reasonably calculated based on the price of the land to be recognized under the economic conditions at the time" of the project.[658] Another judicial precedent interpreted the just compensation as "the full compensation, that is, the compensation which would equalize the property value of the expropriated person before and after the expropriation."[659] The recent judicial precedent referred to both precedents.[660] It implies that the just compensation may reflect on the economic conditions which have been changing in the development process and the substantial impacts of the public project on the interests of the people in the social context at the time of the project. By considering this, the principle to be applied to the just compensation is not a simple commutative justice or corrective justice, but a more comprehensive reallocation of the increased public interests to be generated by the project by taking into consideration of the special sacrifices of the persons who have contributed their property rights to the project if they are compared with other persons (the reallocative justice).[661]

Under this general standard for the just compensation, it is concretely calculated by aggregating: (i) the market value the land, (ii) the expenses to allocate the building and other facilities and business activities on the land, (iii) the expenses for life reconstruction of the interested persons, and (iv) the compensation for the losses due to the injurious affections by the public project.[662] One of the characteristics of Japanese law on compensation for the public takings is that the building and other facilities on the land shall in principle not be taken but be reallocated to the other appropriate place by the appropriate method, because the land and the building are separate properties in Japanese law[663] and the expropriation shall be minimum for the project unless there is any special reason to take not only the land but also the building (the principle of reallocation for building).[664]

658. SCJ (FB) Dec. 23, 1953 Minshu 7-13-1523.
659. SCJ Oct. 18, 1973 Minshu 27-9-1210.
660. SCJ Jun. 11, 2002 Minshu 56-5-958.
661. Matsuo 2011: pp. 38–40, 58.
662. Matsuo 2011: pp. 40–42.
663. *See* paras. 86–90 *supra*.
664. Section 77 Land Expropriation Law, s. 24 (1) Guidelines for Standards of Compensation for Loss Caused by the Acquisition of Land for Public Use was decided by the Cabinet; Matsuo 2011: p. 61. For critical comments to the principle of reallocation for building, *see* Matsuo 2011: pp. 77–80.

Chapter 7. Insolvency

§1. Overview of Insolvencies in Japanese Law

331. In Japanese law four major types of "tosan" [the insolvency] procedure have been currently recognized by the provisions of law.[665] They are: (i) "hasan" [the bankruptcy] regulated by Bankruptcy Law (Law No. 75, 2004), (ii) "minji-saisei" [the civil rehabilitation] regulated by Civil Rehabilitation Law (Law No. 225, 1999), (iii) "kaisha-kosei" [the corporate reorganization] regulated by Corporate Reorganization Law (Law No. 154, 2002), and (iv) "tokubetsu-seisan" [the special liquidation] regulated by Part II, Chapter 9, from sections 510 to 574 and Part VII, Chapter 3, sections 879–902, Company Law (Law No. 86, 2005).

Among those major types (i) the bankruptcy and (iv) the special liquidation are classified into "seisan" [the liquidation] type, while (ii) the civil rehabilitation and (iii) the corporate reorganization are characterized as "saiken" [the reconstruction] type. The liquidation type of insolvency procedure aims to distribute the debtor's properties among creditors as equal as possible. The reconstruction type has been created to reconstruct the debtor's business and economic life so that the creditors may expect to increase the sources of payment for their claims.

From the viewpoint of the person who conducts the insolvency procedure: (i) the bankruptcy procedure and (iii) the corporate reorganization procedure shall be conducted by "kanzai-nin" [the administrator] who is to be appointed by the court as a third party in accordance with the provisions of law. But the debtor loses the right to administer the procedure, dispose of properties and manage transactions. On the other hand, (ii) in the civil rehabilitation procedure "saimusha" [the debtor] shall maintain the right to administer the procedure, dispose of properties and manage transactions. It is the Debtor in Possession (DIP)-type of insolvency procedure, which was received from the U.S. insolvency law.[666] (iv) The special liquidation procedure shall be conducted by "seisan-nin" [the liquidator] who is appointed by the court but recognized as one of the organs of a company (not a third party) in accordance with the provisions of Company Law.[667]

332. In addition to the major types of insolvency procedure, the voluntary process of workout for restructuring debt is often used in practice by way of negotiations and an agreement between a debtor and creditors. It is called "shiteki-seiri" [the private coordination]. If all the parties are cooperative to negotiate on the treatment of the debtor's insolvency and agree to the reconstruction or liquidation plan, it would be the simplest and quickest procedure by saving time and costs for reconstruction or liquidation of the debtor. It may also have an advantage to keep confidential information within the parties. It has been used for liquidation of

665. As for the history of the Japanese insolvency laws, *see* Yamamoto 2018: pp. 10–15.
666. Chapters 11 and 13, Federal Bankruptcy Code in the U.S. were referred to in the drafting process of Civil Rehabilitation Law of 1999.
667. Yamamoto 2018: pp. 15–16.

individuals and small- and medium-sized companies, reconstruction of firms including big companies, etc.[668] From the legal point view, the voluntary workout for restructuring debt is regarded as a collective contract of compromise. It is a characteristic of the voluntary workout that no third party intervenes into the procedure but the process is promoted by all the parties concerned.[669] However, the voluntary workout is only the outcome to be reached at the end of the procedure. The legal relation among the parties in the whole procedure can be explained as a trust in which the debtor is a settlor, the representative of a collective body of creditors who undertakes the workout for restructuring debt and conducts the procedure is a trustee, and the creditors who would be benefitted from the procedure are beneficiaries. If this conception applies, it is said that the representative of creditors, as a trustee, has a duty to administer the trust affairs with the due care of a prudent manager (section 29 (2) Trust Law on the trustee's duty of care) and faithfully on behalf of the beneficiaries (section 30 Trust Law on the trustee's duty of loyalty).[670] As a result, if the representative of creditors received any payment from the debtor's property more advantageously than the other creditors, it would be regarded as against the duty to administer the affairs with due care and faithfully and he/she should be obliged to return the payment to the collective body of creditors.[671]

333. Alternative Dispute Resolution (ADR) procedures may also be available for facilitating the insolvency process without using the formal procedures. It is also different from the voluntary process of workout for restructuring debt as stated above in that a third party shall be appointed as a conciliator who conducts the procedure. For instance, "tokutei-chotei" [the special conciliation] is available for debtors who are in danger of falling into insolvency to be economically rehabilitated. It is based on the Law on the Special Conciliation Procedure for Expediting Arrangement of Specified Debts, etc. (Law No. 158, 1999), which came into effect in February 2000.[672] This procedure may be used either by a natural person or by a legal person, and either by a consumer or by a business person by making an application to the court. It is a special procedure of civil conciliation. In response to the application to the court, it appoints the conciliator who has a professional knowledge of law, tax, finance, corporate finance, asset appraisal, etc.[673]

An administrative organization may become a conciliator. The Small and Medium-Sized Enterprises Revitalization Support Councils (SMERSC) have been established in each prefecture since 2003 and played an important role to support

668. In September 2001, the Guidelines of Workout for Restructuring Debt was arranged by the agreements among representatives from industries and financial institutions. It aims to restructure the debt of a firm which is expected to be reconstructed by the reduction of the debt. Yamamoto 2018: pp. 25–26.
669. Yamamoto et al. 2010: pp. 312–313.
670. As for the duty of care and the duty of loyalty to be taken by the trustee, *see* paras. 401–403 (on the duty of care) and paras. 404–406 (on the duty of loyalty) *infra*.
671. DCJ (Tokyo) Apr. 27, 1981 Hanji 1020-122; DCJ (Tokyo) Apr. 27, 1982 Hanji 1064-79.
672. It is a special law of the Civil Conciliation Law. It aims to dispose of the bad debt of bankrupt companies and the multiple debt of consumers. Yamamoto 2018: p. 32.
673. Yamamoto 2018: pp. 32–38, 47–52.

the reconstruction of the small- and medium-sized companies.[674] The ADR procedure is provided by the Basic Guidelines for Business Implementation by the SMERSC. It is reported that the SMERSC succeeded in achieving the reconstruction plans for 12,098 companies by March 2017 since their establishment in February 2003.[675] They have been playing a crucial role to rehabilitate the local economy through the support of restructuring local SMEs.

A private organization can be a conciliator. For instance, a Special Certified Dispute Resolution Business Operator (SCDRBO) is recognized by the Minister of Economy and Industries from among the Certified Dispute Resolution Business Operators recognized by the Minister of Justice in accordance with the Law on the Promotion of the Use of Alternative Dispute Resolution Procedure (Law No. 151, 2014).[676] The SCDRBO must fulfills requirements provided by the Law on the Strengthening Industrial Competitive Abilities (Law No. 98, 2013). It aims to rehabilitate the business through the conciliation by using the special knowledge of the conciliator.[677] For the bankrupt consumers, the Japan Credit Counseling Organization (JCCO) provides counseling by the counsellors (a lawyer and a consumer life advisor) to make a repayment plan, conclude a compromise contract with the creditor, etc. It has an advantage to provide debtors with educational instructions, which cannot be expected to the ADR procedure led by the court and the administrative organization.[678]

§2. Bankruptcy

334. "Hasan" [the Bankruptcy] is a typical procedure for the purpose of liquidation of a debtor and has been playing a central role in the insolvency process. It is a liquidation process rather than a rehabilitation or reconstruction process of a debtor, and it is regulated by Bankruptcy Law. The purpose of Bankruptcy Law is to specify the procedures for liquidation of property held by a debtor who is unable to pay debts and becomes insolvent and to appropriately coordinate the interests of creditors and other interested persons. It mainly aims to ensure the proper and fair liquidation of debtor's property, but, at the same time, it also aims to secure the opportunity for rehabilitation of debtor's economic life (sections 1 and 2 (1) Bankruptcy Law).[679] For instance, the institution of "menseki" [the discharge, exemption or indemnity] will provide the debtor with the chance to rehabilitate his/her economic life.[680]

674. The SMERSC were established in accordance with the Special Measures Law for Industrial Revitalization and Innovation (Law No. 131, 1999). This special law was a legislation with a specified period of time (to be valid until Mar. 31, 2008, extended until Mar. 31, 2016) and succeeded by the Industrial Competitiveness Enhancement Law (Law No. 98, 2013).
675. Yamamoto 2018: p. 39.
676. The SCDRBO was first introduced by the amendment to the Special Law on the Rehabilitation of Industrial Vitality in 2007.
677. Yamamoto 2018: p. 41.
678. Yamamoto 2018: p. 53.
679. Ito 2006: p. 23.
680. *See* paras. 343–348 *infra*.

335. The bankruptcy procedure shall commence when a debtor becomes unable to pay debts, and the court, upon application, orders commencement of bankruptcy procedure in accordance with section 30 (1) Bankruptcy Law (section 15 (1) Bankruptcy Law).[681] The application for commencement of bankruptcy procedure can be filed by either a creditor or by a debtor (section 18 (1) Bankruptcy Law). If the creditor applies for the procedure, he/she has to make a prima facie proof of the existence of the claim and the constituting grounds for the fact that the debtor is "unable to pay debts" (section 18 (2) Bankruptcy Law), whereas if the debtor applies for the procedure (the self-bankruptcy), the proof is not required, because the fact that the application is made by the debtor can be regarded as the presumption of the grounds for the commencement of bankruptcy procedure.[682] If the application is made against a legal person, such persons may file an application for commencement of bankruptcy as a director of a general incorporated association or a general incorporation foundation, a director of a stock company or a mutual company of the Insurance Business,[683] a managing member of a general partnership company, limited partnership company or limited liability company, and a liquidator of a legal person (section 19 Bankruptcy Law). However, a third person who had established a right of pledge to his/her claim right for the creditor cannot apply for the bankruptcy procedure of the debtor.[684]

336. The bankruptcy procedure shall be processed by a district court before which a bankruptcy case is pending by the application. This court is called "hasan-saibansho" [the bankruptcy court] (section 2 (3) Bankruptcy Law). The jurisdiction is determined by the location of the debtor's property or that of the debtor's business office. If the debtor has engaged in the commercial business, the District Court which has its jurisdiction over the location of the debtor's principal business office may accept the application. If the debtor has engaged in the commercial business and has a principal business office in a foreign country, the jurisdiction is determined by the location of the debtor's principal business office in Japan. If the debtor has not engaged in the commercial business or engaged in commercial business but does not have any business office, the District Court which has its jurisdiction over the location of the debtor's general venue may treat the bankruptcy procedure. If there is no court with jurisdiction to be determined as stated above, the bankruptcy case shall be subject to the jurisdiction of the District Court that has jurisdiction over the location of the debtor's property (section 5 Bankruptcy Law).[685]

---

681. When a debtor "has suspended payment," the debtor shall be presumed to be "unable to pay debts" (s. 15 (2) Bankruptcy Law). However, if the debtor is a juridical person (except for any existing general partnership company and limited partnership company), the term "unable to pay debts" shall be deemed to be replaced with "unable to pay debts or insolvent," which includes the condition in which a debtor is unable to pay its debts in full with its property (s. 16 Bankruptcy Law).
682. Ito 2006: p. 88. It is not always easy for the creditor to prove that the debtor "is unable to pay debts," In practice, if the bill (commercial paper) which was drawn by a debtor is dishonored at a clearing house more than twice within six months, the debtor is deemed to be unable to pay debts. HCD (Fukuoka) Oct. 12, 1977 Hanji 880-42.
683. It is provided by the Insurance Business Law (Law No. 105, 1995).
684. SCD Apr. 16, 1999 Minshu 53-4-740.
685. Ito 2006: pp. 141–148; Yamamoto 2018: p. 71.

If the court finds that the conditions for the commencement of the bankruptcy procedure are met (section 15 (1) Bankruptcy Law), then it shall make an order to commence the procedure and a public announcement (section 32 Bankruptcy Law). At the same time, the bankruptcy court shall appoint one or more "hasan-kanzainin" [the bankruptcy trustee(s)] and specify the period during which proofs of bankruptcy claims should be filed, the date of a creditors meeting that is to be convoked to report the status of the debtor's property, and the period for conducting an investigation of bankruptcy claims (sections 31 and 32 Bankruptcy Law).[686]

By the order of commencement of bankruptcy procedure, properties which belong to the bankrupt debtor shall become "hasan-zaidan" [the bankruptcy estate], for which the bankruptcy trustee has an exclusive right to administer and dispose of it in the bankruptcy procedure (section 2 (14) and (15) Bankruptcy Law). As a result, any law suits concerned with the bankruptcy estate shall be interrupted, because the bankrupt debtor has lost the right to administer and dispose of it (section 44 (1) Bankruptcy Law). A law suit which is not concerned with the bankruptcy claim shall be succeeded by the trustee (section 44 (2) Bankruptcy Law).[687]

337. The bankruptcy trustee(s) appointed by the bankruptcy court shall lead the bankruptcy procedure. On the one hand, the bankruptcy trustee shall succeed the legal status of a bankrupt and may take over the litigation in which the bankrupt had been one of the parties (section 44 (2) Bankruptcy Law).[688]

On the other hand, however, the bankruptcy trustee shall represent the bankruptcy creditors and may exercise the right to terminate a bilateral contract which the bankrupt had not yet completely performed by the commencement of bankruptcy procedure or the right to avoid an action conducted by the bankrupt with the knowledge that it would prejudice bankruptcy creditors (sections 53 and 160 Bankruptcy Law). The legal status of the bankruptcy trustee is regarded as an independent manager.[689] The bankruptcy trustee shall be supervised by the court (section 75 (1) Bankruptcy Law), and the court, upon the application by an interested person or by its own authority, may dismiss a bankruptcy trustee if he/she does not appropriately perform the administration and disposition of property that belongs to the bankruptcy estate, or there are any other material reasons (section 75 (2) Bankruptcy Law). The bankruptcy trustee should bear a duty of care as a good manager.[690]

338. Since the main purpose of bankruptcy procedure is to coordinate the performance of obligations of the bankrupt debtor corresponding to the bankruptcy claims of the creditors from the debtor's properties (bankruptcy estate), it is necessary for the bankruptcy trustee to ascertain the assets and liabilities of the bankrupt debtor. Section 34 (1) Bankruptcy Law provides that "any and all property that

686. Ito 2006: pp. 129–135.
687. Yamamoto 2018: pp. 68–69.
688. Ito 2006: pp. 129–135; Yamamoto 2018: p. 73.
689. SCJ Jan. 14, 2011 Minshu 65-1-1. As for the legal doctrines on the status of the bankruptcy trustee, *see* Ito 2006: pp. 136–140.
690. SCJ Dec. 21, 2006 Minshu 60-10-3964.

the bankrupt holds at the time of commencement of bankruptcy proceedings, irrespective of whether or not it exists in Japan, shall constitute the bankruptcy estate." The bankruptcy estate shall include any claim which may arise in the future and be enforced by the bankrupt based on a cause that has occurred prior to the commencement of bankruptcy procedure (section 34 (2) Bankruptcy Law). For instance, a death insurance claim to be acquired by the bankrupt debtor based on a life insurance contract concluded with an insurance company before the commencement of the bankruptcy procedure should be interpreted to belong to the bankruptcy estate.[691]

339. However, certain properties that may not be seized shall not belong to the bankruptcy estate in principle: section 131 Civil Execution Law provides a series of properties which cannot be seized. They include: (i) clothes, bedclothes, furniture, kitchen utensils, tatami mats and fittings that are indispensable for the living of the obligor, etc.; (ii) food and fuel necessary for one-month living of the obligor, etc.; (iii) money in the amount specified by a Cabinet Order by taking into account an average household's necessary living expenses for two months;[692] (iv) equipment, fertilizers, work animals and their feeds that are indispensable for agriculture as well as seeds and any similar agricultural products that are indispensable for continuing agriculture until the next harvest of a person who engages in agriculture mainly through his/her own labor; (v) fish nets and any other fishing equipment, baits, juvenile fish and any similar fishery products that are indispensable for capturing or farming fishery products of a person who engages in fisheries mainly through his/her own labor; (vi) equipment or any other objects (excluding products) that are indispensable for the work of a technician, an artisan, a laborer or any other person who engages in an occupation or business mainly through his/her own intellectual or physical labor (excluding those prescribed in the preceding two items); (vii) a registered seal or any other seal that is indispensable for an occupation or living; (viii) a Buddha statue, an ancestral memorial table or other object that is indispensable for direct use in a religious service or worship; (ix) a family tree, a diary, commercial books and any similar documents that are necessary for the obligor; (x) a medal or any other object representing honor received by the obligor or his/her relative; (xi) documents and equipment necessary for the debtor, etc. in learning at school or any other educational institution; (xii) any object pertaining to an invention or a copyright work that has yet to be made public; (xiii) a prosthetic arm or hand, a prosthetic leg or foot or any other object used for supplementing body that is necessary for the obligor, etc.; (xiv) firefighting machinery or equipment, fire escape equipment and any other supplies that are required to be put in place in a building or any other structure pursuant to the provisions of laws and regulations for the purpose of preventing disasters or for security.

Section 34 (3) [2] Bankruptcy Law provides that property which may not be seized shall not constitute the bankruptcy estate. However, as for the money which is provided by section 131 [3] Civil Execution Law as above, the amount of 1.5 times of that money shall not belong to the bankruptcy estate (section 34 (3) [1]

---

691. SCJ Apr. 28, 2016 Minshu 70-4-1099.
692. It is JPY 660,000.

Bankruptcy Law).[693] In addition, if the court may, upon application, permit seizure of any of the properties listed in section 131 as above taking into consideration the living conditions of the debtor and the creditors and any other circumstances, then those properties belong to the bankruptcy estate (section 34 (3) [2] Bankruptcy Law).[694]

Besides, a claim to be exclusively attributed to the person of the bankrupt debtor shall not be seized so that it does not belong to the bankruptcy estate. For instance, a claim of the bankrupt debtor for compensation for mental loss caused by defamation should not belong to the bankruptcy estate if the concrete amount of the claim has yet to be determined.[695]

340. A creditor who holds a claim against the bankrupt debtor from a cause that has been created before the commencement of bankruptcy procedure, which is called "hasan-saiken" [the bankruptcy claim] (sections 2 (5) and 97 Bankruptcy Law), may participate in the bankruptcy procedure and will have distribution in that procedure in accordance with the amount of the bankruptcy claim (sections 100 and 103 Bankruptcy Law).[696] A voluntary payment by a debtor from some money which the debtor earned after the commencement of the bankruptcy procedure to a certain creditor of the bankruptcy claim was held to be valid. However, if the creditor required the debtor to pay by any compulsory measure, the payment must be invalid and returned to the debtor.[697]

However, creditors who have a bankruptcy claim for which any general priority right such as a general right of lien on a property that belongs to the bankruptcy estate shall have priority over other bankruptcy claims (section 98 (1) Bankruptcy Law).

In addition, a creditor who has a bankruptcy claim for which a special right of lien, a pledge or a hypothec on a property that belongs to the bankruptcy estate, that is called "betsujo-ken" [the right of separate satisfaction] may exercise it separately from the bankruptcy procedure (sections 2 (9) and 65 (1) Bankruptcy Law). But the creditor can participate in the bankruptcy procedure only for the estimated amount of the bankruptcy claim which will be unable to collect by exercising the right of separate satisfaction (section 108 Bankruptcy Law).

341. A creditor who acquired a claim caused by the contribution to the bankruptcy procedure such as a claim for reimbursement of expenses for the administration, disposition and distribution of the bankruptcy estate can be paid from the bankruptcy estate at any time after the due date without following the bankruptcy

693. It is around JPY 990,000.
694. Ito 2006: pp. 171–174; Yamamoto 2018: pp. 141–142.
695. SCJ Oct. 6, 1983 Minshu 37-8-1041.
696. When both a debtor and a guarantor became bankrupt and the bankruptcy procedure commenced for each of them, a creditor can participate in each bankruptcy procedure in accordance with the full amount of the claim (s. 104 Bankruptcy Law). The creditor is not required to reduce the amount of bankruptcy claim in the guarantor's bankruptcy procedure even if that creditor acquired certain distribution from the debtor's bankruptcy procedure, though the total amount of distribution must be within the amount of bankruptcy claim.
697. SCJ Jan. 23, 2006 Minshu 60-1-228.

procedure. This claim is called "zaidan-saiken" [the claim on the bankruptcy estate] and it shall be paid in preference to the bankruptcy claims (sections 2 (7), 148 (1) [2] and 151 Bankruptcy Law).

The scope of "zaidan-saiken" [the claim on the bankruptcy estate] has been extended by the provisions of law. It includes certain tax claims,[698] claims for salaries of employee, etc. For instance, a claim for salary of an employee of the bankrupt debtor for three months preceding the commencement of bankruptcy procedure is recognized as a claim on the estate (section 149 Bankruptcy Law).

342. The right to administer and dispose of the bankruptcy estate shall exclusively belong to the bankruptcy trustee since the commencement of the bankruptcy procedure (section 78 (1) Bankruptcy Law). Under this authority the bankruptcy trustee shall become the party of juridical act concerned with the bankrupt estate.[699] For instance, the bankruptcy trustee can choose either to exercise a right and perform an obligation created by a contract concluded between a bankrupt debtor and a third party before the commencement of bankruptcy procedure or to terminate the contract if both the right and the obligation has yet to be exercised and performed (section 53 (1) Bankruptcy Law).

The bankruptcy trustee has a right to deny the validity of a contract and other actions made by the bankrupt debtor and a beneficiary before the commencement of bankruptcy procedure (sections 160–176 Bankruptcy Law). This right is called "hinin-ken" [the right to deny the validity of action]. It aims to restore the bankrupt estate to make a fair distribution from the bankrupt estate to the creditors.[700]

Before the distribution, the bankrupt trustee has to investigate and determine the bankrupt claims, and investigate, administer and dispose of the bankrupt estate. In order to determine the bankruptcy claims, the holder of a bankrupt claim is required to notice to the bankrupt court about the amount and the cause of his/her claim (section 111 Bankruptcy Law).[701]

After the determination of the bankruptcy claims (section 124 Bankruptcy Law), the bankruptcy trustee makes a distribution at every appropriate timing before the final distribution. It is called "chukan-haito" [the interim distribution]. When the bankruptcy trustee finds that there exists any money suitable for a distribution which belongs to the bankruptcy estate after the ordinary period for investigation of assets and liabilities has expired or the ordinary date of the investigation has ended for properties which belong to the bankruptcy estate, the distribution can be made (section 209 (1) Bankruptcy Law).[702]

698. A tax claim can be recognized as the claim of the bankruptcy estate only if it is not due date or within one year after the due date at the commencement of bankruptcy procedure (s. 148 (1) [3] Bankruptcy Law).
699. Ito 2006: pp. 252–292; Yamamoto 2018: pp. 88–99.
700. Ito 2006: pp. 369–427; Yamamoto 2018: pp. 109–120.
701. Ito 2006: pp. 433–463; Yamamoto 2018: pp. 120–123.
702. It is necessary for the bankruptcy trustee to obtain permission of the bankruptcy court before making the interim distribution (s. 209 (2) Bankruptcy Law).

When the disposition of the bankruptcy estate to turn it into money completed, the bankruptcy trustee shall make "saishu-haito" [the final distribution] to holders of filed bankruptcy claims without delay (section 195 (1) Bankruptcy Law).[703]

343. A bankrupt debtor "who is an individual" may file an application to the bankruptcy court for grant of "menseki" [the discharge, exemption or indemnity] within a period between the application for commencement of bankruptcy procedure and one month after the order of commencement of bankruptcy procedure (section 248 (1) Bankruptcy Law). This institution of "menseki" [the discharge] was first introduced into the Japanese bankruptcy law in 1952 under the strong influence of the U.S. federal insolvency law to rehabilitate the individual bankrupt.[704]

The applicant for grant of discharge has to submit a list of holders of dischargeable claims stating such matters as specified by the Rules of the Supreme Court (section 248 (3) Bankruptcy Law). It is noted that when a debtor has filed an application for commencement of bankruptcy procedure, he/she shall be deemed to have filed an application for grant of discharge upon filing the application for bankruptcy procedure unless he/she manifested his/her intention to the contrary (section 248 (4) Bankruptcy Law).

When the application for grant of discharge was filed and it found that the expenses for the bankruptcy procedure would not be reimbursed from debtor's property so that an order of discontinuance or termination of bankruptcy procedure is made, the compulsory execution, provisional seizure, and provisional disposition based on the bankruptcy claims shall not be initiated and those which had already proceeded shall be stayed (section 249 (1) Bankruptcy Law). And when the order of grant of discharge becomes final, the compulsory execution and other procedures which had been stayed shall become invalid (section 249 (2) Bankruptcy Law). This is the result of the amendment to the Bankruptcy Law to strengthen the protection of the bankrupt who has applied for discharge.[705]

344. The bankruptcy court shall make an order of grant of discharge if the bankrupt debtor falls under none of those negative requirements for the order as follow (section 252 (1) Bankruptcy Law):[706]

(i) The bankrupt, for the purpose of harming his/her creditors, has concealed or damaged property which belongs or should belong to the bankruptcy estate, disposed of such property in a manner disadvantageous to creditors or conducted any other act that would unduly reduce the value of the bankruptcy estate.

---

703. The bankruptcy trustee has to obtain permission of a court clerk in order to make a final distribution (s. 195 (2) Bankruptcy Law).

704. It was held that the institution of "menseki" [the discharge] was not against Art. 29 CJ (the guarantee of private property), because it should contribute to maintain the public interest by facilitating rehabilitation of the individual bankrupt and earlier application for the commencement of bankruptcy procedure, which will enable to avoid the worst matter. SCD Dec. 13, 1961 Minshu 15-11-2803.

705. Yamamoto 2018: pp. 143–147.

706. Ito 2006: pp. 522–529.

(ii) The bankrupt, for the purpose of delaying the commencement of bankruptcy procedure, has assumed a debt under extremely disadvantageous conditions or purchased goods on credit and disposed of them under extremely disadvantageous conditions.
(iii) The bankrupt, for the purpose of giving a special benefit to a specific creditor to whom he/she owes a debt or for harming other creditors, has conducted an act concerning the provision of security or extinguishment of debt which is not included in the scope of a debtor's obligation in terms of the act itself or the method or time of performance of the act.
(iv) The bankrupt, by conducting extravagant spending, gambling or any other speculative act, has significantly reduced his/her property or assumed excessive debts.
(v) During the period between one year before the application for commencement of bankruptcy procedure and the order of commencement of bankruptcy procedure, the bankrupt, knowing that there is a fact constituting the grounds for the commencement of bankruptcy procedure, has acquired property on credit by fraudulent means so as to make the other party believe that there is no such fact.
(vi) The bankrupt has destroyed, forged or altered books, documents or any other objects concerning the status of his/her business and property.
(vii) The bankrupt has submitted a false list of holders of dischargeable claims.
(viii) The bankrupt has refused to give an explanation or given a false explanation in the investigation conducted by the bankruptcy court in bankruptcy procedure.
(ix) The bankrupt, by fraudulent means, has obstructed the performance of duties of a bankruptcy trustee, provisional administrator, bankruptcy trustee representative or provisional administrator representative.
(x) The application for grant of discharge is filed within seven years from the day on which the order of grant of discharge for the same bankrupt was made and became final and binding, or the day on which the rehabilitation plan for a salaried worker, etc. (section 239 (1) Civil Rehabilitation Law)[707] was executed for the same bankrupt.
(xi) The bankrupt has breached his/her duties provided in Bankruptcy Law.

Besides, even if the bankrupt falls under any of the negative requirements as listed above, the bankruptcy court may make an order of grant of discharge, when it finds it to be appropriate by taking into consideration of all the circumstances (section 252 (2) Bankruptcy Law).[708]

345. When the order of grant of discharge becomes final and binding, "the bankrupt debtor shall be discharged from liabilities for bankruptcy claims" (section 253 (1) Main Text Bankruptcy Law). The meaning of "discharged from liabilities" is disputed in the legal doctrines. The majority opinion understands that the obligation

707. As for the civil rehabilitation, *see* §3 *infra*.
708. Ito 2006: p. 529; Yamamoto 2018: p. 147.

remains to be as a natural obligation so that if the bankrupt debtor performs voluntarily his/her obligation to a holder of the bankruptcy claim, it should be valid.[709] But the dissenting opinion recognizes the extinction of obligation as an effect of the discharge. According to this opinion, the holder of the bankruptcy claim cannot ask the bankrupt debtor to pay voluntarily, and if the creditor receives any payment from the debtor, it should be returned as an unjust enrichment.[710]

However, the following claims are not be discharged (section 253 (1) Bankruptcy Law):[711]

(a) A claim for tax excluding a claim for a foreign tax subject to mutual assistance;
(b) A claim for compensation for damages due to a tort action which harmed the life or body of another that the bankrupt debtor has committed intentionally or by gross negligence, or a tort which the bankrupt debtor has committed in bad faith;
(c) A claim arising from certain duties such as: (i) the duty to cooperate and provide mutual assistance between husband and wife (section 752 CC), (ii) the duty to share expenses arising from marriage (section 760 CC), (iii) the duty concerning the custody of a child (section 766 CC and sections 749, 771 and 788 CC), (iv) the duty to support for certain relatives (section from 877 to 880 CC), (v) the duties arising from any contract concerned with those duties as (i) to (iv) above.
(d) A claim of an employee and a claim for return of an employee's deposit, which have arisen from an employment relationship;
(e) A claim which the bankrupt has not stated knowingly in the list of holders of dischargeable claims excluding a claim held by a person who knew that an order of commencement of bankruptcy procedure for that bankrupt had been made;
(f) A claim for a fine, etc.

346. As an effect of the commencement of bankruptcy procedure, the bankrupt debtor has certain disadvantages such as a certain disqualification. There is no comprehensive list of the disqualification in Bankruptcy Law, provisions of separate laws disqualify or limit the capacity of the bankrupt debtor. For example, the bankrupt cannot become a lawyer, certified public accountant, tax accountant, patent attorney, etc. Besides, he/she may not become a guardian, testamentary executor, director of a juridical person, etc. However, the provision which had disqualified the bankrupt debtor as a director of a company has been deleted so as to facilitate his/her revitalization and to promote the business of the company.[712]

347. While it has been controversial whether and how these limitations on the bankrupt debtor's activities should be reduced, it is necessary for the bankrupt debtor to have restoration of his/her rights so as to promote the rehabilitation of the individual debtor. The bankrupt debtor may restore his/her original qualification

709. Yamamoto 2018: p. 148.
710. Ito 2006: pp. 532–534.
711. Ito 2006: pp. 534–537; Yamamoto 2018: p. 148.
712. Yamamoto 2018: p. 149. *See also* s. 331 Company Law.

with or without application. The bankrupt debtor's rights shall be restored without application if any of the following facts occur (section 255 (1) Bankruptcy Law):[713]

(i) Where an order of grant of discharge has become final and binding;
(ii) Where the order of discontinuance of bankruptcy procedure (section 218 (1) Bankruptcy Law) has become final and binding;
(iii) Where the order of confirmation of the rehabilitation plan has become final and binding; or
(iv) Where ten years have elapsed after the order of commencement of bankruptcy procedure was made, and the bankrupt has not been given a final and binding judgment of conviction for the crime (section 265 Bankruptcy Law) during this period.

348. The bankrupt debtor may restore his/her original qualification by his/her application to the bankruptcy court. When the bankrupt debtor became free from all the liabilities for the bankrupt creditors by payment or any other means,[714] the bankruptcy court has to make the order of restoration of the bankrupt debtor's original qualification in response to the application filed by the bankrupt debtor (section 256 (1) Bankruptcy Law). Against the order of restoration by the bankruptcy court, the immediate appeal may be filed. When the order of restoration becomes final and binding, the original qualification of the bankrupt shall be restored (sections 256 (5) and 255 (1) Bankruptcy Law).[715]

§3. Civil Rehabilitation

I. Overview

349. The Civil Rehabilitation Law was promulgated in December 1999 and came into effect in April 2000. The purpose of this law is to ensure the rehabilitation of economic life of a debtor from financial difficulties by formulating rehabilitation plans which are to be approved by creditors and confirmed by the court so as to appropriately coordinate rights and duties between the debtor and creditors. It is different from the bankruptcy procedure in that the major purpose of the civil rehabilitation is to rehabilitate a debtor and, therefore, the debtor shall administer the rehabilitation procedure (Debtor in Possession: DIP), while the major purpose of the bankruptcy is to liquidate the debtor's properties and its procedure is administered by the bankruptcy trustee as a liquidator. It is also different from the corporate reorganization procedure regulated by the Corporate Reorganization Law in that the corporate reorganization is only applied to stock companies and its procedure is administered by the trustee appointed by the court. The Civil Rehabilitation Law was enacted in 1999 mainly for the reconstruction of small- and medium-sized

713. Ito 2006: p. 541; Yamamoto 2018: p. 150.
714. The grounds for the liberalization from all the liabilities will include payment, exemption, completion of the period for extinctive prescription (limitation period), etc. Ito 2006: p. 542.
715. Ito 2006: pp. 541–542; Yamamoto 2018: p. 150.

enterprises. In addition, it was amended in 2000 in order to extend its coverage over the rehabilitation of individual consumers. The amended Civil Rehabilitation Law which added special provisions on Home Loan Claims (Chapter 10) and those on Rehabilitation for Individuals with Small-Scale Debts and Rehabilitation for Salaried Workers, etc. (Chapter 13) was promulgated in November 2000 and took into effect in April 2001.[716]

II. Application for Commencement of Corporate Rehabilitation Procedure

350. Even if a risk which may be the ground for the commencement of bankruptcy procedure[717] would occur for a debtor,[718] the debtor and a creditor can file an application for the commencement of rehabilitation procedure to the court. In addition, the debtor can file the application for commencement of rehabilitation procedure when the debtor is unable to pay his/her debts which are due "without causing significant hindrance to the continuation of his/her business" (section 21 (1) and (2) Civil Rehabilitation Law). If the court recognizes that one of these requirements is met and that there exist no reasons to dismiss the application as provided by section 25 of the Civil Rehabilitation Law, it shall make an order of the commencement of rehabilitation procedure, and the order shall become effective from when it is made (section 33 (1) and (2) Civil Rehabilitation Law).[719]

According to section 25 Civil Rehabilitation Law, the application shall be dismissed with prejudice on the merit in any of the following cases:[720] (i) when the expenses for the rehabilitation procedure are not prepaid;[721] (ii) when the bankruptcy procedure or the special liquidation procedure are pending before the court, and the court recognizes that either the bankruptcy or the special liquidation procedure conforms better to the common interests of creditors than the rehabilitation procedure; (iii) when it is obvious that a rehabilitation plan is unlikely to be prepared or approved or the rehabilitation plan is unlikely to be authorized by the court; and (iv) when the application for the commencement of rehabilitation procedure is filed for an unjustifiable purpose or it is not filed in good faith. The last one aims to dismiss the abused application.[722]

When the court has made the order of commencement of rehabilitation procedure, it has to immediately make a public notice of the main text of the order and give a notice of that main text to the rehabilitation creditors who have been known to the court (section 35 Civil Rehabilitation Law).

---

716. Yamamoto et al. 2010: pp. 28–29; Yamamoto 2018: pp. 152–155.
717. *See* para. 335 *supra*.
718. From para. 350 to para. 358, a debtor means a corporate debtor such as, typically, a small- or medium-sized company. As for the rehabilitation procedure for an individual debtor, *see* paras. 359 and 360 *infra*.
719. Yamamoto 2018: pp. 155–157.
720. Yamamoto et al. 2010: pp. 409–410; Yamamoto 2018: pp. 161–162.
721. In order to apply for the commencement of rehabilitation procedure, the applicant has to prepay an amount designated by the court as expenses for rehabilitation procedure as provided by s. 24 Civil Rehabilitation Law.
722. HCD (Tokyo) Mar. 9, 2012 Hanji 2151-9.

351. Even after the rehabilitation procedure is commenced, the rehabilitation debtor keeps the right to carry out his/her business or administer or dispose of his/her property irrespective of whether it exists in Japan or not (section 38 (1) Civil Rehabilitation Law). This is one of the salient characteristics of the rehabilitation procedure, which is called the DIP (Debtor in Possession) type of insolvency procedure. It aims to facilitate the efforts of the debtor to promote rehabilitation.[723] The rehabilitation debtor has a duty to exercise that right and conduct rehabilitation procedure in a fair and sincere manner (section 38 (2) Civil Rehabilitation Law).

For that purpose, once the order of commencement of rehabilitation procedure is issued, it is not allowed to apply for any other insolvency procedure such as a commencement of bankruptcy or special liquidation procedure, or to enforce compulsory execution based on a rehabilitation claim. If these procedures have already been initiated against the rehabilitation debtor, the bankruptcy procedure and compulsory execution shall be stayed, and the special liquidation procedure shall become invalid by the effect of the commencement of rehabilitation procedure (section 39 (1) Civil Rehabilitation Law).[724]

352. The rehabilitation procedure is promoted by the rehabilitation debtor. But it is supervised by the court. When the court finds it necessary, it may require the permission of the court for disposition of a property, acquisition of a property and other actions as specified by the provision of law (section 41 (1) Civil Rehabilitation Law).[725]

The court, when it finds it necessary, may appoint one or more supervisors by issuing a supervision order and designate certain actions for which the rehabilitation debtor may not conduct without obtaining the supervisor's consent (section 54 (1) and (2) Civil Rehabilitation Law). The supervision order may also be issued upon the application by an interested person (section 54 (1) Civil Rehabilitation Law).[726] In practice, the court tends to issue the supervision order rather than requires the court permission as stated above.[727] Normally lawyers and/or authorized public accountants are appointed as supervisors. The supervisor(s) shall also supervise the execution of the rehabilitation plan by the rehabilitation debtor (section 186 (2) Civil Rehabilitation Law).[728]

353. When the court makes an order of commencement of rehabilitation procedure, it has to specify a period during which proofs of "saisei-saiken" [the rehabilitation claims] should be filed and the period for conducting the investigation of

723. Yamamoto 2018: p. 163.
724. Yamamoto 2018: p. 164.
725. The action made without the permission of the court shall be void (s. 41 (2) Main Text Civil Rehabilitation Law). However, it cannot be opposable against a third party who did not know that the action was made without the court's permission (a third party in good faith: s. 41 (2) Proviso Civil Rehabilitation Law).
726. The action conducted by the rehabilitation debtor without the supervisor's consent shall be void (s. 54 (4) Main Text Civil Rehabilitation Law). However, it may not be asserted against a third party who did not know that the action was conducted without the supervisor's consent (a third party in good faith: s. 54 (4) Proviso Civil Rehabilitation Law).
727. Yamamoto 2018: p. 166.
728. Yamamoto et al. 2010: pp. 420–421; Yamamoto 2018: pp. 167–168.

rehabilitation claims (section 34 (1) Civil Rehabilitation Law). The rehabilitation claims shall include claims for property interests against the rehabilitation debtor which had been created before the commencement of rehabilitation procedure (section 84 (1) Civil Rehabilitation Law). If A sold a piece of land to B before the commencement of rehabilitation procedure, but the transfer of ownership was registered after its commencement, B cannot acquire ownership of that land unless B was in good faith, that is, the rehabilitation procedure had commenced when B registered the title (section 45 Civil Rehabilitation Law).[729]

After the commencement of rehabilitation procedure, it is not allowed for the rehabilitation debtor to make or receive payment or conduct any other actions which will cause the rehabilitation claims to be extinguished except as provided by the Civil Rehabilitation Law (section 85 (1) Civil Rehabilitation Law). Exceptions provided by the Civil Rehabilitation Law are as follows:

> [1] "Shogaku-saiken" [the small amount claims] can be paid by the rehabilitation debtor (Sec. 85 (5) Civil Rehabilitation Law), because it contributes to the reduction of the number of rehabilitation creditors and the reconstruction of the debtor's business.[730]
>
> [2] The court may permit the rehabilitation debtor to pay a certain claim in whole or in part when small or medium-sized enterprises whose major trading partner is that rehabilitation debtor are likely to suffer significant hindrance to the continuation of their business unless they receive payment of their claim even before the authorization of the rehabilitation plan (Sec. 85 (2) Civil Rehabilitation Law). It is based on the social policy to prevent the chain of bankruptcies.[731]

"Saisei-saikensha" [the rehabilitation creditor: the creditor who intends to participate in the rehabilitation procedure] has to file a proof of his/her claims to the court within the period as specified in the order of commencement of rehabilitation procedure with regard to the content, amount and cause of claims, the expected shortfall, the amount of voting right, etc. (section 94 Civil Rehabilitation Law).[732]

354. The rehabilitation debtor has to prepare a draft of rehabilitation plan and submit it to the court within the period specified by the court after the expiration of the period for filing a proof of rehabilitation claims (section 163 (1) Civil Rehabilitation Law). When the proposed rehabilitation plan is submitted, the court checks whether the period for investigation has expired and certain reports are prepared

---

729. This rule for the transfer of immovable property and ship (s. 45 Civil Rehabilitation Law) was applied to the automobile transaction (a reservation of ownership) which could be valid only if the contract and the registration had been completed before the commencement of rehabilitation procedure. SCJ Jun. 4, 2010 Minshu 64-4-1107.
730. Yamamoto 2018: p. 165.
731. Yamamoto 2018: p. 165.
732. Details are specified by the Rules of the Supreme Court. The amount of voting right shall be determined in accordance with the kind of claims (s. 87 Civil Rehabilitation Law).

required by the law. Then it makes an order to refer the draft of rehabilitation plan to a resolution by the meeting of rehabilitation creditors (section 169 (1) Civil Rehabilitation Law).

The draft of rehabilitation plan must be approved by: (i) the majority of holders of voting right and (ii) the amount of voting right which is not less than a half of the total amount (section 172-3 (1) Civil Rehabilitation Law). However, if the number of the voting rights holders are manipulated by the division of rehabilitation claims or any other means which aim exclusively to collect the majority of voters, it may be recognized as an illegal resolution that will lead to the rejection of the proposed rehabilitation plan by the court.[733]

355. When the draft of rehabilitation plan is approved by the meeting of rehabilitation creditors, then the court has to make an order of confirmation of the rehabilitation plan except in the following cases, for which the court has to make an order of disconfirmation of the rehabilitation plan: (i) when the rehabilitation procedure or the draft rehabilitation plan contravenes provisions of law and that defect is not a minor one so that it cannot be corrected; (ii) when the rehabilitation plan is unlikely to be executed; (iii) when the resolution at the creditors meeting on the draft of rehabilitation plan has been adopted by unlawful means;[734] or (iv) when the resolution on the proposed rehabilitation plan is contrary to the common interests of rehabilitation creditors[735] (section 174 (1) Civil Rehabilitation Law). The rehabilitation plan becomes effective when an order of confirmation is made by the court and thus it becomes final and binding (section 176 Civil Rehabilitation Law).

356. Once the rehabilitation plan becomes final and binding by the court's order, the rehabilitation claims which had been filed by the creditors and those recognized by the debtor shall be altered in accordance with the rehabilitation plan (section 179 Civil Rehabilitation Law). The rehabilitation debtor shall be discharged from liabilities for all claims except for the rehabilitation claims which had been recorded in the rehabilitation plan (section 178 Civil Rehabilitation Law). This is called "menseki-teki-koryoku" [the discharging effect] of the rehabilitation plan.[736] As a result, the rehabilitation claims which had not been filed by the creditors to the court shall become ineffective.

However, the discharging effect of the rehabilitation plan does not apply to certain claims such as: (i) a rehabilitation claim for which the rehabilitation creditor was unable to file a proof within the period as specified in the rehabilitation plan due to the ground which was not attributable to the creditor, (ii) a rehabilitation

733. SCJ Mar. 13, 2008 Minshu 62-3-860.
734. The case referred to in the previous footnote (SCJ Mar. 13, 2008 Minshu 62-3-860) was an example of Item (iii).
735. Item (iv) above would include the case where the bankruptcy procedure will probably be more advantageous for creditors than the rehabilitation procedure. It aims to protect the interest of the minority number of creditors. HCJ (Tokyo) Jul. 25, 2003 Kinsho 1173-9.
736. However, security measures such as a surety, pledge, and hypothec which had been established to secure the rehabilitation claim shall not be affected by the confirmation of rehabilitation plan and its discharging effect (s. 177 (2) Civil Rehabilitation Law). This exceptional provision was held to be constitutional. SCJ (FB) Jun. 10, 1970 Minshu 24-6-499.

claim that has arisen after the order of confirmation of the rehabilitation plan is issued, (iii) a rehabilitation claim which had not been recorded by the rehabilitation debtor in bad faith. These claims can be included in the rehabilitation plan by modifying it (section 181 (1) Civil Rehabilitation Law). Besides, the additional exceptions to the discharging effect can be stipulated in the rehabilitation plan in advance.[737]

357. The rehabilitation debtor has to execute the rehabilitation plan promptly, when the court issued an order of confirmation of the rehabilitation plan. If a supervisor of the rehabilitation procedure was appointed by the court,[738] the supervisor shall supervise the execution of the rehabilitation plan (section 186 (1) and (2) Civil Rehabilitation Law). In this case, the rehabilitation plan can be finalized after three years from the confirmation unless it is completely implemented (section 188 (2) Civil Rehabilitation Law). It would be necessary to restructure the business and secure the reward to be paid to the supervisor(s).[739]

If the clauses of the confirmed rehabilitation plan are recorded in "saisei-saikensha-hyo" [the list of rehabilitation creditors] by the court clerk, the record shall have the same effect as a final judgment against the rehabilitation debtor. Consequently, if the rehabilitation debtor fails to perform any obligation as it is provided in the rehabilitation plan, the rehabilitation creditor may execute the rehabilitation claim according to the clauses of the rehabilitation plan (section 180 (1), (2) and (3) Civil Rehabilitation Law). This is the advantage of the rehabilitation creditors in the rehabilitation procedure.[740]

The court may decide the end of the rehabilitation procedure. It must be after the rehabilitation plan has been completely implemented or three years have passed since the confirmation of the rehabilitation plan was issued, if the supervisor(s) had been appointed (section 188 (2) Civil Rehabilitation Law). Even if the rehabilitation plan has yet to be executed, the rehabilitation debtor can be expected to continue to implement the rehabilitation plan after three years from its confirmation.[741]

358. The Civil Rehabilitation Law was amended in November 2000 to introduce special provisions concerned with individual rehabilitation for the debtor of the housing loan claims in Chapter 10, and for the debtor of the small-scale claims and for the salaried workers, etc. in Chapter 13 in response to the tendency of increasing insolvency of individuals due to the long-standing economic recessions after the burst of the bubble economy.[742]

---

737. SCJ Mar. 1, 2011 Hanji 2114-52.
738. The supervisor(s) may be appointed by the court after the application of the commencement of rehabilitation procedure, and the court may specify the actions for which the rehabilitation debtor is required to have a consent by the supervisor(s). Any actions made by the rehabilitation debtor without the consent of the supervisor(s) shall be void unless the other party was in good faith (s. 54 Civil Rehabilitation Law). In most cases, the lawyer(s) and public accountant(s) are appointed as the supervisor(s). Yamamoto 2018: pp. 167–168.
739. Yamamoto 2018: p. 203.
740. Yamamoto et al. 2010: pp. 447–448; Yamamoto 2018: p. 202.
741. Yamamoto et al. 2010: pp. 448–449.
742. Yamamoto et al. 2010: pp. 534–581; Yamamoto 2018: pp. 206–233.

With regard to a housing loan claim, a rehabilitation plan may specify special clauses on housing loan which will modify the whole or part of the housing loan claim of a rehabilitation creditor (sections 196 [4] and 198 (1) Civil Rehabilitation Law). Those special clauses on housing loan may include: (i) provision of providing an additional period for the delayed payment within five years, (ii) provision of rescheduling the whole payment plan to be extended up to ten years from the final due date in the original payment plan and the age of the rehabilitation debtor as of the final due date as modified by the special clauses shall not exceed seventy years, (iii) provision of a grace period to pay only the principal by rearranging the amount of payment of it in part with paying the agreed interest, or (iv) provision of any other modification to which the consent is obtained from any person who is subject to the modification of rights by the special clauses on housing loan (section 199 Civil Rehabilitation Law).[743]

A proposed rehabilitation plan which includes those special clauses on housing loan may be submitted only by the rehabilitation debtor. However, the rehabilitation debtor has to consult with the creditors of the housing loan claim (section 200 (1) Civil Rehabilitation Law; section 101 Regulation on Civil Rehabilitation). In the creditors meeting to adopt the draft of a rehabilitation plan, a creditor of the housing loan claim and a guarantee company who has acquired a right of reimbursement on the basis of the guarantee for the debt for the housing loan claim do not have any voting right (section 201 (1) Civil Rehabilitation Law). If the draft of the rehabilitation plan that specifies special clauses on housing loan is adopted in the creditors meeting, the court shall issue an order of confirmation of the rehabilitation plan and thus it will become final and binding.[744]

However, the court may, in addition to the general causes of a disconfirmation order of the rehabilitation plan as stated above,[745] the court also has to issue a disconfirmation of the rehabilitation plan in the following cases: (i) when the rehabilitation plan cannot be found feasible for execution; or (ii) when the rehabilitation debtor is likely to lose his/her ownership in the residence or the right to use the land, which is currently used to own the house (section 202 (1) Civil Rehabilitation Law). If the rehabilitation plan which includes the special clauses as mentioned above is feasible, the court may order the suspension of the execution of the right of hypothec established on the house and/or on the land by specifying the reasonable suspension period (section 197 (1) Civil Rehabilitation Law). But, if the rehabilitation plan is not feasible, there should be no justifiable reason for the court to prevent the creditor of the housing loan to execute the right of hypothec.[746]

743. Yamamoto et al. 2010: pp. 575–578.
744. Yamamoto et al. 2010: pp. 578–579.
745. *See* the grounds for disconfirmation order by the court in para. 355 *supra*.
746. Yamamoto et al. 2010: pp. 574, 579.

III. Special Provisions on Rehabilitation for Individuals Who Bear Small-Scale Debts

359. If an individual debtor is likely to earn income continuously or regularly in the future and the total amount of rehabilitation claims owed by him/her (excluding the amount of the housing loan claims, the amount of rehabilitation claims for which payment is expected to be received by exercising a right of separate satisfaction, and the amount of claims for a fine, etc. arising prior to the commencement of rehabilitation procedure) is not more than JPY 50 million, he/she may apply for the implementation of rehabilitation procedure subject to the special provisions on rehabilitation for individuals with small-scale debts (section 221 (1), (2) Civil Rehabilitation Law).[747]

If the court issued the order to commence the rehabilitation procedure, only the rehabilitation debtor may submit the rehabilitation plan (section 238 Civil Rehabilitation Law). In the rehabilitation plan, the content of any alteration of rights shall be equal among rehabilitation creditors except when any special agreement is made between the debtor and creditors. An extension period of the term for debt under the clauses that alter the rights of rehabilitation creditors, unless otherwise agreed as stated above, shall be made based on an installment payment plan, in which the due date shall come more than once in every three months, and the final due date must be fixed within three years (or within five years in cases where any special circumstances are to be found) since the date of the order of confirmation of the rehabilitation plan by the court (section 229 (1) and (2) Civil Rehabilitation Law). These provisions aim to prevent the rehabilitation debtor to make the rehabilitation plan to be unreasonably disadvantageous to the creditors.[748]

The rehabilitation procedure for individuals who bear small-scale debts shall end with the confirmation of the rehabilitation plan (section 233 Civil Rehabilitation Law). There is no supervision process by any third party after the confirmation of the rehabilitation plan. In this sense, the implementation measure of the rehabilitation plan is fairly weak in exchange of the simplicity of the procedure.[749] If the rehabilitation debtor fails to perform the payment in accordance with the rehabilitation plan, the rehabilitation plan may be rescinded by the court (section 189 (1) Civil Rehabilitation Law).

IV. Special Provisions on Rehabilitation for Salaried Workers, Etc.

360. If the individual debtor who is eligible to apply for the commencement of rehabilitation procedure subject to the special provisions on rehabilitation for individuals who bear small-scale debts in accordance as stated above[750] is likely to receive salary or earn similar regular income including a pension and the amount of the salary or income is expected to fluctuate only within a small range, may apply

747. Yamamoto et al. 2010: pp. 559–560.
748. Yamamoto et al. 2010: pp. 566–569.
749. Yamamoto et al. 2010: p. 569.
750. *See* para. 359 *supra*.

for the implementation of rehabilitation procedure subject to the special provisions on rehabilitation for salaried workers, pensioners, etc. (section 239 (1) Civil Rehabilitation Law).[751] The reason for providing the special rules for the salaried workers, etc. is that it is fairly easy to calculate the personal income of the salaried workers, etc., which is the basis for arranging the rehabilitation plan.[752]

The proposed rehabilitation plan needs not to be adopted in the creditors meeting, and it becomes final and binding when the court issues an order of confirmation of a draft of rehabilitation plan. This is the central feature of the rehabilitation procedure for salaried workers, etc. as a special procedure of the rehabilitation for individuals who bear small-scale debts.[753]

However, if the draft of rehabilitation plan is submitted, the court shall hear from creditors who have filed rehabilitation claims whether or not the proposed rehabilitation plan should be appropriate or not (section 240 (1) Civil Rehabilitation Law). In order to issue the confirmation of the rehabilitation plan, the court has to confirm that the total amount of payment stipulated in the draft of rehabilitation plan will be not less than the amount of multiplying the average income for the latest two years after deducting the taxed, social insurances, the amount of certain expenses which are necessary for maintaining the minimum standards of living for the rehabilitation debtor and persons eligible to receive his/her support (section 241 (2) [7] Civil Rehabilitation Law). The rehabilitation debtor has to pay the amount of rehabilitation debts within three years (or within five years in cases where any special circumstances are to be found) since the date of the order of confirmation of the rehabilitation plan by the court.[754] There is a case in which the court did not confirmed the rehabilitation plan, because the rehabilitation debtor did not satisfy the requirement provided by section 241 (2) [7] Civil Rehabilitation Law.[755]

§4. CORPORATE REORGANIZATION

361. "Kaisha-kosei-tetsuzuki" [the corporate reorganization procedure] is an insolvency process of the reconstruction type as a special procedure of the civil rehabilitation, which applies only to a stock company (section 1 Corporate Reorganization Law). It aims to coordinate the interests of stock company which falls in financial difficulties, its creditors, its shareholders and other interested parties by specifying the procedures concerning formulating reorganization plans and implementing them so as to ensure the maintenance and reconstruction of the business to be conducted by that stock company.[756]

On the one hand, the corporate reorganization procedure is more strictly regulated by law than the civil rehabilitation procedure in some aspects. First, different from the general civil rehabilitation procedure, the corporate reorganization procedure is to be conducted not by the debtor in possession but by "kanzainin" [the

751. Yamamoto et al. 2010: pp. 570–572.
752. Yamamoto et al. 2010: p. 571.
753. Yamamoto 2018: pp. 219–220.
754. *See* para. 359 *supra*.
755. HCD (Fukuoka) Jun. 12, 2003 Hanta 1139-292.
756. Yamamoto et al. 2010: pp. 462–509; Yamamoto 2018: pp. 234–262.

trustee] appointed by the court so that the transparency of the procedure can be ascertained more strictly.[757] Second, the exercise of rights of separate satisfaction by the right-holder of collaterals is not allowed outside the reorganization procedure but incorporated into the procedure and rearranged in accordance with the reorganization plan. Once the constitutionality of those rigid restrictions on the property rights of the interested persons was challenged. Although the Corporate Reorganization Law strictly regulates and restricts the right of private properties of those concerned persons, it was held to conform to the constitutional protection of private property (Article 29 CJ) by taking into consideration of the careful and reasonable restrictions by its provisions.[758]

On the other hand, the content of the corporate reorganization plan may include more broadly a variety of organization changes such as division of company, merger, share exchange, and share transfer,[759] for which special procedures shall be required by Company Law if they are implemented according to the civil rehabilitation procedure.[760]

362. The corporate reorganization procedure is initiated either by the stock company to be reorganized (a debtor) or by its creditor or its shareholder.[761] The stock company may apply for commencement of reorganization procedure: (a) when the grounds for commencement of bankruptcy procedure[762] are likely to occur, or (b) when the stock company is likely to suffer significant hindrance to the continuation of its business if it pays its debts which are due. In addition, in the case of (a) above, a creditor and a shareholder may also file an application for commencement of reorganization procedure in the following condition respectively: (i) a creditor who holds claims that account for one-tenth or more of the amount of the stated capital of the stock company; and (ii) a shareholder who holds one-tenth or more of the voting rights of all shareholders of the stock company (section 17 (1), (2) Corporate Reorganization Law).

363. The important features of the corporate reorganization procedure can be found in the preservation measures to be issued by the court, upon the application by the concerned parties or ex officio, before it issues the commencement order of the reorganization procedure.

> First, if the application for the commencement of reorganization procedure is submitted, the court can issue an order against the creditors to suspend not

---

757. However, in practice the manager of the reorganizing company can be appointed as a trustee of the corporate reorganization procedure. In that case, the DIP type of corporate reorganization may be available. It was recognized by the Tokyo District Court in December 2008.
758. SCD (FB) Dec. 16, 1970 Minshu 24-13-2099.
759. For instance, when the Japan Air Line (stock company) fell into insolvent around 2009, it applied for the corporate reorganization procedure in January 2010 so as to reconstruct its business. In accordance with the corporate reorganization procedure, it was incorporated into the Japan Air Line International in December 2010, which has changed its trade name to the Japan Air Line in April 2011.
760. Yamamoto 2018: p. 234.
761. Yamamoto et al. 2010: pp. 467–468; Yamamoto 2018: pp. 237–238.
762. *See* para. 335 *supra*.

only the compulsory execution of their claims but also the execution of collaterals for the claims until it decides on the commencement of reorganization procedure (sections 24 and 25 Corporate Reorganization Law).[763]
Second, the court can appoint the supervisor(s) before the commencement order is issued and order him/her (them) to investigate whether the director(s) and executive officer(s) are appropriate to perform the duties of a trustee(s) (section 37 Corporate Reorganization Law).[764]
Third, in most cases, the court orders the company to be reorganized not to dispose of the properties (section 28 (1) Corporate Reorganization Law)[765] and appoints the preservation manager(s) to keep the properties (section 30 Corporate Reorganization Law).[766]

These preservation measures aim to avoid the loss of properties of the company for the reconstruction and to keep the fairness among the concerned parties.

364. When the application for commencement of reorganization procedure is filed, the court has to issue an order of commencement of reorganization procedure, if it finds that the application meets the requirements as stated above.[767] But the court has to reject the application in any of the following cases: (i) when the expected expenses for reorganization procedure are not prepaid; (ii) when the bankruptcy procedure, rehabilitation procedure or special liquidation procedure are pending before the court, and the promotion of any of those procedures should conform to the common interests of creditors; (iii) when it is obvious that a reorganization plan to maintain the continuation of the business is unlikely to be proposed, approved or confirmed; or (iv) when the application for commencement of reorganization procedure is filed for an unjustifiable purpose or it is not filed in good faith (section 41 (1) Corporate Reorganization Law).[768]

365. When the court issues the order of commencement of corporate reorganization procedure, it has to appoint one or more trustees and specify a period during which proofs of "kosei-saiken" [the claims to be performed in the corporate reorganization procedure, reorganization claims], etc. should be filed and a period for conducting investigation of reorganization claims, etc. (section 42 (1) Corporate Reorganization Law). It should be noted that the manager(s) such as the executive director(s) of the reorganizing company can be appointed as the trustee(s). It becomes evident when section 67 (3) Company Reorganization Law provides that the court cannot appoint, as a trustee, a person who is likely to receive an order to assess his/her liability as the officer in accordance with section 100 (1) of Corporate

763. Yamamoto et al. 2010: pp. 469–470; Yamamoto 2018: p. 238. It was held to be constitutional although it is the strict restraint on the private property. *See* para. 361 *supra* and corresponding decision (SCD (FB) Dec. 16, 1970 Minshu 24-13-2099).
764. Different from the civil rehabilitation procedure, the appointment of the supervisor(s) must be made only before the commencement of the procedure (s. 35 (1) Corporate Reorganization Law).
765. Yamamoto et al. 2010: p. 417.
766. Yamamoto 2018: p. 239.
767. *See* Item (a) and Item (b) in para. 362 *supra*.
768. Yamamoto et al. 2010: pp. 477–478; Yamamoto 2018: pp. 239–240.

Reorganization Law. It means that the managers of the reorganizing company can be appointed as the trustees unless they are expected to receive the order to assess their liability. As a result, the DIP type of corporate reconstruction may be available in the corporate reorganization procedure.[769]

366. The commencement of corporate reorganization procedure becomes effective when the court issues the order to that effect (section 41 (2) Corporate Reorganization Law).[770] The order must be immediately made public through the public notice which contains: (i) the main text of the order of commencement of reorganization procedure, (ii) the name of trustee(s), (iii) the period during which proofs of reorganization claims, etc. should be filed and the period for conducting investigation of reorganization claims, etc., and other matters as provided by the law (section 43 (1) [1], [2] and [3] Corporate Reorganization Law).

As the effects of the order of commencement of reorganization procedure, the right to manage the business and the right to dispose of the properties shall belong to the trustee(s) appointed by the court (section 72 Corporate Reorganization Law). As a result, a possessor of a property belonging to the reorganization company must not deliver the property to the other person(s) than the trustee(s), and a person who owes a debt to the reorganization company must not make payment to that company (section 43 (1) [4] Corporate Reorganization Law).[771] The performance of obligations as well as the exercise of rights must be made by the trustee(s) according to the reorganization plan so as to maintain the fairness among the interested persons.[772]

367. The reorganization procedure is to be promoted by the trustee(s) appointed by the court when it issues the order of commencement of reorganization procedure as stated before.[773] The right to manage business and to administer and dispose of properties of the reorganizing company is vested exclusively in the trustee (section 72 (1) Corporate Reorganization Law).[774] The trustee has to perform his/her duties with due care of a prudent manager (section 80 (1) Corporate Reorganization Law).

The trustee has a right and a duty to prepare a draft of reorganization plan and to submit it to the court by the date the court specifies after the expiration of the period for filing a proof of a claim by a creditor[775] and within one year from the issue of

769. Yamamoto 2018: p. 243. As for the DIP type of reconstruction procedure, *see* para. 349 *supra*.
770. Yamamoto et al. 2010: p. 479.
771. It shall be announced in the public notice as explained in para. 365 *supra*.
772. Yamamoto et al. 2010: pp. 478–479.
773. *See* para. 363 *supra*.
774. However, the court may require the trustee to obtain its prior permission for certain actions such as disposition of property, acceptance of the transfer of property, borrowing of money, and waiver of a right as provided by s. 72 (2) Company Reorganization Law. Any actions conducted without the permission of the court shall be void. However, it may not be asserted against a third party without knowledge of the lack of the permission by the trustee.
775. A creditor who intends to participate in reorganization procedure has to file a proof of the content and cause of his/her claim and other matters as provided by s. 138 (1) Corporate Reorganization Law to the court within a period for filing proofs of claims as specified by the court in accordance with s. 42 (1) of that law. If the creditor fails to file the proof of his/her claims within the date, the

commencement order of reorganization procedure (section 184 (1) and (3) Corporate Reorganization Law). In addition, the reorganizing company, a holder of reorganization claim which was filed to the court with a proof and a shareholder may also have a right to submit a draft of reorganization plan to the court within the same period (section 184 (2) and (3) Corporate Reorganization Law).[776] As a result, the draft of reorganization plan submitted by the trustee and that submitted by the reorganizing company and by the reorganization creditors may be put on the resolution at the stakeholders meeting.[777]

Then the court refers the draft(s) of reorganization plan to the resolution for the approval of stakeholders either at a stakeholders meeting, or by documentary voting or by documentary voting at a stakeholders meeting. The way of resolution and the method of exercising the voting right are specified by the court (section 182 (2) Corporate Reorganization Law). A resolution on the drafts of reorganization plan is usually made separately by each group divided on the basis of right such as a secured reorganization claim, a reorganization claim with a general statutory lien or any other general priority rights, a claim of shareholders, and other claims (section 196 (1) Corporate Reorganization Law).[778] The court can modify the draft of reorganization plan to have approval of the right holders of a dissenting group by providing the protection of their right (section 200 (1) Corporate Organization Law).[779]

368. If the court finds that the resolution on the reorganization plan has been adopted in a fair and sincere manner, the content of that reorganization plan is fair and equitable, and feasible for implementation, it has to issue an order of confirmation of the rehabilitation plan (section 199 (2) Corporate Reorganization Law). Whether the content of reorganization plan is fair and equitable has been often challenged by the stakeholders. It was held to be fair and equitable when the claims of a parent company were subordinated to other claims in the reorganization plan, because it would contribute to realize the substantial equity among stakeholders.[780]

Once the reorganization plan is confirmed by the court, then the rights of stakeholders shall be altered in accordance with the reorganization plan (section 205 Corporate Reorganization Law). The reorganizing company needs to perform the duties corresponding to the altered rights of stakeholders, and it shall be discharged from performing obligations caused by the claims which had not been filed with proof within the period specified by the court (section 204 Corporate Reorganization Law). This exemption is different form the civil rehabilitation procedure where a certain exception to the exemption is recognized for a creditor who could not file a

---

reorganizing company will be discharged from its liabilities for claims by the confirmation of the proposal for reorganization plan (s. 204 (1) Corporate Reorganization Law).

776. In practice, the standard period for its submission specified by the court is around four to nine months after the commencement order. The court may extend the period upon application or by its own authority where any special circumstances exist (s. 184 (4) Corporate Reorganization Law).
777. Ito 2012: p. 602.
778. However, the court may combine or divide those groups for the resolution of the drafts of reorganization plan (s. 196 (2) Corporate Reorganization Law).
779. Yamamoto et al. 2010: pp. 504–506; Yamamoto 2018: pp. 256–258.
780. HCD (Fukuoka) Dec. 21, 1981, Hanji 1046-127.

claim due to the reason not attributable to the creditor.[781] The strengthened exemption aims to stabilize the reorganization plan which should contribute to its implementation.[782]

369. When the reorganization plan is confirmed by the court, a trustee has to initiate promptly the implementation of the reorganization plan (section 209 (1) Corporate Reorganization Law). However, if the right of business administration and property management is granted to the director or the executive officer of the reorganizing company according to the reorganization plan or by the court decision, the trustee shall supervise the business administration and property management of the reorganizing company (section 72 (4) and 209 Corporate Reorganization Law). If the new company is established according to the reorganization plan, the trustee supervises the business administration and property management of that company (section 209 (1) Corporate Reorganization Law).

Before the confirmation of reorganization plan, the reorganization procedure is abolished by the court decision upon application of the trustee or reorganization creditors if the reorganization plan cannot be submitted (section 236 Corporate Reorganization Law) or the reason for the commencement of reorganization procedure disappears (section 237 Corporate Reorganization Law). Then the reorganization creditors can execute their claims on the basis of the list of reorganization creditors.[783]

Even after the confirmation of reorganization plan, the reorganization procedure is abolished by the court decision upon application of the trustee or ex officio if it has become obvious that the reorganization plan is unlikely to be implemented (section 241 Corporate Reorganization Law). In this case, the effect of the court decision to abolish the reorganization procedure shall not affect the validity of actions made after the confirmation of reorganization plan to implement it. The disposition of a property by the reorganizing company shall remain effective even after the decision of abolishment of reorganization procedure.[784]

The reorganization procedure shall be ended by the court decision upon application of the trustee or ex officio: (i) when the reorganization plan has been implemented, (ii) when there has been no default in implementing the reorganization plan at least until the payment for not less than two-thirds of the total amount of monetary claims has been performed, or (iii) if it can be recognized that the reorganization plan will surely be implemented (section 239 Corporate Reorganization Law). Item (ii) and (iii) above aim to promote the reorganization procedure promptly. In practice, right after the confirmation of reorganization plan, the reorganizing company is likely to receive certain amount of money to be paid for the reorganization claims and thus the reorganization procedure is ended by the court decision.[785]

781. *See* para. 356 *supra*.
782. Yamamoto 2018: p. 259.
783. Yamamoto et al. 2010: p. 509; Yamamoto 2018: p. 260.
784. SCJ Oct. 13, 1962 Minshu 15-9-2409 (It is based on the opposite interpretation of s. 54 (1) Corporate Reorganization Law).
785. This type of ending the reorganization procedure has been increasing. Yamamoto 2018: p. 261.

§5. SPECIAL LIQUIDATION

370. The bankruptcy, civil rehabilitation and corporate reorganization as explained above are the major types of insolvency procedure in Japan. However, there is another insolvency procedure of a liquidation type called "tokubetsu-seisan-tetsuzuki" [the special liquidation procedure]. It is provided by the Company Law and only for the stock company which has already been dissolved.[786] It has an advantage as a simpler insolvency procedure than the bankruptcy procedure regulated by Bankruptcy Law.[787] In practice, the special liquidation procedure is also used by a parent company to liquidate a subsidiary to obtain the taxation benefit of deductible for debt exemption.[788]

Before entering into the special liquidation procedure, a company has to make a resolution of dissolution at the shareholders meeting (sections 471 [3] and 309 (2) [11] Company Law).

Creditors, liquidator, company auditor and shareholders may apply for the commencement of special liquidation (section 511 (1) Company Law). The liquidator has a duty to apply for the commencement of special liquidation if the liquidating stock company is suspect to become insolvent (section 511 (2) Company Law).

In response to the application by applicants explained above, the court has to order to commence the special liquidation when it finds that: (i) there are circumstances which will significantly hinder the implementation of the normal liquidation, or (ii) there is a suspicion that the liquidating stock company is "insolvent," which means that it is in the status where the assets of the liquidating stock company is not sufficient to fully discharge its debts (section 510 Company Law).However, the court may reject the application: (a) if it is obvious that the completion of liquidation cannot be expected by special liquidation, (b) if it is evident that the use of special liquidation procedure is contrary to the general interest of creditors, (c) if the application has been filed with a dishonest intention, etc. (section 514 Company Law).[789]

371. Once the commencement order of the special liquidation procedure is issued by the court, all the creditors are forced to exercise their claims only within the special liquidation procedure. As a result, any bankruptcy procedure, compulsory execution, provisional attachment, or provisional disposition procedure must be suspended and any application for those procedures may not be filed, except for the execution based on claims such as caused by the expenses for the special liquidation procedure which have a general priority (section 515 Company Law). The creditors have to participate in this procedure by filing their claims in accordance with the public notice by the Official Gazette to the effect that creditors should file and state their claims during a period determined for not less than two months or in

786. It was first introduced in the Commercial Code by its amendment in 1938 and succeeded by the Company Law in 2005.
787. *See* para. 334 *supra*.
788. Yamamoto 2018: p. 264.
789. Item (b) aims to protect the interest of creditors who would be more advantageous in the bankruptcy procedure in which they may exercise the right of avoidance provided by the Bankruptcy Law than in the special liquidation procedure.

response to the notices to be given separately to each known creditor. Those creditors who did not file their claims in response to those notices shall be excluded from this liquidation procedure (section 499 Company Law). During the period for filing claims the liquidating stock company cannot perform its obligations in principle. However, the liquidating company may perform those obligations, with special permission by the court, as concerning minor claims, claims secured by collaterals over assets of the company or other claims unlikely to be detrimental to other creditors even if they are performed (section 500 Company Law). If the court finds it necessary, it may make an order to evaluate the responsibilities of the executive officers such as directors for the damages to the liquidation stock company in response to the application by the company or ex officio (section 545 Company Law).[790]

372. The special liquidation procedure is to be led by the liquidator(s) of the dissolved stock company under the supervision by the court (section 477 (1) Company Law). The court may appoint investigator(s) to order the investigation of the causes of the special liquidation, the conditions of business and properties of the liquidating company, the necessity of preservation measure, and other matters to be necessary for special liquidation (sections 522 and 533 Company Law).

The creditors' meeting plays an important role in the special liquidation procedure, because the decision-making about how to perform the obligations for the creditors of the liquidating stock company is determined by "kyotei" [the agreement] at the creditors' meeting, though which must be authorized by the court. This is the most advantageous feature of the special liquidation procedure different from the bankruptcy procedure. It enables the liquidating stock company to perform its obligations more flexibly than in the bankruptcy procedure in accordance with the features of each case. The liquidating company may offer the agreement to the creditors' meeting, in which the performance of obligation to each creditor may be arranged on the basis of the substantial equality rather than the strict and formal equality. In the meeting those creditors who hold collaterals or general liens may also be asked to take part in the agreement (sections 563, 565 and 566 Company Law).

At the creditors' meeting, the resolution of the agreement must be adopted by the consent of a majority of the voting right holders attending the meeting and more than two-thirds of the total amount of claims of those voting right holders (sections 522 (1) and 567 Company Law).[791]

The agreement adopted at the creditors' meeting shall take effect when it is authorized by the court (section 570 Company Law). The authorized agreement binds all the creditors who were the parties of the creditors' meeting (section 571 Company Law). However, the court may reject the authorization: (i) when the agreement violates any provisions of law, (ii) when it cannot be expected to be performed, (iii)

---

790. Yamamoto 2018: pp. 265–266.

791. The holders of voting right are the creditors who have filed and stated their claims in response to the notices as stated in para. 371 *supra*. The requirement of more than two-thirds of the total amount of claims of the voting right holders is relaxed from that of more than three-fourths in the provision before the amendment to the Company Law. Yamamoto 2018: p. 269.

when it was made by unlawful means, or (iv) when it is contrary to the general interest of the creditors (section 569 Company Law).[792]

373. The agreement authorized by the court must be implemented by the liquidator(s) of the liquidating stock company. When the special liquidation has been completed, the court has to announce the conclusion of special liquidation in response to the application by the liquidator(s), auditor(s), creditors, shareholders or investigator(s).

On the other hand, if the court finds that the agreement cannot be expected to be implemented or the special liquidation procedure is contrary to the general interest of the creditors, it has to make ex officio the order of commencement of bankruptcy procedure, even after the authorization of the agreement (section 574 (1) Company Law). Before the authorization of the agreement, the court must commence the bankruptcy procedure ex officio when the agreement cannot be expected to be made.

In addition, the court may make ex officio the commencement order of bankruptcy procedure when the agreement was not adopted at the creditors' meeting, or when the agreement was not authorized by the court. In those cases, the agreement for the special liquidation may be rearranged and submitted to the creditors' meeting again (section 574 (2) Company Law). For that purpose, the court has the discretion whether to make the commencement order of the bankruptcy procedure or not.[793]

792. As for Item (iv), if the court finds that the bankruptcy procedure, in which the creditors may exercise the right of avoidance to prevent unfair performance of obligation for a particular creditor in the sacrifice of other creditors, should be more advantageous for the creditors of the liquidating company, then it may reject to authorize the agreement.

793. Yamamoto 2018: p. 269.

Part IV. Trust and Fiduciary Mechanisms

Chapter 1. Administration of Property

§1. Trust Relations in Japanese Law

374. The concept of trust is called "shintaku" in Japanese. It is a combination of the Chinese character of "shin" which means the faith or fiduciary, and that of "taku" which means to entrust. It was first introduced into Japanese law in the Secured Bond Trust Law promulgated in 1905, in which the right of collateral for secured bond was transferred to the trust company as a trustee and the creditors became beneficiary.[794] This scheme was introduced into Japan in order to finance the economic activities just after the Russo-Japanese War which began in 1904.

The term of "shintaku," however, was not defined correctly so that various companies including usury and weak companies used the term "shintaku," because it sounded like good for their company's names. In order to regulate the transactions undertaken under the name of "shintaku," the government enacted the Trust Law and the Trust Business Law in 1922 at the same time. They were modeled on the Indian Trust Law, trust laws in the California Civil Code of the U.S.A. and English case laws.[795]

Those trust laws introduced in Japan were mainly used by financial institutions for finance by collecting money from institutional investors and wealthy persons and operating it for loans and public bonds. Family trust for the purpose of succession of patrimony as developed in the U.K. and the U.S.A. has not become popular in Japan.

375. The use of trust scheme has been gradually extended to various types of property management including the fund trust, pension trust, trust for securitization of company's assets, etc. The Supreme Court recognized the formation of trust relationship when the local government A ordered a public work from the construction company B and paid a certain amount of money for the contract price into B's bank account. In this case, A was recognized as a settlor and B was regarded as a trustee

794. Dogauchi 2007: pp. 19–23. As for the history of the Japanese trust law, *see also* Arai 2014: pp. 3–37.

795. Arai 2014: pp. 12, 15–16; Dogauch 2017a: pp. 12–14.

of the money prepaid into B's bank account as a trust property even though there was no explicit agreement on the formation of trust.[796] Thus the trust has gradually taken its root into the practice.

376. In response to the increasing usage of trust and for its further usage in various types of property management, the Trust Business Law was amended in 2004 (Law No. 154, 2004) and it deregulated former restrictions on trust: (i) before the amendment, the trust property must be a certain amount of money, stocks and bonds, a money claim, a movable property, and a right to land such as ownership, superficies and a land lease right. However, this restriction on the kinds of trust property was removed so that property in general including intellectual property can be an object of trust; (ii) formerly, the business trust must be undertaken by the trust bank recognized in accordance with the law. However, the amendment abrogated this restriction as well. As a result, various companies may become a trustee. These deregulations contributed to the diversification of trust in practice.[797] In response to this amendment to the Trust Business Law in 2004, the Trust Law as a general law of trust relations was totally revised in 2006 (Law No. 108, 2006). It aimed to make the use of trust more flexible in the way of establishment, the types and the content of trust for the diversification of trust relations.[798]

377. In parallel with the introduction of trust laws into Japan through legislation, the legal theory of trust has been developed so as to assimilate the unique nature of trust relations consisting of rights and duties of a trustee, a beneficiary and a settlor into the system of rights in the Japanese civil law which is based on the distinction between real rights and claim rights, though it is not a strict distinction.[799] The central point of discussion has been focused on the nature of duties of the trustee in relation to that of rights of the beneficiary. According to the Trust Law, an ownership right of a trust property shall be transferred from the settlor to the trustee (sections 3 and 4 Trust Law). The trustee has the obligation to manage and dispose of a property which has become the trust property and to conduct any other acts necessary to achieve the purpose of the trust which is provided by terms of trust, while the beneficiary holds a right to receive a beneficial interest corresponding to the obligation of the trustee. Various theories have been developed to explain the nature of the right of beneficiary.[800]

378. The prevailing theory is based on the distinction of real rights and claim rights. It understands that ownership of a trust property shall be completely transferred from a settlor to a trustee, and the trustee only bears the obligation to manage the trust property for a beneficiary in accordance with the trust agreement between the settlor and the trustee. Consequently, the right of beneficiary must be regarded

---

796. SCJ Jan. 17, 2002 Minshu 56-1-20.
797. Arai 2014: pp. 20–25, 30–31; Dogauchi 2017a: pp. 15–16.
798. Arai 2014: pp. 30–31; Dogauchi 2017a: p. 16.
799. As for the distinction between real rights and claim rights in the Japanese civil law, *see* para. 72 *supra*. The Civil Code of Japan was enacted in 1896, which was before the enactment of trust laws since 1905 as explained in para. 374 *supra*.
800. On the development of the trust law theories in Japan, *see* Arai 2014: pp. 39–60.

a claim right against the trustee.[801] However, the trust property shall be managed as an independent property from other properties which belong personally to the trustee. The trustee's right and duty to manage and dispose of the trust property are strictly regulated by the provisions of law for the protection of the beneficiary's right.

379. Another theory explains that ownership of a trust property belongs formally to the trustee but substantially to the beneficiary. More concretely, the rights of owner are functionally divided into the management rights which belong to the trustee and the profit-making rights which belong to the beneficiary.[802] This theory based on the understanding about the nature of trust property which must be managed independently from the trustee's own property for the beneficiary's interest.

380. More advanced theory recognizes that the trust property is substantially a subject of rights and the trustee is an administrator of the trust property, just like a representative director of a company.[803] The beneficiary is vested with the special rights in trust property which include the right to pursue the property at a third party to whom the trustee has disposed of the property in breach of his/her duty.[804]

381. It seems difficult to characterize correctly the nature of trust relations within the rigid distinction between real rights and claim rights. It is due to the history of Trust Law which originated in the U.K. where the strict distinction between real rights and claim rights has not been developed. It is necessary and fruitful to confirm the concrete effects of rights and duties of the trustee, beneficiary and settlor together with the theoretical explanation to maintain the integrity of law in the Japanese legal system that includes Trust Law. A recent theory emphasizes the characteristics of trust relations as an instrument to provide the owner-like legal remedy to the beneficiary without determining whether it is a claim right or not.[805]

§2. Establishment of Trust

382. The Trust Law defines the term "shintaku" [trust] as an arrangement in which a specific person (trustee) administers or disposes a certain property in accordance with a certain purpose, and conducts any other acts that are necessary to achieve such purpose. However, the purpose which "exclusively promotes the person's own interests" shall not be the purpose of a trust (section 2 (1) Trust Law). As the essential nature of a trust lies in the creation of a trust property to be managed

801. Tetsuji Aoki, *Shintaku Ho Ron* [*The Theory of Trust Law*] 299–301 (Zaisei-keizai-jiho-sha 1926); Arai 2014: p. 60.
802. Minoru Tanaka, *Shintaku Ho Nyumon* [*An Introduction to the Trust Law*] 128 (Yuhikaku 1992).
803. Kazuo Shinomiya, *Shintaku Ho* [*The Law of Trust*] 63, 70–74 (Yuhikaku New Edition 1989).
804. However, the beneficiary's right to pursue the property disposed beyond the scope of the right of trustee may be restricted for the protection of a third party. *See* para. 395 *infra*.
805. Dogauchi 2017a: p. 17.

by the trustee independently from the trustee's own property, it would not be necessary to create the trust property if it aims to achieve the trustee's own interests.[806] A trust relation in Japanese law can be established by: (i) contract, (ii) testamentary will, or (iii) unilateral declaration of intention to establish the trust (section 3 Trust Law).

383. (i) The trust may be established by a contract concluded with a specific person to the effect that the person will be assigned a property, that the person will be granted a security interest in the property,[807] or that the property will be disposed of to the person in any other ways, and that the said specific person should administer or dispose of such property in accordance with a certain purpose and carry out any other acts that are necessary for achieving that purpose (section 3 [1] Trust Law). It is not necessary to use the term "trust" explicitly when the trust is established by the contract between the settlor and the trustee.[808] When a local government A concluded a contract with a construction company B to the effect that A would pay a contract price in advance into B's account at the bank C, and that B should return the price if B could not complete the construction work, and A paid the price into B's account at the bank C. After that B became bankrupt and the construction work could not be completed. In this case, it was recognized that the trust was established between A (a settlor and a beneficiary) and B (a trustee) and the money paid by A into B's bank account at C must be recognized as the trust property so that the money should not be included in the bankruptcy estate.[809]

384. (ii) The trust may be created by a testamentary will to the effect that a property will be assigned to a specific person, that a specific person will be granted a security interest in property, or that property will otherwise be disposed of to a specific person, and that the specific person should administer or dispose of such property in accordance with a certain purpose and carry out any other actions that are necessary for achieving such purpose (section 3 [2] Trust Law). The term "trust" is not necessary to be used explicitly in the testamentary will if the intention to establish the trust is evident.[810]

385. (iii) The trust may be set up by a declaration of intention of a specific person to administer or dispose of a certain property which the person holds in accordance with a certain purpose and to conduct any other actions that are necessary for achieving that purpose. The declaration of intention to establish the trust of that person has to be evidenced by a notarial deed or any other document or an electromagnetic record, in which the purpose, the matters necessary for specifying the property, and other matters specified by Ordinance of the Ministry of Justice must be stated or recorded (section 3 [3] Trust Law). It is called "shintaku-sengen" [the declaration of trust] in which the settlor shall become the trustee. In this case, the term

---

806. Dogauchi 2017a: p. 47.
807. The "security interest" includes, for instance, a collateral such as the right of hypothec.
808. SCJ Nov. 16, 1954 Hanji 41-11.
809. SCJ Jan. 17, 2002 Minshu 56-1-20.
810. Dogauch 2017a: p. 59.

"shintaku" must be used in the declaration of intention to establish the trust by that declaration.[811] The declaration of trust may be used, for instance, when a parent of a disabled person will establish a trust on his/her certain property for the purpose of maintaining the support of the life of his/her disabled son or daughter even when the parent would become bankrupt.[812]

386. The trust becomes effective when the contract, testamentary will or declaration of intention becomes effective:[813] (i) the trust established by a contract shall become effective when the contract is concluded between a settlor and a trustee, even before the property as an object of the trust is transferred from the settlor to the trustee; (ii) the trust created by a testamentary will shall become effective when the will takes effect, that is, when the settlor dies (section 965 CC); (iii) the trust created by the declaration of intention shall become effective when a notarial deed or any other document or an electromagnetic record which is authenticated by a notary is executed. If the declaration of intention is made by a document or an electromagnetic record which is not authenticated by a notary, it shall become effective when a notice about the establishment and the content of the trust is given to a beneficiary or anyone of beneficiaries by means of an instrument which includes the authenticated fixed date (section 4 (3) [2] Trust Law). The authentication of the date of the instrument as well as that of the document or the electromagnetic record aims to avoid the forged date of the notice or the declaration of trust.[814]

387. When a settlor has created a trust with the knowledge that it would harm the settlor's creditor, the creditor may, irrespective of whether the trustee had knowledge of the fact that the creditor of the settlor would be harmed or not, request the court for a rescission of the establishment of the trust against the trustee as a defendant (section 11 Main Text Trust Law). However, this right of rescission cannot be exercised when there are any beneficiaries who had no knowledge of the fact that the creditor of the settlor would be harmed when they became aware that they had been designated as beneficiaries or when they acquired any beneficiary's interests (section 11 Proviso Trust Law). This is a special provision of section 424 CC, in which the creditor may rescind the debtor's action only when the other party of the action was aware that the action would harm the creditor. In practice, it is often disputed whether a creditor "would be harmed" by a certain action of establishing trust. For instance, if a settlor A whose total assets were equivalent to USD 1 million and total debts were equivalent to USD 500 thousands has transferred his/her property equivalent to USD 800 thousands to the trustee B as a trust property, a creditor C of A may rescind the action of establishing the trust. However, if A was designated as a beneficiary in that action so that C would not be harmed by that action, then C cannot rescind the action of establishing the trust.[815]

---

811. Dogauchi 2017a: p. 72.
812. Arai 2014: p. 139.
813. They can be subjected to a certain condition or a certain term. In that case, the trust shall be effective when the condition is fulfilled or the term arrives (s. 4 (4) Trust Law).
814. Dogauch 2017a: pp. 69–70.
815. Dogauchi 2017a: p. 123.

§3. Nature of Trust Property

388. In order to establish a trust, some property is necessary as an object of trust. It is the original trust property. The restrictions of the kinds of the trust property was removed by the amendment to the Trust Business Law in 2004.[816] Now various kinds of property may be the trust property including intellectual property, secured interest such as a right of hypothec and other collaterals. In addition to the property specified by the contract, testamentary will or declaration of establishing trust as the original trust property, any property obtained by the trustee as a result of the administration, disposition, loss or damage of, or any other events occurring to the original trust property shall also be regarded as the trust property (section 16 [1] Trust Law). "Any other events" may include the public taking (compulsory purchase) of the trust property. In this case the compensation for the taking shall become the trust property.[817]

389. The trust property transferred from the settlor to the trustee belongs to the trustee. However, the trust property shall be kept independently from the trustee's own property. This independent nature of the trust property is recognized by the Trust Law. For instance, section 23 (1) provides that except for a claim corresponding to an obligation to be performed from the trust property, no execution, provisional seizure, provisional disposition, or exercise of a security interest or an auction nor collection procedure for delinquent national tax may be enforced against the trust property.[818] If any action such as an execution was applied to the trust property, the trustee or the beneficiary may make an objection to prevent it (section 23 (5) Trust Law). It is the right and the duty for the trustee to make the objection (section 29 (1) Trust Law), while it is only the right for the beneficiary, because it is for his/her own interest to make the objection.[819] When there are two or more beneficiaries, each beneficiary may make the objection independently (section 92 [3] Trust Law).

390. The independent nature of the trust property can also be found in the following cases: (i) the creditor of the settlor and the creditor of the trustee for his/her own interest cannot execute the trust property for the reason of non-performance of their claim.[820] When the creditor of the settlor or the creditor of the trustee applies

816. *See* para. 376 *supra*.
817. Dogauchi 2017a: p. 102.
818. When the accession takes place between the trust property and the trustee's own property, ss. 242 to 248 CC shall be applied by treating the trust property as if it is owned by a person other than the trustee (s. 17 Trust Law). And when the right of superficies which had been established on the land owned by the trustee has become a trust property, the superficies shall not be merged into the trustee's own land as s. 179 CC shall not be applied to maintain the independence or the trust property (s. 20 Trust Law).
819. Dogauchi 2017a: p. 112.
820. On the contrary, a claim corresponding to an obligation to be covered by the trust property (an obligation on which the trustee is liable to perform through the use of the trust property including an obligation arising from the management of trust property) may be enforced against the trust property (ss. 23 (1) and 2 (9) Trust Law).

for the execution of the trust property, the trustee in the former case or the beneficiary in the latter case may assert an objection to the execution (section 23 (5) Trust Law). The same applies when the government initiates the collection procedure for delinquent national tax to be imposed on the settlor or the trustee for his/her own duty (section 23 (6) Trust Law).

391. (ii) Even when an order for commencement of bankruptcy procedure is made by the court against the trustee for his/her own debt, the trust property shall not be included in the bankruptcy estate (section 25 (1) Trust Law). The same applies to the cases where an order for commencement of rehabilitation procedure and corporate reorganization procedure is made by the court against the trustee for his/her own debt (section 25 (4), (5), (6) and (7) Trust Law). This is called the advantageous function of the trust called "tosan-kakuri" [the insolvency remoteness].[821]

However, if the trust property may be registered and the acquisition, loss and modification of the property rights may not be opposable against a third party unless it is registered as the trust property. If it is not registered, the trustee or beneficiary may not assert against the creditor of the trustee or of the creditor that the property belongs to the trust property (section 14 Trust Law).

392. A creditor of the trustee's own debt cannot execute the trust property for non-performance of obligation by the trustee. This is one of the important aspects of the independence of trust property.[822]

On the other hand, however, a creditor of the trustee who acted as the manager of trust property and owed obligations to be performed from the trust property[823] may execute not only the trust property but also the trustee's own property as well.[824] This is a result from the fact that the trust property does not have a legal personality so that all the actions such as contracts which the trustee has concluded as a manager of the trust property are also regarded as the actions of the trustee. If the trust property were to have the legal personality like a foundation or the property belongs to a company, any actions made by the manager of the foundation or the company are regarded as actions of the legal person and obligations caused by the actions of the representative of the legal person must be performed only from the legal person's property. For instance, if the manager of the foundation or the company borrowed a certain amount of money from the bank, the obligation to repay the money shall belong to the foundation or the company, not to the manager. But if the trustee borrowed a certain amount of money from the bank for the management of the trust property in accordance with the purpose of the trust, it is the

821. When a trustee dies, the trust property shall become a legal person (s. 74 (1) Trust Law), so that it is not included in the inheritance property of the trustee. Dogauchi 2017a: p. 114.
822. *See* para. 390 *supra*.
823. Obligations to be performed by using the trust property called "shintaku-zaisan-sekinin-hutan-saimu" are listed in s. 21 (1) [1] to [9] Trust Law, which may be classified into: (i) obligations caused by the administration of the trust affairs, (ii) obligations concerned with the beneficiary's interest, and (iii) obligations which had been generated before the creation of the trust. Dogauchi 2017a: p. 114.
824. Arai 2014: p. 356; Dogauchi 2017a: p. 261.

obligation of the trustee to repay the money. Any actions of the trustee for the management of the trust property are regarded as the trustee's actions as the trust property does not have a legal personality.[825] However, if the trustee has performed an obligation caused for the purpose of the trust by using the trustee's own property, he/she can have reimbursement from the trust property (section 48 Trust Law).[826]

393. Obligations to distribute the beneficiary's interest and obligations for which only the trust property shall be liable by the provision of law or by the agreement between the creditor and the trustee can be performed only by the use of trust property (section 21 (2) [1], [3] and [4] Trust Law). In addition, if it is provided by the terms of trust either by contract or testamentary will or unilateral declaration of the will to establish the trust that the trustee is liable to perform obligations caused by the actions for the trust property only by using that trust property (section 216 (1) Trust Law) and a registration to that effect is made in accordance with the provisions of law (section 232 Trust Law), it is called a "gentei-sekinin-shintaku" [the limited liability trust].[827] Once the limited liability trust is established, no execution, provisional seizure, provisional disposition, execution of a security interest, auction to collect delinquent national taxes imposed on the trust property by the trustee's actions for the trust property may be carried out against the trustee's own property except for the obligations caused by tort (section 217 (1) Trust Law). It is similar to the establishment of a limited liability company, in which only the company's property is liable for the obligations caused by the director through the transactions between the company and the other parties, and the director does not have a duty to perform the obligations by using his/her own property.[828]

§4. Rights of Trustee

394. The trustee has the rights to administer or dispose of property which belongs to the trust property and to conduct any other acts that are necessary to achieve the purpose of the trust. As these are comprehensive rights of the trustee to manage the trust property and to maintain the trust relations, the scope of those rights may be restricted by the terms of contract, testamentary will or unilateral declaration of intention that establishes the trust (section 26 Trust Law) as well as by the provisions of law.[829] Those rights are also the duties of the trustee to manage

825. Dogauchi 2017a: pp. 75–76, 114, 216. The distinction between the trustee's action for his/her own interest and that for the trust property depends on the intention of the trustee whether he/she acts for his/her own interest or for the trust property as the trustee. Dogauchi 2007: pp. 108–109.
826. Dogauchi 2017a: p. 114.
827. The terms for the limited liability trust must include: (i) the purpose of the limited liability trust, (ii) the name of the limited liability trust, (iii) the names and addresses of the settlor(s) and the trustee(s), (iv) the place where the ordinary trust management for the limited liability trust are to be administered, (v) the method of administration or disposition of property which belongs to the trust property; and (vi) other matters specified by Ordinance of the Ministry of Justice (s. 216 (2) Trust Law).
828. Arai 2014: pp. 410–411; Dogauchi 2017a: p. 151.
829. Arai 2014: p. 249.

the trust property and to conduct any actions for achieving the purpose, which are ultimately rooted in the intention of the trustee.[830]

395. When the trustee acted beyond the scope of his/her rights restricted by the terms of trust or by the provisions of law, the beneficiary may rescind such an act if: (i) the other party (a third party viewed from the beneficiary) knew, at the time of the act, that the act was conducted for the trust property and (ii) if the other party to the act (the third party) knew or did not know with gross negligence, at the time of the act, that the act did not fall within the scope of the trustee's rights (section 27 (1) Trust Law). It is one of the beneficiary's rights to correct the deviation of the trustee's power in the sacrifice of a third party.[831] The right to rescind the act is regarded as a special right given by the law for the protection of the beneficiary's right if it is understood as a claim right, while it is the restriction of the beneficiary's right to pursue the trust property which was illegally disposed by the trustee for the protection of a good faith acquirer if the right of beneficiary is substantially understood as an ownership right.[832]

If the act conducted by the trustee was to establish or transfer a right concerning the trust property for a third party for which the registration as the trust property can be made in accordance with section 14 of the Trust Law did not fall within the scope of trustee's rights, the beneficiary may rescind that act, only if: (i) the property was registered as the trust property at the time of the act, and (ii) the other party to the act (the third party) knew or did not know with gross negligence, at the time of the act, that the act did not fall within the scope of the trustee's rights (section 27 (2) Trust Law). The requirement (ii) is still necessary, because the transfer of trust property registered as a trust property to a third party is not always beyond the scope of the trustee's rights so that the bad faith or the gross negligence on the party of the third person should be required.[833] The restricted requirements for the beneficiary's right to rescind the act between the trustee and the third party aims to balance the interest of the beneficiary and that of the third party.

396. Another problem is a solution of the case when the trustee acted within the scope of his/her rights, but with the intention to act for his/her own interest or for the interest of his/her interested person other than the beneficiary.[834] For example, the trustee A bought a piece of land from B which was within the scope of the trustee's rights recognized by the contract of trust, but with the intention to acquire it for his/her own interest (such as by reselling it to a third party at a higher price) and on account of his/her own property. However, the trustee may not act on account of the trustee's own property or on account of the trustee's interested person, when the act

830. Dogauchi 2017a: p. 167.
831. As for the content of beneficiary's rights, *see* paras. 414–417 *infra*.
832. As for the nature of beneficiary's right *see* para. 378, 379 and 380 *supra*.
833. Dogauchi 2017a: p. 83.
834. If the trustee acted beyond the scope of his/her rights with the intention for his/her own interest or for the interest of his/her interested person, then the act is effective only for his/her own property or for the property of his/her interested person and the trust property cannot be executed for the non-performance of obligations caused by this act. Dogauchi 2017a: p. 85.

may be carried out as the trust administration within the trustee's rights and the failure to carry it out would be contrary to the beneficiary's interest (section 32 (1) Trust Law).[835] The trustee may act on account of his/her own property or on account of his/her interested person only if: (i) it is allowed by the terms of trust or (ii) the trustee obtains approval from the beneficiary by disclosing relevant facts and it is not prohibited by the terms of trust (section 32 (2) Trust Law).[836] When the trustee has carried out the act on account of his/her own property or on account of his/her interested person in violation of the requirements of (i) or (ii) above, the beneficiary may deem that the act has been conducted on account of the trust property (section 32 (4) Main Text Trust Law). In the case above, the beneficiary C may deem that A bought the land from B on account of the trust property and the land shall belong to the trust property. This is called "kainyu-ken" [the right of intervention] for the beneficiary's interest.[837] But the right of intervention "may not harm the rights of a third party" (section 32 (4) Proviso). It means that, for instance, in the case above C cannot change the content and conditions of the contract concluded by A with B.[838]

397. If a trustee has spent any expenses from his/her own property which are considered to be necessary for the trust administration, the trustee may receive reimbursement from the trust property for the expenses and the interest from the date of payment unless the terms of trust provides otherwise (section 48 (1) Trust Law). The trustee may receive advance payment from the trust property when it is necessary for the trust administration unless the terms of trust provides otherwise (section 48 (2) Trust Law). When the trustee may receive reimbursement for expenses including advance reimbursement from the trust property, the trustee can transfer such amount of money from the trust property to the trustee's own property (section 49 (1) Trust Law). When necessary, the trustee may dispose of the trust property to have reimbursement unless it would make it impossible to achieve the purpose of the trust and the terms of trust provides otherwise (section 49 (2) Trust Law).

The trustee's right of reimbursement became problematic in the development project when the expenses paid by the trustee to maintain the facilities that belonged to the trust property considerably increased because of the unexpected change of economic conditions such as caused by natural disasters and the interests to be distributed to the beneficiary seriously decreased. The claim of reimbursement by the trustees (Trust Banks) against the beneficiary (Hyogo Prefecture, who was also the settlor) was rejected in the District Court for the reason that the right to receive reimbursement should be regarded as waived by the interpretation of the terms in trust contract.[839] However, in response to the appeal by the trustees, the Appellate

835. In this context, it is also the duty of the trustee to refrain from competition with the beneficiary.
836. In this case, the trustee has to give notice to the beneficiary of the relevant facts concerned with the act unless the terms of trust act provide otherwise (s. 32 (3) Trust Law).
837. However, the beneficiary's right of intervention shall be extinguished when one year has elapsed from the time of the trustee's act (s. 32 (5) Trust Law).
838. Dogauchi 2017a: p. 87.
839. District Court (Kobe) Feb. 26, 2009 Kinsho 1324-42.

Court recognized the claim of the trustees for reimbursement against the beneficiary.[840] The reason was that in this case the settlor and the beneficiary was the Prefecture who established the trust on the public land, and it understood well about the risk and return from this trust when it established the trust by concluding the trust contract with the Trust Banks. The Appellate Court decision was affirmed by the Supreme Court.[841]

398. When the trustee suffered any damages during the trust administration without his/her own negligence, he/she may receive compensation for the amount of the damages from the trust property (section 53 (1) [1] Trust Law). In addition, when the trustee has suffered any damages during the trust administration due to the intentional or negligent action of a third party and the negligence of the trustee, the trustee may receive compensation for the amount of damages which may be claimed against the third party (section 53 (1) [2] Trust Law). In the latter case, the amount of damages due to the trustee's own negligence may be reduced from the amount of compensation by the claim of the third party.[842]

In these cases, the trustee may transfer such amount of money from the trust property to the trustee's own property, and when it is necessary, the trustee may dispose of the trust property to receive the amount of damages unless the disposal would make it impossible to achieve the purpose of the trust and the terms of trust provide otherwise (section 53 (2), 49 (1), (2) Trust Law). This method of payment is the same as that for the reimbursement of expenses.[843] If the compensation was paid to the trustee from the trust property, the claim for compensation against the tortfeasor shall belong to the trust property which can be claimed by the trustee.[844]

399. The trustee may receive remuneration from the trust property only when it is provided by the terms of trust to that effect or the trustee is a merchant and he/she has conducted the trust administration within the scope of his/her business (section 54 (1) Trust Law, section 512 Commercial Code). The amount of remuneration depends on the terms of trust. If it was not stipulated in the terms of trust, the trustee may receive "a reasonable amount" from the trust property (section 54 (2) Trust Law). However, in this case, the trustee has to notice to the beneficiary about the amount of remuneration and the basis for calculation of the amount (section 54 (3) Trust Law).[845]

840. HCJ (Osaka) May 14, 2010 Kinsho 1380-36.
841. SCJ Nov. 17. 2011 Kinsho 1380-29.
842. This is a setoff due to the trustee's negligence. Dogauchi 2017a: p. 271.
843. *See* para. 397 *supra*.
844. Dogauchi 2017a: p. 272. It can be based on the substitution of the claim for compensation by the third party's payment (s. 422 CC).
845. In addition, the beneficiary may particularly agree with the trustee about the payment of remuneration even after the establishment of trust (s. 54 (4) Trust Law).

§5. Obligations and Responsibilities of Trustee

400. Trust Law provides basic duties of the trustee: (i) the duty to administer trust affairs in accordance with the purpose of the trust (section 29 (1)); (ii) the duty to manage the trust property with the due care of a prudent manager (section 29 (2)); (iii) the duty of loyalty (sections 30–32); (iv) the duty of impartiality (section 33); (v) the duty to manage the trust property separately (section 34); (vi) the duty to select and supervise the delegated third party (section 35); and (vii) the duty to report on the trust administration (sections 36–38).

As a general duty, the trustee has to manage the trust property in accordance with "shintaku-no-honshi" [the purpose of the trust] (section 29 (1) Trust Law).[846] The purpose of trust does not mean the abstract purpose of trust institution. It is the concrete objective to be achieved by each trust, and it can be identified by the contract, testamentary will or unilateral declaration which established the trust.[847]

The trustee has another general duty to manage the trust property with "zenryo-na-kanrisha-no-chui" [the due care of a prudent manager] unless the terms of trust provide otherwise (section 29 (2) Trust Law). The "due care of a prudent manager" shall be interpreted not by the subjective standard whether the trustee did his/her best or not on his/her own ability, but by the objective standard whether he/she performed the duty of care which is reasonably expected for the trustee in accordance with his/her profession and social status.[848]

401. The duty to manage the trust property with due care of a prudent manager may be implemented in concrete situations. Some of them are stipulated more specifically by the law. For instance, the trustee has to manage the trust property separated from the trustee's own property and the trust property of other trust(s) unless the terms of trust provide otherwise (section 34 (1) Trust Law). It is called "bunbetsu-kanri-gimu" [the duty to manage separately].

(a) If the trust property is a piece of land or any other property which may be registered, it must be registered in the name of the trust property.[849]
(b) For the trust property which cannot be registered: (i) if it is movable property, it must be administered by retaining it separately from the trustee's own property and the other trust property in the manner whereby they can be distinguished from each other on sight; (ii) if it is money or property other than property in (i) above, it must be administered by the method of clarifying the accounting of it; and (iii) if it is property specified by Ordinance of the Ministry

846. As for the general qualification, the trustee must not be a minor, a person under guardianship or curatorship (s. 7 Trust Law).
847. Dogauchi 2017a: pp. 167–168.
848. Dogauchi 2007: pp. 134–135; Dogauchi 2017a: pp. 168–169.
849. The duty to register the registrable property in the name of trust property cannot be removed even by the terms of trust (s. 34 (2) Trust Law), for the registration is important to manage the trust property separated from other properties.

of Justice, it must be administered by a method specified by Ordinance of the Ministry of Justice for the appropriate segregation of the property.[850]

402. If there are two or more beneficiaries, the trustee has a duty to perform his/her obligations equally for those beneficiaries in the trust administration (section 33 Trust Law). This duty is called "kohei-gimu" [the duty of impartiality]. It can be drawn from the general duty to manage the trust property with the due care of a prudent manager (section 29 (2) Trust Law).[851]

However, the trust act may provide the distinction between the preferred beneficiary and the subordinate beneficiary and the content of the beneficiary's rights may differ depending on the terms of trust. The trustee's duty of impartiality means that the trustee must treat the beneficiaries impartially in accordance with the content of the beneficiary's rights.[852]

If the trustee has acted or is likely to act in violation of the duty of impartiality and the act is likely to cause "serious harm" to some of the beneficiaries, those beneficiaries may claim to suspend the act (section 44 (3) Trust Law). However, when the damages have been caused to the trust property by the trustee's act in violation of the duty of impartiality, the affected beneficiary can claim for compensation for damages according to section 40 (1) of the Trust Law.[853]

403. The trustee has a duty to report on the trust administration so that the settlor and the beneficiary can claim the trustee to report on the current state of trust administration and the situation of trust property and the obligations to be performed by using the trust property (section 36 Trust Law). Each settlor and beneficiary may claim for the report individually (section 92 [7] Trust Law), for this duty is fundamental to watch the trust administration and the trust property.[854] In order to prepare for such report, the trustee has to prepare books and other documents or electromagnetic records concerning the trust property which can clarify the accounts on trust administration and the situation of trust property and the obligations to be covered by the trust property (section 37 (1) Trust Law).

In addition, the trustee has to prepare a balance sheet, a statement of profit and loss and any other documents or electromagnetic records specified by Ordinance of the Ministry of Justice, once a year, at a certain time, as provided by Ordinance of the Ministry of Justice (section 37 (2) Trust Law).[855]

When the trustee has prepared the documents or electromagnetic records such as a balance sheet and a statement of profit and loss, he/she has to report to a beneficiary, or a trust administrator if any, on their content unless the terms of trust provide otherwise (section 37 (3) Trust Law). Those documents and electromagnetic records are called "shintaku-chobo" [the trust account book]. The trustee has to keep

---

850. Properties specified by Ordinance of the Ministry of Justice (s. 34 (1) [3] Trust Law) include the transfer bond and transfer public bond, for which the registration as the trust property and the method of clarifying the accounting of it is necessary.
851. Dogauchi 2017a: p. 187.
852. Arai 2014: pp. 279–281; Dogauchi 2017a: pp. 186–188.
853. Arai 2014: p. 281.
854. Dogauchi 2017a: p. 193.
855. Arai 2014: pp. 304–305; Dogauchi 2017a: pp. 193–194.

them for ten years after they are prepared or until the liquidation of the trust is completed unless they or their copies are delivered to the beneficiary (section 37 (4) Trust Law).

404. The trustee must administer the trust affairs "faithfully for the beneficiary" (section 30 Trust Law). This is called "chujistu-gimu" [the duty of loyalty] and it is implemented by the provisions of law in some concrete situations.[856]

(a) The trustee cannot acquire any benefit[857] from the trust property under any name except for the case in which the trustee can benefit from the trust property as one of the beneficiaries (section 8 Trust Law).[858]
(b) The acts of trustee which lead to the conflict of interests are restricted. The trustee cannot carry out: (i) acts which will make the trust property to belong to the trustee's own property or make the trustee's own property to belong to the trust property (section 31 (1) [1] Trust Law); (ii) acts which will make the trust property to belong to the trust property of another trust (section 31 (1) [2] Trust Law); (iii) acts for the trust property with a third party for whom the trustee will serve as an agent (section 31 (1) [3] Trust Law); and (iv) acts which will establish a security interest on the trust property in order to secure a claim corresponding to an obligation that the trustee is liable to perform only by using the trustee's own property, or any other acts with a third party for the trust property which will create a conflict of interest between the trustee or his/her interested person and the beneficiary (section 31 (1) [4] Trust Law).

When the acts of the conflict of interests as listed in Item (i) and (ii) above are carried out in breach of the restriction, they are void (section 31 (4) Trust Law). However, they shall become effective from the time of the acts, if they are ratified by the beneficiary (section 31 (5) Trust Law).

When the trust property which had been made to belong to the trustee's own property or the trust property of another trust in breach of the restriction by Item (i) and (ii) above has been transferred to a third party, the beneficiary may rescind the transaction only if the third party knew or did not know with gross negligence that the acts were carried out in breach of the restriction (section 31 (6) Trust Law).

And when the acts of the conflict of interests as listed in Item (iii) and (iv) above are carried out in breach of the restriction, the beneficiary may rescind the act only if the third party knew or did not know with gross negligence that the acts were carried out in breach of the restriction (section 31 (7) Trust Law).

Item (i) to Item (iv) in the category above are the comprehensive list of the conflict of interests between the trustee and the beneficiary. They regulate broadly the trustee's acts including the act which will make the trustee's own property to belong to the trust property such as a donation from the trustee's own property to the trust

---

856. Arai 2014: pp. 256–279; Dogauchi 2017a: pp. 203–235.
857. The benefit referred to here is different from the remuneration that may be lawfully acquired by the trustee. *See* para. 399 *supra*.
858. The trustee can be one of the beneficiaries. However, if the trustee is only a beneficiary, the trust can be recognized only within one year (s. 163 [2] Trust Law).

property. For example, if a piece of land which was included in the trustee's own property is donated to the trust property, it will cause a damage to the trust property and affect the interest of the beneficiary if the land was contaminated by pollutant substance. However, it is not always the case. There are exceptions which may validate the act of conflict of interests.[859]

405. The trustee are allowed to carry out the acts which are listed as the conflict of interests[860] in the following cases unless the terms of trust provide otherwise: (i) if the terms of trust provide that the trustee is allowed to carry out those acts (section 31 (2) [1] Trust Law); (ii) if the trustee has disclosed the relevant facts and obtained approval from the beneficiary of carrying out those acts (section 31 (2) [2] Trust Law); (iii) if a part of the trust property has been included in the trustee's own property by succession (section 31 (2) [3] Trust Law); and (iv) if it is considered reasonably necessary for the trustee to carry out those acts so as to achieve the purpose of the trust, and it is clear that those acts to be conducted by the trustee would not harm the interest of the beneficiary, or if there is a justifiable ground for the trustee to carry out those acts in light of the impact of those acts on the trust property, the purpose and manner of the acts, the state of a substantial relationship between the trustee and the beneficiary, and the other relevant circumstances (section 31 (2) [4] Trust Law).

For instance, the donation from the trustee's own property to the trust property may be allowed as an exception to the regulation of the conflict of interests (section 31 (2) [4] Trust Law).[861] There is a judicial precedent which held that the donation from the parent to the child who was a minor could not be regarded as the conflict of interests.[862] Although the parent is not the trustee of his/her minor child, this judicial precedent can be analogically applied to the trust relation, because the conflict of interests between the parents and their minor child is also regulated by the provision of law (section 826 (1) CC).

406. Another important implementation of the duty of loyalty by the provision of law can be found in "kyogyo-hishi-gimu" [the duty to refrain from competitive business] with the beneficiary (section 32 (1) Trust Law). For instance, the trustee found a piece of land which is appropriate to carry out the trust administration, however, he/she bought it not to belong to the trust property but to belong to the trustee's own property, because the price of the land was expected to increase rapidly. But the trustee is not allowed to carry out this act on account of his/her own property or his/her interested person's property, because "the failure to carry out" this act on account of the trust property is "contrary to the interest of the beneficiary" (section 32 (1) Trust Law) and thus regarded as a breach of the duty of loyalty. This is a prohibition of the competitive business. Once it was carried out by the trustee, the beneficiary can deem the act had been conducted in the interest of and on

859. *See* para. 405 *infra*. The case of donation from the trustee's own property to the trust property may be valid if it meets the requirement (s. 31 (2) [4] Trust Law).
860. These acts are listed from Item (i) to Item (iv) in Category (b) in para. 404 *supra*.
861. Dogauchi 2017a: p. 206.
862. STJ Nov. 24, 1931 Minshu 10-1103.

account of the trust property (section 32 (4) Trust Law). This is called "kainyu-ken" [the right of intervention] as explained above.[863]

However, the trustee can carry out the act of competitive business if it is allowed in the terms of trust (section 32 (2) [1] Trust Law), or if the trustee obtained the approval from the beneficiary after disclosing the relevant facts about the act unless the terms of trust provide otherwise (section 32 (2) [2] Trust Law).

In practice, it is not always easy to judge whether "the failure to carry out" of a particular act on account of the trust property is "contrary to the interest of the beneficiary" (section 32 (1) Trust Law) or not. The trustee is not liable for all the failure to carry out the act on account of the trust property contrary to the beneficiary's interest. The trustee may be exempted from the liability by proving that he/she has performed the duty to administer the trust affairs with the due care of a prudent manager (section 29 (2) Trust Law).[864]

407. If the trustee acted in breach of his/her duties as explained above[865] and caused any loss for the beneficiary due to that breach, the beneficiary may claim the trustee to take appropriate measures to recover the loss: (i) if any loss to the trust property has occurred due to that breach, the trustee has to compensate for the loss (section 40 (1) [1] Trust Law); (ii) if any change to the trust property has occurred due to that breach, the trustee has to restore the trust property (section 40 (1) [2] Trust Law).

The beneficiary can choose the remedy among the measures as provided above. However, if any loss remains after the restoration, the beneficiary can still claim for compensation for the remaining loss.

As for the claim for compensation for the loss, the scope of compensation shall be limited within the predictability for the trustee about the possible damages by applying the general rule of the Civil Code (section 416 CC).[866]

However, if the trustee acted in breach of the duty of loyalty including its implementation by the provisions of law (sections 30, 31 (1), (3) and 32 (1), (2) Trust Law),[867] the amount of the profit obtained by the trustee or by his/her interested person can be presumed to be the loss for the trust property (section 40 (3) Trust Law). This presumption of loss could have a meaning of a sanction on the trustee who acted in breach of the duty of loyalty, which has the fundamental importance in the trust relations.

408. As for the claim for restoration of the trust property, it is advantageous for the beneficiary, because it is not necessary to prove the amount of the loss as in the case of the claim for compensation.[868] However, the beneficiary cannot claim for restoration of the trust property: (i) if it is extremely difficult to restore the trust

863. *See* para. 396 *supra*. The beneficiary has to exercise the right of intervention within one year from the time of the act (s. 32 (5) Trust Law).
864. Dogauchi 2017a: pp. 224–226. As for the due care of a prudent manager, *see* para. 400 *supra*.
865. *See* paras. 400 to 406 *supra*. As for the comprehensive list of the trustee's duties, *see* para. 400 *supra*.
866. Dogauchi 2017a: pp. 243–244.
867. *See* para. 404 *supra*.
868. Dogauchi 2017a: p. 241.

property, (ii) if the restoration should require excessive expenses, or if there are any other special circumstances in which it is inappropriate to have the trustee restore the trust property (section 40 (1) Proviso Trust Law).

If the trustee would not compensate for the loss or restore the trust property, even though the beneficiary's claim was recognized by the final judgment, the beneficiary can execute the judgment only by the indirect enforcement (section 172 Civil Execution Law), because the trustee's action is necessary to execute the compensation or the restoration.[869] Finally, the beneficiary and the settlor can dismiss the trustee (section 58 Trust Law) and appoint the new trustee, and the new trustee can claim for compensation or restoration against the former trustee (section 75 (5) Trust Law).

Both the beneficiary's claim for compensation and that for restoration may be extinguished by the extinctive prescription (sections 167 and 724 CC). However, the extinctive prescription shall not begin to run until the beneficiary becomes aware that the beneficiary has been designated as a beneficiary or, if there is no beneficiary, until the trust administrator is appointed (section 43 (3) Trust Law).

409. When a defective building or any other structure on a land caused any loss to a person, the injured person can claim for compensation against the possessor of the structure (section 717 CC).[870] If that structure belonged to the trust property, the trustee is liable as a possessor of the trust property by the interpretation of law and bears primarily the liability to compensate for the damages caused by the defect in installation or maintenance of that structure on the land.[871]

410. Duties of the trustee shall terminate when the following grounds take place (section 56 Trust Law): (i) the death of the trustee;[872] (ii) the judgment for commencement of guardianship or curatorship for the trustee unless the terms of trust provide otherwise ; (iii) the order for commencement of bankruptcy procedure against the trustee unless the terms of trust provide otherwise; (iv) the dissolution of the trustee who has been a juridical person for reasons other than a merger; (v) the resignation of the trustee;[873] (vi) the dismissal of the trustee;[874] (vii) any grounds specified by the terms of trust.

The former trustee has to give notice to the beneficiaries about the termination of the duties in the cases of Item (iii) to Item (vii) above (section 59 (1) Main Text

869. Dogauchi 2017a: p. 247.
870. Section 717 (1) CC provides that if a defect in installation or maintenance of any structure on a land has caused damages to others, the possessor of the structure shall be liable to the victims to compensate for the damages; provided that if the possessor has used a necessary care to prevent the damages, the owner must compensate for the damages.
871. DCJ (Tokyo) Feb. 7, 2012 Hanta 1404-200.
872. When the trustee dies, the trust property shall not be succeeded by the trustee's successor(s) but it shall be incorporated as a juridical person (s. 74 (1) Trust Law). However, where two or more joint trustees exist, the remaining trustee(s) shall succeed the rights and duties of the deceased trustee (s. 86 (4) Trust Law).
873. The trustee can resign with the approval of the settlor and the beneficiary; otherwise the trustee can resign with the permission of the court (s. 57 Trust Law).
874. The trustee may be dismissed by the agreement between the settlor and the beneficiary (s. 58 Trust Law).

Trust Law), while the successor of the trustee in the case of Item (i) above and the guardian or curator of the trustee in the case of Item (ii) above have to give the same notice to the beneficiaries who are known to them (section 60 (1) Main Text Trust Law).

The new trustee shall be appointed by the terms of the trust, the agreement between the settlor and the beneficiaries, or the decision by the court as provided by the provisions of law (section 62 (1), (2), (3), (4) Trust Law). Until the new trustee becomes able to administer the trust affairs, the former trustee (in the cases of Item (iv) to (vii) above), the successor (in the case of Item (i) above) or the guardian or curator (in the case of Item (ii)above) have to carry out the necessary actions for the new trustee to take over the trust affairs unless the terms of trust provide otherwise (sections 59 (3), 60 (2) Trust Law).[875]

§6. Status of Beneficiary

411. In normal cases, there is one or more beneficiaries in a trust. The beneficiary may be fixed or specified by the trust act, or it may be appointed or altered by the person who is assigned by the trust act (section 89 Trust Law).[876]

The settlor may become the beneficiary. If the settlor is the beneficiary, it is called "jieki-shintaku" [the self-benefit trust]. If the settlor is not the beneficiary, it is called "taeki-shinntaku" [the others-benefit trust].[877]

The trustee can be one of the beneficiaries, and for the purpose of trust administration, the trustee can tentatively become the only one beneficiary in accordance with the trust act.[878] But if the trustee is only a beneficiary, the trust can be recognized only within one year, and after that the trust shall terminate (section 163 [2] Trust Law).

The trust can be established in which no beneficiary exists. It is a trust for its own purpose.[879]

412. A person who is designated as a beneficiary by the trust act shall acquire a beneficiary's right when the trust is established unless the terms of trust act provides otherwise (section 88 (1) Trust Law). If there is a person who has a right to designate or change the beneficiary, the beneficiary is determined by that person's manifestation of intention to the trustee (section 89 (1) Trust Law). The person who hold the right to designate the beneficiary can make a testamentary will to designate or alter the beneficiary (section 89 (2) Trust Law). If that person designates or alters

875. Dogauchi 2017a: pp. 278–289. In the case of Item (iii) above, the bankruptcy trustee shall take over the management of trust property in response to the notice from the former trustee (s. 59 (2) Trust Law).
876. Arai 2014: pp. 223–226; Dogauchi 2017a: pp. 295–303.
877. However, if the beneficiary's right is transferable, the self-benefit trust can be transformed into the others-benefit trust, and vice versa.
878. However, the "purpose" of the trust cannot be the purpose of "exclusively" promoting the trustee's own interests (s. 2 (1) Trust Law). *See also* para. 404 (a) *supra*.
879. *See* para. 418 *infra*.

the beneficiary by testamentary will, the acquisition of the beneficiary's right cannot be asserted against the trustee unless the trustee knows of the designation or alteration (section 89 (3) Trust Law).[880]

The beneficiary may waive the right of beneficiary by a manifestation of intention to the trustee unless the beneficiary is the settlor or the trustee (section 99 (1) Trust Law).[881] A person should not be forced to become a beneficiary against his/her will. In this case, the beneficiary shall be deemed to have never held the beneficiary's right (section 99 (2) Main Text Trust Law). However, it may not prejudice a third party's rights (section 99 (2) Proviso Trust Law). For instance, if a creditor of the beneficiary executed his/her claim right and attached the beneficiary's interest, then the beneficiary cannot waive the right of beneficiary. This restriction to waive the beneficiary's right which has the retroactive effect would not prevent the waiver of the beneficiary's right for the future.[882]

413. The beneficiary may be specified not only as fixed person(s) but also by general terms. For instance, the settlor A may conclude a trust contract with the trustee B to the effect that the first beneficiary is A's wife C, and if C dies, C's eldest son D shall become the new beneficiary, and if D dies, the beneficiary's eldest son (including adopted child) shall become the new beneficiary. It is called "jyuekisha-renzoku-shintaku" [the successive beneficiaries trust].[883] However, if the trust shall continue too long, the trust property would continue to be bound by the trust terms for a long time, which might affect the property transactions. If it is recognized as against the principle of public order and good morals (section 90 CC),[884] the trust shall be void.[885] Another problem is that the successive beneficiaries trust may change the succession law by the intention of an individual.[886]

414. From this viewpoint, the Trust Law regulates the successive beneficiaries trust. If a trust act stipulates to the effect that upon the death of the previous beneficiary, another person (such as the eldest son including the adopted child) shall become the beneficiary, and a person who is alive after thirty years have passed since the trust was established "becomes the beneficiary according to the trust act," the trust shall be valid until this beneficiary dies or his/her beneficiary's right is extinguished (section 91 Trust Law). In the previous example,[887] if C still alive when thirty years have passed since the trust contract was concluded between A and B, and at that time C's eldest son D was born and still alive, D "becomes" the beneficiary according to the trust contract when C died, and the trust shall terminate

880. Arai 2014: p. 225; Dogauchi 2017a: pp. 301–302.
881. Arai 2014: p. 231.
882. It is valid by the declaration to the trustee, and the beneficiary shall lose the beneficiary's right from the time of the waiver for the future. Arai 2014: p. 233; Dogauchi 2017a: p. 331.
883. Arai 2014: pp. 226–227; Dogauchi 2017a: pp. 306–309.
884. A juridical act which is against the principle of public order and good morals shall be void (s. 90 CC).
885. Dogauchi 2017a: p. 309.
886. Arai 2014: p. 226.
887. *See* para. 412 *supra*.

when D dies or D's beneficiary's right is extinguished. Even if D's eldest son E was born and still alive when D dies, E cannot become the beneficiary.[888]

As a result, the successive beneficiaries trust may be valid around 100 years. This regulation can be one of the standards by which the validity of a long-standing trust in conformity to the principle of public order and good morals (section 90 CC) may be judged.[889]

415. The right of beneficiary is called "jueki-ken." It is defined as "a claim based on the terms of trust concerning the obligation of a trustee to distribute property that comes under trust property to a beneficiary or to make any other distribution from the trust property (hereinafter referred to as the 'beneficiary's distribution claim'), and the right to request a trustee or any other person to carry out certain acts under the provisions of this law" (section 2 (7) Trust Law). The content of the beneficiary's distribution claim is determined by the trust act. It can be the right to use the trust property, the right to take any profits from the trust property, the right to receive a certain amount of money from the trust property, or any other interests unless it is against the principle of public order or good morals (section 90 CC).[890]

Corresponding to the beneficiary's distribution claim, the trustee bears obligation and responsibility to perform in accordance with the purpose and terms of the trust as specified by the trust act. The trustee is liable to perform obligations for the beneficiary by using the trust property (section 100 Trust Law), and he/she is not liable for performing those obligations by using his/her own property, even if the trust property is not enough to perform those obligations for the beneficiary. In addition, the beneficiary's rights against the trustee to claim for any interest specified by the trust act shall be subordinated to the claims of creditors with whom the trustee transacted for the trust administration and any other claims to be covered by the trust property. These claims are "sintaku-saiken" [the trust claim] (section 101 Trust Law).[891]

416. The beneficiary may transfer the beneficiary's right to the other person in accordance with the terms of trust act unless the nature of the right does not allow the transfer (section 93 (1) Trust Law). It can be restricted by the terms of trust, however, the restriction cannot be opposable against a third party who did not know without gross negligence about the restriction (section 93 (2) Trust Law).[892] This regulation is the same as the transfer of claim rights (section 466 CC). If there is a restriction on the transfer of the beneficiary's right by the trust terms, the creditor of

888. If D was born and C died and D becomes the beneficiary before thirty years have passed since the establishment of the trust, and after thirty years have passed since the establishment of the trust D died and E is alive, then E becomes the beneficiary according to the trust contract and the trust shall be valid until E dies or E's beneficiary's right is extinguished.
889. Dogauchi 2017a: p. 309.
890. Arai 2014: pp. 233–236; Dogauchi 2017a: pp. 309–314.
891. The trust claim means a claim which corresponds to an obligation to be covered by the trust property other than the beneficiary's distribution claim (s. 21 (2) [2] Trust Law).
892. Dogauchi 2017a: pp. 322–324.

the beneficiary can attach the beneficiary's right to execute the claim, because the settlor cannot create any special property which are free from the attachment by the creditor of the beneficiary.[893]

The transfer of the beneficiary's right may not be asserted against the trustee and a third party unless the transferor gives notice of the transfer to the trustee or the trustee has acknowledged the transfer (section 94 (1) Trust Law). The notice by the transferor to the trustee and the acknowledgement by the trustee cannot be opposable against the third party unless it is made by means of an instrument authenticated with a certified date (section 94 (2) Trust Law).[894] This regulation is the same as the transfer of claim rights (section 467 CC).

The regulations of transferability and requirements of the beneficiary's right shall apply to the establishment of the right of pledge on the beneficiary's right (sections 96, 97 Trust Law; section 364 CC).[895]

417. In order to maintain the interest of the beneficiary, the beneficiary has some auxiliary rights other than the beneficiary's distribution claim. The beneficiary can request the trustee, by specifying the reason, to inspect or copy the documents or the electromagnetic records concerned with the trust administration (section 38 (1) Trust Law). In order to specify the reason for the request, the beneficiary does not need to prove that the suspected fact actually exists.[896] The trustee cannot refuse the request unless the request is for the purpose of disturbing the trust administration or harming the common interests of the beneficiaries, or for other purposes as provided by the law (section 38 (2) Trust Law). If the beneficiary administers a competitive business with the trust administration, the trustee can refuse the request for the reason of possible disturbance of the trust administration and possible loss to the trust property without proving that the beneficiary has an intention to use the information for the advantage of his/her own business.[897] When the trustee refuses the beneficiary's request for the reason of the confidentiality of the other beneficiary, the requesting beneficiary needs to prove the probability of the breach of the duty of the trustee.[898]

If two or more beneficiaries exist, each beneficiary can request the trustee, by specifying the reason, to disclose the name and address of the other beneficiaries and the content of the beneficiary's right held by other beneficiaries unless the terms of trust provide otherwise (section 39 (1), (3) Trust Law). The trustee cannot refuse the request unless the request is for the purpose of disturbing the trust administration or harming the common interests of the beneficiaries, or for other purposes as provided by the law unless the terms of trust provide otherwise (section 39 (2) Trust

893. The judicial precedent on the restriction on the transfer of claim right (SCJ Apr. 10, 1970 Minshu 24-4-240) is interpreted to apply to the restriction on the transfer of beneficiary's right.

894. Arai 2014: p. 230; Dogauchi 2017a: pp. 322–326.

895. Arai 2014: p. 230; Dogauchi 2017a: pp. 327–329.

896. The judicial precedent on the stakeholder's right to the director of the company (SCJ Jul. 1, 2004 Minshu 58-5-1214) is interpreted to apply to the beneficiary's right to the trustee.

897. The judicial precedent on the stakeholder's right to the director of the company (SCJ Jan. 15, 2009 Minshu 63-1-1) is interpreted to apply to the trustees refusal to the beneficiary's request.

898. DCJ (Tokyo) Feb. 1, 2001 Hanta 1074-249. On the duty of the trustee to report on the trust administration, *see* para. 404 *supra*.

Law). The beneficiary's right to request disclosure of other beneficiaries' name, address, etc. aim to negotiate with other beneficiaries for the collective decision-making by the beneficiaries on the matters specified by the provisions of law (sections 105 and 106–122 Trust Law) and by the terms of trust act.[899] The appropriateness of the trustee's refusal should be judged in light of this purpose of the beneficiary's right.

418. The trust may be established if there is no specific beneficiary. It is called "mokuteki-shintaku" [the trust for its own purpose]. For example, the trust for the promotion of public interest does not presuppose the existence of any specified beneficiaries. The Trust Law of 2006 provides in Chapter XI "Special Rules for a Trust with No Provisions on Beneficiaries." The trust with no provisions on the beneficiary including provisions on the method for specifying a beneficiary may be established only by the trust contract between the settlor and the trustee or by the testamentary will of the settlor (section 258 (1) [1], and section 3 [1] and [2] Trust Law).[900]

The rationality of the trust without beneficiary is recognized if it is reasonable to achieve the purpose specified by the trust act (section 3 [1], [2] Trust Law). For instance, the settlor will provide a certain property and agree with the trustee to use it for the community activities or for the charitable activities, or to distribute scholarship for certain students, etc.[901] However, it can be abused by the settlor to separate a certain property and avoid the attachment as the execution of claims by his/her creditors. For the restriction on the possible abuse, once the trust without beneficiary is established, the beneficiary cannot be newly appointed by the alteration of the trust (section 258 (2) Trust Law), while once the trust with beneficiary is established, the provision on the beneficiary in the trust terms cannot be abolished by the alteration of the trust (section 258 (3) Trust Law).[902] In addition, the trust without beneficiary must be within twenty years (section 259 Trust Law).

When the trust without beneficiary is established by the contract of trust, the beneficiary's right to supervise the trust administration by the trustee shall be vested to the settlor and it cannot be changed by the alteration of trust (section 260 (1) Trust Law). In order to establish a trust without beneficiary by the testamentary will, the terms of trust should include a provision to designate a trust administrator (section 258 (4) Trust Law). The trust administrator is a person who shall play the role of beneficiary to supervise the trustee's administration of trust (section 259 Trust Law). If the provision is not included in the trust terms, the executor of the will, if any, has to appoint the trust administrator (section 258 (5) Trust Law). If the executor of

899. Arai 2014: p. 307; Dogauchi 2017a: pp. 200–201.

900. The trust without beneficiary (the trust for its own purpose) cannot be established by the declaration of intention to establish a trust (s. 3 [3] Trust Law). If there is no beneficiary, the supervision of the trust should depend only on the settlor or the trust administrator (the appointment of the trust administrator is necessary for the trust established by a testamentary will [ss. 258 (4) to (6) Trust Law]). However, in the declaration to establish the trust, the settlor becomes the trustee and the trust administrator is not necessary so that it is difficult to supervise the trustee's administration of trust. Dogauchi 2017a: pp. 317–318, 367.

901. As for the examples of trust without beneficiary, *see* Arai 2014: pp. 431–432.

902. Dogauchi 2017a: p. 320.

the will does not appoint the trust administrator or there is no executor of the will, the court can appoint the trust administrator upon the request by the interested persons (section 258 (6) Trust Law). However, if the appointed trust administrator refused to take the office or the interested person did not apply for the appointment of the trust administrator and one year has passed without the trust administrator, the trust without beneficiary established by the testamentary will shall be extinguished (section 258 (8) Trust Law). Thus the trust without beneficiary can be administered by the trustee under the supervision by the settlor and the trust administrator.[903]

§7. Status of Settlor

419. Even after the establishment of the trust, the settlor can keep certain rights on the administration of trust property.[904] Certain rights are vested to the settlor by the provisions of law, though they can be excluded by the trust act (section 145 (1) Trust Law).[905] For instance, the settlor may dismiss the trustee with the approval of the beneficiary unless the trust act provides otherwise (section 58 (1), (2), (3) Trust Law). Even if the beneficiary does not agree, the settlor may ask the court to dismiss the trustee when the trustee has caused a substantial detriment to the trust property through a breach of the duties or if there are other relevant reasons for the dismissal (section 58 (4) Trust Law). The settlor may permit the trustee to resign with the approval of the beneficiary (section 57 (1) Trust Law). If the trustee's duty has been terminated on any of the grounds, the settlor may appoint the new trustee with the approval of the beneficiary unless the trust terms provide otherwise (section 62 (1) Trust Law).

In addition, certain rights can be added by the trust act (section 145 (2) [1] to [15] Trust Law). These rights aim to supervise the trustee to facilitate the trust administration.[906]

§8. Termination of Trust

420. The trust shall terminate by: (i) the agreement between the settlor and the beneficiary (section 164 (1) Trust Law), and (ii) the provisions of law (section 163 Trust Law). However, the trust continues to exist even after the termination for the purpose of liquidation (section 146 Trust Law). The termination means the commencement of liquidation procedure.[907]

903. The trust administrator can be appointed when the settlor exists. Dogauchi 2017a: pp. 318–319.
904. Arai 2014: p. 204; Dogauchi 2017a: pp. 382–386.
905. The reason is that the settlor is the party to the trust act so that it is based on his/her own intention. But, in the case of the trust without beneficiary, the settlor shall be deemed to have certain rights to supervise the trust administration which are listed in s. 145 (2) Trust Law. In this case, those rights of settlor cannot be changed by the alteration to the trust (s. 260 (1) Trust Law). *See also* para. 418 *supra*.
906. Arai 2014: p. 204; Dogauchi 2017a: pp. 384–386.
907. Dogauchi 2017a: p. 403.

The settlor and the beneficiary may terminate the trust at any time by the agreement between them unless the trust act provides otherwise (section 164 (1) Trust Law). It is a kind of contract to terminate the trust. However, the beneficiary is not a party to the trust act so that it is different from the termination contract but a special cause to terminate the trust.[908]

421. Trust Law provides the legal grounds for the termination of trust (section 163 Trust Law). They include the cases: (a) when the purpose of trust has been achieved or it has become impossible to achieve the purpose of trust; (b) when the trustee has continuously held all beneficial interests in the form of the trustee's own property for one year; (c) when the trust lacks the trustee and the duties have not been filled by a new trustee for one year; (d) when the trustee has terminated the trust for the reason of shortage of the trust property to reimburse the expenses spent by the trustee;[909] (e) when the trust is merged with another trust; (f) when the court has made a decision to order the termination of the trust for the reason of emerging unexpected circumstances[910] or securing the public interest;[911] (g) when the court order for the commencement of bankruptcy procedure has been entered against the trust property; (h) when the settlor is given the court order for the commencement of bankruptcy, rehabilitation or reorganization procedure, and the trust contract has been terminated according to the provisions of law; or (i) when any grounds specified by the terms of trust occur.[912]

422. When the trust has terminated for the reasons as stated in paragraph 421 *supra* except for the reason of the merger (Item (e) in paragraph 421 *supra*) and for the reason of the court order for commencement of bankruptcy procedure against the trust property and that given to the settlor (Item (g) and (h) in paragraph 421 *supra*), the trust enters into the liquidation procedure, which is to be led by the trustee (section 175 Trust Law).[913]

Even after the trust has terminated, it is deemed to continue to exist until the liquidation is completed (section 176 Trust Law). The trustee, as the liquidation trustee, has to perform obligations, exercise rights and do any other things in accordance with the provisions of law (sections 177 and 178 Trust Law).

---

908. Arai 2014: pp. 387–388; 390–391. The settlor has the interest to achieve the purpose of trust and the beneficiary has the interest to receive distribution, while the trustee should not have the interest from the administration of trust. *See* Dogauchi 2017a: p. 409.
909. Dogauchi 2017a: pp. 412–413.
910. Section 165 (1) Trust Law. *See* Dogauchi 2017a: pp. 409–410.
911. Section 166 (1) Trust Law. *See* Dogauchi 2017a: pp. 410–411.
912. In practice, this is the normal ground for the termination of trust. For instance, the case when the term of duration has expired as stipulated by the trust act. *See* Arai 2014: p. 390.
913. Arai 2014: pp. 392–405; Dogauchi 2017a: pp. 413–424.

Residual assets shall vest in the person designated by the trust act as: (i) the person who is the beneficiary and will have the distribution of residual assets (the beneficiary for residual assets) and (ii) the person who is not the beneficiary and will only be vested with residual assets should be vested (the holder of the vested right) (section 182 (1) Trust Law).[914]

423. In the case of a limited liability trust, a liquidation trustee must give public notice in the Official Gazette without delay after assuming the office to the effect that trust creditors are requested to file their claims during a certain period of time (not less than two months) and that the trust creditors who fail to file their claims within that period shall be excluded from the liquidation. Besides, the liquidation trustee must give the same notice to each known trust creditors respectively (section 229 Trust Law). This procedure is necessary, because the liquidation trustee is not responsible for the payment of debt from his/her original assets against trust creditors.[915]

914. Arai 2014: pp. 395–397; Dogauchi 2017a: pp. 418–421. If the trust act contains no provisions on the designation of the person who will receive the residual assets, or all of beneficiaries for residual assets or the holders of the vested rights have waived their rights on residual assets, the settlor or settlor's heir or other successor is deemed to be designated as the holder of the vested right (s. 182 (2) Trust Law). When the residual assets still remain which have not been vested to anybody, they shall be vested to the liquidation trustee (s. 182 (3) Trust Law).

915. Dogauchi 2017a: pp. 423–424. However, if residual assets remain after the liquidation, the trust creditors who did not file their claims within the designated period can still claim for the payment (s. 231 (2) Trust Law).

Chapter 2. Security

§1. Trust for Security Purpose

424. The trust may be used for security purposes in various ways:[916] (i) the beneficiary may use the beneficiary's rights as collateral; (ii) the trustee may use the trust property as collateral or become a guarantor as a part of trust administration in accordance with the purpose and terms stipulated in the trust act; (iii) the settlor may establish the trust for security purposes. The first and second type of trust usages (Item (i) and (ii) above) are the simple and normal usages of trust scheme. The third type of trust usage (Item (iii) above) should be discussed as the use of trust for security purpose in a narrow sense (trust for security). In order to secure the performance of obligations of the debtor corresponding to the claims of the creditor, the provision of collateral such as a hypothec and a mortgage and the arrangement of suretyship provided by the guarantor have been often used in the practices in Japan. However, the types and the content of collateral is fixed by the law[917] and the use of suretyship depends on the consent of the guarantor. Recently the use of trust has been extended to the transactions which have security purposes. This trust scheme is used in the equipment trust, the trust of the intracompany savings for corporate employees, the trust for the separate management of customer assets, the trust for debt assumption, etc.[918]

425. One of the typical examples of trust for security purpose which is used in business practice can be found in the trust for retirement benefits. For instance, a company may establish the trust by making contract with a trust bank as the trustee for the purpose of secure the funds for retirement benefits to be paid to the employees when they retire, and transfer certain assets such as stocks and bonds which the company holds to the trust bank as the trustee. The trust bank administers, manages and dispose of those assets in accordance with the trust contract. The beneficiaries are employees, but it is also advantageous for the company as the settlor. By using this trust scheme, the company may utilize the assets for making profits of them, for securing the funds for retirement benefits and for fulfilling the requirement as pension assets provided by the Accounting Standard Concerning Retirement Benefits Reserves[919] and Operational Guidelines Concerning Retirement Benefits Reserve Accounting[920] at the same time. Thus it may be the viable measure to make up the lack of reserves which is required by the Accounting Standards. According to the terms of the trust act, the company may continue to exercise the voting right, even when the company has transferred the stocks to the trust bank as the trust property.

916. Hiroto Dogauchi, "Tanpo-toshite-no-shintaku" [Trust as Security], Kinpo 1881 (2007) pp. 26–31.
917. The principle of numerus clausus also applies to the types of collateral as real rights. However, some types of collateral as real rights such as a transfer of ownership for the purpose of collateral (the conveyancing mortgage) and the reservation of ownership have been created as the customary law and recognized by the case law. *See* paras. 493, 524, 526 *infra.*
918. Arai 2014: pp. 480–483.
919. Business Accounting Council, Jun. 16, 1998.
920. Report No. 13, Accounting System Committee of the Japanese Institute of Certified Public Accountants.

The trust scheme like this shows the possibility of more flexible usage of trust for security purposes than the existing secured transactions such as collateral and suretyship.

§2. Security Interest for Trust Property

426. The security interest as a property right may be the trust property in response to the need of business practices in Japan. It is called a "security trust." The settlor establishes the trust by concluding a trust contract with the trustee and transfers the security rights such as the rights of hypothec to the trustee and the creditors who hold claim rights to be secured by those security rights become the beneficiaries.[921]

427. For instance, the company A needs finance of JPY 10 billion (equivalent to around EUR 7 billion and USD 8 billion) for the construction of a new factory, and Bank B, Bank C and Bank D agree with A to lent money of JPY 5 billion, JPY 3 billion and JPY 2 billion respectively to A. A establishes the right of hypothec on the land and factory as the factory foundation for B, C and D and they agree that the priority order among them is the same rank. In this type of syndicate loan, it would be convenient for B, C and D to establish the trust to administer and exercise the right of hypothec uniformly. Otherwise, it would be costly for D, for instance, to transfer the claim right of JPY 2 billion to Company E, because D and E need to change the name of the holder of right of hypothec in the registration book.

428. Further, it would be complicated if Bank C and Bank D want to execute the right of hypothec, but Bank B would like to postpone the due date of repayment and suspend the execution of the right of hypothec, when the company A delays to repay the debt to B, C and D. In order to avoid the inconvenience, B, C and D may agree to establish the trust to administer and exercise the right of hypothec uniformly and to appoint B as the trustee and B, C and D become the beneficiaries. B has to administer and exercise the right of hypothec in accordance with the purpose and terms provided by the trust contract. If D wants to sell his/her claim right to E, D may transfer (assign) it to E with the beneficiary's right and D and E do not need to change the holder's name of the right of hypothec in the registration book, in which it remains to be registered in the name of B as the trustee. The Trust Law of 2006 recognizes this type of trust explicitly. It provides that the trust may be established to the effect that "the person will be granted a security interest in property" (section 3 [1] and [2] Trust Law). And it also provides that in the case where the trust is established for a security interest to the effect that the trust property is the security right and the beneficiary is the creditor of the claim to be secured by the security right, the trustee may, as the holder of the security right, apply for its enforcement and receive money as proceeds of the auction or payment for the debt within the scope of trust administration (section 55 Trust Law).[922]

---

921. Dogauchi 2007: pp. 69–70; Arai 2014: pp. 150–156.
922. Dogauchi 2007: p. 70; Arai 2014: pp. 152–153.

Part V. Security

Chapter 1. Securities in Immovable Property

§1. Introduction

429. In the historical development of the Japanese economy, the financial transactions have developed in the business practices even before the Meiji period. But they have become more widespread in the modernization process since the end of the nineteenth century under the government policy of "shokusan-kogyo" [the investment to encourage new industries].[923] With the expansion of the credit economy, the need for various types of secured transaction have been promoted. The general introduction of the private landownership since 1871[924] has greatly contributed to the use of securities in immovable property in Japan. The central role has been played by the hypothec established on the land.[925]

430. Types of securities in Japanese law can be divided into two categories. They are: (i) "butteki-tanpo" [the security by property] and (ii) "jinteki-tanpo" [the security by person]. The former is the security by a certain property which the debtor or a third party provides for the creditor, while the latter is the security by a personal liability backed by the assets and incomes of that person.

(i) The major types of "butteki-tanpo" [the security by property] are collateral rights provided by the Civil Code. They are: (a) the right of retention, (b) the right of lien, (c) the right of pledge and (d) the right of hypothec. They are all classified into "bukken" [real rights] in the Civil Code (sections 295 to 398-22 CC). The first two, (a) the right of retention and (b) the right of lien, are statutory collateral rights which are established by the effect of law (ipso iure) without any agreement between the parties. The last two, (c) the right of pledge and (d) the right of hypothec, are collateral rights by agreement. The first three ((a), (b) and (c) above) can be established in both immovable and movable property, while (d) the right of

923. *See* paras. 38 and 59 *supra*.
924. *See* para. 70 *supra*.
925. Matsuo and Kozumi 2008: pp. 244–245. *See* §5 (paras. 462 to 487 *infra*).

hypothec is established in immovable property in the Civil Code.[926] These four types are provided in the Civil Code so that they are called "typical" collateral rights.[927]

In addition, (e) "the security right preserved by provisional registration" was created by the customary law and recognized by the special law,[928] and (f) the right of conveyancing mortgage and (g) the reservation of ownership are created by the customary law and recognized by the case law. They are called "atypical" collateral rights.[929]

These collateral rights, (a) to (g) above, are all recognized as real rights called "tanpo-bukken" [the collateral real rights, the real rights for the purpose of security]. Besides, one more type of secured transaction on the basis of a property is (h) "kaimodoshi-no-tokuyaku" [the special agreement on the redemption] of an immovable property, which is provided in the chapter of contract as an additional agreement to the contract of sale (sections 579–585 CC).[930] The redemption agreement must be put at the same time as the conclusion of the sales contract, and the object of the redemption agreement is limited to the immovable property (section 579 CC). In this case, a certain amount of finance is created in the form of a purchase money provided by the lender as a purchaser, and the property as a collateral to secure the repayment of money is provided by the borrower as a seller. The special agreement on the redemption of immovable property can be registered in the registration book (section 581 (1) CC, section 96 LRIP).[931]

431. (ii) The major type of "jinteki-tanpo" [the security by person] is (a) the suretyship (sections 446 to 465-5 CC). In addition to the suretyship (b) the indivisible obligation to be borne by two or more persons (section 430 CC) and (c) the joint obligation to be borne by two or more persons (sections 436–445 CC) will also strengthen the right of creditor, because every debtor has a duty to perform obligation to the full for the interest of the creditor (sections 430 and 436). For instance, if A and B jointly borrowed an apartment house from C and agreed to pay the rent of JPY 100,000 per month to C. The obligation to pay the lent is interpreted as the indivisible obligation (section 430 CC) and C can claim either A or B to pay the full amount of JPY 100,000 (sections 430, 436 CC)[932] even though A and B agreed to share the rent of JPY 50,000 respectively. If A and B jointly injured C and C acquired a claim to pay compensation for the damage of JPY 50,000 (sections 709, 710 CC), C can claim either A or B to pay the full amount of JPY 100,000 (sections

926. However, special laws recognize the right of hypothec in certain movables such as a car, ship, and airplane. *See* para. 523 *infra*.
927. Matsuo and Kozumi 2008: pp. 241–245.
928. The Law on the Contract for Security Right Preserved by Provisional Registration (Law No. 78, 1978).
929. Matsuo and Kozumi 2008: pp. 250, 396–434.
930. Hoshino 1981: pp. 220, 317.
931. The similar agreement used in the practice is the reservation agreement to resale the immovable property, the right to complete the reservation can be registered as the provisional registration in the registration book (ss. 2 [2], 105 [2], 107, 108 LRIP).
932. STJ Nov. 24, 1922 Minshu 1-670.

719, 436 CC). In this sense, the indivisible obligation and joint obligation virtually mean the security to perform the obligation to be borne by another person.[933]

§2. RIGHT OF RETENTION

432. If a person A possesses a thing which belongs to another person B and A has a claim right which has been created "with respect to that thing," A can refuse B's claim to return the thing and retain it until B performs the obligation corresponding to A's claim on that thing (section 295 (1) CC Main Text). This right of A to retain the thing is called "ryuchi-ken" [the right of retention]. For example, B asked A to repair a construction machine and delivered it to A. A fixed it up, but B did not pay a remuneration which B agreed with A. B claimed against A to return it on the basis of his/her ownership. However, A can make a counterclaim asserting that he/she can retain the machine until the remuneration is paid in full on the basis of his/her right of retention. The right of retention is a security right provided by law for the purpose of keeping fairness between the owner of a thing and a creditor who has a claim right on that thing.[934]

In the previous case B can make a re-defense when the claim is not due (section 295 (1) Proviso CC). In addition, if A had acquired its possession by means of "a tortious act," the right of retention cannot be recognized for A (section 295 (2) CC). This is another re-defense for B.

The similar effect as the right of retention can be enjoyed by using "doji-riko-no-koben" [the defense to ask the simultaneous performance of obligation] (sections 533, 546 CC). In the previous case, when A is asked from B to return the machine after A repaired it but without payment which B agreed to pay, A can make a defense that A will return it in exchange of the payment. A can choose to make a defense either based on the right of retention or by the simultaneous performance.[935] The defense of simultaneous performance (section 533 CC) can be exercised on the basis of contractual relation between A and B. If B has sold the machine to C and C asks A to return it, A can exercise the right of retention which is the real right to be asserted even against a third party with whom A does not have any contractual relation. However, the defense of simultaneous performance can be recognized when a contract was terminated for any reason after the performance of obligations between the parties. If A sold a piece of land to B and delivered it to B in exchange of the partial payment, however, A terminated the contract, because B did not pay the rest of the purchase money as promised, then A can claim B to return the land. B can make a defense to retain the land either based on the right of retention or by the simultaneous performance. But if B lent the land to C without A's permission, B's right of retention shall be extinguished by the counter-defense of A (section 298 (3) CC). However, even in that case B can still use the defense of simultaneous performance between the return of the partial payment and the return of the land.[936]

933. Matsuo and Kozumi 2008: pp. 251–253; Matsuo 2016: pp. 311–314.
934. Matsuo and Kozumi 2008: pp. 254.
935. Matsuo and Kozumi 2008: pp. 255–256.
936. HCJ (Tokyo) Jul. 14, 1949 Kominshu 2-2-124.

433. The right of retention can be created on a thing when the claim is caused "with respect to that thing" (section 295 Main Text CC).[937] The close relation between the claim and the thing is required for the right of retention. For instance, the right of retention was not recognized in the following case. B, who owned a piece of land, leased it to A for twenty years, but A's right of lease was not registered. After 7 years passed B sold the land to C and C registered the acquisition of ownership and claimed against A to vacate the land. A refused to return it on the basis of his/her prior right of lease. However, C may re-defense by asserting that A's right was not be opposable against a third party like C without registering the right of lease (section 177 CC, section 3 [8] LRIP). Then, A alleged that A had acquired a claim to pay compensation for damages against B because of the breach of the contract of lease concluded between A and B, and in order to secure the claim A should be able to retain the land on the basis of the right of retention (section 295 Main Text CC). But, the Supreme Court denied A's defense for the reason that the right of retention could not be recognized in this case, because the claim right for compensation could not be recognized as created "with respect to that thing" (section 295 Main Text CC) but should be recognized as caused by B's breach of the contract of lease.[938] The relation between the claim and the thing seems to be interpreted as being more direct.

434. Similarly, if B, an owner of a building, sold and delivered it to A but A's acquisition has not been registered, and B sold it to C and C registered his/her acquisition and claimed against A for the vacation of that building. A made a defense against C on the basis of his/her prior acquisition of ownership, however, C made a re-defense that A's ownership was not opposable without the registration (section 177 CC). Then A alleged that A had a claim for compensation against B because of the breach of the sales contract and in order to secure that claim A should be able to retain the building on the basis of the right of retention (section 295 Main Text CC). However, the Supreme Court denied A's defense for the reason that the right of retention could not be recognized in this case, because the claim for compensation could not be recognized as created "with respect to that thing" (section 295 Main Text CC) but should be recognized as caused by B's breach of the sales contract.[939] In addition to the remoteness between the thing and A's claim for compensation caused by B's breach of contract, if the right of retention were to be recognized for A in this case, the normative value of section 177 of the Civil Code must be ruined.[940]

---

937. However, this relation between the claim and the thing can be relaxed for the claim which is created in the transaction between the merchants. When a claim is created in the commercial transaction for both parties who are the merchants and the claim is due, the creditor can retain the thing or the stocks and bonds which is owned by the debtor and possessed by the creditor through the commercial transaction until the obligation corresponding to the claim is performed unless the parties have agreed otherwise (s. 512 Commercial Code). It aims to facilitate the commercial transactions between the merchants. Matsuo and Kozumi 2008: p. 256.
938. STJ Aug. 21, 1922 Minshu 1-498.
939. SCJ Nov. 21, 1968 Minshu 22-12-2765.
940. Matsuo 2016: pp. 527–528.

435. If the right of retention is recognized for the creditor, he/she can possess the whole thing until the obligation corresponding to his/her claim is fully performed (section 296 CC). The creditor who holds the right of retention must possess the thing with "the due care of a prudent manager" (section 298 (1) CC), and he/she cannot use, lease or establish a collateral right on that thing without the consent of a person who delivered it to the creditor or its owner except for the use necessary for the preservation of the thing (section 298 (2) CC). The example of "the use necessary for the preservation of the thing" is the use of a building by a tenant who possesses the building after the lease was over and claims the owner of that building to reimburse the expenses to reserve the building.[941]

If the creditor obtains the consent to use or make a profit of it, he/she can use for him/herself or collect fruits from the thing, and assign those profits to the satisfaction of his/her claim prior to other creditors (section 297 (1)).[942] The profits collected by the creditor from the thing must be assigned first to the payment of interest on the claim, and the remainder, if any, must be assigned to the satisfaction of the principal of the claim (section 297 (2) CC).

436. If A, the holder of the right of retention, did not retain the thing with the care of a good manager, or he/she used or leased the thing without a necessary consent of B who delivered it to A or its owner, B can claim for extinction of the right of retention (section 298 (3) CC). The claim for extinction can be recognized even if the use or lease was over or B suffered any substantial damages.[943] When B sold the thing to a third party C, C can claim for extinction[944] unless B had given A a consent to use or lease the thing.[945] B may also make a claim for the extinction of the right of retention by tendering a reasonable collateral (section 301 CC).

437. When the debtor is in default, the holder of the right of retention may execute it by applying for the auction to the court (section 195 Civil Execution Law). If the thing is sold, the court has to pay the holder of the right of retention a certain amount corresponding to his/her claim from the purchase money paid by the buyer at the auction before the distribution of it to the other creditors of the debtor, otherwise the buyer cannot acquire the possession.[946]

When the owner of the thing claims to return it on the basis of ownership, the holder of the right of retention can make a defense based on that right, and the court should hold that the holder of the right of retention must return the thing in exchange of the provision of money corresponding to his/her claim.[947]

---

941. STJ May 13, 1925 Minshu 14-876. If the tenant acquired any profits from the use, he/she can assign it to the satisfaction of the claim (Matsuo and Kozumi 2008. p. 263).
942. The creditor can use the thing and assign the profits from the use of that thing to the satisfaction of his/her claim prior to other creditors without the consent of a person who delivered it to the creditor or its owner, if the use is necessary for the preservation of the thing (s. 298 (2) Proviso CC). *See* Matsuo and Kozumi 2008: p. 263.
943. SCJ May 51, 1963 Minshu 17-4-570.
944. SCJ Jul. 15, 1965 Minshu 19-5-1275.
945. SCJ Jul. 3, 1997 Minshu 51-6-2500.
946. Matsuo and Kozumi 2008: p. 264.
947. SCJ Mar. 13, 1958 Minshu 12-3-524.

Thus the right of retention has an effect to receive performance of obligation corresponding to the claim prior to the other creditors though it is not explicitly provided in the Civil Code.[948]

However, as the right of retention cannot be registered in the registration book and thus lacks publicity, it may affect the other creditors even though they had registered their secured interest such as a hypothec. There is a legal doctrine that the immovable property should be excluded from the object of right of retention.[949]

§3. Right of Lien

I. Overview

438. Among various kinds of claim rights generated from a variety of causes, certain claim rights are given priority over others by the provisions of law (sections 303–341 CC). This priority right given to creditors of those certain claims is called "sakidori-tokken" [the right of statutory lien (hereinafter "the right of lien")] (section 303 CC). This institution was introduced from the French Civil Code, though the corresponding right did not exist in the German law.[950] It is one of the statutory security rights together with the right of retention which are established without any agreement between the parties. According to the provisions of law, the right of lien is recognized in: (i) assets as a whole (the general right of lien), (ii) a particular movable property (the special right of lien in movable), or (iii) a particular immovable property (the right of lien in immovable) which belongs to the debtor: (i) the general right of lien and (iii) the special right of lien in immovable property will be treated in this section, and (ii) the special right of lien in movable property will be explained in the next Chapter on the Securities in Movable Property.[951]

439. The right of lien can be exercised to the substituting things of the object such as money which the debtor has received as a result of the sale, lease or loss of, or damage to the object of the statutory lien (section 304 (1) Main Text CC). However, it is necessary for the creditor (the holder of the right of lien) to attach the money before the payment to the debtor (the owner of the object) (section 304 (1) Proviso CC). This is called "butsujo-daii" [the substitution of the object]. The same shall apply if a real right is established on the object of the right of lien and the payment is agreed between the parties such as a rent for a superficies established on a land, and the creditor can attach the rent before it is delivered to the debtor, the owner of the land (section 304 (2) CC). It is the special extension of security interest to a claim to be created from the object of the right of lien by the provision of law.[952]

948. Matsuo and Kozumi 2008: p. 264.
949. Kenzaburo Kozumi, "Ryuchiken-no-shatei-oyobi-seishitsu-ni-kansuru-ichkosatsu" [A Reflection on the Scope and the Nature of the Right of Retention], Hogaku-shinpo, Vol. 111, No. 3 and 4 (2004) p. 1.
950. Matsuo and Kozumi 2008: p. 269.
951. *See* Ch. 2, §2 (paras. 501 to 512 *infra*).
952. Matsuo and Kozumi 2008: pp. 276–278, 322–333.

II. General Right of Lien

440. A person who has a claim right which arose from the following causes shall have a right of lien in the entire property of the debtor: (i) expenses for the common benefit; (ii) an employer-employee relationship; (iii) funeral expenses; and (iv) a supply of daily necessaries (section 306 CC). It is called "ippan-no-sakidoritokken" [the general right of lien], for the creditor of claims which are generated from the causes listed above has a right of lien in the properties as a whole that belong to the debtor. These claims are recognized as to be strongly protected to maintain the fairness among the creditors and to secure the necessary expenses for the life of the debtor.[953]

441. (i) The general right of lien for expenses for the common benefit shall exist with respect to the claim for expenses of preservation, liquidation or distribution of the property of the debtor incurred for the common benefit of all creditors (section 307 (1) CC). If the expenses were not beneficial for all the creditors, the general right of lien can be asserted only against creditors who received a benefit as a result of that expenses (section 307 (2) CC).[954]

442. (ii) The general right of lien for employer-employee relationship shall exist with respect to the claim for salaries and other claims such as a claim for compensation for damages which were generated between the employer (debtor) and the employee (creditor) relationship (section 308 CC).[955]

443. (iii) The general right of lien for funeral expenses shall exist with respect to the claim for reasonable expenses of a funeral held for the debtor (section 309 (1) CC) and for his/her relatives whom the debtor was bound to support (section 309 (2) CC). It aims to secure the funeral which is appropriate for the deceased person. The "reasonable" expenses should be determined by considering the social status of the debtor.[956]

444. (iv) The general right of lien for daily necessities shall exist with respect to the claim for supply of food and drink, fuel and electricity for the latest six months required for the household of the debtor, his/her relatives who reside with him/her and whom the debtor is bound to support, and the domestic servants of the debtor (section 310 CC). It aims to secure the supply of the daily necessities.[957]

445. The priority order among the general rights of lien is given to: (i) the claim caused by expenses for the common benefit (sections 306 [1], 307 CC); then (ii) the claim caused from an employer-employee relationship (sections 306 [2], 308 CC);

953. Matsuo and Kozumi 2008: p. 269.
954. Matsuo and Kozumi 2008: pp. 269–270; Ohmi 2020b: p. 44.
955. It will include the employee's claim for compensation for damages caused by the defects of the facilities in the workplace managed by the employer. Matsuo and Kozumi 2008: p. 270; Ohmi 2020b: pp. 44–45.
956. Matsuo and Kozumi 2008: p. 270.
957. Matsuo and Kozumi 2008: p. 270.

then (iii) the claim caused by funeral expenses (sections 306 [3], 309 CC); and then (iv) the claim caused by the supply of daily necessities (section 306 [4]), 310 CC) (section 329 (1) CC). This priority order is based on the fairness among the creditors and the legal policy to protect the certain claims. The claim for the common benefit ((i) above) is the first priority, because all the creditors enjoy this benefit. The priority order between the claim caused from an employer-employee relationship ((ii) above) and the claim for funeral expenses (Item (iii) above) was changed in 1949 to strengthen the protection of employees.[958]

446. The priority order between the general right of lien and the special right of lien, the special right of lien shall prevail over the general right lien in principle (section 329 (2) Main Text CC). The reason is that the special right of lien is recognized on the particular property, while there may be other objects for the general right of lien.[959] However, exceptionally, the general right of lien to secure the claim caused by expenses for the common benefit prevails over all other creditors who received the benefit of those expenses (section 329 (2) Proviso CC). This exception can be justifiable for it is fair among all the creditors who have benefitted from those expenses.

447. When the debtor is in default, the creditor who holds the general right of lien may exercise the right and apply for the auction of the debtor's property and receive payment for the claim prior to other creditors from the price of the property at the auction. In the bankruptcy procedure, the general right of lien is treated as the "preferred bankruptcy claim" which is prior to other bankruptcy claims but inferior to the right of separate satisfaction that may be exercised without involving in the bankruptcy procedure and thus receive performance prior to bankruptcy claims (section 98 (1) Bankruptcy Law).[960]

III. Special Right of Lien in Immovable Property

448. The special right of lien in immovable property is recognized by the provisions of law in a particular immovable property to secure the claims caused by: (i) the preservation, (ii) the construction work, and (iii) the sale of that immovable property (sections 325, 326, 327 and 328 CC).

(i) The special right of lien for the preservation of an immovable property shall exist to secure the claims for expenses required for preservation of that immovable property or for preservation, approval or execution of rights in that immovable property (section 325 [1], 326 CC). It aims to restore the fairness among the creditors. An example of "the preservation of immovable

958. Dogauchi 2007b: p. 76.
959. Dogauchi 2007b: p. 76.
960. On the right of separate satisfaction, *see* para. 340 *supra*.

property" is the repair to keep its value,[961] and that of "the preservation or approval of rights" is to make a lawsuit against or to ask approval of a third person who possesses the immovable property and thus prevent the acquisitive prescription. The execution of rights means, for instance, to receive a delivery of the immovable property from a possessor on behalf of its owner (debtor).[962]

(ii) The special right of lien for the construction work of an immovable property shall exist to secure the claims for the existing increased value resulting from the expenses for construction work performed by a person who designed, carried out or supervised construction work regarding that immovable property (sections 325 [2], 327 CC).[963] This also aims to keep the fairness among the creditors who have benefitted from the construction work.[964]

(iii) The special right of lien for the sale of an immovable properties shall exist to secure the claim for purchase price and its interest of that immovable property (sections 325 [3], 328 CC). It also intends to keep the fairness among the seller and the creditors of the buyer (debtor) for they will benefit from that immovable property which had been sold by the seller.[965]

449. In order to preserve the validity of the rights of lien in an immovable property, the Civil Code requires the creditor to register the rights of statutory lien in the registration book:

(i) In the case of the right of lien for the preservation of an immovable property, registration must be carried out immediately after the completion of the act of preservation (section 337 CC). The reason is that the registered right of lien for the preservation of an immovable property shall be given priority even against the existing registered right of hypothec (section 339 CC) so that the publicity of the right of lien should be implemented as fast as possible.[966]

(ii) As for the right of lien for the construction work of an immovable property, the estimated expenses of the construction work must be registered in advance before the commencement of the construction. If the actual expenses of that construction work exceed the estimated amount, the right of lien shall not exist with respect to the exceeding amount (section 338 (1) CC). The reason for the registration is the same as the right of lien for the preservation of an immovable property (Item (i) above).[967] The registered right of lien for the construction work shall also be given priority against the existing registered right of hypothec (section 339 CC).

---

961. If it increases the value of the immovable property, it will be the construction work to which the right of lien for the construction work (ss. 325 [2], 327 CC) shall apply.
962. Dogauchi 2017b: pp. 60, 63.
963. The amount of increased value of the immovable property due to the construction work shall be evaluated by an appraiser appointed by the court at the time of the creditors' participation in the distribution procedure after auction (s. 338 (2) CC).
964. Dogauchi 2017b: p. 64.
965. Dogauchi 2017b: pp. 61, 64.
966. Dogauchi 2017b: p. 63. *See also* para. 452 *infra*.
967. Dogauchi 2017b: p. 63.

(iii) In the case of the right of lien for the sale of an immovable property, a statement that the purchase price of the immovable property or its interest has not been paid must be registered simultaneously with the conclusion of the sales contract (section 340 CC). However, different from the right of lien for the preservation and construction work, the right of lien for the sale of an immovable property cannot be given priority against the registered right of hypothec.[968] However, once the right of lien is registered earlier than the right of hypothec, the right of lien shall prevail. In this sense, the earlier registration is recommended by this provision.

450. The priority order between the rights of lien in an immovable property and other rights is provided by the provisions of law: (a) the rights of lien in an immovable property shall prevail over the general rights of lien except for the general right of for the expenses for the common benefit, which prevails over all creditors who were benefited from those expenses (section 329 (2) CC).[969]

451. (b) Among the rights of lien in an immovable property, the priority is given to that: (i) for the preservation, then (ii) for the construction work, and then (iii) for the sale of an immovable property (section 331 (1) CC).[970] This priority order is justifiable in considering the fairness among creditors. The seller of an immovable property should enjoy the benefits by the preservation and the construction works in the immovable property. If the preservation work of the immovable property was implemented after the construction work, the creditor of the construction work should be benefitted by the preservation. However, if the construction work was completed after the preservation, there would be no reason to give priority to the right of lien for the preservation.[971]

If there are two or more registered rights of lien for the preservation or for the construction work, the priority is given to the latest one by the analogical interpretation of section 330 (1) Second Sentence CC, because it currently contributes to maintain or increase the value of the immovable property.[972]

But if there are two or more registered rights of lien for the sale of the same immovable property (the case of successive sales), the priority order shall be given to the first seller, then the second, etc. following the chronological order of the sale (section 331 (2) CC). For the transfer of ownership by the later sale depends on that of the earlier sale, and the later seller could have known the existence of the right of lien for the earlier seller by confirming the registration.[973]

968. In this sense, the reason for the simultaneous registration of the right of lien for the sale of an immovable property with the conclusion of sales contract seems to be vague (Dogauchi 2017b: p. 65).
969. *See* para. 446 *supra.*
970. It is presupposed that the rights of lien in an immovable property are all registered in accordance of the provisions of law. Without registration they are not valid (ss. 337, 338, 340 CC). *See* para. 449 *supra.*
971. Dogauchi 2017b: p. 80.
972. Dogauchi 2017b: p. 80.
973. Dogauchi 2017b: pp. 79–80.

452. (c) The priority order between the rights of lien in an immovable property and the right of hypothec or the right of pledge in the immovable property depends on the content of the statutory lien in the immovable property: (i) the priority between the right of lien for the sale of an immovable property and the right of hypothec or the right of pledge in the immovable property is determined by the time of registration.[974] However: (ii) the right of lien for the preservation and that for the construction work in the immovable property which are registered shall prevail over the right of hypothec and the right of pledge in that immovable property, even though the registration of the right of hypothec or the right of pledge was earlier than that of the rights of lien for the preservation or for the construction work (sections 339 and 361 CC). The reason is that the preservation and construction work for an immovable property are also beneficial for the creditor who holds right of hypothec or the right of pledge in the immovable property.[975]

453. When the debtor is in default, the creditor who holds the right of lien in an immovable property can exercise the right by applying for the auction of the immovable property and receive payment for the claim prior to other creditors from the purchase money of the immovable property. In the bankruptcy procedure, the right of lien in an immovable property is treated as the right of separate satisfaction which may be exercised without involving in the bankruptcy procedure and thus receive payment prior to other creditors (sections 2 (9) and 65 Bankruptcy Law).[976]

§4. Right of Pledge

454. The right of pledge called "shichi-ken" in Japanese is defined as the right of a creditor (the pledgee) to possess a thing, either immovable or movable, provided by a debtor or a third party (the pledgor) so as to secure the performance of obligation corresponding to the claim and to enjoy the performance of obligation prior to the other creditors from the thing sold at auction (section 342 CC). The establishment of the right of pledge shall take effect by delivering the thing to the pledgee (section 344 CC). In addition, the pledgee cannot allow the pledgor to possess the thing pledged on behalf of the pledgee (section 345 CC). The pledgee can retain the thing pledged until his/her claim is satisfied unless a person who is given priority against the pledgee claims to deliver it (section 347 CC). Different from the right of retention and the right of lien, the right of pledge is established by the agreement between the pledgor and the pledgee.[977]

974. The right registered earlier prevails over that registered later (ss. 341 and 373 CC).
975. Dogauchi 2017b: p. 80. *See also* para. 449 *supra*.
976. On the right of separate satisfaction, *see* paras. 340 and 447 *supra*.
977. Matsuo and Kozumi 2008: pp. 282–283; Dogauchi 2017b: pp. 83–85; Ohmi 2020: pp. 88–101.

455. The right of pledge can be established on an immovable property (sections 356–361 CC), though the actual usage of it has been decreasing.[978] It can be registered in the registration book in order to be opposable against a third party (section 177 CC). The duration of pledge in an immovable property may not exceed ten years. If a longer period is provided for in the act of establishing the pledge, the duration shall be ten years (section 360 (1) CC). When the duration expires, the pledgee must return the immovable property to the pledgor.[979] The right of pledge may be renewed, but the duration may not exceed ten years from the time of the renewal (section 360 (2) CC). This restriction aims to avoid the inefficient usage of the pledgor's immovable property to be caused by the pledgee's long-standing continuous retention for the purpose of security.[980] Once the right of pledge was established on an immovable property, registered, and the pledgee acquired the possession of it (section 344 CC), and then the pledgee returned the possession to the pledgor, the right of pledge was interpreted not to be extinguished though it is provided that the pledgee cannot allow the pledgor to possess the thing pledged on behalf of the pledgee (section 345 CC).[981] The reason is that once the right of pledge was established and registered, it is publicly announced by the registration book and opposable against a third party, so that the possession is no longer necessary to maintain the validity of the right of pledge. However, there are dissenting opinions in the legal doctrine that if the pledgee returned the object to the pledgor, the right of pledge shall cease to exist because the possession of the object is an essential and indispensable element of the right of pledge.[982] The registered right of pledge can still be valid although the pledgee returns the immovable property to the pledgor. But the pledgee should be able to claim the pledgor to return the possession.

456. The pledgee of an immovable property can use and receive profits from the immovable property pledged in accordance with the appropriate usage for it (section 356 CC). It may be the advantage for the pledgee. However, in that case, the pledgee has to pay expenses necessary to administer the immovable property (section 357 CC)[983] and cannot ask the debtor to pay the interest of the claim (section 358 CC) unless the pledgee and the pledgor have agreed otherwise[984] or the execution procedure on the profits derived from that immovable property (section 180 [2] Civil Execution Law) has commenced (section 359 CC). These provisions presuppose that the profits to be drawn from the immovable property can be regarded as equivalent to the interest of the claim and expenses necessary to manage the property.[985] They should have been based on the agricultural economy and applied to

978. Dogauchi 2017b: p. 84.
979. STD Jan. 18, 1918 Minroku 24-1.
980. Matsuo and Kozumi 2008: p. 294; Dogauchi 2017b: p. 88.
981. STJ Dec. 25, 1916 Minroku 22-2509.
982. *See* Ohmi 2020b: pp. 90–92.
983. The pledgee has to possess the thing pledged with the care of a good manager (ss. 350, 298 (1) CC).
984. This agreement can be registered in the registration book (s. 95 (1) [6] LRIP). *See* para. 458 *infra*.
985. Dogauchi 2017b: p. 95.

the agricultural land.[986] However, the socioeconomic conditions for the use of the right of pledge on an immovable property seem to have been significantly changed since the Civil Code was enacted.

457. The scope of a clam which can be secured by the right of pledge may include the principal, interest, penalty, expense of executing the pledge, expense for preserving the thing pledged and the compensation for damages arising from non-performance of obligations or latent defect in the object unless the pledgee and the pledgor have agreed otherwise (section 346 CC). However, the amount of the claim, interest, penalty and compensation for damages due to the non-performance must be registered in the registration book (section 95 (1) [1], [2] LRIP), and the interest, penalty, and compensation shall be limited within the latest two years (sections 361, 375 CC) to protect an interested third party who may appear after the establishment of the right of pledge on an immovable property.[987]

458. As explained above, the pledgee of an immovable property has to pay expenses for the management of the property (section 357 CC) and cannot claim for interest of the claim (section 358 CC), while the pledgee can use and make profits of the pledged immovable property.[988] However, the pledgee and the pledgor may agree otherwise (section 359 CC). But in order to assert this agreement against a third party, the registration to that effect is necessary (section 177 CC; section 95 (1) [6] LRIP). In order to adapt to the change of the socioeconomic conditions for the use of the right of pledge on an immovable property since the enactment of the Civil Code, the special agreement the pledgee and the pledgor and its registration should be used for the development the right of pledge in an immovable property.

459. If the pledgee may claim, based on the agreement with the pledgor, for periodical payment such as the interest of the principal (section 359 CC), he/she can exercise the right of pledge regarding the periodical payment with priority against other creditors only for the latest two years after it has fallen due unless the special agreement which extends the scope of interest is registered after the periodical payment has fallen due (sections 361 and 375 CC; section 177 CC; section 95 (1) [2] LRIP). However, as this restriction aims to protect the interest of a third party such as the mortgagee who registered his/her right of hypothec after the registration of the pledgee, it is applied only the case where the third party appears.[989] If no third

---

986. Matsuo and Kozumi 2008: pp. 292–293.
987. It means that there is no limit on the amount of claim, interest, penalty, expenses, and compensation between the pledgee and the pledgor unless they are invalid due to the violation of the law of compulsory application (s. 91 CC) or the principle of public order and good morals (s. 90 CC). *See* para. 459 *infra*.
988. *See* para. 456 *supra*.
989. Dogauchi 2017b: pp. 93, 163–164.

party has appeared, the pledgee may claim the pledgor to perform all the obligations even beyond the two-year restriction on the periodical payment such as the interest as long as they may be covered by the value of the pledged immovable property.[990]

460. The scope of the object of the right of pledge in an immovable property may extend to the things which are the integral part of the immovable property as the object of the right of pledge except for the building on the pledged land unless the pledgee and the pledgor have agreed otherwise (sections 361, 370 CC). However, there is a dissenting opinion in the legal doctrine which denies the application of section 370 CC, because it presupposes that the mortgagor may keep the possession of the immovable property, while the pledgor has to transfer the possession to the pledgee.[991]

461. When the debtor is in default, the pledgee may exercise the right of pledge and apply for the auction of the immovable property and receive payment for the claim prior to other creditors from the purchase money of or the profits from the immovable property (section 342 CC; section 181 (1) [3] Civil Execution Law).[992] In the bankruptcy procedure, the right of pledge in an immovable property is treated as the right of separate satisfaction which may be exercised without involving in the bankruptcy procedure and thus receive performance prior to other creditors (section 342 CC, and sections 2 (9) and 65 Bankruptcy Law).[993]

§5. Right of Hypothec

I. Overview

462. The right of hypothec, called "teito-ken" is defined as the right of a creditor (mortgagee, hypothecate [hereinafter the term "mortgagee" shall be used in this sense]) to receive performance of the claim prior to other creditors from the immovable property provided by a debtor or a third party (mortgagor, hypothecator [hereinafter the term "mortgagor" shall be used in this sense]) to secure performance of the debtor's obligation without transferring possession of the immovable property (section 369 (1) CC). Among the various types of security interest in the immovable property, the right of hypothec has been playing the central role, because it has the advantage for the owner of the immovable property to maintain the possession and the use of it, which enables him/her to continue economic activities on that

990. A third party may include the acquirer of the pledged immovable property. However, the judicial precedent seems to exclude the transferee, because it regards the acquirer of the immovable property as succeeding the status as the pledgor. *See* STJ Sep. 15, 1915 Minroku 21-1469 (on the right of hypothec) and para. 468 *infra*.

991. Dogauchi 2017b: p. 90.

992. Matsuo and Kozumi 2008: p. 295; Dogauchi 2017b: pp. 102–104.

993. On the right of separate satisfaction, *see* paras. 340, 447, 453 *supra*.

property even after the establishment of the right of hypothec.[994] However, the security interest of a creditor must be coordinated with the right of owner, particularly after the due date of the payment of debt. This problem lies in the forefront of discussions concerning the security interest in the immovable property.[995]

II. Establishment of Hypothec

463. The right of hypothec is established by the agreement between the mortgagee and the mortgagor by specifying: (i) the object of the right and (ii) the claim to be secured by the right of hypothec: (i) the object of right of hypothec is ownership of the immovable property (section 369 (1) CC), superficies and emphyteusis on the land (section 369 (2) CC). Since the land and the building on it are the separate immovable property in the Japanese law,[996] the right of hypothec may be established on the land, on the building or on both of them (section 370 CC).[997]

464. (ii) A claim right must exist to establish the right of hypothec which aims to secure the performance of obligation corresponding to that claim. If there exists no claim or the claim has extinguished, the right of hypothec shall not be established or become invalid ipso iure even though it is registered in the registration book. It is called "fuju-sei" [the subordinate nature] of the right of hypothec to the claim. When the claim secured by the right of hypothec extinguishes, then that right of hypothec ceases to exist ipso iure and the right of hypothec of the next priority order promotes ipso iure instead of the previous one.[998] It is called "jun-i-shojun-no-gensoku" [the principle of the ipso iure promotion of the priority order] of the right of hypothec.[999]

However, the coexistence of a claim and a right of hypothec to secure that claim are not always strictly required. The right of hypothec which was agreed before the claim has been generated may be interpreted as valid, if the claim has actually come into existence. The right of hypothec was regarded as valid, even when the claim has not yet been created but would appear in the future as long as the creation of claim could be specified by its cause and content.[1000] Thus the subordinate nature of

---

994. Matsuo and Kozumi 2008: pp. 303–307; Dogauchi 2017b: pp. 121–124.
995. *See* paras. 472, 473 and s. V *infra*.
996. *See* para. 86 *supra*.
997. If the creditor acquired the right of hypothec only on the building and it was sold at the auction by the execution of hypothec, the statutory superficies shall be established for the interest of the buyer of the building and the amount of lent to be paid to the landowner shall be determined by the court (s. 388 CC). The same applies to the case where the right of hypothec was established only on the land on which there was a building owned by the landowner, and the statutory superficies shall be established for the interest of the owner of the building. For more detail, *see* para. 482 *infra*.
998. As for the priority order between the two or more rights of hypothec on the same immovable property *see* para. 465 *infra*.
999. Matsuo and Kozumi 2008: p. 307; Ohmi 2020b: pp. 115–116.
1000. STJ May 8, 1913 Minroku 19-312.

the right of hypothec to the claim may be relaxed in accordance with the need of the security in the practice as long as the claim may be reasonably specified.[1001]

465. The agreement to establish the right of hypothec must be registered for the mortgagee to assert the right to a third party (section 177 CC). Two or more mortgagees may establish the rights of mortgage on the same immovable property and register them. The priority order between the two or more rights of hypothec on the same immovable property shall be determined by registration (section 373 CC; section 4 (1) LRIP), which shall be determined by the reception number at the registration office (sections 19, 20 LRIP). The right of hypothec is registered in the form of electromagnetic record, and it must include the content of the right of hypothec such as the amount of principal of the claim, interest rate and other matters required by the Law on the Registration of Immovable Property (sections 83 (1), 88 (1) LRIP). They are important information for the publicity of the right of hypothec, which will enable the concerned parties to utilize the value of the immovable property. The right of hypothec which can be established without the transfer of possession and made public through registration has been the institutional basis for the development of financial transactions on the credit economy in Japan.[1002]

III. Effects of Hypothec

A. *Scope of Secured Claim*

466. The claims to be secured by the right of hypothec will include the principal, interest and compensation for damages due to non-performance of obligation in accordance with the agreement between the mortgagee and the mortgagor. But, there is a restriction on the scope of claim to the effect that even if the mortgagee can claim for periodical payment including interest based on the agreement with the mortgagor, the mortgagee can exercise the right of hypothec with respect to periodical payment only for the latest two years which has fallen due unless the special agreement on the extension of the scope of payment is registered after the periodical payment has fallen due (section 375 (1) CC). This restriction aims to guarantee the foreseeability of a third party who intends to make a transaction with the mortgagor by establishing the right of hypothec, purchasing the mortgaged immovable property, and other creditors.[1003] If there appears no third party, all the claims including those beyond the scope of two-year restriction can be covered by the right

1001. The relaxation of the subordinate nature of the right of hypothec can be found in the revolving hypothec (ss. 398-2 to 398-22 CC). *See* s. VII *infra*.

1002. Matsuo and Kozumi 2008: p. 304.

1003. Matsuo and Kozumi 2008: pp. 312–313; Dogauchi 2017b: pp. 161–162. However, it is disputed whether the acquirer such as a purchaser should be protected by this restriction on the scope of the claims as a third party. *See* para. 468 *infra*.

of hypothec. As the right of hypothec continues to exist until all the claims including those beyond the scope of two-year restriction are satisfied, the mortgagor needs to satisfy all the claims to remove the registration of the right of hypothec.[1004]

467. This restriction also applies to the case where the mortgagee has a right to claim for compensation for damages resulting from non-performance of obligation corresponding to the claim such as the special interest calculated by the increased interest rate (section 375 (2) Main Text CC). In this case the aggregate period including the interest and other periodical payment may not exceed two years (section 375 (2) Proviso CC). However, if the special agreement on the extension of the scope of payment is registered after the periodical payment has fallen due, it shall be valid (section 375 (2) Main Text, section 375 (1) Proviso CC).[1005] As the aim of this restriction is the same as that of interest explained in the previous paragraph, the mortgagee can exercise the right of hypothec to collect all the debts including those beyond the scope of two-year restriction if there appears no third party, and the mortgagor needs to pay all the debts to remove the registration of hypothec, because the right of hypothec continues to exist until all the claims are fulfilled.

468. The problem is whether the restriction on the scope of claims as explained above[1006] should apply to the acquirer (such as a purchaser) of the mortgaged immovable property. The judicial precedent and the majority of legal doctrines held that the acquirer has become the owner of the mortgaged immovable property and thus succeeded the status of the mortgagor so that he/she cannot be protected by the restriction on the scope of claims.[1007] The dissenting opinion holds that the acquirer such as a purchaser will estimate the value of the mortgaged immovable property when he/she decides to acquire it, so that in order to protect the expectation of the acquirer to be equated with that of the typical third party who intend to provide finance to the debtor by acquiring the right of hypothec, the restriction on the scope of claims should be applied to the acquirer.[1008]

On the one hand, it is concerned with the legal policy in the Japanese civil law. The protection of the acquirer should increase the foreseeability of the possible acquirer and promote the transaction of the mortgaged property. On the other hand, the protection of the creditor who holds the right of hypothec should be taken into consideration. In addition, there are other measures to protect the acquirer of the mortgaged property.[1009] From the comprehensive perspective, the majority opinion and the judicial precedent seem to prevail.

1004. Matsuo and Kozumi 2008: pp. 312–313.
1005. Matsuo and Kozumi 2008: p. 312.
1006. *See* paras. 466 and 467 *supra*.
1007. STJ Sep. 15, 1915 Minroku 21-1469; Matsuo and Kozumi 2008: p. 313; Ohmi 2020b: p. 157.
1008. Dogauchi 2017b: p. 164.
1009. *See* s. VI (paras. 484 and 485) *infra*.

B. Scope of Object

469. The scope of the object of the right of hypothec not only reaches the immovable property such as the land but also extends to the thing which is regarded as an integral part of the immovable property except for the building on the mortgaged land unless the mortgagee and the mortgagor have agreed otherwise (section 370 CC). As the land and the building on it are separate immovable properties in the Japanese legal system,[1010] the effect of right of hypothec established on the land cannot be extended to the building and the effect of the right of hypothec established on the building may not be extended to ownership of the land.[1011]

470. Except for the building, the registered cluster of trees, and other fixtures to the land which are regarded as independent properties from the land,[1012] the effect of right of hypothec established on the land shall be extended to things which are regarded as the integral part of the land, even though they become attached to the land after the right of hypothec was established (section 370 CC).[1013] The reason is that the right of hypothec is established without the transfer of possession of the object, it is still used by the mortgagor until the mortgagee executes that right, so that the mortgaged property may be improved during the use by the mortgagor, and it can be expected by the mortgagee and the mortgagor.[1014]

471. When a part of the object of the right of hypothec was removed and moved away from the mortgaged land or the building by a third party without any approval of the mortgagee and the mortgagor, then the mortgagee may pursue the removed thing to a person who possesses it on the basis of the right of hypothec. But if the person has acquired the thing through any transaction such as a sales contract in good faith and without negligence, the possessor can acquirer ownership by the provision of law (section 192 CC).[1015]

However, when the thing was removed and moved away from the mortgaged land or the building by the mortgagor (the owner of the mortgaged land or the building) without any approval of the mortgagee, then the mortgagee may pursue the thing to a person who possesses it on the basis of the right of hypothec. The possessor may make a defense that he/she will not recognize the removed thing as the object of the right of hypothec for the lack of opposable requirement (possession according to section 178 CC) and will state that the mortgagee has lost the right on the removed thing because the possessor has acquired ownership of the removed thing by fulfilling the opposable requirement (possession according to section 178 CC). The mortgagee may make a counter-defense by proving that the possessor acquired the

---

1010. *See* paras. 86–89 *supra*.
1011. However, the right of hypothec established only on the building should be associated with any right to use the land to be established by the agreement between the mortgagee and the landowner or by the provisions of law. *See* paras. 482 and 483 *infra*.
1012. *See* para. 93 *supra*.
1013. STJ Jul. 8, 1921 Minroku 27-1313, STJ Jul. 2, 1934 Minshu 13-1489.
1014. Matsuo and Kozumi 2008: p. 313; Matsuo 2016: p. 550.
1015. SCJ Mar. 12, 1982 Minshu 36-3-349. It is called the immediate acquisition (or the good faith acquisition). *See* paras. 260–270 *supra*.

thing with the knowledge that the thing was a part of the mortgaged property (in bad faith) and in a manner which was against the principle of good faith and fair dealing (section 1 (2) CC).[1016]

472. Even after the establishment of the right of hypothec, the mortgagor can continue to use the object of the right of hypothec and take profits from it and thus enjoy its fruits. But if the debtor falls into a default with respect to a claim secured by the right of hypothec, the object of the right of mortgage shall be able to extend to the fruits of the immovable property to be collected after the default (section 371 CC). On the basis of this rule the mortgagee may execute the right of hypothec on the fruits in accordance with the procedure provided by the Civil Execution Law (sections 181, 188, 88, 91, 93, 94 and 95 Civil Execution Law).[1017]

473. The right of hypothec can also be extended to the claim for money or other things which the mortgagor may receive as a result of the sale, lease or loss of, or damage to the object of the right of hypothec (sections 372 and 304 (1) Main Text CC). However, the mortgagee has to attach them before payment of the money or delivery of the things (sections 372 and 304 (1) Proviso CC). It is called "butsujo-daii" [the substitution of the object], which is the special extension of security interest to a claim to be created from the object of the right of hypothec by the provision of law.[1018]

The substitution of the object can be classified into two categories: (a) the substitution in place of the object (such as the claim for payment as a result of the sale and loss of the object) and (b) the substitution in addition to the object (such as the claim for payment as a result of the lease of and damage to the object).[1019]

As for (a) the substitution in place of the object, the right of hypothec may not need to be extended to the claim for purchase money which the mortgagor will receive as a result of the sale of the object, because the mortgagee can still keep the right of hypothec even if the immovable property is sold to the purchaser and execute it when a debtor becomes in default. For this reason the majority opinion in the legal doctrines denies this substitution,[1020] while some affirm the substitution.[1021]

As for (b) the substitution in addition to the object, the claim for rent to be paid to the mortgagor as a result of the lease of the mortgaged immovable property may be included in the object of the right of hypothec.[1022] In this case, the mortgagee may execute the right of hypothec on the claim for rent either according to the specific procedure for the execution of the fruits from the mortgaged immovable property (sections 181, 188 Civil Execution Law), or by attaching the claim for rent to

---

1016. As for the counter-defense based on the principle of good faith and fair dealing (s. 1 (2) CC), *see* paras. 253 and 254 *supra*.
1017. Matsuo and Kozumi 2008: p. 321; Dogauchi 2017b: p. 147.
1018. *See* para. 439 *supra*. Matsuo and Kozumi 2008: pp. 322–333.
1019. Dogauchi 2017b: p. 148.
1020. Matsuo and Kozumi 2008: p. 323; Dogauchi 2017b: pp. 149–150.
1021. Ohmi 2020b: p. 144.
1022. SCJ Oct. 27, 1989 Minshu 43-9-1070; Matsuo and Kozumi 2008: pp. 323–324; Dogauchi 2017b: 150–152; Ohmi 2020b: pp. 147–148.

be paid after the default of the debtor (section 371 CC) and before the payment to the mortgagor (sections 372, 304 (1) Proviso CC).[1023] However, it cannot include the claim for rent to be paid by the subtenant, because it is not recognized as the claim for money or other things which the debtor should receive, but it is received by the tenant (a third party) of the debtor (sections 372, 304 (1) Main Text CC).[1024]

The claim for compensation for the loss of or the damage to the mortgaged immovable property can be included into the object of the right of hypothec (section 304 (1) Main Text CC).[1025] In this context, the claim for insurance money to be received by the mortgagor due to the fire by which the mortgaged building was burnt down.[1026]

C. *Remedies Against Infringement*

474. When a person physically damages the mortgaged immovable property, not only the mortgagor as the owner of the property, but also the mortgagee can claim that person for removal of existing disturbance and injunction of future disturbance, because not only the ownership of the mortgagor but also the right of hypothec of the mortgagee is regarded as infringed by the person's action.[1027] The purchase price of the mortgaged immovable property should be reduced by the physical damage to the property. However, the mortgagee cannot claim for compensation for damages against that person, because the mortgagee can attach the claim for compensation money to be paid to the mortgagor (the owner of the damaged property) as a substitution of the object (sections 372, 304 (1) CC).[1028]

475. When a person possesses the immovable property without any title, not only the mortgagor but also the mortgagee may claim the possessor for vacation of the immovable property under the condition that the possession is recognized as disturbing the execution of the right of hypothec, because the very nature of the right of hypothec is to execute it and sell it compulsorily at auction to receive performance of obligation of the debtor in default.[1029]

476. When a person possesses the immovable property with a title such as a right of lease established by the agreement between the possessor (as a tenant) and the mortgagor (as a landlord), the mortgagee may claim the possessor for vacation of the immovable property under the condition that the possessor has an intention to disturb the execution of the right of hypothec and the possession is objectively

1023. Matsuo and Kozumi 2008: p. 324; Dogauchi 2017b: pp. 150–153.
1024. SCD Dec. 14, 2000 Minshu 54-4-1552; Matsuo and Kozumi 2008: p. 324; Dogauchi 2017b: p. 152; Ohmi 2020b: pp. 152–153.
1025. STJ Jun. 28, 1916 Minroku 22-1281; Matsuo and Kozumi 2008: p. 325; Dogauchi 2017b: pp. 149–150.
1026. STJ Mar. 12, 1907 Minroku 13-265; STJ (FB) Apr. 7, 1923 Minshu 2-209; Matsuo and Kozumi 2008: pp. 325–326; Dogauchi 2017b: p. 153; Ohmi 2020b: p. 146.
1027. STJ Apr. 20, 1932 Shinbun 3407-15.
1028. *See* para. 473 *supra*.
1029. SCJ (FB) Nov. 24, 1999 Minshu 53-8-1899.

recognized as disturbing its execution.[1030] In this case, it is important to coordinate the mortgagor's interest to use and make profits from the mortgaged immovable property and the mortgagee's interest to execute the right of hypothec promptly when the debtor is in default. The point in this case is that the mortgagee was in the process of execution of the right of hypothec after the debtor had become in default. This is the reason why the intervention by the mortgagee into the use of the mortgaged property which was originally allowed to the mortgagor but was to be taken by the mortgagee after the execution procedure when the execution was disturbed by that use caused by the agreement between the possessor and the mortgagor.[1031] The judicial precedent can be interpreted that it coordinated the interest of the mortgagor to use the mortgaged property and that of the mortgagee to execute the right of hypothec and secure the prioritized fulfillment of the claim.

IV. Execution of Hypothec

477. When the debtor is in default, the mortgagee can execute the right of hypothec by applying auction to the court. The mortgagee has to submit the document to prove the right of hypothec such as a certificate of registered matters (sections 180, 181 Civil Execution Law). If the court makes the order of commencement of auction for the execution of a security right, it attaches the immovable property, determines the standard price, collects applicants for purchase, and determines the purchaser, normally who offered the highest price (sections 188, 60, 64 (2), 69 Civil Execution Law). The mortgagee and an acquirer of the immovable property can be the purchaser at the auction, but the debtor in default cannot become the purchaser (section 390 CC; sections 188, 68 Civil Execution Law). The purchaser acquires the ownership by paying the purchase price and the acquisition is registered and the registration of the right of hypothec is deleted ex officio (sections 188, 79, 82 Civil Execution Law). The court distributes the purchase money to the mortgagees and other creditors in accordance with the priority order after it withholds the expenses incurred by a person and reimburses them. The surplus, if any, is to be distributed to the mortgagor (section 391 CC, and sections 188, 84 and 87 Civil Execution Law).[1032]

478. When the court makes the order for commencement of bankruptcy procedure, the right of hypothec is treated as the right of separate satisfaction which may be exercised without involving in the bankruptcy procedure and thus the mortgagee can receive performance prior to other creditors (sections 2 (9) and 65 (1) Bankruptcy Law).[1033]

1030. SCJ Mar. 10, 2005 Minshu 59-2-356. In this case the right of hypothec on an immovable property had already been established and registered before it was lent to the possessor, so that the right of hypothec of the mortgagee shall prevail over the right of lease of the possessor.

1031. Matsuo and Kozumi 2008: pp. 338–339.

1032. Matsuo and Kozumi 2008: pp. 340–345; Dogauchi 2017b: pp. 200–205; Ohmi 2020b: pp. 163–169.

1033. On the right of separate satisfaction, *see* paras. 340, 447, 453, 461 *supra*.

479. The prompt, efficient and costless execution is crucial for the use of the right of hypothec. Some amendments to the Civil Code and Civil Execution Law and creation of case laws have contributed to the reform of its execution process in Japanese law.[1034] This problem is intimately concerned with the development of the conveyancing mortgage which has been recognized by case laws.[1035]

V. Coordination of Hypothec with the Right to Use the Property

480. The feature of the right of hypothec is that the mortgagor can keep possession, use and make profits of the mortgaged immovable property. But, this interest of the mortgagor needs to be adequately coordinated with the security interest of the mortgagee. If A, the owner of the land and building, borrowed a certain amount of money from B and established the right of hypothec on both the land and building for B and registered them, A can still use the land and the building for him/herself or lend them to a third person to collect a rent. A, for instance, concluded a lease contract of the building with C and C possessed the building. It is no problem and A did not need to have C's consent about the lease.

However, when A becomes in default and cannot repay the money, B needs to execute the right of hypothec on the land and the building. The problem is whether the purchaser at the auction can claim for vacation of the building against C. If the registration of B's right of hypothec was earlier than the registration of C's right of lease (sections 177, 605 CC), if any, and C's possession of the building (section 31 (1) LLLB),[1036] C's right of lease cannot be opposable against B, and the purchaser at auction can claim for vacation of the building against C. However, even in that case, C's interest still needs to be coordinated with the interest of the purchaser, because it will contribute to the coordination of the interests between the mortgagor and the mortgagee.[1037]

481. Section 395 (1) CC provides that a person who uses a mortgaged building or receives profits from a mortgaged building on the basis of a right of lease which is not opposable against the mortgagee shall not be claimed to vacate the building to the purchaser at auction until six months have passed from the time when the purchaser purchased that building at auction, if: (i) the person has been using or receiving profits from the building since before the commencement of auction procedure; or (ii) the person is using or receiving profits from the building on the basis of a

1034. The execution of the right of hypothec on the fruits to be drawn from the mortgaged immovable property has been introduced in 2003 by the Amendment to the Civil Execution Law (s. 180 [2] Civil Execution Law). It was also amended to exclude the possessor of the mortgaged immovable property without title and introduced the temporary restraining order for auction (ss. 188, 55 Civil Execution Law), delivery order (ss. 188 and 83 Civil Execution Law). *See also* judicial precedents concerning the exclusion of possessors who disturbed the execution of the right of hypothec cited in paras. 475 and 476 *supra*.

1035. *See* §7 *infra*.

1036. As for s. 31 (1) LLLB, *see* Part I, Ch. 4, §5 *supra*.

1037. Matsuo and Kozumi 2008: pp. 353–355; Dogauchi 2017b: p. 176.

right of lease established by the administrator of the compulsory administration procedure or of the execution procedure for profits from secured immovable property after the commencement of auction procedure. This institution is the suspension of the vacation for the use of mortgaged building. It is also beneficial for the mortgagor who can use and make profits from the mortgaged building by taking into consideration of this institution.[1038]

In addition, section 387 CC provides the special treatment of the right of lease on the mortgaged land and building to secure the stable usage of the mortgaged immovable property. If all persons who hold the right of hypothec on the immovable property, even though the registrations of which preceded the registration of a lease, give their consent to the restriction on their priority, and such consents are registered, the right of lease registered even after the registration of the rights of hypothec is opposable against those mortgagees who gave their consent (section 387 (1) CC).[1039] For example, if A, the landowner, plans to construct a building for lease and borrowed money from B, and A established the right of hypothec on the land and the building for B and registered them. A wants to lease the building to C1 to C10, but C1 to C10, the tenants, are anxious about the possibility of the execution of the right of hypothec held by B. The lease contract of this building to those tenants is advantageous not only for A but also for B, because B can receive A's performance of obligation from the rent to be collected by A from C1 to C10, B may give consent to the restriction on the priority of his/her right of hypothec to the right of lease to be held by those tenants. It will contribute to increase the stability of the use of mortgaged immovable property.[1040]

482. If the land and the building on it belong to the same owner A, A can establish the right of hypothec only on the land or on the building, or on both the land and the building. When A establishes the right of hypothec only on the land for his/her creditor B, and B executed the right of hypothec established on the land, and C purchased the land at auction, which resulted in the creation of different owners such as the owner of the land is C and the owner of the building is A, it shall be deemed that a right of superficies has been established for the interest of A's building (section 388 First Sentence CC). B could foresee this result. In this case, the rent shall be fixed by the court at the request of the parties such as C (section 388 Second Sentence CC).

When A establishes the right of hypothec only on the building for his/her creditor B, and B executed the right of hypothec established on the building, and D purchased the building at auction, which resulted in the creation of different owners such as the owner of the land is A and the owner of the building is D, it shall be

1038. Matsuo and Kozumi 2008: p. 355; Dogauchi 2017b: pp. 176–179; Ohmi 2020b: pp. 206–208.

1039. When the mortgagees give their consent to the restriction on their priority, the approval of the persons who hold rights on the right of hypothec and other persons who will suffer any disadvantage as a result of the consent of the mortgagees must be obtained (s. 387 (2) CC).

1040. Matsuo and Kozumi 2008: pp. 355–356; Dogauchi 2017b: pp. 179–183; Ohmi 2020b: pp. 208–210.

deemed that a right of superficies has been established for the interest of D's building (section 388 First Sentence CC). A could foresee this result. In this case, the rent shall be fixed by the court at the request of the parties such as A (section 388 Second Sentence CC).

This is called "hotei-chijo-ken" [the right of statutory superficies] and it enables the owner of the building (A or D in the cases above) to continue to use the building.[1041]

483. The right of statutory superficies is not deemed to be established if there was no building on the land when A, the owner of the land, established the right of hypothec on the land for the creditor B, and after that A constructed a building on it. In this case, the effect and scope of the right of hypothec on the land cannot reach the building, because the land and the building are separate properties in Japanese law (section 370 CC).[1042] If B, the mortgagee on the land, executed the right of hypothec and C purchased the land at auction and paid price, C can claim A to remove the building and vacate the land because there was no building when B's right of hypothec was established on the land so that the right of statutory superficies cannot be recognized for the interest of A (section 388 First Sentence CC) for the reason that B did not take into account of the construction of the building and expect the land value without building. If A and C cannot reach the agreement on the treatment of the building, and C execute the vacation of the land and the removal of the building, the value of the building, if any, may be lost. In order to avoid this result and keep the value of the building from the viewpoint of social economy, A can apply to sell the building together with the land at auction (section 389 (1) Main Text CC). In this case, B's right of priority to receive the purchase money at auction may be exercised only for the purchase money of the land (section 389 (1) Proviso CC). This institution called "ikkatsu-baikyaku-ken" [the right to sell collectively] aims to maintain the value of the building under the principle of separate property between the land and the building on it.[1043]

VI. Coordination of Hypothec with a Third-Party Acquirer

484. Once the right of hypothec is established on the immovable property, its transaction is restrained for fear of the execution of the right of hypothec. In order to avoid this risk, a person who wants to buy the mortgaged immovable property need to perform obligation corresponding to the claim secured by the right of hypothec. If the person performs obligation, it is the performance by the third party (section 474 CC), and the acquirer of the mortgaged property has a legitimate interest to perform obligation corresponding to the claim secured by the right of

1041. Matsuo and Kozumi 2008: pp. 356–367; Dogauchi 2017b: pp. 215–227; Ohmi 2020b: pp. 187–203.

1042. *See* para. 86 *supra*.

1043. Matsuo and Kozumi 2008: pp. 367–368; Dogauchi 2017b: pp. 160–161, 216–217; Ohmi 2020b: pp. 189–190.

hypothec.[1044] The acquirer will have a claim for reimbursement of the expenses against the seller (section 570 CC), and he/she can set off the seller's claim for purchase money with the claim for reimbursement. However, it would be a heavy burden to perform obligation as a third party and to fulfill the claim. In order to further facilitate the transactions of the mortgaged immovable property, the law provides some incentives for the acquisition of the mortgaged property.

(i) If a third party who purchased ownership or superficies of the mortgaged immovable property pays, at the request of the mortgagee, the price of the right of hypothec to that mortgagee, the right of hypothec shall be extinguished for the benefit of the third-party acquirer (section 378 CC). It is called "daika-bensai" [the payment of the price of the right of hypothec]. In this case, the initiative is taken by the mortgagee, and the agreement is necessary to extinguish the right of hypothec. The price of the right of hypothec offered by the mortgagee may be lower than the amount of claim secured by the right of hypothec which must be fulfilled when the acquirer would perform as a third party.[1045]

485. (ii) The third-party acquirer may take the initiative to extinguish the right of hypothec by making a claim for the extinction of the hypothec before attachment for auction to execute the right of hypothec takes effect (sections 379, 382 CC). It is called "teito-ken-shometsu-seikyu" [the claim for extinction of the right of hypothec]. The third-party acquirer of the mortgaged immovable property who intends to make a claim for the extinction of the right of hypothec must send the documents to all the registered mortgagee: (i) a document which specifies the cause and date of the acquisition, the name and address of the transferor and the acquirer, the nature, location and price of the mortgaged immovable property and burdens of the acquirer; (ii) a certificate of registered matters regarding the mortgaged immovable property; and (iii) a document to the effect that if the mortgagee does not apply for auction by executing the right of hypothec within two months, the third-party acquirer of the immovable property will pay or deposit the price provided in (i) above or an amount specifically designated in accordance with the order of priority of claims (section 383 CC). The right of hypothec shall be extinguished if all the registered mortgagees approved or are deemed to have approved the price or amount offered by the third-party acquirer, and the third-party acquirer has paid or deposited the price or the approved amount (section 386 CC).[1046]

This claim for the extinction of the right of hypothec by the initiative of the third-party acquirer may be successful when the price of the immovable property has

1044. STJ Jun. 2, 1920 Minroku 26-839.

1045. Matsuo and Kozumi 2008: pp. 368–369; Dogauchi 2017b: pp. 168–170; Ohmi 2020b: pp. 212–214.

1046. The mortgagees who received the document as stated above shall be deemed to have approved the price or the amount that the third-party acquirer has offered in that document, (i) if the mortgagee does not apply for auction by executing the right of hypothec within two months after he/she received the document, (ii) if the mortgagee withdraws the application for the auction, (iii) if the court dismiss the application for the auction, or (iv) if the court rescinds the auction procedure (s. 384 CC).

been decreasing and the purchase price at auction by the execution of the right of hypothec seems to be lower than the amount of the claim secured by the hypothec.[1047]

VII. Revolving Hypothec

486. The subordinate nature of the right of hypothec which means that the claim must preexists the hypothec[1048] has been relaxed through the needs in the business practices. This movement was initiated by "ne-teito" [the revolving hypothec], which was introduced into the Civil Code in 1971 (sections 398-2 to 398-22 CC). It recognizes that the right of hypothec can be established to secure "unspecified claims of a certain scope, up to the limit of a maximum amount" (section 398-2 (1) CC). It aims to secure the collective claims which will be created continuously in the future from the continuous contractual relationship between the particular parties. For instance, if a bank A agrees with a company B to lend a certain amount of money every month for two years at the request of B for its business activities, B can establish a right of hypothec on B's land to secure A's claim to be created from the continuous transaction between A and B on the basis of that agreement. By establishing the right of revolving hypothec A and B can save the cost to establish the right of hypothec and register it every month when B borrows money from A to secure A's Claim. It is also frequently used to secure the claims to be generated from the continuous transaction between the manufacturer and the wholesaler.[1049]

The revolving hypothec originated in the customary law on the security transactions since the end of the nineteenth century. It was recognized by the judicial precedents[1050] and the registration practices, while the Ministry of Justice denied the validity of "comprehensive revolving hypothec" which shall secure all the claims created between the particular parties in 1955 and the registration office refused to accept the application for such revolving hypothec. In order to put an end to the confusion, the Civil Code was amended in 1971 to regulate the requirement for the valid revolving hypothec. Then it has become very popular in the financial transactions between the banks and companies.[1051]

The important requirement is the scope of claims to be secured by the valid revolving hypothec. The scope of claims can be identified as "claims arising from a specific contract for continuous transaction with the obligor" or "claims arising from a certain kind of transactions with the obligor" (section 389-2 (2) CC). The scope of claims must be registered (section 88 (2) [1] LRIP). For instance, "claims to be generated from the bank transactions" was recognized to meet the requirement of "claims arising from a certain kind of transactions with the obligor."[1052] In

1047. Matsuo and Kozumi 2008: pp. 370–373; Dogauchi 2017b: pp. 170–175; Ohmi 2020b: pp. 214–217.
1048. *See* para. 464 *supra.*
1049. Matsuo and Kozumi 2008: p. 382; Dogauchi 2017b: pp. 238–239.
1050. STJ Oct. 25, 1901 Minroku 7-9-137; STJ Jan. 27, 1902 Minroku 1-72.
1051. The number of registration of the revolving hypothec occupies around one sixth to one fifth among the total number of the registration of the right of hypothec. Dogauchi 2017b: p. 239.
1052. SCJ Jan. 19, 1993 Minshu 47-1-41.

addition, claims which will arise continuously from a specific cause with the obligor, claims relating to negotiable instruments or checks, or electronically recorded monetary claims (section 2 (1) Law on the Electronically Recorded Monetary Claims, Law No. 102, 2007) shall be treated as claims which can be secured by the right of revolving mortgage (section 398-2 (3) CC).

487. Another requirement for the valid revolving hypothec is the stipulation of "kyokudo-gaku" [the limit of a maximum amount] of the claim (section 398-2 (1) CC). The limit of a maximum amount of claims must also be registered (section 88 (2) [1] LRIP). Even if the total amount of claims consisting of a principal and periodic payments including interest and compensation for loss or damage due to non-performance of obligation exceeds the limit of a maximum amount, the creditor can collect up to the limit of a maximum amount (section 398-3 (1) CC), even though the purchase price of the object at auction was more than the total amount of claims.[1053] The revolving hypothec is a right to receive performance only within the limit of a maximum amount through the execution procedure.

In order to execute the right of revolving hypothec, the principal must be fixed. The principal shall be fixed by the following reasons: (i) the principal shall be fixed on the date which the mortgagee and the mortgagor agreed. creditor and the agreement on the date of fixation (section 398-6 (1) CC). It must be within five years (section 398-6 (3) CC). It can be renewed; however, the renewed date must be within five years from the date of the renewal (section 398-6 (1), (3) CC). The agreement of the date can be registered (section 88 (2) [3] LRIP); (ii) even if the date of fixation is not agreed, the mortgagee can require the fixation at any time, and then the principal shall be fixed at the time of request (section 398-19 (2) CC); (iii) the mortgagor and the acquirer of the object can require the fixation after three years since the establishment of the revolving hypothec (section 398-19 (1) CC), and then the principal shall be fixed after two weeks from the time of request (section 398-19 (1) CC); (iv) in addition, the principal shall be fixed when the mortgagee applies for auction, execution on the fruits to be collected from the object,[1054] attachment on the claim for substitution of the object,[1055] which must be followed by the actual commencement of those procedures; when two weeks have passed since the mortgagee was aware of the commencement of the procedure for auction initiated by a third party or the attachment by the central or local government on the mortgaged property for the reason of tax delinquency; or when the commencement order of bankruptcy procedure is issued for the debtor or the mortgagee (section 398-20 CC). In these cases, the mortgagee will require the payment of claims with priority so that the principal must be fixed.[1056]

When the principal is fixed, the mortgagee can execute the right of hypothec to collect all of the fixed principal and periodical payments including the interest and compensation for loss or damage due to non-performance of obligation (section

1053. SCJ Oct. 4, 1973 Hanji 723-42.
1054. It is the execution of the right of hypothec on the fruits in accordance with the procedure provided by the Civil Execution Law (ss. 181, 188, 88, 91, 93, 94 and 95 Civil Execution Law). *See* para. 472 *supra*.
1055. *See* para. 473 *supra*.
1056. Dogauchi 2017b: pp. 255–256.

398-3 (1) CC). It means that the restriction of the scope of claims on the periodical payment such as the interest within the latest two years (section 375 CC)[1057] shall not be applied to the revolving hypothec because the interest and compensation cannot be calculated until the principal is fixed. As a result, the mortgagee of revolving hypothec can require to collect the interest for more than the latest two years as long as it is within the limit of a maximum amount of claim.[1058]

§6. Security Interest Preserved by Provisional Registration

488. The parties to secured transaction can establish the right of security interest preserved by provisional registration. For instance, if A borrows certain amount of money from B, A may agree with B that A must transfer the immovable property which A owns when A becomes in default. In order to secure the acquisition of the immovable property by B as a substitute performance in case of A's default and the liquidation for the interest of A, A and B can agree to establish the provisional registration of the acquisition of the immovable property to be caused by the conditional transfer or by the reservation of the transfer of ownership (sections 105–110 LRIP). It is one of the atypical types of collateral which include the conveyancing mortgage, the reservation of ownership, etc.[1059] It aims to save the cost by bypassing the court procedure to execute the right of hypothec and to maintain the fairness between the creditor and the owner of the immovable property by liquidating the value of the property and the amount of debt.[1060]

489. In the case above (paragraph 488) when A is in default, B can assert the fulfillment of the condition or exercise the right to complete the reservation for the transfer of ownership and claim A for the registration of the transfer of ownership of the immovable property from A to B. If A refuses to cooperate with the registration, or if A transferred the same property to C and registered it for C after the provisional registration for B, B can bring the case to the court on the basis of the agreement between A and B. B can win the case and apply for the registration of the transfer of ownership from A to B by showing the final judgment in favor of B at the registration office without approval of A. If the registration for B was completed, the incompatible registration for C shall be deleted ex officio because B's provisional registration was earlier than the registration for C (section 109 (2) LRIP).[1061]

1057. *See* paras. 466, 467 *supra.*
1058. Dogauchi 2017b: p. 257.
1059. *See* paras. 493, 524, 526 *infra.*
1060. Matsuo and Kozumi 2008: pp. 398–399; Dogauchi 2017b: p. 272; Ohmi 2020b: pp. 288–289.
1061. Matsuo and Kozumi 2008: pp. 67–68; para. 242 *supra.* However, in order to transfer ownership of the immovable property, A must give a notice to B about the estimated amount of liquidation (s. 2 (1) LCSPPR), and A should also give a notice to C that A has given the notice to B, it reached B, and the content of the notice for the interest of C (s. 5 (2) LCSPPR). *See also* paras. 491 and 492 *infra.*

490. This secured transaction by using the provisional registration was initially created in the business practice because it was advantageous for B to acquire the immovable property without the liquidation of the difference between the amount of B's claim and the value of A's immovable property. In order to maintain the fairness between A and B, the Law on the Contract of Security Preserved by Provisional Registration (LCSPPR) was enacted in 1978 (Law No. 78). It provides that when the creditor who has the security interest preserved by provisional registration based on the contract with the owner of an immovable property (a debtor or a third party) execute his/her right, he/she must notice to the other party of the contract the estimated amount of liquidation, and the transfer of ownership from the owner to the creditor shall take place when two months have passed since the notice reached the other party of the contract (section 2 (1) LCSPPR). This two-month period is called "seisan-kikan" [the liquidation period] during which the other party of the contract (the owner of the property) can keep ownership of the property and perform obligation to remove the provisional registration.[1062]

491. The creditor's duty to pay liquidation must be simultaneously performed with the other party's duty to deliver the immovable property (section 3 (1) and (2) LCSPPR). In addition, even after the liquidation period as explained in the previous paragraph, if the creditor has yet to perform the duty to pay liquidation, the other party can still redeem ownership of the immovable property by providing the creditor with the amount of money corresponding to that of the claim until five years have passed since the notice of the estimated liquidation reached the other party or a third party has acquired ownership from the creditor (section 11 LCSPPR). However, even when the third party acquired ownership of the property and registered the transfer of ownership, the other party of the security contract with the creditor can refuse to deliver it to the third party and retain the property on the basis of the right of retention until the liquidation money is paid to him/her.[1063]

492. When the creditor gives a notice to the other party (the owner of the immovable property) about the estimated amount of liquidation (section 2 (1) LCSPPR), and he/she should also give a notice to the other creditors who have the right of lien, the right of pledge, the right of hypothec who do not prevail over the creditor secured by the provisional registration to the effect that the creditor has given the notice to the other party, it reached him/her, and the content of the notice (including the amount of liquidation) for the interest of those inferior creditors (section 5 (2) LCSPPR). They can apply for auction within the liquidation period even though their claims have not fallen due (section 12 LCSPPR). Alternatively, those inferior creditors may attach the owner's claim for liquidation as the substitution of the object (sections 304, 361, 372 CC).[1064] If the creditor secured by the provisional registration did not give the notice to those inferior creditors, they can apply for auction even after the liquidation period was over.[1065]

1062. Ohmi 2020b: p. 291.
1063. SCJ Mar. 31, 1983 Minshu 37-2-152.
1064. *See* paras. 439, 473 *supra*.
1065. SCJ Apr. 11, 1986 Minshu 40-3-584.

The creditor secured by the provisional registration should also give a notice to a third party who has acquired the immovable property after the creditor's provisional registration that the creditor has given the notice to the other party (the owner of the property), it reached him/her, and the content of the notice (including the amount of liquidation) for the interest of the third-party acquirer (section 5 (2) LCSIPR). The acquirer may perform the debtor's obligation as a third party (section 474 CC) to remove the provisional registration before the liquidation period, and exercise the owner's right of redemption (section 11 LCSPPR) by way of a creditor's right to subrogate the exercise of debtor's right (section 423 (1) Main Text CC) even after the liquidation period was over unless the liquidation money has yet to be paid. If the creditor secured by the provisional registration fails to give the notice to the third-party acquirer, the creditor cannot be opposable against the acquirer so that the acquirer may deny the transfer of ownership to the creditor even after the liquidation period and the payment of the liquidation money.[1066]

§7. Conveyancing Mortgage

493. In the business practices, "jyoto-tanpo" [the conveyancing mortgage] has been frequently used, and it has been recognized by the court as the real right for the security interest based on the customary law. It is recognized as one of the atypical types of collateral right. It has been created to save the cost to execute the right of hypothec. For example, when A borrows money from B, A and B may agree that A transfers the ownership of his/her property, either immovable or movable,[1067] to B for the purpose of security interest, so that B must return the property when A perform his/her obligation in accordance with the agreement between A and B. When the object of conveyancing mortgage is an immovable property, the registration is made and the name of the owner is changed from A to B.[1068] As for the possession, A usually keeps the actual and direct possession of the property by declaring that A intends to possess the thing on behalf of B. By this declaration of intention of A called "senyu-kaitei" [the constructive transfer of possession], B is legally recognized as acquired the possession of the property (indirect possession: section 183 CC) and satisfies the opposability requirement for the acquisition of ownership of movable property (delivery: section 178 CC).[1069]

1066. Dogauchi 2017b: p. 283.

1067. Intangible things such as claim rights, collective monetary claims, bills and checks, stocks, claim for insurance money, and intellectual property may also be the object of conveyancing mortgage. Dogauchi 2017b: pp. 349–364.

1068. In registration, the cause of transfer of ownership may be recorded as "jyoto-tanpo" [the conveyancing mortgage] so that the security purpose can be identified by confirming registration. However, in the practice of conveyancing mortgage, the cause of transfer of ownership has been frequently recorded as "bai-bai" [the sale] even when the actual purpose of transfer of ownership is conveyancing mortgage. Dogauchi 2017b: pp. 311–312.

1069. *See* para. 256 *supra*.

494. The transfer of ownership for security purpose seems to be achieved by "kaimodoshi-no-tokuyaku" [the special agreement of redemption] which is explicitly provided by the Civil Code (sections 579–585). But it is limited to the immovable property (section 579 CC), and the term of redemption is limited within five years if there is no agreement on it and within ten years by any agreement (section 580 CC). And the last but not least, the redemption agreement is not always used for security purpose, and the possession of the object of redemption is normally transferred to the buyer. If the possession of the immovable property is kept by the seller and is not delivered to the purchaser, it should be interpreted as the conveyancing mortgage even though the contracting parties use the term of "kaimodoshi" [the redemption] unless the special circumstance cannot be found.[1070] As a result, the redemption agreement would be better to see a difference from the conveyancing mortgage.

495. There are several reasons for the development of conveyancing mortgage. First, it may save time and cost of executing the right of hypothec due to the court procedure by maintaining its advantage of keeping possession of the property in the hands of mortgagor and continuing the mortgagor's activities by using the property.[1071] Second, the conveyancing mortgage may be used for movable property, for which the right of hypothec is not recognized by existing laws except for limited types of movable property.[1072] Third, the conveyancing mortgage can be established for collective things within a certain scope as an object of conveyancing mortgage by one agreement.[1073] Fourth, the conveyancing mortgage may be established on claim rights or other intangible things including a certain scope of collective and future claim rights.[1074]

496. It is difficult to characterize the nature of the conveyancing mortgage in a simple expression. It has been discussed much in the legal doctrine concerning the legal status of conveyancing mortgagee. It seems to be between the true ownership and the right of hypothec. In the case of the corporate reorganization procedure which was commenced for the conveyancing mortgagor A, the court decided that the right of conveyancing mortgagee B of an immovable property as the object of conveyancing mortgage and in the possession of A should be treated as the reorganization security right (section 2 (10) Corporate Reorganization Law).[1075] As long as this judicial precedent is concerned, the right of conveyancing mortgagee seems to be regarded as a kind of security rights. After that, judicial precedents stipulate that by the conveyancing mortgage, the transfer of ownership of the object takes place for the purpose of security interest so that "the effect of transfer of ownership

1070. SCJ Feb. 7, 2006 Minshu 60-2-480.
1071. Dogauchi 2017b: p. 309.
1072. *See* para. 523 *infra*.
1073. SCJ Nov. 10, 1987 Minshu 41-8-1599. There are special laws which recognize collective assets such as land, buildings, machines and other facilities used in a factory, or all assets of a company as an object of a right of collateral. *See* paras. 97, 98, 99 *supra*.
1074. SCJ Nov. 22, 2001 Minshu 55-6-1056, SCJ Feb. 15, 2007 Minshu 61-1-243.
1075. SCJ Apr. 28, 1966 Minshu 20-4-900.

can be recognized only within the scope of achieving the security purpose."[1076] This seems to be the main stream of the judicial precedents, though different views still exist. The majority of the legal doctrines have moved from the understanding that the conveyancing mortgagee's right is ownership to the understanding that the conveyancing mortgagee's right is a collateral right and there remains a real right in the hand of the conveyancing mortgagor. The understanding of the legal status of the conveyancing mortgagee and that of the conveyancing mortgagor will influence the solution of the problem between the conveyancing mortgagor and a third party and that between the conveyancing mortgagee and a third party.

497. The problem between the conveyancing mortgagor and a third party will occur, for instance, when A borrowed a certain amount of money from B and established the conveyancing mortgage on A's immovable property for B, and the registration was completed. A is the conveyancing mortgagor and B is the conveyancing mortgagee. After that B's creditor C attached this immovable property as it was registered in the name of B and B was in default and could not perform obligation for C. But it was before the due date of B's claim B against A so that A was not in default. In this case, the Supreme Court held that the conveyancing mortgagor A can claim against C to restore the immovable property and can make an action based on the third party objection (section 38 Civil Execution Law) to exclude the execution by C.[1077] It presupposed that before the due date of B's claim against A, transfer of ownership of the property could not be recognized for B and B was not substantially the owner of the property though the registration was completed for B, while A was regarded as retaining the real right to exclude C's execution like the owner of the property.[1078] For the protection of C, C may allege that A should be blamed to have made the registration to the effect that ownership was transferred from A to B, and C believed that the property belonged to B, so that A cannot be opposable against B who was in good faith (the protection of a bona fide third party by analogical application of section 94 (2) CC).[1079]

Similarly, when the conveyancing mortgagee B has become bankrupt before the due date of B's claim against A, A may claim the bankruptcy administrator C to restore the immovable property by performing his/her obligation.[1080]

If the conveyancing mortgagee B sold the immovable property to a third party C before the due date of B's claim against A, A should be able to claim against C to restore the immovable property on the basis of ownership or the retained real right to restore the property. C may make a defense that C acquired the registration from B before A restores the registration from B (section 177 CC). A will allege that A

1076. SCJ Sep. 29, 1982 Hanji 1062-81; SCJ Feb. 26, 1993 Minshu 47-2-1653; SCJ Nov. 10, 1995 Minshu 49-9-2953; SCJ Oct. 20, 2016 Minshu 60-8-3098.

1077. SCJ Oct. 20, 2006 Minshu 60-8-3098.

1078. Kozumi and Matsuo 2008: pp. 409, 413–415; Dogauchi 2017b: p. 322.

1079. Dogauchi 2017b: p. 322. After the due date of B's claim against A, B can execute the conveyancing mortgage (*see* para. 499 *infra*), and if B becomes the owner of the property and then C attaches the property, C's attachment is valid. However, after the due date of B's claim against A, but before the execution of the conveyancing mortgage, C can still be protected by the analogical application of s. 94 (2) CC. *See* Dogauchi 2017b: p. 329.

1080. STJ Oct. 12, 1938 Minshu 17-2115.

could not restore the registration before the due date of B's claim against A, so that section 177 CC should not be applied to this case.[1081] Then C may make another defense that A should be blamed to have made the registration to the effect that ownership was transferred from A to B, and C believed that the property belonged to B, so that A cannot be opposable against B who was in good faith (the protection of a bona fide third party by analogical application of section 94 (2) CC).

After the due date of B's claim against A, if B sold the immovable property to C and registered the transfer of ownership from B to C, A cannot claim C to restore the property, even though the liquidation money has yet to be paid to A and A provided B with performance of obligation.[1082]

498. The problem between the conveyancing mortgagee and a third party will occur, for instance, when A borrowed a certain amount of money from B and established the conveyancing mortgage on A's immovable property for B, and the registration was completed. A is the conveyancing mortgagor and B is the conveyancing mortgagee. After that A's creditor D (a creditor of the conveyancing mortgagor) attached the property which was the object of the conveyancing mortgage and possessed by A. B made an action against D to exclude the execution based on the objection by the third party (section 38 Civil Execution Law). The court recognized B's claim to exclude the execution by D.[1083] The court regarded B (the conveyancing mortgagee) as the owner of the property. In this case, the object of conveyancing mortgage was the movable property, for which B may acquire possession as the requirement for the opposability against a third party D (section 178 CC) through the constructive transfer of possession by A's declaration of intention that he/she will possess the thing on behalf of B (section 183 CC).[1084] However, in the case of the commencement of corporate reorganization procedure for A, the Supreme Court held that B's right should be treated as the reorganization security right provided by section 2 (10) of the Corporate Reorganization Law.[1085]

499. As for the execution of the conveyancing mortgage, after the due date of the claim, the conveyancing mortgagee has to give a notice to the conveyancing mortgagor about the execution of the conveyancing mortgage and can either assign the object as his/her own property or sell the object to a third party and appropriate the purchase price to satisfy the claim depending on the agreement at the establishment of the conveyancing mortgage. In either case, if the value of the property as the object of conveyancing mortgage is beyond the amount of claim (including the

---

1081. Matsuo and Kozumi 2008: p. 415.

1082. SCJ Feb. 22, 1994 Minshu 48-2-414. The Supreme Court held that the acquirer C has acquired ownership "definitely," so that A cannot redeem ownership by performing obligation to B. *See also* para. 499 *infra.*

1083. STJ Nov. 2, 1914 Minroku 20-865, SCJ Dec. 17, 1981 Minshu 35-9-1328, SCJ Feb. 24, 1983 Hanji 1078-65.

1084. In the case of an immovable property, as the transfer of ownership from A to B is registered and the name of the owner is changed from A to B, D, the creditor of A, cannot attach the immovable property registered in the name of B.

1085. SCJ Apr. 28, 1966 Minshu 20-4-900. *See also* para. 496 *supra.*

interest, compensation for damages, etc.),[1086] the conveyancing mortgagee has a duty to pay the difference to the conveyancing mortgagor as a liquidation money.[1087] Until the conveyancing mortgagee complete the liquidation, the conveyancing mortgagor may redeem the property by providing the conveyancing mortgagee with obligation. However, judicial precedents deny the redemption when the conveyancing mortgagee sold the immovable property to a third party and register the transfer of ownership even though the liquidation money has yet to be paid to the conveyancing mortgagor.[1088] But if the conveyancing mortgagor still possesses the immovable property, he/she can refuse to deliver it to the acquirer by exercising the right of retention until the payment of liquidation money.[1089] If the acquirer did not know that the property was the object of conveyancing mortgage, he/she can make a defense that the conveyancing mortgagor cannot be opposable against the bona fide third party (by the analogical application of section 94 (2) CC).[1090]

1086. As for the scope of claims to be secured by the conveyancing mortgage, there is no restriction like the s. 375 for the right of hypothec. However, if the conveyancing mortgage should be understood as a collateral right (*see* para. *supra*), the analogical application may be considered. *See* Matsuo and Kozumi 2008: p. 412.
1087. SCJ Mar. 25, 1971 Minshu 25-2-208.
1088. SCJ Jan. 22, 1982 Minshu 36-1-92; SCJ Feb. 22, 1994 Minshu 48-2-414.
1089. SCJ Apr. 11, 1997 Shumin 183-241.
1090. Dogauchi 2017b: p. 329.

Chapter 2. Securities in Movable Property

§1. Right of Retention

500. The right of retention may be established in iure on the movable property as well. The same principles as explained for the right of retention on the immovable property shall apply to the movable property.[1091]

§2. Special Right of Lien in Movable

501. The general right of lien and the special right of lien in an immovable property have been explained in paragraphs 448–453 *supra*. In this section, the special right of lien to be recognized on a movable property will be treated. A person who has a claim that has been created from the following eight causes shall have the special right of lien on a particular movable which belongs to the debtor (section 311 CC): the claim caused by: (i) the lease of an immovable property; (ii) the lodging at hotels or inns; (iii) the transportation of passengers or luggage; (iv) the preservation of movables; (v) the sale of a movable; (vi) the supply of seeds or fertilizers including eggs of silkworms or mulberry leaves used to feed silkworms; (vii) the agricultural labor; or (viii) the industrial labor. In these cases, the creditor of the claim which has been created from the causes listed above shall have the right of lien in the particular movable as specified by the provisions of law. These special rights of lien on a particular movable property are recognized by the provisions of law without any agreement between the parties. They are based on the presumption of the parties' intention, the principle of fairness between the parties or the legal policy to protect a certain claim.[1092]

502. (i) The special right of lien for the lease of an immovable property shall exist on certain movables owned by the lessee to secure claims which are caused by the lease of the immovable property such as a claim for rent and compensation for damages due to non-performance of obligation. It is based on the presumption of the parties' intention to secure those claims. For instance, the special right of lien for the lease of a land shall exist on the movables attached to the land and buildings for the use of that land, the movables provided for the use of that land, and the fruits collected from that land and possessed by the lessee (section 313 (1) CC).

The special right of lien for the lease of a building shall exist on the movables "attached" to the building by the lessee (section 313 (2) CC). However, the judicial precedent interprets the term "attached" not strictly. It held that the movables attached to the building should include not only those equipped to the building but also placed continuously for a certain period.[1093]

1091. *See* Ch. 1, §1 *supra*.
1092. Matsuo and Kozumi 2008: pp. 270–273.
1093. Matsuo and Kozumi 2008: p. 271.

Even if a movable property attached to the building (or placed continuously for a certain period in the building) does not belong to the debtor, the creditor (the lessor) may be protected when he/she attached the movable believing reasonably that it belonged to the lessee (in good faith without negligence) and he/she can execute the special right of lien on that movable (sections 319, 192–195 CC). This is the immediate (good faith) acquisition of the special right of lien on the other person's movable.[1094]

When the lessor A leased his/her immovable property to B, and then B sublet it to C with the approval (section 612 CC), the special right of lien on the movable attached to the building shall include the movables which C attached or placed continuously for a certain period (section 314 First Sentence CC) and a claim for rent to be received by B from C (section 314 Second Sentence CC). These are regarded as the substitution of the object (section 304 CC).[1095]

All the claims which the lessor can acquire from the lessee shall be secured by the special right of lien on the movables attached to the immovable property. However, if all of the lessee's property is to be liquidated such as in the bankruptcy procedure, the special right of lien of the lessor shall secure only claims for the rent of previous, current and next terms, for compensation for damages that arose in the previous and current terms (section 315 CC). In addition, if the lessor has received a security deposit from the lessee, the special right of lien of the lessor can secure only the portion of the claim which will not be satisfied by that security deposit (section 316 CC). These restrictions on the scope of claims aim to prevent the unfair reduction of the bankruptcy estate.[1096]

503. (ii) The special right of lien for the lodging at a hotel shall exist on the hand luggage which was brought into the hotel by the guest. It will secure the claim for room charges and food and beverage charges that should be borne by the guest (section 317 CC). It is based on the presumption of the parties' intention that the luggage shall be the collateral to secure the claim for charges to room, food, drink, etc.[1097] Consequently, the hotel's expectation that the claim for hotel fee can be secured by the guest's luggage should be protected. Even when the luggage did not belong to the guest, the hotel may be protected if it possessed some pieces of luggage believing reasonably that they belonged to the guest (in good faith without negligence). In this case, the hotel can execute the special right of lien on the luggage (section 319, 192–195 CC).

504. (iii) The special right of lien for the transportation shall exist on the luggage possessed by the transporter to secure the claim for transportation charge for passenger or luggage and related expenses (section 318 CC). It also aims to protect the transporter's expectation that the luggage which it possesses should be the collateral to secure the claim for transportation charge. As a result, even when the luggage did not belong to the passenger or the sender, the transporter may be protected

1094. As for the immediate (good faith) acquisition of a movable property, *see* paras. 260 to 267 *supra*.
1095. Matsuo and Kozumi 2008: p. 271.
1096. Matsuo and Kozumi 2008: pp. 271–272.
1097. Matsuo and Kozumi 2008: p. 272.

if it possessed some pieces of luggage believing reasonably that they belonged to the passenger or the sender (in good faith without negligence). In this case, the transporter can execute the special right of lien on the luggage (sections 319, 192–195 CC).[1098]

505. (iv) The special right of lien for preservation of a movable shall exist on the movable to secure the claim for expenses spent for the preservation (such as the repair) of that movable or expenses spent for the preservation of a right relating to that movable (such as the action to prevent the acquisitive prescription), recognition of the right (such as asking the possessor to recognize that the movable belongs to the debtor to prevent the acquisitive prescription) or execution of the right (such as exercising the debtor's claim for delivery of that movable by way of the creditor's subrogation [section 423 CC]) (section 320 CC). It aims to maintain the fairness between the creditor who spent expenses for the preservation and other creditors who may be benefitted by the preservation of that movable.[1099]

506. (v) The special right of lien for the sale of a movable shall exist on the movable to secure the claim for the purchase money of that movable and its interest (section 321 CC). The seller can assert and execute this special right of lien for the sale of a movable even after the movable was delivered to the buyer until it has been delivered to a third party (section 333 CC).[1100] It aims to maintain the fairness between the seller of a movable who are not paid and the other creditors of the owner of that movable.[1101]

507. (vi) The special right of lien for the supply of seeds or fertilizers shall exist on fruits which are derived from the land where the seeds or the fertilizers were used within one year from that use so as to secure the claim for price of the seeds or the fertilizers and its interest (section 322 CC). It aims not only to maintain the fairness between the supplier and the other creditors of the owner of the fruits but also to sustain the agriculture by protecting the supplier of materials.[1102]

508. (vii) The special right of lien for the agricultural labor shall exist on fruits which are produced by the labor in order to secure the claim for wages within the latest one year of the person who engaged in that labor (section 323 CC). It aims to maintain the fairness between the worker and other creditors of the owner of the fruits as well as to guarantee the life of that worker from the viewpoint of social policy.[1103] The general right of lien for employer-employee relationship (sections 306 [2], 308 CC) will also be available for the worker.[1104]

1098. Matsuo and Kozumi 2008: p. 272.
1099. Dogauchi 2017b: pp. 60–61.
1100. *See also* para. 512 *infra*.
1101. Matsuo and Kozumi 2008: p. 272.
1102. Dogauchi 2017b: pp. 61–62.
1103. Dogauchi 2017b: p. 62.
1104. *See* para. 442 *supra*. The object of the general right of lien for employer-employee relationship shall include all the assets of the employer, not limited to the fruits from the labor.

509. (viii) The special right of lien for the industrial labor shall exist on manufactured goods which are produced by the labor in order to secure the claim for wages within the latest three months of the person who engaged in that labor (section 324 CC). The purpose of this right of lien is the same as that for the agricultural labor, though the priority is given only the latest three months for the industrial worker.[1105]

510. If the special rights of lien on a movable property conflict each other, the priority order shall be fixed by the following principles stipulated in section 330 CC. They are based on the presumption of the parties' intention and the principle of fairness:[1106]

(i) The first priority is given to the special right of lien for the lease of an immovable property, the lodging at hotels and the transportation.
(ii) The second priority lies in the special right of lien for the preservation of a movable.
(iii) The third priority is put on the special right of lien for the sale of a movable, the supply of seeds or fertilizers, agricultural labor and industrial labor (section 330 (1) CC).

As for Item (ii) above, if there are two or more preservers concerned with the special right of lien for the preservation of a movable, a new preserver shall prevail over previous preservers (section 330 (1) CC).

Throughout these priorities if there are two or more holders of the right of lien who have the same priority rank on the same property, they shall be paid in proportion to the amounts of their claims (section 332 CC).

However, there are three exceptions to those priority principles. First, if the holder of the special right of lien ranked first (see (i) above) knew at the time of the acquisition of the claim about the existence of the holder of the special right of lien of the second or the third rank, he/she cannot exercise the right against those persons (section 330 (2) First Sentence CC). The reason is that the special right of lien for the lease of an immovable property, the lodging at hotels and the transportation are based on the presumption of the parties' intention and the protection of the creditor's expectation.[1107]

Second, the person who preserved the movable for the holder of the special right of lien of the first rank prevails over the latter (section 330 (2) Second Sentence CC). It is based on the fairness, because the latter is benefitted by the former.

Third, as far as the fruits are concerned, the first rank belongs to persons who engage in agricultural labor, the second rank belongs to persons who supplied seeds or fertilizers, and the third rank is given to lessors of a land (section 330 (3) CC).

1105. The reason for the difference is that the source of the agricultural wage is usually from the annual crops (Dogauchi 2017b: p. 62). The general right of lien for employer-employee relationship (ss. 306 [2], 308 CC) will also be available for the industrial worker as well (*see* the previous footnote).

1106. Dogauchi 2017b: pp. 77–78.

1107. Dogauchi 2017b: pp. 77–78.

This priority is based on the causality of the fruits, the protection policy of the agricultural workers and the existence of alternative objects for the right of lien.[1108]

511. When the debtor is in default, the creditor who holds the special right of lien in a movable property may exercise the right and apply for the auction of the movable property (section 190 (1), (2) Civil Execution Law) and receive payment for the claim prior to other creditors from the purchase money of that movable. In the bankruptcy procedure, the special right of lien in a movable property is treated as the right of separate satisfaction which may be exercised without involving in the bankruptcy procedure and thus receive performance prior to other creditors (sections 2 (9) and 65 Bankruptcy Law).[1109]

512. The right of lien cannot be exercised on the movable which has been "delivered" from the debtor to a third-party acquirer (section 333 CC). The court held that the delivery provided by section 333 CC may include the constitutive delivery (section 183 CC). For instance, A sold a machine to B and delivered it to B before the payment of purchase money. B sold it to C and then agreed that B would keep possession of that machine on behalf of C and kept in B's warehouse. In this case, the Supreme Court held that A cannot exercise the special right of lien for the sale of a movable (section 321 CC), because the machines had already been "delivered" to C in the sense of section 333 CC.[1110] This broad interpretation of the term "delivered" seems to have protected the transaction by using the constructive delivery such as establishing the conveyancing mortgage on the movables.[1111]

§3. Right of Pledge

513. The right of pledge may also be established on a movable property by the agreement between the pledgee (the creditor) and the pledgor (the debtor or the third party) and by delivering the movable as its object to the pledgee (section 344). The pledgee may not have the pledgor to possess the object on behalf of the pledgee (section 345 CC). In addition, as the right of pledge on the movable cannot be registered unless it is recognized by the special laws,[1112] it is necessary for the pledgee of movable to continue possession of the object pledged in order to assert his/her right of pledge against a third party (section 352 CC). Two or more pledges may be established on the same movable property, though it is not often if the pledgor and the pledgee agree to it. In this case, the priority order shall be decided following the chronological order of the establishment (section 355 CC). For instance, A borrowed a certain amount of money from B and established the righto of pledge on the movable owned by A and delivered it to B. Then A borrowed money from C and agreed to establish the right of pledge on the movable on which B's right of

1108. Dogauchi 2017b: p. 78.
1109. On the right of separate satisfaction, *see* paras. 340, 447, 453, 461, 478 *supra*.
1110. STJ Jul. 27, 1917 Minroku 23-1203, SCJ Nov. 10, 1987 Minshu 41-8-1559.
1111. As for the establishment of the conveyancing mortgage on movables by the constructive delivery, *see* para. 524 *infra*.
1112. *See* §4 *infra*.

pledge has already established. In order to deliver it to C as required by sections 344, 345 and 352 CC, A can order B to possess the movable not only for B but also for C and if C agrees to it, the delivery to C can be recognized (section 184 CC). It is "sashizu-niyoru-sen-yu-iten" [the transfer of possession by way of the order to a third party].[1113] However, the priority is given to B who first acquired the right of pledge and the delivery (section 355 CC).[1114]

514. The pledgee of the movable property cannot use, lease or provide as a collateral the object pledged unless he/she obtains consent from the pledgor except for the use for preservation of the object. When the pledgee breaches this restriction, the pledgor can claim that the right of pledge shall be extinguished (sections 350, 298 CC). This restriction on the usage of the pledged movable by the pledgee is different from the pledgee of an immovable property, who has a right to use and take profits from the pledged immovable property unless agreed otherwise (section 359 CC).[1115]

515. The scope of clams which can be secured by the right of pledge on a movable property may include the principal, interest, penalties, expenses of executing the pledge, expense for preserving the thing pledged and compensation for damages arising from non-performance of obligations or latent defects in the object pledged unless the pledgee and the pledgor have agreed otherwise (section 346 CC). It is broader than the scope of claims of the right of hypothec (section 375 CC), because it is seldom that two or more creditors have the right of pledge on the same movable property.[1116]

516. The scope of the object of the right of pledge on a movable property may not extend to "jyubutsu" [the appurtenance to the principal thing] unless the appurtenance is also delivered to the pledgee together with the principal thing (section 87 (2) CC). However, if "fugobutsu" [the accessory] is attached to the object of the right of pledge as a result of accession (sections 243 and 244 CC), the scope of the right of pledge extends to the accessory.[1117]

517. The pledgee can exclude the infringement on the object on the basis of the right of pledge. For instance, if a third party is damaging the object, the pledgee can claim for suspension of the damage and for compensation to remove the disturbance on the basis of the right of pledge. However, if the object of pledge was deprived of the pledgee by a third party, the pledgee cannot claim for recovery on the basis of the right of pledge but can bring the possessory action for recovery (sections 353, 200 CC).[1118] The reason is that the exercise the right of pledge on the

1113. As for "sashizu-niyoru-sen-yu-iten" [the transfer of possession by way of order to a third party], *see* paras. 256, 289 *supra*.
1114. Dogauchi 2017b: p. 87.
1115. *See* para. 456 *supra*.
1116. Dogauchi 2017b: p. 92.
1117. Matsuo and Kozumi 2008: p. 286; Dogauchi 2017b: p. 90. As for the accession of a movable to a movable, *see* para. 311 *supra*.
1118. As for the possessory action for recovery, *see* para. 297 *supra*.

movable is established and becomes opposable against a third party with the possession of the object (sections 344, 352 CC) and is not registered for the publicity, the effect shall become weak if the pledgee has lost the possession.[1119] However, if the pledgee brings the possessory action for recovery, the possession shall be regarded as never has been interrupted (section 203 Proviso CC).

518. When the debtor is in default, the pledgee may exercise the right of pledge and apply for the auction of the movable property and receive payment for the claim prior to other creditors from the price of the immovable property. In the bankruptcy procedure, the right of pledge on a movable property is treated as the right of separate satisfaction which may be exercised without involving in the bankruptcy procedure and thus receive performance prior to other creditors (section 342 CC; section 190, 133 Civil Execution Law; section 2 (9), 65 Bankruptcy Law).[1120]

However, this formal execution procedure may be too costly for the value of the movable as the object of the right of pledge. For the purpose of avoiding this inconvenience, when there is a justifiable reason, the pledgee may apply the court for recognizing the object of the right of pledge as assigned to the pledgee as performance of the claim in accordance with evaluation of an appraiser (section 354 First Sentence CC). In this case the pledgee must notify the debtor about the application to the court in advance (section 354 CC Second Sentence). The cost for the application to the court including the expenses for appraisal can be included in the scope of claim to be secured by the right of pledge (section 346 CC).[1121]

It should be noted that this is the special rule in the execution process. On the contrary, the pledgee and the pledgor cannot agree at the conclusion of contract to establish the right of pledge that the object shall belong to the pledgee or shall be disposed of in the ways other than the provisions of law as a performance of obligation in advance (section 346). The purpose is to avoid the possible unfair agreement between the creditor and the debtor in the negotiation process of the contract of establishing the pledge.

519. The right of pledge may be established on property rights such as claims, shares of the company, and corporate bonds. When the pledge is established on a claim right, the right of pledge cannot be asserted and opposable against a third party including the debtor of that claim unless a notice of the establishment of the pledge is given to the debtor of that claim or the debtor of that claim acknowledges the establishment of the pledge in accordance with the provision of section 467 CC on the transfer (assignment) of a claim right (sections 362, 364 CC). For example, A has a claim right to receive payment of JPY 1,000,000 from B (the debtor of the claim) after six months when the claim shall become due. A borrowed JPY 800,000 from C and established the right of pledge on that claim. In order to make C's right of pledge on that claim opposable against B, C needs to have a notice of the establishment of the pledge for C to be delivered by A to B, or to have a recognition from B (sections 364, 467 (1) CC). In addition, C needs to have A's notice to B or B's

1119. Dogauchi 2017b: p. 94.

1120. On the right of separate satisfaction, *see* paras. 340, 447, 453, 461, 478, 511 *supra*.

1121. Section 346 CC mentions about it as "expenses of executing the pledge," *See* para. 515 *supra*.

recognition to be made by the certificate with fixed date (such as a notary deed and a mail the content of which is recorded for the proof at the post office) in order to be opposable against a third party except for B such as D who is another creditor of A and attached that claim right (sections 364, 467 (2) CC).

The delivery of the document to prove the claim was necessary from the creditor of the claim to the pledgee (old section 363 CC). However, it was removed by the amendment to the Civil Code in 2017. This is the result of the movement toward the paperless transaction.[1122]

520. Shareholders may establish the right of pledge on their shares (section 146 Company Law). However, the right of pledge on the shares of a company which issues the share certificate cannot become effective unless the share certificates of the pledged shares are delivered to the pledgee (section 146 (2) Company Law). The right of pledge on the shares cannot be asserted and opposable against the stock company and other third parties unless the name and address of the pledgee is stated or recorded in the shareholders' registry (section 147 (1) Company Law) and the pledgee continuously possess the share certificates for the pledged shares (section 147 (2) Company Law). The pledgor of the shares may request that the stock company should state or record such matters as: (i) the name and address of the pledgee, and (ii) the shares as the object of the pledge (section 148 Company Law). In this case, the pledgee may request the stock company to deliver the document which states those matters or provide the electromagnetic records which record those matters (section 149 (1) Company Law). By this statement or record, the right of pledge on the shares will be effective and strengthened. However, it is seldom in the practice.[1123]

521. The same as the pledge on shares will apply to that on corporate bonds. The right of pledge on corporate bonds cannot become effective unless bond certificates concerning the pledged bonds are delivered to the pledgee (section 692 Company Law), and it cannot be asserted and opposable against the bond-issuing company and other third parties unless the name and address of the pledgee is stated or recorded in the bond registry (section 693 (1) Company Law). Besides, the pledgee of bonds of the company which issues bond certificates cannot assert his/her right of pledge against the bond-issuing company and other third parties unless he/she continuously possesses the bond certificates (section 693 (2) Company Law).

The pledgor of the bonds can request the bond-issuing company to state or record the name and address of the pledgee and the bonds as the object of the pledge unless the bond certificate is issued (section 694 Company Law). The pledgee for whom those matters are stated or recorded in the bond registry may request that the bond-issuing company should deliver document stating matters stated or recorded in the bond registry or should provide the electromagnetic record on those matters (section 695 (1) Company Law). By this statement or record the right of pledge on the bonds will be effective and strengthened.

1122. Matsuo and Kozumi 2008: p. 297; Dogauchi 2017b: pp. 108–109.
1123. Dogauchi 2017b: p. 107.

522. In the case of the pledge on the claim right, the pledgee may directly receive performance of obligation corresponding to the claim which was pledged (section 366 (1) CC). In this case the thing received by the pledgee become the object of the pledge (section 366 (4) CC). If money is the object of the claim which is pledged, the pledgee may collect money to the extent of the portion that corresponds to the amount of the pledgee's own claim (section 366 (2) CC). It can save time and cost to execute the right of pledge on the monetary claim. If the scope of claim of the pledgee is not evident, the debtor of the pledged claim should be able to deposit money as performance of the pledged claim for the reason that the creditor is uncertain (section 494 (2) CC).[1124]

If the due date of the pledged claim arrives earlier than the due date of the pledgee's claim, the pledgee can ask the debtor of the pledged claim to deposit that amount to be paid to the pledgee. In this case, the right of pledge shall exist on the deposited amount (section 366 (3) CC).

§4. Right of Hypothec

523. For certain kinds of movable property, the right of hypothec can be established in accordance with the provisions of special laws. They include ships (sections 687 and 848 (3) Commercial Code), construction machines (section 7 (1) Law for Hypothec on Construction Machines), automobiles (section 5 (1) Law for Hypothec on Automobile), airplanes and helicopters (section 5 Law for Hypothec on Aircraft), farming machines (section 13 Law on Financing for Farming Machine), etc. In order to establish the right of hypothec on these movables they must be registered in the registration book.[1125]

A small boat such as a pleasure boat and a cruiser may also be registered in the registration book in accordance with section 4 of the Law on Registration of Small Boats. However, the law does not recognize neither the hypothec nor the pledge to be established on the small boat because the need for secured transaction of it in practice was thought to be not much.[1126]

§5. Conveyancing Mortgage

524. As for "jyoto-tanpo" [the conveyancing mortgage], the basic structure and the major principles are explained by using examples of the immovable property in Chapter 1, §7 above.[1127] The conveyancing mortgage may also be established on a movable property in accordance with the agreement between the parties. However, since the registration system is not introduced for the transaction of movables in general, the establishment of conveyancing mortgage on a movable property can be asserted and opposable against a third party by the delivery of the object (section

1124. Dogauchi 2017b: p. 119.
1125. *See* Part II, Ch. 1, §3 *supra.*
1126. Matsuo and Kozumi 2008: p. 114; Matsuo 2016: p. 363.
1127. *See* paras. 493–499 *supra.*

178 CC). Mostly, "sen-yu-kaitei" [the constitutive delivery, the constructive transfer of possession] (section 183 CC) or "sashizu-niyoru-sen-yu-iten" [the transfer of possession by way of the order to a possessing third party] (section 184 CC) is used for the purpose of a delivery of the object. For instance, if A borrows certain amount of money from B and establishes the conveyancing mortgage on the movables which A keeps in its warehouse, A may agree with B that A will possess the movable on behalf of B and thus the movables are legally regarded as delivered from A to B (section 183 CC). Or if A wants to establish the conveyancing mortgage on the movables which A keeps in C's warehouse, A can give instruction to C that C should possess them on behalf of B, and if B consents to it, then A's right of conveyancing mortgage can be asserted and opposable against the third party such as A's creditor D who attached A's claim for recovery of the movables to execute his/her claim or the acquirer E who bought those movables from B.[1128]

525. However, a special law was enacted which recognizes the registration of conveyance and conveyancing mortgage. According to section 3, paragraph (1) of the Law on Special Provisions of the Civil Code Concerning Requirements for the Opposability of Transfer of Movables and Claims,[1129] if a juridical person has transferred movables and the transfer is recorded in the registration file with regard to the conveyance and the conveyancing mortgage of the movables, it is deemed that the movables have been delivered in accordance with section 178 CC. It means that the registration shall replace the delivery in the sense of section 178 CC. In addition, movables to be registered in the registration file shall be identified by the kind and place of them so that the conveyance and conveyancing mortgage of collective movables can be made and registered.[1130]

When the movables are possessed by a third party, the conveyance or the conveyancing mortgage can be made between the owner of those movables (the transferor or the conveyancing mortgagor) and the transferee or the conveyancing mortgagee without telling the third party who possess it for the owner. In this case, if the third party is requested by the person who is registered as the transferee to deliver the movables, then the third party can notify the principal who had asked the third party to possess those movables without delay that he/she should make an objection, if any, to the transferee's request for delivery within a reasonable period of time. If the principal has made no objection within that period, the third party should not be liable to compensate for any damage that may be caused to the principal due to the delivery of those movables to the transferee (section 3 (2) Law on Special Provisions of the Civil Code Concerning Requirements for the Opposability of Transfer of Movables and Claims).[1131]

1128. However, D and E may be protected by the immediate acquisition (s. 192 CC) when they acquired possession of them believing reasonably that the movables had belonged to A (in good faith without negligence). As for the immediate acquisition of a movable property, *see* para. 260 *supra*.
1129. Law No. 104, Jun. 12, 1998.
1130. Matsuo 2016: pp. 363–364.
1131. Matsuo and Kozumi 2008: p. 115; Matsuo 2016: pp. 363–364.

§6. Reservation of Ownership

526. In installment sales of goods such as cars and machines, "shoyuken-ryuho" [the reservation of ownership] is often used for security purpose. It is an agreement attached to the contract of sale that the ownership shall be transferred when the purchase money is paid in full, even though the object is delivered to the purchaser.[1132] Since the reserved ownership aims to secure the seller's claim for payment, the purchaser may possess, use and take profits from the object. The ownership reserved in the hand of seller is just for the purpose of security interest, whereas the right of purchaser is substantially similar to ownership restricted by the security interest. It has been much discussed in the legal doctrines on how to characterize the nature of the reserved ownership of the seller and the right of purchaser in the object.

(a) On the one hand, there is a view that the seller is the owner of the object until the price is fully paid though it can be restricted by the contractual agreement between the seller and the purchaser.[1133] (b) On the other side of the view, the reserved ownership of the seller is regarded as collateral right like the right of hypothec, while the purchaser acquires ownership on which the seller's collateral right is established.[1134] By this view, the seller's right is regarded as a right of hypothec or called the reserved right for the seller, while the purchaser's right is regarded as ownership or the expectation right which has the nature of real right.[1135] Currently, the latter view (Item (b) above) is thought to have become the majority in the legal doctrines and the judicial precedents.[1136] However, in the judicial precedents, the former view (Item (a) above) seems to be kept in some cases.

527. When the purchaser's creditor attached the object to initiate the compulsory auction, the seller brought an action as a third party objection based on ownership to seek for non-permission of the compulsory execution by the purchaser's creditor (section 38 Civil Execution Law). The Supreme Court recognized the seller's action of a third party objection.[1137] It implies that when the purchaser B sold the object in his/her possession and deliver it to a third party C even though he/she has not fully paid the purchase money to the seller A, A can claim against C to return it on the basis of A's reserved ownership.[1138]

However, when the seller A, a dealer of cars, sold a car to a sub-dealer B with the agreement of reservation of ownership, and B sold the car to a customer C and C paid the purchase money in full to B, but A terminated the contract with B because B did not perform the obligation to pay the purchase money to A, and A claimed

---

1132. The reservation of ownership is presumed to be agreed in the installment sales (s. 7 Law on Installment Sales).
1133. Matsuo and Kozumi 2008: p. 431.
1134. Akira Yonekura, *Shoyuken-ryuho No Kenkyu* [*A Study of the Reserved Ownership*] (Shinsei-shuppan 1997) p. 378.
1135. Dogauchi 2017b: pp. 367–368.
1136. Ohmi 2020b: p. 339.
1137. SCJ Jul. 18, 1984 Minshu 28-5-743.
1138. However, C may be protected by the immediate acquisition if C was believing reasonably that B was the owner of the object (in good faith without negligence), when B bought the object from B (s. 192 CC). *See* para. 260 *supra*.

against C to return the car on the basis of the reserved ownership. The Supreme Court did not recognized A's claim for the reason that A, the car dealer, was aware of the resale to be concluded between B and C and had cooperated with B's resale, so that A's claim against C was in contradiction with A's former attitude and amounted to the abuse of rights (section 1 (3) CC).[1139] It presupposed that A has been keeping ownership of the car, but the claim against C on the basis of ownership could not be allowed because of the abuse of ownership. There is another explanation in the legal doctrine. In this case B was regarded as having been authorized by A to sell the car to C so that the ownership of the car can be regarded to have transferred from A to C if C paid the purchase money in full to B.[1140]

In another case, A sold a car and delivered it to B with the reservation of ownership until the full payment. But B did not pay the purchase money as promised with A, and left the car in the parking lot owned by C without paying the parking fee, and disappeared. C claimed against A as the owner of the car to remove it from the parking lot on the basis of ownership of the parking lot (section 206 CC) and to pay compensation for damages on the basis of tort liability (section 709 CC). The Supreme Court held that the seller who reserved ownership of the car until the full payment should not have a duty to remove the car and a tort liability to pay compensation before the purchaser has become in default. But after the purchaser has become in default, then the seller should have a chance to terminate the sales contract and take back the possession of the car so that the seller should have a duty to remove it from the parking lot. However, as for the tort liability, the seller should become liable to pay compensation when the seller knew the fact that the car is disturbing ownership of a third party in such a way that the third party tell the fact to the seller.[1141]

The Supreme Court seems to have interpreted the seller's right as a kind of collateral right, which should not include the right to remove the object before the purchaser has become in default.[1142] However, the seller's duty to remove the car and pay compensation as the owner of the car can be explained to be restricted by the purchaser's right to use and manage the car until the purchaser has become in default. In this sense the main stream of the judicial precedents seems to follow the view that the seller's right is ownership of the object until the full payment (Item (a) in the previous paragraph).

528. The practical problem which accompanies the reservation of ownership on the movable is the lack of publicity. There was a case in which A sold a certain amount of metal scrap and delivered it to B with the reservation of ownership until the full payment of purchase money. B borrowed money from C and established the conveyancing mortgage on the collection of the metal scrap with the agreement of

1139. SCJ Feb. 28, 1975 Minshu 29-2-193.
1140. Ohmi 2020b: pp. 342–343.
1141. SCJ Mar. 10, 2009 Minshu 63-3-385.
1142. In the insolvency procedure the judicial precedent treated the reserved ownership of the seller as "betsujo-ken" [the right of separate satisfaction] in the same way as the collateral right such as the special right of lien, the right of pledge and the right of hypothec, which may be exercised separately from the bankruptcy procedure (s. 2 (9), s. 65 (1) Bankruptcy Law; s. 53 Civil Rehabilitation Law). *See* SCJ Jun. 4, 2010 Minshu 64-4-1107.

constructive delivery to C (section 184 CC) and registered it according to section 3 (1) of the Law on Special Provisions of the Civil Code Concerning Opposability Requirements for the Transfer of Movables and Claim Rights. When B became in default, A terminated the sales contract with B and took back the metal scrap for which purchase money had not been paid. C claimed against A to pay compensation for the damages for the reason that the metal scrap belonged to C because C executed the conveyancing mortgage and it became opposable against a third party by the constructive delivery (sections 178, 184 CC). The Supreme Court held that C cannot acquire the conveyancing mortgage on the metal scrap for which the purchase money had not been paid because the ownership is still reserved by A.[1143] A's priority was recognized without delivery and registration because the metal scrap has been owned by A and has never been transferred to B. C needs to confirm whether the object of the conveyancing mortgage is the object of the reservation of ownership, and if it is, C needs to confirm and prove that the payment of purchase money has been completed. The last measure for C's protection will be given by the immediate acquisition (section 192 CC) when C believed reasonably that the object of the conveyancing mortgage was not the object of the reservation of ownership or, if it was, the purchase money was already paid in full (in good faith without negligence).[1144]

1143. SCJ Dec. 7, 2018 Minshu 72-6-1044.

1144. However, the judicial precedents held that the constructive delivery is not enough to be protected by the immediate acquisition (s. 192 CC), which is interpreted to require "the situational change of the possession that can be confirmed from the outlook" (STJ May 5, 1916 Minroku 22-961; SCJ Dec. 27, 1957 Minshu 11-14-2485; SCJ Feb. 11, 1960 Minshu 14-2-168). *See* para. 263 *supra*.

Selected Bibliography

English Translation of Japanese Law

Japanese Law Translation, available at http://www.japaneselawtranslation.go.jp/?re=02.

Japanese Geography, History and Society

Geospatial Information Authority of Japan, Ministry of Land, Infrastructure, Transport and Tourism, Maps & Geospatial Information, available at http://www.gsi.go.jp/ENGLISH/page_e30031.html (accessed November 1, 2020).

Gordon, Andrew, *A modern history of Japan: from Tokugawa times to the present* (3rd ed., Oxford University Press, 2014).

Henshall, Kenneth G., *A History of Japan: From Stone Age to Superpower* (3rd ed., Palgrave Macmillan, 2012).

Huffman, James L., *Japan in World History* (Oxford University Press, 2010).

Mason, R. H. P. and J. G. Caiger, *A History of Japan* (Revised Edition, Tuttle Publishing, 1997).

Ramseyer J. Mark and Frances McCall Rosenbluth, *Japan's Political Marketplace, with a New Preface* (Harvard University Press, 1997).

Statistics Bureau, Ministry of Internal Affairs and Communications, *Japan Statistical Year Book 2020*, available at http://www.stat.go.jp/english/data/nenkan/ (accessed November 1, 2020).

Totman, Conrad, *A History of Japan* (2nd ed. Malden, Mass.: Blackwell Publishing, 2005).

World Development Indicators, Japan, available at http://data.worldbank.org/country/japan (accessed November 1, 2020).

Japanese Law in General

Dean, Meryll, *Japanese Legal System* (2nd ed., Cavendish Publishing Ltd., 2002).

Foote, Daniel H. (ed.), *Law in Japan: A Turning Point* (University of Washington Press, 2007).

Goodman, Carl F., *The Rule of Law in Japan: A Comparative Analysis* (3rd revised ed., Wolters Kluwer, 2012).

Haley, John O., "Judicial Independence in Japan Revisited," *Law in Japan*, Vol. 25 (1995[a]), pp. 1–15.

Haley, John O., "Political Culture and Constitutionalism in Japan," in: Daniel P. Franklin and Michael J. Baun (eds.), *Political Culture and Constitutionalism: A Comparative Approach* (M. E. Sharpe, 1995[b]), pp. 98–115.
Hozumi, Nobushige, *Ancestor-Worship and Japanese Law* (Z. P. Maruya & Co., Ltd., 1901).
Hozumi, Nobushige, *Lectures on the New Japanese Civil Code as Material for the Study of Comparative Jurisprudence* (2nd and Revised ed., The Maruzen Kabushiki-kaisha, 1912).
Hozumi, Nobushige, *Horitsu Shinka Ron* [*Theory of Legal Evolution*], Vols. 1, 2, 3 (Iwanami-shoten, 1924, 1924, 1927).
Jones, Colin P.A. and Frank S. Ravitch, *The Japanese Legal System* (West Academic Publishing, 2018).
Katsuta, Aritsune, "Japan: A Gray Legal Culture," in: Esin Örücü, Elspeth Attwooll and Sean Coyle (eds.), *Studies in Legal Systems: Mixed and Mixing* (Kluwer Law International, 1996), pp. 249–264.
Kawaguchi, Yoshihiko, *Nihon Kindai Ho Shi* [*A Modern Japanese Legal History*] (Shinseisha, 1998).
Noda, Yosiyuki, translated and edited by Anthony H. Angero, *Introduction to Japanese Law* (University of Tokyo Press, 1976).
Oda, Hiroshi, *Japanese Law* (3rd ed., Oxford University Press, 2011).
Röhl, Wilhelm (ed.), *History of Law in Japan since 1868* (Koninklijke Brill, 2005).
Upham, Frank, "Mythmaking in the Rule-of-Law Orthodoxy," in: Thomas Carothers (ed.), *Promoting the Rule of Law Abroad: In Search of Knowledge* (Carnegie Endowment for International Peace, 2006), pp. 75–104.
Venoverbeke, Dimitri, Jeroen Maesschalck, David Nelken and Spephan Parmentier (eds.), *The Changing Role of Law in Japan: Empirical Studies in Culture, Society and Policy Making* (Edward Elgar, 2014).

§4. Property Law (including Secured Transactions)

Dogauchi, Hiroto, *Tanpo Bukken Ho* [*The Law of Real Rights for Security*] (Yuhikaku, 2017b).
Funabashi, Jun-ichi, *Bukken Ho* [*The Property Law*] (Yuhikaku, 1960).
Hirano, Hiroyuki, *Bukken Ho* [*The Property Law*] (Nihonhyoronsha, 2016).
Hironaka, Toshio, *Bukken Ho* [*The Property Law*, 2nd and Enlarged ed.] (Seirinshoin, 1987).
Hoshino, Eiich, *Minpo Gairon II* [*Outline of the Civil Law*] (Ryoshofukyukai, 1976)
Inamoto, Yonosuke, *Minpo II: Bukken* [*Civil Law, Vol. II: Real Rights*] (Seirinshoin-shinsha, 1983)
Ishida, Minori, *Minpo Taikei II: Bukken Ho* [*System of the Civil Law II: Law of Real Rights*] (Shinzansha, 2008)
Ishida, Minori, *Minpo Taikei III: Tanpo-Bukken-Ho* [*System of the Civil Law III: Law of Collateral Real Rights*] (Shinzan-sha, 2010).
Kawakami, Shoji, *Bukken Ho Kogi* [*Lecture on the Property Law]* (Nihonhyoronsha, 2012).
Kawashima, Takeyoshi and Ken Kawai (eds.), *Shinban Chushaku Minpo II, VI, VII* [*The New Series of Commentary on the Civil Law, Vols. II, VI, VII*] (Yuhikaku, 1991, 1997, 2007).

Matsuo, Hiroshi, *Minpo No Taikei* [*A System of Civil Law*] (6th ed., Keio University Press, 2016).
Matsuo, Hiroshi, *Kazoku Ho Kaisei Wo Yomu* [*Reading the Family Law Reform*] (Keio University Press, 2019).
Matsuo, Hiroshi and Kenzaburo Kozumi, *Bukkenn Tanpo Bukken Ho* [*The Property Law and the Security Law*] (2nd ed., Kobundo, 2008).
Matsuoka, Hisakazu, *Bukken Ho* [*The Property Law*] (Nihonhyoronsha, 2017).
Ohmi, Koji, *Minpo Kogi II* [*Lecture on the Civil Law, Vol. II*] (4th ed., Seibundo, 2020a).
Ohmi, Koji, *Minpo Kogi III* [*Lecture on the Civil Law, Vol. III*] (3rd ed., Seibundo, 2020b).
Ozawa, Michikazu, *Tochi Shuyo Ho I, II* [*The Land Expropriation Law, Vols. I, II*] (3rd ed., Gyosei, 2012).
Suekawa, Hiroshi, *Bukken Ho* [*The Property Law*] (Nihonhyoronsha, 1956).
Tayama, Teruaki, Yukihiko Sawano and Masamichi Nozawa (eds.), *Shakuchi-Shakka-Ho* [*Law on the Lease of Land and Building*] (2nd ed., Nihonhyoronsha, 2019).
Tomii, Masaaki, *Minpo Genron II* [*The Basic Theory of Civil Law, Vol. II*] (Yuhikaku, 1923).
Ume, Kenjiro, *Minpo Yogi I, II* [*The Essence of the Civil Law, Vols. I, II*] (Yuhikaku, 1911).
Wagatsuma, Sakae and Toru Ariizumi, *Bukken Ho* [*The Property Law*] (New ed., Iwanami-shoten, 1983).
Yamanome, Akio, *Bukken Ho* [*The Property Law*] (5th ed., Nihonhyoronsha, 2012).

Insolvency Law

Ito, Makoto, *Hasan Ho* [*The Bankruptcy Law*] (4th and complementary ed., Yuhikaku, 2006).
Ito, Makoto, *Kaisha Kosei Ho* [*The Corporate Reorganization Law Law*] (Yuhikaku, 2012).
Ito, Makoto, *Hasan Ho and Minji Saisei Ho* [*The Bankruptcy Law and the Civil Rehabilitation Law*] (4th ed., Yuhikaku, 2018).
Ito, Makoto, Takashi Sonoo and Makoto Tahira (eds.), *Tosan Ho no Jissen* [*Practices of the Insolvency Law*] (Yuhikaku, 2016).
Taniguchi, Yasuhei, *Tosan Shori Ho* [*The Insolvency Treatment Law*] (Chikumashobo, 1980)
Yamamoto, Kazuhiko, *Tosan Shori Ho Nyumon* [*Introduction to the Insolvency Treatment Law*] (5th ed., Yuhikaku, 2018)
Yamamoto, Kazuhiko, Tadashi Nakanishi, Masatoshi Kasai, Masami Okino, and Hironori Mizumoto, *Tosan Ho Gaisetsu* [*Outline of the Insolvency Law*] (2nd ed., Kobundo, 2010).

Trust Law

Arai, Makoto, *Shintaku Ho* [*The Trust Law*] (4th ed., Yuhikaku, 2014).
Dogauchi, Hiroto, *Shintaku Hori To Siho Taikei* [*Principles of Trust Law and the System of Private Law*] (Yuhikaku, 1996).

Selected Bibliography

Dogauchi, Hiroto, *Shintaku Ho Nyumon* [*Introduction to the Trust Law*] (Nikkei-bunko, 2007).
Dogauchi, Hiroto, *Shintaku Ho* [*The Trust Law*] (Yuhikaku, 2017a).
Dogauchi, Hiroto, "Overview of Trust Law in Japan," available at: http://www.law.tohoku.ac.jp/kokusaiB2C/link/dogauchi.html
Nomi, Yoshihisa, *Gendai Shintaku Ho* [*The Contemporary Trust Law*] (Yuhikaku, 2004).
Shinomiya, Kazuo, *Shintaku Ho* [*Trust Law*] (2nd ed., Yuhikaku, 1989).

Index

The numbers given refer to paragraphs.

Index

Index

www.ingramcontent.com/pod-product-compliance
Ingram Content Group UK Ltd.
Pitfield, Milton Keynes, MK11 3LW, UK
UKHW020135290926
15471UKWH00003B/503

9 789403 534756

SIMPLICIUS

On Aristotle

Physics 8.1-5